Essentials of Language Do

edited by

Jost Gippert
Nikolaus P. Himmelmann
Ulrike Mosel

Mouton de Gruyter
Berlin · New York

Mouton de Gruyter (formerly Mouton, The Hague)
is a Division of Walter de Gruyter GmbH & Co. KG, Berlin.

Published with support of VolkswagenStiftung, Hannover, FRG.

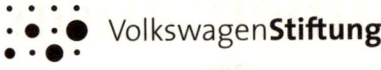 Volkswagen**Stiftung**

The hardcover was published in 2006 as volume 178
of the series *Tends in Linguistics Studies and Monographs.*

♾ Printed on acid-free paper which falls within the guidelines
of the ANSI to ensure permanence and durability.

The Library of Congress has cataloged the hardcover edition as follows:

Essentials of language documentation / edited by Jost Gippert, Niko-
laus P. Himmelmann, Ulrike Mosel.
    p. cm. − (Trends in linguistics. Studies and monographs ; 178)
Includes bibliographical references and index.
ISBN-13: 978-3-11-018864-6 (cloth : alk. paper)
ISBN-10: 3-11-018864-3 (cloth : alk. paper)
    1. Linguistics − Documentation.   2. Language and languages −
Documentation.   I. Gippert, Jost.   II. Himmelmann, Nikolaus P.,
1959−   III. Mosel, Ulrike   IV. Series
    P128.D63E85   2006
    025.06'41−dc22
                                     2006001315

ISBN-13: 978-3-11-018406-8
ISBN-10: 3-11-018406-0

Bibliographic information published by Die Deutsche Bibliothek

Die Deutsche Bibliothek lists this publication in the Deutsche Nationalbibliografie;
detailed bibliographic data is available in the Internet at <http://dnb.ddb.de>.

Cover design: Martin Zech, Bremen.
Printed in Germany.

Essentials of Language Documentation

Editors' preface

Language documentation is concerned with the methods, tools, and theoretical underpinnings for compiling a representative and lasting multipurpose record of a natural language or one of its varieties. It is a rapidly emerging new field in linguistics and related disciplines working with little-known speech communities. While in terms of its most recent history, language documentation has co-evolved with the increasing concern for language endangerment, it is not only of interest for work on endangered languages but for all areas of linguistics and neighboring disciplines concerned with setting new standards regarding the empirical foundations of their research. Among other things, this means that the quality of primary data is carefully and constantly monitored and documented, that the interfaces between primary data and various types of analysis are made explicit and critically reviewed, and that provisions are taken to ensure the long-term preservation of primary data so that it can be used in new theoretical ventures as well as in (re-)evaluating and testing well-established theories.

This volume presents in-depth introductions into major aspects of language documentation, including a definition of what it means to "document a language," overviews on fieldwork ethics and practicalities and data processing, discussions on how to provide a basic annotation of digitally-stored multimedia corpora of primary data, as well as long-term perspectives on the preservation and use of such corpora. It combines theoretical and practical considerations and makes specific suggestions for the most common problems encountered in language documentation.

The volume should prove to be most useful to students and researchers concerned with documenting little-known languages and language varieties. In addition to linguists and anthropologists, this includes students and researchers in various regional studies and philologies such as African Studies, Indology, Turkology, Semitic Studies, or South American Studies. The book presupposes familiarity with the basic concepts and terminology of descriptive linguistics (for example, basic units such as *phoneme* or *lexeme*), but most chapters will also be accessible and useful to non-specialists, including educators, language planners, politicians, and government officials concerned with linguistic minorities.

Nearly all chapters of this volume are based on a series of lectures and seminars presented during the *First International Summer School on Language Documentation: Methods and Technology* held in Frankfurt/Main (Sept. 1–11, 2004). While not a textbook in the strict sense (which would include exercises, etc.), the volume is designed to serve as the main source of readings for a university class on language documentation (for third-year students and above). Parts of it can also be used as readings in fieldmethod classes and classes in linguistic anthropology. However, it is not a guide to linguistic fieldwork. Instead, it focuses on issues which are typically not mentioned at all, or all too briefly, in fieldwork manuals such as, for example, the cooperative interaction between researcher(s) and speech community, orthography development, the function of metadata, archiving recordings and transcripts. When used as a textbook in a language documentation class, it should be complemented with readings on linguistic fieldwork and linguistic anthropology from other sources (see further Section 5 of Chapter 1).

Of major import to documentary linguistics is the technology used in recording and preserving linguistic primary data, most of which is IT-related today. Since this is a rapidly changing field, we have kept the discussion of specific technological aspects and procedures to an absolute minimum, focusing on conceptual issues and practicalities which we believe will stay with us for some time to come. Nevertheless, a considerable number of technical standards, software programs, and institutions concerned with corpus building and preservation are mentioned in this book in order to provide examples for a given conceptual issue or a recommended general procedure. The appendix provides an alphabetical list of all the abbreviations used in this regard, as well as internet links providing more up-to-date information on them. This information is continuously updated on the book's website at:

http://titus.uni-frankfurt.de/ld

On this website, the reader will also find video and audio files for some of the examples given in this book as well as links and suggestions for topics which could not be adequately dealt with here.

Finally, it bears emphasizing once again that language documentation in many ways is still a rather new discipline where many basic concepts and procedures are in the process of being tested and fully elaborated (see also Section 3.2 in Chapter 1). In particular, while considerable progress has been made in recent years with regard to the compilation and archiving aspects of language documentation, to date there is very little experience indeed with regard to actually working with digitally-stored multimedia corpora of lesser-known languages. In the coming years, we expect to see major developments here with regard to the etiquette of working with such corpora (How are they evaluated? How are they referred to in publications? How can work by different investigators on the same variety be combined into a single coherent corpus?) as well as with regard to the technology used in exploring them and extracting relevant information for a specific project. We also expect an impact on the methodological and theoretical debate in the subject areas working most intensively with data from such corpora, including linguistic typology, linguistic anthropology, and oral literature. As a part of these developments, it may well turn out that some of the suggestions made in this book, e.g. with regard to the structuring of the corpora or the format for annotations, will need to be revised or perhaps even be discarded. Still, we trust that the discussion of the basic conceptual issues as laid out here will be of continued interest and relevance for many years to come and thus truly merit to be considered "essentials of language documentation."

Nikolaus P. Himmelmann, Bochum
Jost Gippert, Frankfurt
Ulrike Mosel, Kiel

Acknowledgements

We gratefully acknowledge the very generous support of the Volkswagen-Stiftung (http://www.volkswagenstiftung.de) which has been instrumental in producing this book. The foundation not only funded the summer school for which most chapters were drafted, but also provided the means to distribute a substantial number of copies of this book free of charge outside of Western Europe, North America, and Japan. By granting a research fellowship for Himmelmann in 2004–2005, it has allowed him to focus his research on the issues dealt with in Chapters 7 and 10 and to engage in the editing of the book in a way which otherwise would not have been possible. Through its *DoBeS Programm* (Documentation of Endangered Languages program), which started in the year 2000, it has made a major contribution to the development of documentary linguistics as an innovative field of study and practice within the humanities.

Our sincerest thanks are due to the contributors of the volume who spent a lot of time on conceiving their chapters and have always been ready to cooperate with us in the difficult task of preparing a consistent book.

We also gratefully acknowledge much practical help we have received in putting the volume together. Marcia Schwartz checked English and style conventions; Judith Köhne compiled the combined list of bibliographical references at the end. At Mouton, Ursula Kleinhenz did a great job of seeing the book through to press. Many thanks to all of you.

Contents

Chapter 1

Language documentation:
What is it and what is it good for?

Nikolaus P. Himmelmann

Introduction

This chapter defines language documentation as a field of linguistic inquiry and practice in its own right which is primarily concerned with the compilation and preservation of linguistic primary data and interfaces between primary data and various types of analyses based on these data. Furthermore, it argues (in Section 2) that while language endangerment is a major reason for getting involved in language documentation, it is not the only one. Language documentations strengthen the empirical foundations of those branches of linguistics and related disciplines which heavily draw on data of little-known speech communities (e.g. linguistic typology, cognitive anthropology, etc.) in that they significantly improve accountability (verifiability) and economizing research resources.

The primary data which constitute the core of a language documentation include audio or video recordings of a communicative event (a narrative, a conversation, etc.), but also the notes taken in an elicitation session, or a genealogy written down by a literate native speaker. These primary data are compiled in a structured corpus and have to be made accessible by various types of annotations and commentary, here summarily referred to as the "apparatus". Sections 3 and 4 provide further discussion of the components and structure of language documentations. Section 5 concludes with a preview of the remaining chapters of this book.

1. What is a language documentation?

An initial, preliminary answer to this question is: **a language documentation is a lasting, multipurpose record of a language**. This answer, of course, is not quite satisfactory since it immediately raises the question of what we mean by "lasting", "multipurpose" and "record of a language". In the following, these constituents of the definition are taken up in reverse order, beginning with "record of a language".

At first sight, a further definition of "record of a language" may look like a bigger a problem than it actually is since it involves the highly complex and controversial issue of defining "a language". The main problem with defining "a language" consists in the fact that the word *language* refers to a number of different, though interrelated phenomena. The problems in defining it vary considerably, depending on which phenomenon is focused upon. That is, different problems surface when the task is to define *language* as opposed to *dialect*, or *language* as a field of scientific enquiry, or *language* as a cognitive faculty of humans, and so on. Unless we want to postpone working on language documentations until the probably never arriving day when all the conceptual problems of defining *language* in all of its different senses are resolved and a theoretically well-balanced delimitation of "a language" for the purposes of language documentations is possible, we need a pragmatic approach in dealing with this problem.

The basic tenet of such a pragmatic approach is implied by the qualifiers *multipurpose* and *lasting* in the definition above: The net should be cast as widely as possible. That is, a language documentation should strive to include as many and as varied records as practically feasible, covering all aspects of the set of interrelated phenomena commonly called *a language*. Ideally, then, a language documentation would cover all registers and varieties, social or local; it would contain evidence for language as a social practice as well as a cognitive faculty; it would include specimens of spoken and written language; and so on.

A language documentation broadly conceived along these lines could serve a large variety of different uses in, for example, language planning decisions, preparing educational materials, or analyzing a set of problems in syntactic theory. Users of such a multipurpose documentation would include the speech community itself, national and international agencies concerned with education and language planning, as well as researchers in various disciplines (linguistics, anthropology, oral history, etc.). In fact, the qualifier *lasting* adds a long-term perspective which goes beyond current issues and concerns. The goal is not a short-term record for a specific purpose or interest group, but a record for generations and user groups whose identity is still unknown and who may want to explore questions not yet raised at the time when the language documentation was compiled.

Obviously, this pragmatic explication of "lasting, multipurpose record of a language" rests on the assumption that it is possible and useful to compile a database for a very broadly defined subject matter ("a language") without being guided by a specific theoretical or practical problem in mind which could be resolved on the basis of this database. With regard to its use in scientific inquiries, the validity of this assumption is shown by the success of all those social and historical disciplines working with data not specifically produced for research purposes. Thus, for example, cave dwellers in the Stone Age did not discard shellfish, animal bones, fragments of tools, and the like within the cave with the purpose in mind of documenting their presence and aspects of their diet and culture. But archeologists today use this haphazardly discarded waste as the primary data for determining the length and type of human occupation found in a given location. Similarly, inscriptions on stones, bones, or clay tablets were not produced in order to provide a record of linguistic structures and practices, but they have successfully been used to explore the structural properties of languages such as Hittite or Sumerian, which had already been extinct for millennia before their modern linguistic analysis began.

However, it is also well known that historical remains and records tend to be deficient in some ways with regard to modern purposes. Stone inscriptions and other historic documents with linguistic content, for example, never provide a comprehensive record of the linguistic structures and practices in use in the community at the time when these documents were written. Thus, given that the Hittite records discovered to date mostly pertain to matters of government, law, trade, and religion, it remains unknown how Hittite adolescents chatted with each other or whether it was possible to have the verb in first position in subordinate clauses.[1]

The experience with historical remains and records thus is ambivalent: On the one hand, it clearly shows that they may serve as the database for exploring issues they were not intended for. On the other hand, they show that haphazardly compiled databases hardly ever contain all the information one needs to answer all the questions of current interest. Based on this observation, the basic idea of a language documentation as developed here can be stated as follows: The goal is to create a record of a language in the sense of a comprehensive corpus of primary data which leaves nothing to be desired by later generations wanting to explore whatever aspect of the language they are interested in (what exactly is meant by "primary data" here is further discussed in Section 3.1.1 below).

Put in this way, the task of compiling a language documentation is enormous, and there is no principled upper limit for it. Obviously, every specific documentation project will have to limit its scope and set specific targets. Guidelines and suggestions as to how to go about setting such limits and targets are further discussed below and in the remaining chapters of this book. But to begin with, the fundamental importance of taking a pragmatic stance in all matters of language documentation needs to be emphasized once again. There are major practical constraints on the usefulness of targets and delimitations for language documentations which are exclusively based on theoretical considerations regarding the nature of language and speech communities. In most if not all documentation settings, the range of items that can be documented will be determined to a significant degree by factors that are specific to the given setting, most importantly, the availability of speakers who are willing and able to participate in the documentation effort. In fact, recent experiences make it clear that encouraging native speakers to take an *active* part in determining the contents of a documentation significantly increases the productivity of a documentation project. Consequently, a theoretical framework for language documentation should provide room for the active participation of native speakers. While the input of native speakers and other factors specific to a given setting is not completely unpredictable, it clearly limits the level of detail of a general framework for language documentation which can be usefully explored in purely theoretical terms.

This assessment, however, should not be construed as denying the relevance of theorizing language documentations. Not everything in a documentation is fully determined by the specifics of a given documentation situation. Speakers and speech communities usually do not have a fully worked-out plan for what to document. Rather, the specifics of a documentation are usually established interactively by communities and research teams. On the part of the research team, this presupposes a theoretically grounded set of basic goals and targets one wants to achieve.

Furthermore, without theoretical grounding language documentation is in the danger of producing "data graveyards", i.e. large heaps of data with little or no use to anyone. While language documentation is based on the idea that it is possible and useful to dissociate the compilation of linguistic primary data from any *particular* theoretical or practical project based on this data, language documentation is not a theory-free or anti-theoretical enterprise. Its theoretical concerns pertain to the methods used in recording, processing, and preserving linguistic primary data, as well as to the question how it can be ensured that primary data collections are indeed of use for a broad range of theoretical and applied purposes.

Among other things, documentation theory has to provide guidelines for determining targets in specific documentation projects. It also has to develop principled and intersubjective means for evaluating the quality of a given documentation regardless of the specific circumstances of its compilation. A further major concern pertains to the interface between primary data and analysis in a broad range of disciplines. Based on a detailed investigation and evaluation of basic analytical procedures in these disciplines, it has to be determined which type and format of primary data is required for a particular analytical procedure so that it can be ensured that the appropriate type of data is included in a comprehensive documentation.

The present book provides an introduction to basic practical and theoretical issues in language documentation. It presents specific suggestions for the structure and contents of language documentations as well as the methodologies to be used in compiling them. To begin with, it will be useful briefly to address the question of what language documentations are good for. That is, why is it a useful enterprise to create lasting, multipurpose records of a language?

2. What is a language documentation good for?

From a linguistic point of view, there are essentially three reasons for engaging in language documentation, all of them having to do with consolidating and enlarging the empirical basis of a number of disciplines, in particular those branches of linguistics and related disciplines which heavily draw on data of little-known speech communities (e.g. descriptive linguistics, linguistic typology, cognitive anthropology, etc.). These are language endangerment, the economy of research resources, and accountability.

Certainly the major reason why linguists have recently started to engage with the idea of multipurpose documentations is the fact that a substantial number of the languages still spoken today are threatened by extinction (see Grenoble and Whaley 1998; Hagège 2000; Crystal 2000; or Bradley and Bradley 2002 for further discussion and references regarding language endangerment). In the case of an extinct language, it is obviously impossible to check data with native speakers or to collect additional data sets. Creating lasting multipurpose documentations is thus seen as one major linguistic response to the challenge of the dramatically increased level of language endangerment observable in our times. In this regard, language documentations are not only seen as data repositories for scientific inquiries, but also as important resources for supporting language maintenance.

Creating language documentations which are properly archived and made easily accessible to interested researchers is also in the interest of research economy. If someone worked on a minority language in the Philippines 50 years ago and someone else wanted to continue this work now, it would obviously be most useful if this new project could build on the complete set of primary data collected at the time and not just on a grammar sketch and perhaps a few texts published by the earlier project. Similarly, even if a given project on a little-known language is geared towards a very specific purpose – say, the conceptualization of space – it is in the interest of research economy (and accountability) if this project were to feed *all* the primary data collected in the project work into an open archive and not to limit itself to publishing the analytical results plus possibly a small sample of primary data illustrating their basic materials.

While the set of primary data fed into an archive in these examples would surely fail to constitute a comprehensive record of a language, it could very well be of use for purposes other than the one motivating the original project (data from matching tasks developed to investigate the linguistic encoding of space, for example, are also quite useful for the analysis of intonation, for conversation analytic purposes, for grammatical analysis, and so on). More importantly, if it were common practice to feed complete sets of primary data into open archives (which do not necessarily have to form a physical unit), comprehensive documentations for quite a number of little-known languages could grow over time, which in turn would strengthen the empirical basis of all disciplines working on and with such languages and cultures. That is, while much of the discussion in this chapter and book is concerned with projects specifically targeted at creating substantial language documentations, the basic idea of creating lasting, multipurpose documentations which are openly archived is not necessarily tied to such projects. It is very well possible and desirable to create such documentations in a step-by-step fashion by compiling and integrating the primary data sets collected in a number of different projects over an extended period of time. In fact, it is highly likely that in most instances, really comprehensive documentations can only be created in this additive way.

Finally, establishing open archives for primary data is also in the interest of making analyses accountable. Many claims and analyses related to languages and speech communities for which no documentation is available remain unverifiable as long as substantial parts of the primary data on which the analyses are based remain inaccessible to further scrutiny. Accountability here is intended to include all kinds of practical checks and methodological tests with regard to the empirical basis of an analysis or theory, including replicability and falsifiability. The documentation format developed here encourages, and also provides practical guidelines for, the open and widely accessible archiving of *all* primary data collected for little-known languages, regardless of their vitality.[2]

3. A basic format for language documentations

This section presents a basic format for language documentations and then highlights some features which distinguish this format from related enterprises.

3.1. The basic format

3.1.1. Primary data

Continuing the argument developed in the preceding sections, it should be clear that a language documentation, conceived of as a lasting, multipurpose record of a language, should contain a large set of primary data which provide evidence for the language(s) used at a given time in a given community (in all of the different senses of "language"). Of major importance in this regard are specimens of **observable linguistic behavior**, i.e. examples of how the people actually communicate with each other. This includes all kinds of communicative activities in a speech community, from everyday small talk to elaborate rituals, from parents baby-talking to their newborn infants to political disputes between village elders.

It is impossible to record *all* communicative events in a given speech community, not only for obvious practical, but also for theoretical and ethical reasons. Most importantly, such a record would imply a totalitarian set-up with video cameras and microphones everywhere and the speakers unable to control what of their behavior is recorded and what not. A major theoretical problem pertains to the fact that there is no principled way for determining a temporal boundary for such a recording (all communicative events in one day? two weeks? one year? a century?).

Consequently, there is a need to sample the kinds of communicative events to be documented. Once again, we can distinguish between a pragmatic guideline and theoretically grounded targets. The pragmatic guideline simply says that one should record as many and as broad a range as possible of communicative events which commonly occur in the speech community.

The theoretically grounded sampling procedure will be determined to a significant degree by the purposes and goals of the particular project. The rather broad and unspecific goal of a lasting, multipurpose record of a language envisioned here implies that, as much as possible, a sufficiently large number of examples for every type of communicative event found in a given speech community is collected. This in turn raises the highly complex issue of how the typology of communicative events in a given speech community can be uncovered. Within sociolinguistics, the framework known as the *ethnography of communication* provides a starting point for dealing with this issue. Chapter 5 provides a brief introduction to major concepts relevant here. Chapter 8 lists a range of important topics and parameters.

Besides observable linguistic behavior, is there anything else that needs to be documented in order to provide for a lasting, multipurpose record of a language? Or can all relevant information be extracted from a comprehensive corpus of recordings of communicative events? One aspect of "a language" that is not, or at least not easily, accessible by analyzing observable linguistic behavior is the tacit knowledge speakers have about their language. This is also known as **metalinguistic knowledge** and refers to the ability of native speakers to provide interpretations and systematizations for linguistic units and events. For example, speakers know that a given word is a taboo word, that speech event X usually has to be followed by speech event Y, or that putting a given sequence of elements in a different order is awkward or simply impossible. Similarly, metalinguistic knowledge as understood here also includes all kinds of linguistically based taxonomies, such as kinship systems, folk taxonomies for plants, animals, musical instruments and styles, and other artifacts, expressions for numbers and measures, but also morphological paradigms.

The documentation of metalinguistic knowledge, while not involving principled theoretical or ethical problems, is also not a straightforward task because much of it is not directly accessible. To be sure, in some instances there are conventional speech events involving the display of metalinguistic knowledge, such as reciting a genealogy or lengthy mythological narratives which sketch a cognitive map of the landscape. In many societies, there are also a number of well established and much discussed topics where speakers engage in metalinguistic discussions regarding the differences between different varieties (in village X they say "da" but we say "de"; young people cannot pronounce our peculiar /k/-sound correctly anymore, etc.). Furthermore, transcripts prepared by native speakers without direct interference by a linguist often provide interesting evidence regarding morpheme, word, and sentence boundaries (see Chapters 3 and 10 for further discussion). But very often documenting metalinguistic knowledge will involve the use of a broad array of elicitation strategies, guided by current theories about different kinds of metalinguistic knowledge and their structure. One very important type of elicited evidence are monolingual definitions of word meanings provided by native speakers. See Chapters 3 and 6 for further discussion and exemplification.

The documentation of metalinguistic knowledge as understood here includes much of the basic information that is needed for writing descriptive grammars and dictionaries. In particular, it includes all kinds of elicited data regarding the grammaticality or acceptability of phonological or morphosyntactic structures and the meaning, use, and relatedness of lexical items. However, it should be clearly understood that documentation here means that the elicitation process itself is documented in its entirety, including the questions asked or the stimuli presented by the researcher as well as the reaction by the native speaker(s). That is, documentation pertains to the level of primary data which provide evidence for metalinguistic knowledge, i.e. what native speakers can actually articulate regarding their linguistic practices or their recordable reactions in experiments designed to probe metalinguistic knowledge.[3] A grammatical rule as stated in a grammar or an entry in a published dictionary are not primary data in this sense, even though some linguists may believe that they are part of a native speakers' (unconscious) metalinguistic knowledge. In this view, grammatical rules and dictionary entries are *analytical formats* for metalinguistic knowledge. Whether and to what extent these have a place in a language documentation is an issue we will take up in Section 4.2.

It is also worth noting that the documentation of observable linguistic behavior and metalinguistic knowledge are similar in that they basically consist of records of communicative events. In the case of observable linguistic behavior, the communicative event involves the interaction of native speakers among themselves, while in the case of metalinguistic knowledge it involves the interaction between native speakers and documenters. There is a superficial difference with regard to the preferred documentation format in that it is now standard practice to make (video) recordings of observable linguistic behavior, while for the elicitation of metalinguistic knowledge it is still more common simply to take written notes. In principle, (video-)recording would also be the better (i.e. more reliable and comprehensive) documentation format for elicited metalinguistic knowledge, but there may often be practical reasons to stay with paper and pencil (among other things, native speakers may be more comfortable to discuss metalinguistic knowledge without being constantly recorded). But, to repeat, regardless of the recording method, records of observable linguistic behavior and metalinguistic knowledge both contain primary data documenting linguistic interactions in which native speakers participate.

In the following, we will use the label *corpus of primary data* as a shorthand for *corpus of recordings of observable linguistic behavior and metalinguistic knowledge* for this component of a language documentation. Throughout this book it is assumed that this corpus is stored and made available in digital form.

To date, there is very little practical experience with regard to structuring and maintaining such digital corpora. Consequently, no widely-used and well-tested structure exists for them. Within the DoBeS program, it is a widespread practice to operate with two basic components in structuring primary data: records of individual communicative events and a lexical database (this obviously follows a widespread practice in linguistic fieldwork where apart from transcripts of recordings and fieldnotes the compilation of a lexical database is a standard procedure).

Records of individual communicative events are called **sessions** (alternative terms would be "document", "text", or "resource bundle"). In the manual for the IMDI Browser,[4] a session is defined as "a meaningful unit of analysis, usually [...] a piece of data having the same overall content, the same set of participants, and the same location and time, e.g., one elicitation session on topic X, or one folktale, or one 'matching game', or one conversation between several speakers." It could also be the recording of a two-day ceremony. Sessions are typically allocated to different sets defined according to parameters such as medium (written vs. spoken), genre (monologue, dialogue, historical, chatting, etc.), naturalness (spontaneous, staged, elicited, etc.), and so on. It is too early to tell whether some of the various corpus structures currently being used are preferable to others.

There are two reasons why a **lexical database** appears to be a useful format for organizing primary data. On the one hand, there is a need to bring together all the information available for a given item so that one can make sure that the meaning and formal properties of the item are well understood.[5] On the other hand, and perhaps more importantly, a list of lexical items is a very useful resource when working on the transcription and translation of recordings. One of the most widely used computational tools in descriptive linguistics, the program *Toolbox* (formerly *Shoebox*),[6] allows for the semi-automatic compilation of a lexical database when working through a transcript, and the existence of this program is certainly one reason why the compilation of a lexical database currently is almost an automatic procedure when working with recordings. However, as with all other aspects of organizing a digital corpus of primary data, it remains to be seen and tested further whether this is indeed a necessary and useful procedure.

3.1.2. Apparatus

Inasmuch as linguistic and metalinguistic interactions cover the range of basic interactional possibilities,[7] a documentation which contains a comprehensive set of primary data for both types of interactions is logically complete with regard to the level of primary data. However, it is well known that a large corpus of primary data is of little use unless it is presented in a format which ensures accessibility for parties other than the ones participating in its compilation. To be accessible to a broad range of users, including the speech community, the primary data need to be accompanied by information of various kinds, which – following philological tradition – could be called the **apparatus**. The precise extent and format of the apparatus is a matter of debate, with one exception: the uncontroversial need for **metadata**.

Metadata are required on two levels. First, the documentation as a whole needs metadata regarding the project(s) during which the data were compiled, including information on the project team(s), and the object of documentation (which variety? spoken where? number and type of records; etc.). Second, each session (= segment of primary data) has to be accompanied by information of the following kind:[8]

- a name of the session which uniquely identifies it within the overall corpus;
- when and where was the data recorded?;
- who is recorded and who else was present at the time?;
- who made the recording and what kind of recording equipment was used?;
- an indication of the quality of the data according to various parameters (recording environment and equipment, speaker competence, level of detail of further annotation);
- who is allowed to access the data contained in this session?;

- a brief characterization of the content of the session (what topic is being talked about? what kind of communicative event [narrative, conversation, song, etc.] is being documented?);
- links between different files which together constitute the session, e.g. a media file (audio or video) and a file containing a transcription, translation, and various types of commentary relevant for interpreting the recording contained in the media file (on which see further below).

The metadata on both levels have two interrelated functions. On the one hand, they facilitate access to a documentation or a specific record within a documentation by providing key access information in a standardized format (what, where, when, etc.). In this function, they are similar to a catalogue in a library and we can thus speak of a *cataloguing* function.[9] On the other hand, they have an *organizational* function in that they define the structure of the corpus which, in particular in the case of documentations in digital format, in turn provides the basis for various procedures such as searching, copying, or filtering within a single documentation or across a set of documentations. Obviously, a metadata standard which targets the organizational function has to be richer and more elaborate than one which targets the cataloguing function. The former is actually a corpus management tool, which defines digital structures and supports various computational procedures, rather than just a standard for organizing a catalogue.

Currently there exist two metadata standards which in fact complement each other in that they target these different functions. The OLAC standard targets exclusively the cataloguing function and provides an easy and fast access to a large number of diverse repositories of primary data on a worldwide scale (in both digital and non-digital formats). The IMDI standard, which incorporates all the information included in the OLAC standard and hence is compatible with it, is actually a corpus management tool which primarily targets digitally archived language documentations. Further discussion of metadata concepts and standards is found in Chapters 4 and 13.

Apart from metadata, there is in most instances also a need for further information accompanying each recording as well as the documentation as a whole in order to make the corpus of primary data useful to users who do not know the language being documented. On the level of individual sessions, such additional information is called here an **annotation**.[10] Thus, in the case of audio or video recordings of communicative events, it is obviously useful to provide at least a transcription and a translation so that users not familiar with the language are able to understand what is going on in the recording.

However, the exact extent and format of the annotations that should be included in each session is a matter of debate. It is common to distinguish between minimal and more elaborate annotation schemes. A widely assumed minimal annotation scheme consists of just a transcription and a free translation which should accompany all, or at least a substantial number of, primary data segments. More elaborate annotation schemes include various levels of interlinear glossing, grammatical as well ethnographical commentary, and extensive cross-referencing between the various sessions and resources compiled in a given documentation. See further Chapters 8 and 9.

On the level of the overall documentation, information accompanying the primary data set other than metadata is, for lack of a well-established term, subsumed here under the heading **general access resources** (alternatively, it could also simply be called "annotation"). Such general (in the sense of: relevant for the documentation as a whole) access resources would include:

– a general introduction which provides background information on the speech community and language (language name(s), affiliation, major varieties, etc.), the fieldwork setting(s), the methods used in recording primary data, an overview of the contents, structure, and scope of the primary data corpus and its quality;
– brief sketches of major ethnographic and grammatical features being documented;
– an explication of the various conventions that are being used (orthography, glossing abbreviations, other abbreviations);
– indices for languages/varieties, key analytic concepts, etc.;
– links and references to other resources (books and articles previously published on the variety or community being documented; other projects relating to the community or its neighbors, etc.).

For further discussion of some aspects of relevance here, see Chapters 8 and 12.

Table 1 provides a schematic overview of the components of the language documentation format sketched in this section.

Table 1. Basic format of a language documentation

Primary data	Apparatus	
	Per session	For documentation as a whole
recordings/records of observable linguistic behavior and metalinguistic knowledge (possible basic formats: session and lexical database)	*Metadata* – time and location of recording – participants – recording team – recording equipment – content descriptors ... *Annotations* – transcription – translation – further linguistic and ethnographic glossing and commentary	*Metadata* – location of documented community – project team(s) contributing to documentation – participants in documentation – acknowledgements ... *General access resources* – introduction – orthographical conventions – ethnographic sketch – sketch grammar – glossing conventions – indices – links to other resources ...

3.2. What's new?

Language documentation in the way depicted in Table 1 is not a totally new enterprise. The compilation of annotated collections of written historical documents and culturally important speech events (legends, epic poems, and the like) was the major concern of philologists in the nineteenth century. Linguistic and anthropological fieldwork in the Boasian tradition has also always put major emphasis on the recording of speech events. Within linguistic anthropology, recording and interpreting oral literature is a major task. All of these traditions have had a major influence on documentary linguistics as developed in this book.

Nevertheless, the idea of a language documentation as sketched above is new for mainstream linguistics, and even compared to these earlier approaches, it is new with regard to the following important features:

– *Focus on primary data*: The main goal of a language documentation is to make primary data available for a broad group of users. Unlike in the philological tradition, there is no restriction to culturally or historically "important" documents, however such importance may be defined.
– *Explicit concern for accountability*: The focus on primary data implies that considerable care is given to the issue of making it possible to evaluate the quality of the data. This in turn implies that the field situation is made transparent and that all documents are accompanied by metadata which detail the recording circumstances as well as the further steps undertaken in processing a particular document.
– *Concern for long-term storage and preservation of primary data*: This involves two aspects. On the one hand, metadata are crucial for users of a documentation to locate and evaluate a given document, as just mentioned. On the other hand, long-term storage is essentially a matter of technology, and while compilers of language documentations do not have to be able to handle all the technology themselves, they need to have a basic understanding of the core issues involved so that they avoid basic mistakes in recording and processing primary data. Among other things, the quality of the recording is of utmost importance for long-term storage and hence needs explicit attention. See further Chapters 4, 13, and 14.
– *Work in interdisciplinary teams*: Work on a truly comprehensive language documentation needs expertise in a multitude of disciplines in addition to the basic linguistic expertise required in transcription and translation. Such disciplines include anthropology, ethnomusicology, oral history and literature, as well as all the major subdisciplines of linguistics (socio- and psycholinguistics, phonetics, discourse analysis, corpus linguistics, etc.). There are probably no individuals who are experts in all of these fields, and few who have acquired significant expertise in a substantial number of them. Hence, good documentation work usually requires a team of researchers with different backgrounds and areas of expertise.
– *Close cooperation with and direct involvement of speech community*: The documentation format sketched above strongly encourages the active involvement of (members of) the speech community in two ways. On

the one hand, as mentioned above, native speakers are among the main players in determining the overall targets and outcomes of a documentation project. On the other hand, a documentation project involves a significant number of activities which can be carried out with little or no academic training. For example, the recording of communicative events can be done by native speakers who know how to handle the recording equipment (which can be learned in very short time), and it is often preferable that they do such recordings on their own because they know where and when particular events happen, and their presence is frequently felt to be less obtrusive. Similarly, given some training and regular supervision, the recording of metalinguistic knowledge and also the transcription and translation of recordings can be carried out by native speakers all by themselves. See further Chapter 3.

3.3. Limitations

As with most other scientific enterprises, the language documentation format developed here is not without problems and limitations. Some of the theoretical and practical problems have already been mentioned in the preceding discussion, and it will suffice here to emphasize the fact that the documentation format in Table 1 is based on a number of hypotheses which may well be proven wrong or unworkable in practical terms (see further Section 4 below). In addition to theoretical and practical problems, there are also ethical problems and limitations which are related to the fact that even the most circumspectly planned documentation project has the potential to profoundly change the social structure of the society being documented. This may pertain to a number of different levels, only two of which are mentioned here (see Wilkins 1992, 2000; Himmelmann 1998; and Grinevald 2003: 60–62 for further discussion).

On a somewhat superficial level, there are usually a few, often not more than one or two native speakers who are very actively involved in the project work. Through their work in the project, their social and economic status may change in a way that otherwise may have been impossible. This in turn may lead to (usually minor) disturbances in the wider community, such as inciting the envy or anger of relatives and neighbors. It is also not unknown that affiliation with an externally funded and administered project is used as an instrument in political controversies and competitions within the speech community.

On a more profound level, in non-literate societies the documentation of historical, cultural, and religious knowledge generally introduces a new way for accessing such knowledge and thereby may change the whole psycho-social fabric of the society (Ong 1982). This is particularly true of societies where much of the social fabric depends on highly selective access to cultural and historical knowledge, transmission of such knowledge thus involving different levels of secrecy (see Brandt [1980, 1981] for a pertinent example). That is, in some instances a documentation project may contribute to the demise of the very linguistic and cultural practices it proposes to document. In these instances, it would appear to be preferable *not* to document, but rather to support language maintenance in other ways, if necessary and possible.

Note that in general, language documentation and language maintenance efforts are not opposed to each other but go hand in hand. That is, it is an integral part of the documentation framework elaborated in this book that it considers it an essential task of language documentation projects to support language maintenance efforts wherever such support is needed and welcomed by the community being documented. More specifically, the documentation should contain primary data which can be used in the creation of linguistic resources to support language maintenance, and the documentation team should plan to dedicate a part of its resources to "mobilizing" the data compiled in the project for maintenance purposes. Chapter 15 elaborates some of the issues involved here.

4. Alternative formats for language documentations

The format for language documentations sketched in the preceding section is certainly not the only possible format. In fact, within structural linguistics there is a well-established format for language documentations consisting primarily of a grammar and a dictionary. In this section, I will first briefly present some arguments as to why this well-established format is strictly speaking a format for language *description* and not for language *documentation* proper, and thus is not a viable alternative to the basic documentation format of Table 1. In Section 4.2, we will then turn to the question of whether it makes sense to integrate the grammar-dictionary format with the basic documentation format of Table 1 and thus make fully worked-out grammars and dictionaries essential components of language documentations.

It should be clearly understood that this section is merely intended to draw attention to this important topic at the core of documentation theory. It barely scratches the surface of the many complex issues involved here. For more discussion, see Labov (1975, 1996), Greenbaum (1984), Pawley (1985, 1986, 1993), Lehmann (1989, 2001, 2004b), Mosel (1987, 2006), Himmelmann (1996, 1998), Schütze (1996), Keller (2000), Ameka et al. (2006), among others.

4.1. The grammar-dictionary format

The grammar-dictionary format of language description targets the language system.[11] That is, it is based on the notion of a language as an abstract system of rules and oppositions which underlies the observable linguistic behavior. In this view, documenting a language essentially involves compiling a grammar (= set of rules for producing utterances) and a dictionary (= a list of conventional form-meaning pairings used in producing these utterances). To this core of the documentation, a number of texts are often added, either in the form of a text collection or in the appendix to the grammar, which have the function of extended examples for how the system works in context. These texts are usually taken from the corpus of primary data on which the system description is based, but they do not actually provide access to these primary data because they are edited in various ways. Providing direct access to the complete corpus of primary data is typically not part of this format.

The compilation of grammars and (to a lesser extent) dictionaries is a well-established practice in structural linguistics, with many fine specimens having been produced in the last century. But even the best structuralist grammars and dictionaries have been lacking with regard to the goal of presenting a lasting, multipurpose record of a language. Major problems with regard to this goal include the following points:

a. Many communicative practices found in a given speech community remain undocumented and unreconstructable. That is, provided with a grammar and a dictionary it is still impossible to know how the language is (or was) actually spoken. For example, it is impossible to derive from a grammar and a dictionary on how everyday conversational routines look like (how does one say "hello, good morning"?) or how one linguistically interacts when building a house or negotiating a marriage.

b. In line with the structuralist conception of the language system, grammars and dictionaries contain abstractions based on a variety of analytical procedures. With the data contained in grammars and dictionaries, most aspects of the analyses underlying the abstractions are not verifiable or replicable. There is no way of knowing whether fundamental mistakes have been made unless the primary data on which the analyses build are made available *in toto* as well.

c. Grammars usually only contain statements on grammatical topics which are known and reasonably well understood at the time of writing the grammar. Thus, for example, grammars written before the advent of modern syntactic theories generally do not contain any statements regarding control phenomena in complex sentences. Many topics of current concern such as information structure (topic, focus) or the syntax and semantics of adverbials have often been omitted from descriptive grammars due to the lack of an adequate descriptive framework. As pointed out in particular by Andrew Pawley (1985, 1993, and elsewhere), there is a large variety of linguistic structures often subsumed under the heading of *speech formulas* which do not really fit the structuralist idea of a clean divide between grammar and dictionary and thus more often than not are not adequately documented in these formats.

d. Grammars and (to a lesser extent) dictionaries provide little that is of direct use to non-linguists, including the speech community, educators, and researchers in other disciplines (history, anthropology, etc.).

These points of critique mostly pertain to the fact that structuralist language descriptions are reductionist with regard to the primary data on which they are based and do not provide access to them. Or, to put it in a slightly different and more general perspective, they document a language only in one of the many senses of "language", i.e. language as an abstract system of rules and oppositions. Inasmuch as structuralist language descriptions are intended to achieve just that, the above "critique" is, with the possible exception of point (b), not fair in that it targets goals for which these descriptions were not intended.[12]

In this regard, it should be emphasized that the above points in no way question the usefulness and relevance of descriptive grammars and dictionaries with regard to their main purpose, i.e. to provide a description and documentation of a language *system*. While there is always room for improvement (compare points (b) and (c) above), there is no doubt about the fact that grammars and dictionaries are essentially successful in delivering system descriptions. What is more, the above points also do not imply that grammars and dictionaries do not have a role to play in language documentations, as further discussed in the next section. The major thrust of the critical observations above is that a description of the language system as found in grammars and dictionaries by itself is not good enough as a lasting record of a language, even if accompanied by a text collection. And it is probably fair to say that the way primary data have been handled in the grammar-dictionary format is now widely seen as not adequate and thus in need of improvement.

From this assessment, however, it does not necessarily follow that the basic format of Table 1 is the only imaginable format for lasting, multipurpose records of a language. Instead, it may reasonably be asked, why not combine the strong sides of the two formats discussed so far and propose that language documentations consist of the combination of a large corpus of annotated primary data as well as a full descriptive grammar and a comprehensive dictionary? This is the question to be addressed in the next section.

4.2. An extended format for language documentations

Assuming that the structuralist notion of a language as a system of rules and oppositions is a viable and useful notion of "a language", though not necessarily the only useful and viable one for documentary purposes, and assuming further that a descriptive grammar and a dictionary provide adequate representations of this system, it would seem to follow that a truly comprehensive language documentation does not simply consist of a large corpus of annotated primary data – as sketched in Section 3 – but instead should also include a comprehensive grammar and dictionary. Along the same lines, one may ask why the apparatus in Table 1 should only contain a sketch grammar and not a fully worked-out comprehensive grammar, thus replacing the format in Table 1 with the one in Table 2.[13]

Table 2. Extended format for a language documentation

Primary data	Apparatus	
	Per session	For documentation as a whole
recordings/records of observable linguistic behavior and metalinguistic knowledge	*Metadata* *Annotations* – transcription – translation – further linguistic and ethnographic glossing and commentary	*Metadata* *General access resources* – introduction – orthographical conventions – glossing conventions – indices – links to other resources …
		Descriptive analysis – ethnography – descriptive grammar – dictionary

The difference between the basic format for language documentations in Table 1 and the extended format depicted in Table 2 pertains to the addition of fully worked out descriptive analyses on various levels (as indicated by the shaded area in Table 2), replacing the corresponding sketch formats (sketch grammar, ethnographic sketch) under *general access resources* in the basic format. Whether this is in fact a fundamental difference or rather a gradual difference in emphasis, is a matter for further debate. In actual practice, the difference may not be as relevant as it may appear at first sight, as we will see at the end of this section. Still, in the interest of making clear what is involved here, it will be useful to highlight the differences between the two formats and to indicate some of the problems that are created by incorporating comprehensive descriptive formats in the extended documentary format. There are at least two types of such problems, one relating to theoretical issues, the other to research economy.

The theoretical problem pertains to the fact that it is not at all clear how exactly the descriptive grammar (or the ethnography or the dictionary)[14] should look that is to be regarded as an essential part of a language documentation. As is well known, for much studied languages such as English,

Latin, Chinese, Arabic, Tagalog, Quechua, or Fijian, there exist not only different types of grammars (pedagogical, historical, descriptive) but also different descriptive grammars, each having its particular emphasis and way of presenting the structure of the language system. This simply reflects the fact that at least according to the current state of knowledge, there is not just exactly one descriptive grammar which correctly and comprehensively captures the system of a language. Instead, any given descriptive grammar is a more or less successful attempt to capture the system of a language (variety), rarely if ever comprehensive, and usually also including at least some contested, if not clearly wrong, analyses.

As a consequence of this state of affairs, the following problem arises with regard to the extended format for language documentations in Table 2. Either one has to specify a particular type of descriptive grammar as the one which is the most suitable one for the purposes of language documentations and thus is able to provide a reasonably precise definition of this part of a documentation. Alternatively, one allows for a multitude of descriptive grammars to be included in a documentation, thus declaring it a desirable goal to include a number of different analyses of the language system as part of the overall documentation of a language. The latter option clearly raises the issue of practical feasibility, which leads us to the second problem mentioned above, i.e. the essentially pragmatic problem of research economy.

Practical feasibility also is an issue if just one analysis of the grammatical system is assumed to be an essential part of a language documentation, for the following reason. It is a well-known fact that it is possible to base elaborate descriptive analyses exclusively on a corpus of texts (either texts written by native speakers or transcripts of communicative events) – and most good descriptive grammars are based to a large degree on a corpus of (mostly narrative) texts. A large corpus of texts in fact provides for the possibility of writing a number of interestingly different descriptive grammars, targeting different components of the language system and their interrelation. Consequently, one could argue that even if one accepts the claim that a comprehensive documentation should also document the language system, there is no need to include a fully worked-out descriptive grammar in a language documentation. The information needed to write such a grammar is already contained in the corpus and the resources needed to extract this information and to write it up in the conventional format of a descriptive grammar are not properly part of the documentation efforts. In this view, resources allocated to documentation should not be "wasted" on writing a grammar but are better spent on enlarging the corpus of primary data, the quantity or quality of annotations, or on the "mobilization" of the data (mobilization is further discussed in Chapter 15).

The major counterargument against this position would be the claim that actually producing a descriptive grammar is a necessary part of a language documentation because otherwise, essential aspects of the language system would be left undocumented. The evaluation of this claim rests on the question of whether there is some kind of important evidence for grammatical structure which, as a matter of principle, cannot be extracted from a sufficiently large and varied corpus of primary data as sketched in Section 3 above. As far as I am aware, there is especially one type of evidence of this kind, i.e. negative evidence. Obviously, illicit structures cannot be attested even in the largest and most comprehensive corpora.[15]

However, the lack of explicit negative evidence in a corpus of texts does not per se necessitate the inclusion of a descriptive grammar in a language documentation. On the one hand, with regard to the usual way of obtaining negative evidence (i.e. asking one or two speakers whether examples x, y, z are "okay"), it is doubtful whether this really makes a difference in quality compared to evidence provided by the fact that the structure in question is not attested in a large corpus. Elicited evidence is only superior here if it is very carefully elicited, paying adequate attention to the sample of speakers interviewed, potential biases in presenting the material, and the like. On the other hand, and more importantly, the basic documentation format of Table 1 does not only consist of a corpus of more or less natural communicative events but also of documents recording metalinguistic knowledge. Metalinguistic knowledge includes negative evidence for grammatical structuring, as already mentioned above.

Obviously, gathering negative evidence on grammatical matters presupposes that the researcher asks the right questions, which in turn presupposes grammatical analysis. In this regard, it bears emphasizing that documentation does not exclude analysis. Quite the opposite: analysis is essential. What the documentary approach implies, however, is that the analyses which are carried out while compiling a documentation do not necessarily have to be presented in the format of a descriptive grammar. Instead, analyses can (or should) be included in a documentation through (scattered) annotations on negative evidence, the inclusion of experiments generating important evidence for problems of grammatical or semantic analysis, and so on (see further Chapters 8 and 9).

The major reason for choosing a distributed grammatical annotation format instead of the established descriptive grammar format is one of time economy. The writing of a descriptive grammar involves to a substantial degree matters of formulation (among other things, the search for the most suitable terminology) and organization (for example, chapter structure or the choice of the best examples for a given regularity; see Mosel 2006 for further discussion and exemplification). These are very time consuming activities which in some instances may enhance the analysis of the language system, but in general do not contribute essential new information on it. Thus, with regard to the economy of research resources, it may be more productive to spend more time on expanding the corpus of primary data rather than to use it for writing a descriptive grammar.

In short, then, the difference between the basic and the extended formats as conceived of here is one between different formats or "styles" for the inclusion of analytical insights in a documentation. In the basic format, analyses are included in the form of scattered annotations and cross-references between sessions (and, of course, indirectly also by the fact that for topics for which little or no data can be found in the recordings of communicative events, elicited primary data are included). In the extended format, analyses are presented as such in full, i.e. as descriptive statements about the language system, usually accompanied by (links to) relevant examples.

In actual practice, there will be many instances where this apparently clear difference will become blurred. For example, when the number and types of communicative events that can be recorded in a given community is severely limited, it may be more useful to work on full, and fully explicit, descriptions of aspects of the grammatical system not represented in the texts, rather than recording more texts of the same kind with the same speaker. Furthermore, on a much more mundane level, there are (individually widely diverging) limits as to the time and energy that can be productively spent on the not always thrilling routine work involved in documentation (filling in metadata, checking translations and glossing, etc.), and it would be a counterproductive and rather ill-conceived idea generally to restrict work with a speech community to "pure" documentation to the exclusion of all fully explicit (= publishable) analytic work. It is thus unlikely that linguists undertaking language documentations will stick to the basic format in its purest form and refrain from working on aspects of a fully explicit descriptive analyses while compiling the annotated corpus of primary data. It should, then, also not come as surprise that many researchers – including some of the contributors to this volume – tend to ignore the difference between the two formats and to remain implicit as to what exactly they have in mind when referring to grammatical analyses and dictionaries.

Most language documentations that have been compiled in recent years are actually hybrids with regard to the two formats. They tend to include many scattered analytical observations as well as substantial fully worked-out descriptive statements of some aspects of the language system (rarely comprehensive grammars). It remains to be seen whether this practice is actually viable in the long-term or whether there are clear advantages attached to adhering to either the basic or the extended format as discussed in this section.

5. The structure of this book

The following chapters provide in-depth discussions and suggestions for various issues arising when working on and with language documentations. While the authors have slightly different views of what a language documentation is (or should be) and clearly differ with regard to their major topics of interest and theoretical preferences, they share a major concern for the maintenance of linguistic diversity, including the quality, processing, and accessible preservation of linguistic primary data, which in some way or other all these chapters are about.

The focus of each chapter is on a topic which is rarely dealt with within descriptive linguistics (and mainstream linguistics in general), reflecting the fact that issues relating to the collection and processing of primary data have been widely neglected within the discipline until very recently. For each topic, both theoretical and practical issues are discussed, although the chapters differ quite significantly as to how much space they allot to either, in accordance with the topic being dealt with.

Apart from the present introduction, there are roughly four parts to this book which, however, are closely linked to, and overlap with, each other.

Chapters 2 to 4 deal with general (i.e. not specifically linguistic) ethical and practical issues which have to be considered and reconsidered from the earliest planning stage of a documentation project through to its completion. The guiding questions here are: How to interact with speech communities and individual speakers; and how to capture, store, and process relevant data. These issues are interrelated, in that data capture and processing is not just a technological issue, but also has to pay attention to sensitivities and interests of the speech community and the individual speakers contributing data. Chapter 3 includes suggestions for getting started with the actual linguistic documentation work in the field.

The next eight chapters (Chapters 5 to 12) pertain to the recording and processing of primary linguistic data from an anthropological and linguistic point of view. The first three of these chapters (Chapters 5 to 7, but also a considerable part of Chapter 8) are primarily concerned with the issue of how and what to document, given the goal of creating a lasting and multi-functional record of a language. Chapter 5 provides an introduction to a cultural and ethnographic understanding of language. This is essential for the success of a documentation project, not only with regard to the necessity of being able to identify the types of communicative events that should be recorded, but also for being able to successfully interact within a speech community which has a different set of norms of interaction. In the latter regard, Chapter 5 complements and expands Chapters 2 and 3.

Chapter 6 addresses the issue of how to access and represent meta-linguistic knowledge, focusing primarily on lexical knowledge. Chapter 7 briefly discusses the kinds of data needed for prosodic analysis, while Chapter 8 reports on the demands of anthropologists for language documentations, which complements the discussion of this topic in Chapter 5.

Chapter 8 also addresses the issue of ethnographically relevant annotation and commentary and thus forms a group with the next four chapters (Chapters 9 to 12) all of which are concerned with the part of a documentation called "apparatus" in Table 1. That is, they deal with the processing of primary data necessary for them to become useful and accessible to a broad range of users. While Chapters 8 and 9 provide an overview of the basic structure and various practical aspects of ethnographic and linguistic annotation and commentary, respectively, the following two chapters address some more specific issues with regard to the written representation of recorded communicative events. Chapter 10 is concerned with one major aspect of transcription, namely, the need to segment the continuous flow of spoken language into smaller units, in particular words and intonations units. Issues relating to the development of a practical orthography which can be used for the written representation of the recordings, for educational materials, etc., and which is acceptable and accessible to the speech community are discussed in Chapter 11. The final chapter in this part of the book, Chapter 12, discusses the structure and format of the sketch grammar which is part of the overall apparatus of the documentation, intended to facilitate access to the primary data themselves as well as the grammatical information to be found in sessions and lexical database.

The last part of the book, consisting of the final three chapters, relates to the long-term perspectives of a documentation, in particular, archiving issues and its use in language maintenance. Apart from an obvious focus on technological issues, the main concern of Chapter 13 on "Archiving challenges" is a critical review of the different interests and goals of the three major groups involved in the archiving process: the donators (the people handing material to the archive), the archivists (the people running and maintaining the archive), and the users of archival sources. Chapter 14 takes up one particularly critical issue in long-term preservation, i.e. the changing standards in character and text structure encoding which very easily render digitally-stored information uninterpretable. Finally, Chapter 15 focuses on speech communities as potential users and argues that there is a need for elaborate and creative concepts for mobilizing primary data, i.e. creating language resources from archival data which are of interest and use to a given community.

There are a number of important topics which actually should also be dealt with in a book such as the present one but which unfortunately and for reasons beyond the control of the editors could not be included at this point. In particular, the following three topics are also of critical importance to language documentation (see the book's website for additional and up-to-date information on these and other topics).

– One major aspect of linguistic interactions which has to be attended to in documentations are so-called paralinguistic features, in particular gesture. The recent textbook on gesture by Kendon (2004) provides a thorough general introduction to this topic. See also Section 2.5 in Chapter 9 for a brief note on paralinguistics.

– There is no chapter on the basics of producing high-quality audio and video recordings. While this topic in part involves a lot of technological aspects which change rather rapidly and thus would in any event not have been included in this book, there is a need to be aware of what defines good recordings. In addition to the book's website, see the *Language Archiving Newsletter* and the DoBeS and ELDP websites for relevant pointers and links.

– Apart from the kind of mobilization of primary data for language maintenance purposes discussed in Chapter 15, there are also more traditional, but equally important contributions that a language documentation can make to language maintenance efforts. These include, in particular, the development of teaching materials in the documented variety. See von Gleich (2005) for a brief discussion and references.

The book is also heavily biased towards the more narrowly linguistic approaches to language. Documentary work that aims at a truly comprehensive record of a language also has to engage with ethnobotany, musicology, human geography, oral history, and so on. We hope that it will be possible before too long to compile a further introductory volume where the core issues and methodologies of these and related disciplines are presented from the point of view of enhancing language (and culture) documentations.

Even though the focus is on linguistic approaches to language, it should be clearly understood that even for this domain the ability to engage in language documentation projects cannot be gained by mastering only the topics and techniques presented here. Ideally, training in language documentation includes a training in the basics of a broad range of linguistic subdisciplines and neighboring disciplines. Training in descriptive and anthropological linguistics is indispensable.

The latter two topics are not dealt with here because good textbooks for them are readily available. As for descriptive linguistics, the classic textbooks by Hockett (1958) and Gleason (1961) still provide an excellent introduction which, however, should be complemented by typologically grounded surveys of major categories and structures as, for example, in the second edition of Shopen's *Language Typology and Syntactic Description* or in Kroeger (2005). As for anthropological linguistics, Duranti (1997) introduces the most important concepts and issues, which could be complemented with the more in-depth discussion of the ethnography of communication by Saville-Troike (2003). Finally, the contributions in Newman and Ratliff (2001) combine descriptive and ethnolinguistic topics and insights and complement the discussion of linguistic fieldwork in Chapters 2 and 3 of this volume.

In conclusion, it may be worthwhile to emphasize the fact that documentary linguistics is an emerging field where many things are still in flux. Most importantly perhaps, large multimedia corpora on lesser-known languages are very new and largely unexplored entities. It is very well possible that new techniques for working with such corpora will emerge before too long, requiring major adjustments to the format for language documentations discussed in this chapter and book. But rather than a shortcoming, this should be seen as one of the exciting aspects of language documentation. Apart from being a useful introduction to language documentation, providing theoretical grounding as well practical advice, this book should make it clear that language documentation is an important, engaging and rewarding enterprise with many repercussions for linguistics and other language-related disciplines and projects.

Acknowledgements

I wish to thank my co-editors and Eva Schultze-Berndt for critical discussion of many of the issues touched upon here, as well as helpful comments on the draft version of this chapter.

Notes

1. With regard to the latter point, compare the following quote from Luraghi (1990: 128 FN1) which nicely illustrates the problems arising when data types are missing in a given corpus: "As to the position of the verb, the most important difference [between main and subordinate clauses, NPH] lies in the absence of VSO sentences in subordinate clauses. It can of course be objected that this may be due simply to the shortage of sources, since VSO sentences are on the whole very infrequent. However, in the light of comparative data from other Indo-European languages, this objection could perhaps be rejected …"
2. The major limitation here are restrictions on access to recordings imposed by speakers or communities which, of course, should be observed.
3. "Experiment" here is to be taken in a broad sense, including, for example, the testing of the acceptability of invented examples.
4. IMDI = ISLE Metadata Initiative. The manual can be downloaded at http://www.mpi.nl/IMDI/tools.
5. Note that this does not necessarily imply that all the information for a lexical item has to be gathered in a single location (i.e. an entry in the database), as it is currently done by most researchers. Alternatively, the lexical database could consist simply of links to all the sessions where the item in question occurs. This could include a session where the item is elicited as part of the elicitation of a word list or semantic field, a session where the item has been recorded in a list of items or a carrier phrase in order to document characteristic sound patterns, and a session where it occurs as part of a procedural text.
6. Please refer to the appendix for further information on this program.
7. Note that *linguistic interaction* here includes interactions with native speakers of other varieties inasmuch as they are a common occurrence in the speech community which is being documented.
8. The following list takes an audio or video recording as its main example. Of course, the same type of metadata is needed for primary data gathered in a different way such as written fieldnotes or photos.
9. Note that the term *cataloguing* is used here in a somewhat broader sense than in Chapter 4 where it is used to refer to one particular subtype of metadata.
10. Strictly speaking, "annotations" could also be called metadata since the term "metadata" in general refers to all kinds of data about data. However, within the

context of language documentations it is useful to distinguish between different types of metadata (in this broad sense), and it is now a widely-used practice to use the term "metadata" in the context of language documentations exclusively for data types which have a cataloguing or organizational function and to use "annotation" (or "commentary") for other types of information accompanying segments of primary data.

11. The structuralist idea of language as an abstract system has been articulated in a variety of oppositions including the well-known Sassurean distinction of *langue* vs. *langage* vs. *parole* and the Chomskyan distinction of *competence* vs. *performance*. For the present argument, the details of how the abstract language system is conceived of do not matter and thus are ignored.

12. With regard to falsifiability (point (b)), not providing access to the primary data is indeed a major problem for the scientific status of these descriptions. However, the basic assumption here appears to have been that whoever wanted to replicate and possibly falsify a descriptive analysis on the basis of material other than the one made available in examples and texts could compile their own set of primary data. This assumption is no longer viable in the case of endangered languages and, as already pointed out in Section 2, it is hence not by chance that a close connection exists between language endangerment and the recent increased concern for the preservation of primary data in linguistics and related disciplines.

13. The part called "descriptive analysis" in the rightmost column could also be added in other ways to the overall format, for example as an additional column of its own, on a par with "primary data" and "apparatus". While there are theoretical issues associated with these alternative overall organizations, these do not play a role for the argument in this section and hence can be safely ignored.

14. Essentially the same points made here and in the following with regard to descriptive grammars could also be made with regard to conventional dictionaries and ethnographic monographs (see Chapter 6 for a brief discussion of different types of dictionaries, which is also relevant here). Including these two other main analytical formats in the discussion would, however, unnecessarily complicate the exposition. Hence, dictionaries and ethnographies are not further discussed in this section. The choice of descriptive grammars as the main example is simply due to the fact that it is the format the author is most familiar with.

15. Very occasionally, though, especially in the interaction between parents and children, unacceptable or highly marked structures might be attested in admonishments of the form: Don't say X, say Y.

Chapter 2

Ethics and practicalities
of cooperative fieldwork and analysis

Arienne M. Dwyer

Introduction

This chapter examines central ethical, legal, and practical responsibilities of linguists and ethnographers in fieldwork-based projects. These issues span all research phases, from planning to fieldwork to dissemination. We focus on the process of language documentation, beginning with a discussion of common ethical questions associated with fieldwork: When is documentation appropriate in a particular community, and who benefits from it? Which power structures are involved, both in and out of the field? Section 1 explores key concepts of participant relations, rights, and responsibilities in fieldwork in the context of ethical decision-making. It introduces a set of guiding principles and examines some potential pitfalls. Section 2 discusses the legal rights issues of data ownership (intellectual property rights and copyright) and data access. Such information aids planning before fieldwork and especially the archiving phase.

Sections 3 and 4 cover the more concrete practical aspects of the fieldwork situation: developing a relationship with a speech community and organizing and running a project. We survey what may be termed "the five Cs" critical to planning and executing a project: criteria (for choosing a field site), contacts, cold calls, community, and compensation. Finally, since even the best-planned projects encounter logistical and interpersonal challenges, we present several generic case studies and some possible methods of resolving such disputes.

Such ethical and logistical planning is essential to successful community-centered knowledge mobilization, from which documentation products useful for both academics and community members are produced in an environment of reciprocity. It is the linguist's responsibility to focus on *process* (Rice 2005: 9)[1] as much as the end goals.

1.   Ethics

1.1. Research as mediation

Ethical behavior is often assumed to flow intuitively from the noble goals of scientific research. Most fieldworkers consider themselves well-intentioned, rational people. But have all participating individuals and groups been considered in these research goals? Have their ethical standards been considered?

Fieldwork methodology has in the last decades progressed from a typically non-cooperative model (research *on* a community) to a cooperative model which in its strongest form explicitly empowers speech communities (research *on, for,* and *with* a community) (Cameron et al. 1992: 22–24). Assumptions about what is ethical for a particular field situation are best avoided, especially assumptions on the part of the researcher about what participants want.[2] The researcher should also have a grasp of the legal implications (local, national, and international) of data ownership.[3] An understanding of ethical and legal responsibilities also facilitates the building of trust – and thus a successful relationship – with a community research team. Finally, making ethical and legal premises explicit, helps to anticipate and avoid problems. A field researcher *mediates* between speakers, their communities and the fieldworker's own community, which includes an institution, a funding body, and possibly an archive. Inevitably, all participants in a language documentation will face ethical dilemmas, in which no course of action seems quite satisfactory. There may be "no right decision, only... [one] 'more right' than the alternatives" (Hill, Glaser and Harden 1995: 19).

Distilled to its essence, the ethics of field research entails indigenous people and field researchers mediating each other's cultural imperatives. This contextualization of ethical principles can only occur through productive mutual negotiation at the local level. The ethical principles presented here may seem as both imperious and overly generic, given that in this chapter broad-brush principles are often preceded by the cajoling imperative *should* or the bossy *must*. But these are suggestions awaiting contextualization in a particular research situation. And this mediation of ethical principles by all participants forms the nucleus of any research project.

1.2. Normative ethics

The ethical decisions made during fieldwork belong to the domain of *professional ethics*. Since many field research networks also create codes of conduct, we are also concerned here with *normative ethics*. Normative practices attempt to prescribe best-practice standards for field situations.

A research team might make the normative decision to adhere to a detailed set of ethical *principles* determined in advance, asking "is our aim just to evaluate the resolution of past ethical dilemmas in the field by consensus?" Normative guidelines generally follow a deductive or an inductive approach. Some researchers review such a list of field experiences and attempt to achieve consensus on future ethical research behavior.

Another less normative approach might simply be to observe and note the ethical dilemmas that appear. This descriptive list of relevant field dilemmas and how they were resolved could serve as a reference for future field researchers. An example of a less normative approach is the "do no harm" credo discussed below.

The dangers of excessive normativity are well-known; colonial subjugation, religious or cultural conversion-induced linguicide, and business profit are all examples of normative frameworks which are tendentially destructive. Such frameworks are assumed by their proponents to be universally held, and universally beneficial.

1.2.1. Documenting endangered languages as a normative framework

Claiming that languages *should* be documented before they disappear is also a normative act, and it is a framework in which not everyone believes.[4] But most researchers strongly support the documentation of endangered languages, arguing that a decline in linguistic diversity constitutes a decline in specific forms of knowledge and expression. Speakers of endangered languages also often support such a normative framework, since language is a central part of culture and of ethnic identity. Should a language be documented when its speakers would prefer it to disappear? How should community priorities and external western-scientific priorities be weighed? Many would argue that documentation should make the language available to future generations; most would also argue that both sets of priorities should be accommodated, to the extent possible.

1.2.2. Balancing priorities

Since field linguistic situations are so diverse, one-size-fits-all codes of conduct are impractical. Codes of conduct are voluntary and often largely unenforceable, but good guidelines help ensure good working relationships and a positive research outcome. For the sake of methodological transparency, and for smooth communications between all parties, some norms are always part of the field experience.

Most research teams choose a pragmatic approach, making use of both explicit ethical guidelines as well as drawing observations from specific field experiences.[5] No matter what form is chosen, research teams would do well to make explicit the ethical norms of their particular project.

1.2.3. Normative ethics in language documentation

Individual teams should establish a code of ethical norms specific to their particular area for a given research project. This code would encompass detailed guidelines on consultation and negotiation between indigenous people and researchers for all phases of the research, including planning and dissemination.

Since such voluntary normative approaches have proven useful, the scientific community can aim at establishing a two-tiered, flexible ethical code for linguistic field research: a *generic code* of putatively universal ethical norms, and as above a specific *individual code* for a research on an ethnic group in a particular area, created by individual researchers.

At present, linguists lack a generic code of conduct. Ideally, field linguists will work with the country's linguists and social scientists to devise this generic code. This code would be specific for field linguistics but could be modelled on existing well-articulated guidelines (such as the Australian Institute of Aboriginal and Torres Strait Islander Studies' *Guidelines for ethical research in indigenous studies* [AIATSIS 2000], the African Studies Association's *Guidelines for ethical conduct in research and projects in Africa* [African Studies Association n.d.], and the American Anthropological Association's *Code of ethics* [AAA 1998]). Though the above are designed as regional codes, they are actually generic enough as to be potentially applicable to any world region.

A generic statement on ethical principles should address all phases of research: planning, fieldwork, analysis, archiving, and end products. Planning ethically for each phase entails assessing the roles played by participants and the potential benefits and detriments of research; it also ideally includes local participants' participation at every phase. In the *planning* phase, researchers should identify all the potential participants (see Section 1.3 below), including sponsoring institutions, and estimate remuneration for local participants. During *fieldwork*, the researchers establish and maintain relationships, and negotiate contracts or protocols for obtaining data. It is at this crucial phase that the researchers must obtain informed consent (see Sections 1.5 and 2.2.1 below). The *analysis* phase includes such normative ethical decisions as the number of minimally adequate levels of annotation. Annotation decisions are questions of ethics, as what annotation is included will determine the accessibility of the materials to particular audiences.[6] During the *archiving* phase, the researcher must carry through the wishes of consultants in terms of anonymity and recognition by making speakers anonymous; decisions must be taken on user access to the materials (community, scientific researchers, general public) and which materials are to be accessed.

In the longer term, such codes of conduct could be developed for specific regions (countries or ethnolinguistic areas), based on a comparison of individual codes of conduct from the same area. This would result in a third tier of guidelines, a *regional code*. Though regional codes are the least critical of the three types of guidelines, such a code would outline certain region- or country-specific practices spanning a number of ethnic groups for a given area, e.g. archival practices for material from a consultant who passed away since the data collection.

1.3. Players

The practical application of ethical principles entails the specification of ethical and legal relationships between all participants in the documentation process. These relationships should be made explicit and clearly differentiated.

First, consultants (speakers/singers) are part of a certain sociocultural context in a certain country (see Figure 1). The sociocultural context consists not only of the speaker community itself but its relationship nested within local society. Then, the interaction between researcher(s) and consultant(s) occurs within a regional and national context, which includes governments, officials, subject experts, and eventually users of the analyzed data. Speaker-consultants are part of both linguistic and administrative communities; language communities are usually part of larger ethnolinguistic or ethnoreligious regions. These regions, in turn, may be contiguous with or reach across provincial or national boundaries.

The roles and perspectives of participants are gradient and dynamically created. We can use "insider/outsider" as shorthand to describe two extremes of how a researcher situates himself or herself with regards to the research situation, as well as how other participants view that researcher. The researcher might be an insider (i.e. accepted as a member of that community) or an outsider (from a distant community, whether in that country or in another). These roles are gradient rather than absolute, since a foreign researcher and a native speaker from a distant community may both be considered "outsiders" from the community under investigation. A local researcher often assumes multiple insider/outsider roles: it is often the case that a researcher is part of the ethnolinguistic group, but not or no longer from the particular community. In this situation, that researcher is both an insider and an outsider. The distinction may be relevant for research planning, as it often facilitates research to work with a person from the actual community under investigation.

Furthermore, researchers' institutional connections play an important role in determining both the direction and scope of the research. Every institution has its own agenda. If a researcher is funded by a university in that nation's capital, for example, in some cases he/she might be expected to produce a study that enhanced that country's ethnic policy. A researcher from overseas might, in contrast, be subtly pressured by the home university or the funding agency to quickly obtain a lot of data and produce publications, while overlooking the need for reciprocity with the speech community. Creating research products useful to communities is an issue which will become more and more central to the ethical practice of the research enterprise, though currently grant funding is mostly limited to products for a scientific audience.

Institutional affiliations almost invariably insinuate themselves into the power relationships between players. Though outsiders may be regarded with more suspicion than insiders, the affiliations of outsiders generally are seen as prestigious. Usually enhancing this prestige is the economic means of the researcher as a result of the funding.

Then in this web of relations there is the archive, in which the researcher deposits his or her materials. Though requirements of the granting agency vary, each has specific guidelines for data depositing and use. Finally, the archive disseminates data to users.

That these players – individual fieldworkers, communities, research consortia, funding agencies, archives and users – may all be located in different countries has legal implications for the storage, ownership, transfer, and publication of the data (see Section 2 below). But more important to the success or failure of a given research collaboration are the shifting and highly contextual nets of power and belonging (insider/outsider) between these players. A research project on any scale would do well to evaluate both these legal and social relationships in the planning stage.

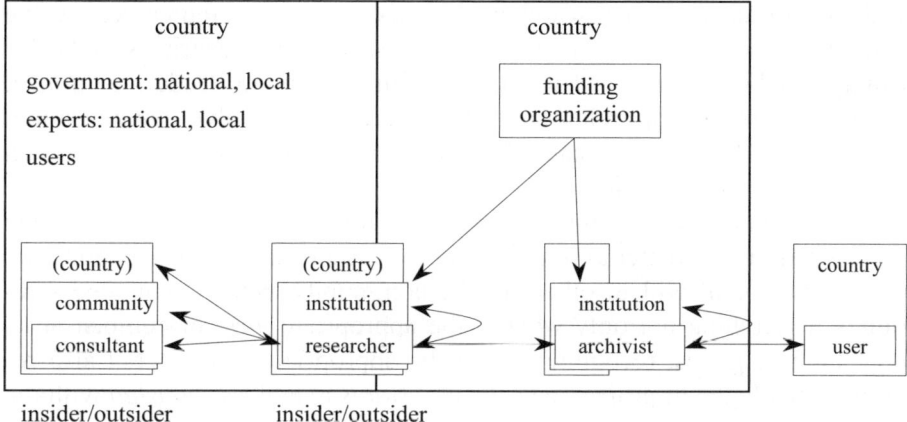

Figure 1. Participants in linguistic fieldwork (adapted from Hiß 2001, Wittenburg 2001–2004)

1.4. Ethical principles

> Heritage can never be alienated, surrendered or sold, except for conditional use. Sharing therefore creates a relationship between the givers and receivers of knowledge. The givers retain the authority to ensure that knowledge is used properly and the receivers continue to recognize and repay the gift.

> (Daes 1993: 9)

We can outline the following five fundamental ethical principles for language documentation:

Principle 1: Do no harm (including unintentional harm)

Though inarguable, this maxim requires individuals to specify what "harm" means in the specific local context. Since research is a kind of prying, protecting privacy largely concerns deciding which information to protect from public view. Harm to privacy may come from revealing information that discredits a person (Thomas and Marquart 1987: 90).

There are, of course, many kinds of inadvertent harm. For example, publicizing one person's name might result in embarrassment, whereas *not* publicizing another's name may be viewed as a slight. Moreover, the people with whom an outsider-researcher associates could be stigmatized by the community for giving away cultural or even national security secrets, for example, which might lead to trouble with community leaders or police. Also, since many researcher-consultant exchanges involve compensation, unintentional harm can be caused by arousing financial or material envy in the indigenous community.

Part of fairness is being attentive to relative compensation: what one person acquires in material or political gains as a result of participation may cause envy or ill will in others in the community. Such attentiveness requires researching not only what is the appropriate *form* of compensation (e.g. money, goods, recognition) and the appropriate *amount,* but also requires knowledge of project participants' *status* in and *relationship* with the community (see Section 3.5).

Gifts or payments of goods or money, where culturally appropriate, compensate for both the expertise of another individual and the inconvenience caused him or her. Even where no overt compensation changes hands, the core participants create a dynamic of reciprocity, whereby the gift of language knowledge is reciprocated by the researcher in some way, e.g. by compiling a community course book. After all, the term compensation literally means 'hanging together.' Underlying this equilibrium is the second principle that we might simply articulate as:

Principle 2: Reciprocity and equity

The research relationship must be *consultative, continuously negotiated,* and *respectful.* Accommodate community input into your research goals, or, better yet, plan the research collaboratively with the indigenous community. Re-negotiation of methodologies and goals is a normal part of this process. Part of the culture of respect is acknowledging that one's viewpoints may not be universally held. The researcher should also respect both the indigenous knowledge system under study and respect the confidence and trust of individual participants.

One area of normative ethics that modern researchers generally think of right away is the idea of "giving something back" to the community. This notion is not altruistic, but rather reflects the consideration that when researchers enter a community, they disturb it at least temporarily, and also take data away. Even with compensation, research behavior is nearly always a lopsided proposition, with clear benefits accorded more to the researcher than the community. Thus, many researchers in recent years have come to feel strongly that they should additionally compensate communities with scientific products or even economic development aid. Therefore, our generic code also includes:

Principle 3: Do some good (for the community as well as for science)

What constitutes a generous act of "giving back" varies greatly depending on community needs. Such acts are more abstract than mere compensation for a consultant's time; they are also never 1:1, in the sense that a researcher can never repay a community for the rich but nonetheless snapshot-like view of the culture obtained during a particular field research experience.

The most common examples of "giving back" include preparing pedagogical and cultural materials useful to the community, such as promulgating an orthography, developing textbooks and primers, making audio CDs, VCDs and documentary film, and creating picture books on material culture, e.g. embroidery or architecture.

Principle 4: Obtain informed consent before initiating research

It is critical for the researcher to establish an agreement with data producers (speakers, singers and/or a community) to record, archive and disseminate these data. Researchers are ethically obligated to inform data producers of all possible uses of the data so as to implement the do no harm principle above. Permission should be recorded in a culturally appropriate form: written, video or audio-taped. A detailed discussion of the issues and procedures in informed consent are found below in Section 2.2.1.

Such mandatory contracts certainly encourage researchers to document permissions. However, in some local situations, unrecorded oral contracts may be most conducive to mutual trust, though they usually do not fulfil the legal requirements of IRBs (Institutional Review Boards).

Principle 5: Archive and disseminate your data and results

Researchers must avoid being buried with their unpublished field notes and recordings. Within bounds of informed consent, those working with endangered-language communities have an obligation to appropriately store and publish data and analyses. Even in imperfect form, ordered, shared data are more useful than no data; disseminating or at least properly archiving collected data is far more respectful to a speaker community than piling it in the back of a closet. Hence, many field researchers now believe that best-practice archiving (cf. EMELD 2000–2005) and dissemination (in any format) should be a requirement of fieldwork.

Such principles sketch out the bare minimum in ethical linguistic fieldwork practice. For more elaborated documents, see AIATSIS (2000) and the African Studies Association (n.d.).

1.5.   Potential problems: some examples

1.5.1. *The observer's paradox and covert research*

The requirement of obtaining informed consent rules out *covert research*, i.e. recording without speaker's knowledge. The deception inherent in covert research renders it taboo for many who do fieldwork. Yet many social scientists routinely pretend to be ordinary citizens in order to obtain a naturalistic view of their research subjects: they, for example, join a group that believes in UFOs, work desk jobs for the sensationalist newspaper *Bild Zeitung,* or staff a Wal-Mart store to reveal the group or corporate practices (Wallraff 1977, Ehrenreich 2002). Such fieldworkers and journalists will vociferously defend their enterprise.

In anthropology and linguistics fieldwork, a researcher's presence changes the phenomena under observation, often making conversation less spontaneous. Most field workers simply attempt to minimize the intrusiveness of their presence (the so-called *observer's paradox* [Labov 1971: 171]) by, for example, using a small recording device, or by having native-speaker insiders conduct the field research. These methods have provided adequate data and have been seen as ethically sound by the majority of field linguists and community researchers.

However, since the observer is always intrusive to some extent, some language researchers have decided to make surreptitious recordings. This issue is so controversial among language researchers and language activists that it is usually dismissed out of hand. But such practices do exist, and therefore merit some discussion here. Covert recording has been reviewed by Allen (1997) and defended by Larmouth et al. (1992), who examined U.S. state and federal laws. Harvey (1992) argues that occasional surreptitious recording simply constitutes a greater degree of non-disclosure in a research environment where all researchers inevitably withhold some information from native speaker-consultants. (For example, a researcher may ask a consultant to converse freely when she is really only interested in the relative clauses produced.) When not based on clearly-delineated ethical principles, though, this rationalization for covert research is untenable.

When might covert research be acceptable for some linguists, then? One technique which appears to satisfy both the need for spontaneity and informed consent is the following: (1) recordists and speakers already have a trusting working relationship; (2) the researcher surreptitiously records spontaneous speech of said speakers, if and only if (3) the subject of the speech is estimated to be non-sensitive, and (4) the speakers are *immediately* afterwards given the option of informed consent, i.e. they listen to the recording to decide whether or not it should be erased or kept.

Community members and outside researchers together must develop a policy on covert recording for every research project. If covert research is allowed, then the terms should be specified. One model is the American Sociological Association's statement (1997: sect. 12.05).[7]

Nonetheless, the ethics of covert research are far from clear-cut. Thomas and Marquart (1987: 11–12) argue that ethics codes and academic goals are often completely contradictory. They suggest that rather than rationalizing behavior, academic researchers should instead squarely face each ethical dilemma as a matter of *honor*: "The operative question should not be 'Does behaviour violate the ASA ethical code,' but instead 'Did the researcher, in this given situation, act honourably?'" Most important, however, is whether or not local people accept as ethical post-facto consent to surreptitious recordings. If there is any doubt, it is best to avoid covert recording entirely.

1.5.2. Change in permissions

Sometimes a speaker who has given permission for material to be used in research and/or publicly disseminated later wants it removed. The researcher or archivist faces the dilemma of whether or not to remove the material, even though archiving was one of the original goals of that recording session. It is best to be explicit about the consultant's future rights to the recording at the time of recording.

1.5.3. When a previously uninvolved party becomes involved

A linguist wants to contribute a legacy recording[8] to an archive, but then a grandson of the speaker objects, saying that the rights to the recording now belonged to him. If an archive does not have an explicit policy, then the two parties must attempt to mediate these situations, based on the original agreement and on the cultural norms of the speaker community.

1.5.4. Ensuring accessibility

What good is an electronic archive to native speaker communities, especially if they lack Internet access? In addition to "giving back" tangible research products such as primers, the researcher should find ways to get offline electronic data to the communities. A researcher could even consider establishing WiFi (wireless) networks, if appropriate.[9]

1.5.5. Management of the resources

When material is in an archive or a private collection, the question arises as to who represents the annotated data: the community, the researcher, or the archivist? Since it is inevitably some combination of these actors, it is wise to specify decision-making power in advance for the concerned parties. When one party, for example, wants to close the resource to the public, it is best to have protocols for making ultimate decisions.

2.   Rights

2.1.   Scope

Participants in linguistic fieldwork are subject to at least three separate juridical realms: (1) the laws of the country in which data recording takes place; (2) the laws of the researcher's country; and (3) international law. Additionally, researchers may be subject to a regional transnational law, such as EU law for the DoBeS archive in the Netherlands. Within each of these realms, the distinction between *intellectual property rights*, *copyright*, and *access* is useful. Note that these issues are moot unless these rights are exercised (e.g., through a claim of ownership of material in an archive). Even then, there is little legal precedent testing protocols on rights and access to linguistic resources, until language archives accumulate several decades of experience with data rights.

2.2. Intellectual Property Rights (IPR)

Intellectual property rights concern the individual, group, local, and national ownership of so-called "creations of the mind," e.g. books, musical performances, films and even folklore. The western notion of property rights may well have no indigenous conceptual counterpart. Nonetheless, a number of documents on indigenous knowledge and property rights have successfully attempted to respectfully address indigenous issues. These include Hansen and VanFleet (2003); AILLA (n.d.a) IPR; and for New Zealand, Sullivan (2002).

2.2.1. *Informed consent*

At a recording's origin (i.e. at taping), it is necessary to obtain the informed consent of all parties. *Informed consent* is a negotiation between researcher and data producer/consultant of all future uses of the material: who will access the data, where will the data be housed, in what form will it be stored, and who will make future decisions over its use. Informed consent does *not* simply entail the researcher informing the consultant of to what use he/she intends to put the data. Of course, linguistic and anthropological goals often overlap with but differ from community goals, so part of the consent process entails community members convincing outsider linguists of practical data uses, and vice-versa.

Though informed consent has both ethical and juridical dimensions, academic institutions in certain countries have emphasized the legal aspects of such contracts. Many field researchers today, particularly those in North America and Australia, find that any of their projects involving direct work with people are subject to an obligatory institutional screening process.[10] Though such informed consent contracts are a positive development, universities need to establish a generic and more flexible consent template for linguistic and social science research in non-clinical settings under different cultural circumstances. For now, each researcher must tailor his/her own contract with his/her own Institutional Research Board.

There are three major types of consent documentation: written, verbal, and third-party.

– *Written consent*
The advantage of having so-called "Human Subject Consent" forms is that both parties have a written record of their agreement. The disadvantages, though, are legion among linguists: they require the anonymity of consultants (which is often inappropriate) and the written forms may breed mistrust. Therefore, field researchers often resort to verbal consent.

– *Verbal consent*
Verbal contracts should be recorded with audio or video devices if at all possible. Though western societies are insistent that written contracts are the only really binding forms of agreement, in many contexts a verbal contract can be equally or more powerful and binding than a written one. A spoken agreement requires at least two parties physically present, it requires eye contact, and it carries with it all the intertwining obligations and respect of a personal relationship between two people bound together in a social network. For a written agreement, by contrast, both parties need not be present nor have or maintain any sort of personal relationship. And this is why many people (e.g. indigenous peoples of the Americas) find oral contracts more binding than written ones: written ones can be torn up and forgotten, but not ones sealed by physical contact.

Furthermore, in a society with varying degrees of literacy, the written contract may wisely be viewed with suspicion, as it has often been the medium used historically by colonial powers to wrest property and land from indigenous peoples.

It has been difficult in the past to convince IRBs of the appropriateness of oral contracts in certain contexts. Even now, a researcher must make a case to these boards, who by definition represent the legalistic and writing-centered aspect of academic culture. However, today most IRBs accept oral contracts as legitimate.

– *Third-party consent*
The last type of consent entails making use of an intermediary such as a village leader to negotiate a contract between participants. The consent

contract may be written or verbal, but using an intermediary may be the best way to quickly establish a modicum of trust between parties, and to facilitate communication between the research world and the community's world.

Issues requiring our attention with regard to consent include attending to *sufficient explanation*, that is, ensuring that one's goals are explained clearly in a culturally appropriate manner. Additionally, participants should anticipate as many future uses of the data as possible.

2.2.2. Some laws governing consent

Though it is not feasible to survey the consent laws of dozens of countries here, even when laws exist on the books in countries, these laws are too loosely defined to protect speakers and singers. Under U.S. law, for example, though the basic law is intended to protect data producers, certain details allow for an unacceptable degree of leeway. A person may generally record, film, broadcast or amplify any conversation where all the parties to it "consent." Yet the consent of data producers is presumed without asking, as long as the recording device is in plain view.[11] Such flexibility, though pragmatically appealing, leaves open the possibility of unethical behavior. U.S. federal publications do recommend (but do not require) obtaining consent individually from *all* parties recorded. We can only second that recommendation here: Permission should always be obtained except where truly impractical, e.g. in a crowd situation with dozens of spontaneous performers.

2.2.3. World Intellectual Property Organization (WIPO)

The primary concern of the World Intellectual Property Organization is to protect the commercial value of intellectual property. When the data producer has a solid legal contract recognized by commercial institutions (e.g. as a recording artist would have with a recording company), then the WIPO generally protects both the data producer and the data recordist/mediator. When, however, the data producer–data mediator relationship is not part of a commercial enterprise (such as that of endangered language researchers and native speaker-consultants), the WIPO basically serves to open up language materials to potential commercial exploitation.

There are various proposals by the World Intellectual Property Organization for new *sui generis* rights in databases, folklore, and life forms. These independent rights essentially specify that rights can be bought and sold; thus a film company or a pharmaceutical enterprise could even buy rights to a certain body of folklore. Once purchased, "an utilization, even by members of the community where the expression has been developed and maintained, requires authorization if it is made outside such a context and with gainful intent" (WIPO 1998: 7; WIPO 1998–1999: 33). Critics see this as a potential for tyranny by the governments who would be authorized to enforce these ownership rights.

Enforcing such rights also has enormous practical barriers. "The fact that ethnic groups do not exactly coincide with national boundaries will make it hard to figure out which government would get to authorize activities and collect the tariffs for which body of folklore. For instance, would a Chicago polka band need [to] get clearance from and pay royalties to the Polish government?" (Liberman 2000/2001).

Even if intellectual property rights are not a pressing legal issue in a given country or society, they are generally still an underlying ethical issue. These western, business-oriented notions must in one way or the other be squared with indigenous knowledge systems so that "intellectual property rights" as conceived by WIPO and other organizations do not go against the interests of indigenous peoples.

2.3. Copyright

The preponderance of resources on ethics and rights deal with copyright as a financial issue. *Copyright* refers to the ownership and distribution of a particular work: who owns what aspects of the result, and whether it is legitimate to distribute or publish the result. As a form of property, copyright can be inherited, given away, or sold.

The focus of copyright law is monetary: if a copyright is violated, the originator of the material will lose profits due her/him. This pecuniary focus is irrelevant for language documentation projects, since they are generally money-*losing* propositions, yet the inappropriateness of copyright laws does not prevent documentation projects from being subject to those laws.

Copyright law applies where the *copying* of the work is being done, not where the work copied was created. So if a theater piece or a story was performed in Latin America but written down or reproduced in Canada, it would be subject to Canadian copyright law.

There are a number of common misconceptions about copyright law, for example:

- The publisher automatically owns the copyright. (This is not necessarily so.)
- The language community owns the copyright for traditional material. (In Western law, this is not so, though it could be given to a legal persona.)
- Owning the copyright to the collection means owning the copyright to the parts. (Not so, since editing is an act in its own right, creating a unique work.)
- The speaker owns the rights to a recorded text. (Translations are derivative works which are separately owned, but the publication of it still requires the speaker's permission; cf. Whalen/SALSA 2001.)

In a collaborative effort, deciding who owns rights can get complicated. In some projects, one native speaker may collect and do a rough transcription and translation of the data, another regularizes it, another person does a translation into another language, and a fourth and fifth may add morphological annotation. Under such circumstances it is best to note each person involved in the process.

In some countries, copyright law distinguishes being paid for doing *part* of a work from being paid to do an *entire* work. In the United States paid employment for part of a work is known as "works made for hire." In this case, the employer and not the employee is considered to be the author (U.S. Copyright office 2004). If this route is taken and the project is subject to U.S. law, then sub-contractors who do part of the work should be made aware in writing of these restrictions right at the beginning of the project. Note that the concept of "works made for hire" may be different or even non-existent in the copyright law of other countries.

Recommendations:

- Make liberal assumptions about what copyrights may exist;
- Make copyright arrangements from the beginning of the project:
- Be explicit about what is "work for hire";
- In other cases, explicitly assign copyrights in writing, where possible to a single entity.

Copyright law is not a very good conceptual fit to the purposes of language documentation, but we must use it as we can. Some have recommended non-exclusive licenses for appropriate research and educational use for use in different language documentation situations (Whalen/SALSA 2001). Fortunately, excellent resources are available on copyright, e.g. the National Library of Australia (n.d.), the U.S. Copyright office (2004), and Nimmer (1998).

2.4. "Moral rights" – non-economic rights

Independent of an originator's copyright (economic rights) there are non-economic, so-called *moral rights* to a given work. The Berne Convention, which was established to protect artistic works, states in part: "*Even after the transfer of the said rights, the author shall have the right to claim authorship of the work and to object to any distortion,* mutilation or other modification of, or other derogatory action in relation to the said work, which would be prejudicial to his honor or reputation." (WIPO International Bureau 1886–1979: Article 6(1), emphasis added). This convention ensures at least theoretically that a data originator (e.g. storyteller, speaker, singer) will always have some legal rights to his or her work. Whether or not these rights can be exercised over the work in the absence of economic rights remains a largely untested question, at least for language data originators. Until the legal strength of "moral rights" is evaluated empirically, the interests of both communities and researchers are usually best protected by ensuring that the economic rights are secured by the most appropriate parties. Data originators and analysts or one of the two are often the most appropriate choice; another possibility would be a data archive.

2.5. Access

During fieldwork, it may seem far from the concern of researchers to intensively ponder the uses of a data set in future years and decades, but the time to ask speaker/singers' permission for access is precisely at the moment of recording, when researchers are still in the field.

Concerns about the privacy or, conversely, the recognition of data contributors apply not only to these speakers and singers, but also to all other people mentioned in the recording. (Thus, if a person talks about her sister's wedding and uses her sister's name, then the sister should be involved in decisions of access.) Furthermore, access concerns apply also to all researchers and helpers on site, including e.g. local researchers and facilitators.

Disputed questions of access very often create ethical issues. One such example is when villagers allow full access including crediting recordings to their name, but local coordinators, possessing an overview of social issues, suggest anonymity for political reasons. Generally, it is best to err on the side of caution and make the names anonymous.

An archive mediates between its collections and the public. The concept most central to this mediation is *graded access*, which allows different degrees of accessibility of materials and to users. The best currently available reference point is AILLA's (n.d.b) graded access system. Types of graded access generally include:

- Fully open;
- Partially open: speaker-based/materials-based/user-based;
  - Speaker-based: e.g. texts from Speakers 1–20 are open, those from Speakers 21–25 not;
  - Materials-based: e.g. taboo or secret material is closed; general material is open;
  - User-based: e.g. only open to researchers, not commercial firms;
- Fully closed.

Most researchers are creating digital repositories, even if these are often ad hoc. These data must be accessible to the native community. Whether the data are deposited in an established archive or on an office shelf, it often falls to the researcher to make relevant material available in a format that the native community can use, which is often not internet-based (see Section 3.5 below).

2.6. Legal requirements for research

In addition to the legal requirements of the researcher-consultant relationship (informed consent) and of the collected and annotated data (e.g. copyright and access), project planning must include obtaining legal permission for personal logistics, the most important of which are:

- Appropriate visas (e.g. tourist/student/research/visiting scholar)
- Residence permits

– Health exams (for longer-term foreign residents many countries require testing for chronic illnesses such as HIV or tuberculosis)
– Research permits (national and/or local) – permission may in some countries or locales require employing certain people not of the researcher's choice, e.g. bureaucrats, known local authorities, and/or "minders."

2.7. In sum: ethics and rights

For planning fieldwork and especially for archiving and disseminating data, being informed of the national and international treaties is very useful, even if national or international treaties on data ownership may not seem to affect a research project.

The ethical requirements of fieldwork-based investigation are complex, as they demand that the researcher attend both to a respectful and reciprocal relationship with the language community and produce a documentation meeting the standards of the academic community and the funding agency. The latter requires ensuring quality (observational adequacy) as well as quantity (working with reasonable efficiency and having adequate coverage) (Krauss 2005); the former entails a duty to consult, to share benefits as well as the management and control of data (Castellano 2005).

3. Practicalities I: How to find a community and develop a cooperative relationship

Two factors are crucial for successful outcomes in linguistic fieldwork: a good relationship between researchers and indigenous partners, and a well-organized work plan based on knowledge sharing and mutually negotiated goals. The more researchers understand both the local culture and their indigenous partners' goals, and the more indigenous consultants understand the researcher's goals, the more nuanced the research results (cf. Chapter 3).

When a researcher lacks a previous working or personal relationship with a specific community of speakers, he or she must identify one, establish contact, and build a cooperative working relationship to that community. Even for a researcher with prior connections, protocols and participant roles must be negotiated cooperatively for each new project. Both kinds of researchers undergo a process of establishing "the five C's": criteria, contacts, (avoiding) cold calls, community, and compensation. Much of this section is designed to be employed as a checklist in advance of field research.

3.1. Criteria

Four criteria generally dictate a researcher's initial decision about research location and variety: With which communities and language variety do I work?

– *Linguistic diversity and/or conservativeness*

If you have the freedom to choose the language variety you will work on, your *linguistic* criteria for deciding may be typological (language *x* is unusual or typologically interesting in some way), and/or that the variety preserves an earlier stage of the language very well.

– *Political expediency*

Certain places may be open or closed to your research team for reasons of regional or national security. Local authorities may prefer that you go to only certain places, for reasons of personal safety or "turf."[12]

– *Logistical expediency*

It may be only practical to combine work in a limited number of regions, if one is working in remote or inaccessible places. This logistical limitation may require the linguist to redefine the theoretical or scientific goals of the project.

– *Interpersonal expediency*

Certain language varieties may already be dominated by a national researcher of great stature, who would resent the competition you represent (see political expediency above). Conversely, certain villages have no such reservations, but they either lack a sufficient number of consultants who are able to produce the phenomenon under investigation, or the local research talent on your team knows more people somewhere else.

3.2. Contacts

– Native speaker-consultants

Of all your contacts, consultants are the most important, and are best found via introductions from intermediaries. Creating the conditions for introductions requires patience, as establishing a consultant-researcher relationship is usually only possible after a period of trust-building with intermediaries.[13]

Native speakers are all potential teachers to the outsider-researcher and crucial to any research project. Rather than zeroing in on a single consultant for the entire research, most projects benefit from a pool of consultants, so as to avoid inadvertently producing a study of for example one person's peculiar idiolect, or a study of male language.[14] Working with a number of consultants allows the researcher to draw on each consultant's strengths, and also to correlate sociolinguistic parameters such as sex, age, place of origin and languages spoken with linguistic parameters.

– Academics

Scholars based in the country or region in question are often a crucial aid to jump-starting our research. We often rely on their prior work, even if only in a related field, e.g. local history. Discussions with these scholars can give you the lay of the land, and may yield valuable contacts.

As these relationships, are also based on equitable exchange, it is important that the outsider-investigator offers something genuinely useful to such scholars, e.g. copies of publications, offers of academic collaboration, and/or volunteering to send hard-to-find books from overseas. It may or may not be appropriate to include some academics in your project.

– Officials

Although most bureaucrats in any country seem to have been put on this earth to hamper research, some can be surprisingly helpful. Brace yourself for the worst while maintaining a pleasant and undemanding demeanor. On the occasion when they are helpful, one is pleasantly surprised. Officials are of course often crucial in obtaining research permission; and they may provide valuable (or dreadful) introductions. In some cases it may be better to keep them abreast of project developments only in the vaguest way – for often these contacts are very political, and could hamper the project or even endanger consultants, depending on local conditions.

– *Local people (non-native speakers)*

Other local people outside of the target language group often provide an etic-emic perspective (outsider-insider) on the group you are actually investigating. They can constitute an important control group for a sociolinguistic or language-contact investigation.[15]

– *A long-term view of contacts*

It is not an exaggeration to suggest that if you are an outsider-researcher, that you plan to continue returning to communities for several decades if you really want successful and mutually satisfying research results. Even though in many cases these iterative visits are impractical, maintaining contact is desirable.

From the view of western academia, repeated field research in the same community is unfortunately not yet encouraged; in fact, many academics are under pressure to do precisely the opposite, undertaking many different projects for typological comparison or for demonstrating "scholarly breadth." Yet depth – the thorough understanding of a particular language family or area and an ability to speak and think in its languages – is often sacrificed for breadth.

Recent developments, lead by endangered-language linguists and anthropologists, indicate a trend toward depth *and* breadth. The key is to work cooperatively with speaker communities and with other scholars. In this way, one can undertake diverse projects *and* continue to work with previous communities.

3.3. (Avoiding) "cold calls"[16]

If a researcher has no connections to the community, region, or even country, her work is very difficult – people will understandably mistrust her, she'll spend a lot of time explaining what she's doing and attempting to build trust among some members of a community. Basically, successful initial fieldwork planning is about *avoiding* this situation, by being introduced by an individual or individuals and building trust – however tenuously – with a community.

That facilitating person should be as local as possible; a villager is usually more trusted than one from the nearest town, and a town resident is usually better than a person from the regional capital, and a person from the regional capital is usually better than one from the national capital – the more local the person is, the more reliable she is perceived.

Of course, the issue of *prestige* sometimes skews this hierarchy, so that sometimes an outsider with the right credentials has a surprising amount of access into a society. (For example, in a society in which the local authorities are detested, someone from the distant capital or even from overseas may be seen as more trustworthy.) However, an outsider having connections is no substitute for local knowledge. Only a villager can identify where the men who know the origin story live, which of them have the teeth to articulate dentals, where the medicinal herbs grow, and who is not speaking to whom.

3.4.   Community: cooperative work between consultants and researchers

3.4.1. Lone-ranger linguistics vs. research teams

– *Lone-ranger linguistics*

What I term *lone-ranger linguistics* (with a nod to America's colonial past) represent the old go-at-it alone model of linguistic research: go in, get the data, get out, publish. It had its advantages: no negotiation was necessary, and it seemed that the one researcher was alone capable of wonders. Its disadvantages, however, are chiefly that it is inefficient and tends to promote ill-will. It is inefficient use of time, money, and other resources for an outsider to travel long distances for short periods and learn a language poorly; it promotes ill-will by giving the researcher no incentive to treat contacts in an egalitarian manner, to maintain relationships, nor to reciprocate the community's generosity.

– *Community-researcher teams*

Cooperative arrangements between community members and outside researchers have a number of convincing advantages: they are enormously efficient in terms of human and economic resources, matching local skills to local tasks and transferring technology; they provide linguistic and ethnographic field methodology training in loco; they tend to produce huge quantities of data; and the "observer's paradox" (at least that of an *outside* observer) is not so strong, since it is generally community members themselves who are conducting the fieldwork. There are some disadvantages to cooperative arrangements of this sort: they are logistically challenging, as greater numbers of people are involved, hence more intercultural mediation; a longer training period is required; and the data produced usually require more regularization before analysis.

3.4.2. Developing a mutual learner-teacher relationship

The linguist should ideally first acquire the mindset: "I am here to learn; can you teach me?" In return, he should make clear what skills, equipment, and/or resources he has to offer, for example, technology, an orthography, or help with grant applications. Many excellent works have been devoted to developing and maintaining the relationship between researcher-learner and community member-consultant-teacher; see e.g. McCarty, Watahomigie, and Yamamoto (1999), Hinton et al. (2002), Grinevald (2003: 57–60), and Chapter 3.

3.4.3. Organization of a community research team

Developing a smooth and mutually agreeable workflow entails the cooperative organization of some kind of community research team, the organization of the researcher's own tasks, and regular mutual consultation and exchange. This collaboration often entails the following steps:

– Assemble trusted local colleagues:
  If a researcher lacks local contacts, she should probably first "introduce herself" to the community, either directly via a pilot research project or indirectly by working in a nearby town (e.g. as an English teacher or development volunteer);

– Propose a research plan;

– Get their feedback and suggestions on the research plan:
  Ideally, before even applying for funding, the researcher should plan the project and budget with input from local colleagues;

– Narrow the scope consultatively:

In each research locale, a researcher should work together with his local team person and village elders, if appropriate, to focus the research plan, including:

- For an overall documentation, make an emic list of all the discourse genres that local people feel are important to document;
- For a project on a specific topic, make a list of all potential interviewees;
- For a sociolinguistic survey, plan with and train the researchers, and obtain necessary permissions, as well as notifying the villagers via a trusted leader that the research will be carried out;

- Archive materials locally *and* remotely (e.g. at the researcher's university and in the local partners' town);

- Work with small, stable, offline software;

- Work with computer programs with which your local partners are comfortable;[17]

- Keep checking in with team members:
Regular consultations by the researcher or local manager are crucial both for logistical and technical support as well as to keep the momentum going;

- Make sure the local researchers see interim and final products:
If it is feasible, show them not just the texts and translations they have worked on, but a complete session consisting of a recording with time-linked annotation should be demonstrated. If appropriate demonstration equipment is lacking, sharing data printouts, photos, sketches or even fieldnotes is important in maintaining a relationship of reciprocity.

3.5. Compensation

Common practices include:

- *For consultant time and expertise: money or gifts?*

A local contact person in the pilot stages is invaluable for advice about what kind of compensation is appropriate. If it is monetary compensation, should it be time- (per hour) or piece-based (per text)? The same compensation for the same work is recommended for every participant.

If compensation is given in the form of gifts, popular items include foods, candy, tea, or cloth. Note that some presents such as tobacco or liquor will only benefit one part of a family, and may, in some situations, delight one family member while angering another.

– *Common-courtesy compensation: media*

Audio and visual media of all types are among the nicest ways to "give something back" to a consultant or a community. Some common examples include:

– Audio and video recordings[18] copied onto more accessible formats (cassette, CD, VCD);
– Written material printed in a format useful to the community, e.g. texts in a practical orthography (without excessive linguistic or computational markup);
– Photos, sketches, and maps reproduced in pamphlet, album, or book form.

– *For communities*

At present, most researchers present native speaker consultants with small tokens of cooperative work, such as photographs and copies of recordings. In the future, documentary activity may well be coupled with or followed by providing primers, texts, and dictionaries to the community. Given that both academic funding and linguists' time is extremely limited, these products may best be created by research partners (e.g. pedagogy specialists) funded by nonacademic sources (e.g. economic development funding). Though such product development at present remains beyond the scope and funding of a scientific project, if the linguist is still able to catalyze this work, the community will benefit greatly.

4. Practicalities II: Common problems and some solutions

4.1. Money, gifts, and other obligations

What constitutes respectful and commensurate compensation will vary widely from region to region, but some form of compensation is obligatory. If community members have played a major role in creating the compensation structure, and if that structure is transparent, then the chances of difficulty will be minimized. Even so, the material and/or interpersonal advantages conferred by project work can still create tensions between researchers and community members, or between community members themselves.

4.1.1. Between outsider-researchers and consultants/community members

Scenario #1:

One common ethical dilemma resulting from ignoring participants' community roles is dealing with the outrage of an uncompensated community leader upon discovering that a young, non-prominent member received remuneration for project work. Similar cases of envy may arise in a community when people hear what a consultant got paid or given, while the clearly unqualified son of the village head wants that much too. If the researcher does not pay the son, the village head may well withdraw permission for the researcher to do the sociolinguistic survey. (Solution: Be pragmatic. If a researcher must, the son can be paid or given something, but hopefully prevented from harming the project.)

Scenario #2:

One of your local team members is certain that she is not getting her "share" of the budget, and furthermore is convinced that the outsider-researcher is making thousands of Euros every day on this project. (Possible solution: If there is enough trust between you, share the project budget with the team member and explain allocations. If this is not possible, review and reach an agreement with her over adequate compensation.)

Often no amount of discussion can ever totally subdue the suspicion that the P.I is horribly wealthy (which in comparison with local people at least is often true), and also making a fortune off the project. In situations of mutual trust, an open budget may be appropriate. In other situations, a fully open budget might exacerbate perceptions of inequity. Core indigenous research partners should in any case be central to budget and compensation planning, and should have a clear idea of the scope of the project. The outsider-researcher can go a long way to dispelling perceptions of inequity (real or imagined) by modelling parsimonious conduct, i.e. by living inexpensively as much as possible. Care with expenditures (but not stinginess) can also help. Also, he should avoid answering questions about how much recording equipment costs, as it really is shockingly expensive. Instead, he can just say, "Oh, pretty much" or "Yeah, it's a good tape recorder."

4.1.2. Between researchers and their funding agencies

Researchers who wish to produce lasting and useful products for communities are in a bit of a bind. On the one hand, they are universally grateful for the academic research funding they receive. On the other hand, scientific funding agencies are not in the business of technology or pedagogical materials transfer to the community; their primary goal is to support the analytical by-products of research on an international standard, such as books, articles, analytical databases, and of course annotated data with associated metadata. The production and transfer of materials to a community, from the point of view of a funding agency, is not quite science and a Pandora's box of endless expenses.

In the longer term, as ethical documenters we must do a better job of convincing both academic and development funding agencies that linguistic fieldwork – unlike much of natural science research, to which these funding agencies are oriented – entails a *long-term* commitment (however superficial) to the communities, and thus the production of at least minimal materials *for the communities* is essential to doing fieldwork. Scientific funding agencies will justifiably argue that they are not in the business of economic development, but with endangered languages these issues simply cannot be separated; economic impoverishment so often goes hand in hand with language endangerment. Diversifying funding sources from non-governmental development organizations may well be a workable future solution.

4.1.3. Between the outsider-researchers and communities

The compensation discussed above – photos, tapes, and gifts or contract payments in the short term, a dictionary and/or grammar in the longer term – is fully adequate. However, such compensation may still seem lacking, given the time lag in producing reference works and their possible irrelevance for the parts of the community not involved in language maintenance or revitalization. Some PIs, therefore, may be motivated to apply for economic development funding. Such funding exponentially increases the long-term contributions of a research collaboration to a community, for under ideal circumstances scientific research has thus contributed to both cultural and economic development.

4.2. Organization

Though an entire chapter could be written on project organization, we will restrict ourselves to two brief remarks on management. The first is *time management*. Building a cooperative work team is much more time-consuming (but also more rewarding) than working alone. Allow three times as much time as you estimate for a project of any size. Secondly, a linguistic research project entails both *data* and *personnel management*. While under older colonialist models, outsider-researchers would typically be responsible for both, the experience of diverse cooperative research projects has shown that the more local partners manage both data and personnel, the more likely it is that these community members consider themselves genuine shareholders in the project. And if local partners consider it their own project, then it has a much greater chance of being self-sustaining and self-perpetuating after the external funding runs out. Thus, if appropriate to the local situation, make sure that local team members with a talent for organization are actually *managing* the project; make sure that they have mirror archives of any annotated data archived elsewhere.

5. Conclusions

> There is… an inherent contradiction…, namely that we have predefined the issues … in a non-aboriginal context. The concepts of intellectual property and heritage resources arise out of a way of viewing the world that either excludes or is antithetical to that of many First Nations and therefore precludes a real understanding of aboriginal culture and society.
>
> (Marsden 2004, by permission)

Clearly, a grasp of the legal requirements for both the researcher-consultant relationship (informed consent) and for the data produced and analyzed (e.g. copyright and access) is important for any project. Such requirements are complex since they involve a web of participants subject to laws often of more than one country. But it is the attentiveness to ethical issues which can determine a project's success. If the researcher is an outsider, the real challenge lies in learning and mediating between at least two ethical systems: that of the researcher, and that of the community. Only with an understanding of both systems – and this applies equally to outsider-academics[19] and insider-community members – can ethical and honorable behavior be determined and evaluated.

Notes

1. References to unpublished papers and web resources on ethics and rights are listed at the end of this chapter.
2. The following adage is useful if raffish: *assume* makes an *ass* out of *u* and *me*.
3. For example, in the dominant legal systems of Europe and North America, it is often assumed that a speaker owns the rights to a *translation* of her text, yet in fact she usually does not, if the translation was done by someone else. (The speaker must first of course be asked permission to publish the translation.) In an aboriginal context, the concept of data "ownership" itself may not even exist.
4. Cf. Kenan Malik's 2000 article "Let them die" Online: http://www.kenanmalik.com/essays/die.html.
5. The DoBeS groups, for example, have used both normative and non-normative solutions: for fieldwork, many individual teams relied on the non-normative list method. At the same time, participants in the pilot projects developed an overall ethics and rights framework for not only fieldwork teams but including, importantly, the archivist and the end users. A summary of the rights issues they identified is Hiß 2001; a later, amended version appeared as Wittenburg 2001–2004.
6. Annotation solely in linguistic transcription and/or very theoretical linguistic tiers (e.g. prosody and syntax) would be impractical for the vast majority of speaker-community members. If other tiers are included (e.g. a practical orthography tier and a translation into the major regional language), however, the additional inclusion of linguistics-oriented tiers is not at all problematic.
7. The American Sociological Association's statement reads in part:
    (a) Sociologists do not use deceptive techniques (1) unless they have determined that their use will not be harmful to research participants; is justified by the study's prospective scientific, educational, or applied value; and that equally effective alternative procedures that do not use deception are not feasible, and (2) unless they have obtained the approval of institutional review boards or, in the absence of such boards, with another authoritative body with expertise on the ethics of research.
    (b) Sociologists never deceive research participants about significant aspects of the research that would affect their willingness to participate, such as physical risks, discomfort, or unpleasant emotional experiences.

(c) When deception is an integral feature of the design and conduct of research, sociologists attempt to correct any misconception that research participants may have no later than at the conclusion of the research.

(d) On rare occasions, sociologists may need to conceal their identity in order to undertake research that could not practicably be carried out were they to be known as researchers. Under such circumstances, sociologists undertake the research if it involves no more than minimal risk for the research participants and if they have obtained approval to proceed in this manner from an institutional review board or, in the absence of such boards, from another authoritative body with expertise on the ethics of research. Under such circumstances, confidentiality must be maintained unless otherwise set forth in 11.02(b).

8. A *legacy recording* is a recording made a number of years previously, usually on a project that is no longer active.

9. A former journalist named Bernard Krisher heads a successful solution to Internet access problems in impoverished areas. WiFi base stations mounted on motorcycles in northern Cambodia allow drivers to exchange email with networked schools and health clinics. Data is then posted on the Internet via satellite (Japan Relief for Cambodia 2003).

10. In North America, the process is often known as Human Subjects Consent, obtained from a so-called Institutional Research Board (IRB) (known elsewhere as Research Ethics Boards, Institutional Ethics Committees, Human Investigation Committees, or Human Research Committees). This process was instituted in the mid-20th century as a belated reaction to egregious medical experimentation. The IRBs therefore generally have a medical bias, so that the process typically requires the linguist to explain social-science consent procedures to the IRB, establishing alternatives to written consent. For example, it is assumed that research occurs in the home country (and therefore legal system) of the IRB, in a clinical setting, and that all participants are literate, and have no reason to mistrust legal contracts. None of these assumptions is true in most endangered-language fieldwork settings.

     Researchers in many European countries are not yet legally bound to obtain consent of any kind. Increasingly, however, academics from European institutions are ethically bound to do so.

11. "In 38 of 50 [U.S.] states, the consent of only one party is required to make it legal to record a conversation. This is also the Federal law…" (Reporters' Committee for Freedom of the Press (RCFP) 2004).

12. Neither scholars nor local officials are on every occasion completely immune to possessively viewing an academic topic or a place as our own "turf," or personal territory.

13. As one student was about to depart for doctoral fieldwork, her friend commented, "Oh, you're going for two years? That should be just about enough time to make some contacts." The student laughed at the time, but the friend was

right: it took over a year to have the contacts to really do productive field work, and seven years passed before the student and an indigenous colleague were able to record a particularly rare form of love song – trust simply requires time.

14. A significant number of grammars written on highly sex-segregated societies have been produced only by interviewing men, simply because the researcher was male. Since female speakers maybe tend to be more conservative of older features and since female language can differ in e.g. discourse significantly from that of men, these "androgrammars" can be considered inadequate, indeed, half-grammars. Even if the original objective is a gender-based study, some comparative data from the opposite sex is presumably required.

15. When I first investigated Salar, a southwestern Turkic language spoken in northern Tibet, I did a full syntactic survey of the local Chinese dialect in order to identify contact effects in Salar syntax.

16. *Cold calls* is a term from telemarketing or advertising, when a person with a service to offer calls another business or a customer without any prior contact.

17. Many people, including the vast majority of academics, have favored software; some software such as Microsoft Word gets a lot of bad knocks from computational specialists. Project partners may well be willing to learn a new program, and if they are not, programs that do not structure data well can be forced to do so (e.g. by using the Table function in MS-Word).

18. Some countries have disincentives embedded in their copyright laws. If a U.S.-based researcher is planning to make a documentary film, for example, any clip which has been "distributed" (including as common-courtesy compensation) can, according to the law, *never* be included in a publicly- or commercially-distributed documentary film. A researcher will therefore not be able to obtain funding for or submit a film to a public television station or a film festival with that clip in it. Nonetheless, most documenters are not intent on making documentary films and have no legal barriers to sharing the data.

19. Indigenous people may also find themselves in the role of outsider-academics.

Web resources and unpublished papers on ethics and rights

African Studies Association
n.d.   Guidelines of the African Studies Association for Ethical Conduct in Research and Projects in Africa. http://www.africanstudies.org/asa_guidelines.htm

AIATSIS
2000   Australian Institute of Aboriginal and Torres Strait Islander Studies, *Guidelines for Ethical Research in Indigenous Studies*. http://www.ling.helsinki.fi/uhlcs/agreements/agreement-data.html

AILLA
  n.d.a   Archive of the Indigenous Languages of Latin America, Intellectual
           property rights. http://www.ailla.utexas.org/site/ipr.html
  n.d.b   Archive of the Indigenous Languages of Latin America, The graded
           access system. http://www.ailla.utexas.org/site/gas.html
American Anthropological Association
  1998   Code of Ethics. June. http://www.aaanet.org
American Folklore Society
  1998   A Statement of Ethics for the American Folklore Society *AFS News-
           letter* volume 17, no. 1. http://afsnet.org/aboutAFS/ethics.cfm
American Folklore Society
  n.d.   Statement of the American Folklore Society on Research with Human
           Subjects. http://afsnet.org/aboutAFS/humansubjects.cfm
American Sociological Association
  1997   Code of Ethics. http://www.asanet.org/ecoderev.htm
Castellano, Marlene Brant
  2005   Towards new TCPS guidelines for research involving Aboriginal peo-
           ples: the emerging process. Congress of the Humanities and Social
           Science, University of Western Ontario, June 2005; in Rice 2005: 2.
Daes, Erica-Irene
  1993   Discrimination against Indigenous peoples: Study on the protection
           of the cultural and intellectual property of indigenous peoples. Paper
           presented to the 45th session of the Commission on Human Rights,
           Economic and Social Council, United Nations, New York.
EDUCAUSE
  2004   Digital Millennium Copyright Act: Issue Brief.
           http://www. educause.edu/ir/library/pdf/NET0303.pdf
EMELD = Electronic Metastructure for Endangered Languages Data
  2000–05 School of Best Practice. http://emeld.org/school/
Hansen, Steven A. and Justin Van Fleet
  2003   *AAAS Handbook on Intellectual Property and Traditional Knowl-
           edge*. AAAS Project on Traditional Ecological Knowledge. Washing-
           ton, D.C.: American Association for the Advancement of Science
           (AAAS). http://shr.aaas.org/tek/handbook/
Hiß, Reinhard
  2001   DoBeS Rechtsfragen. DoBeS internal document 7 March.
Holton, Gary
  2005   Ethical practices in language documentation and archiving languages.
           http://www.language-archives.org/events/olac05/olac-lsa05-holton.pdf
Japan Relief for Cambodia/American Assistance for Cambodia
  2003   Press Release: Remote Cambodian villages to send and receive email
           vial moto-bikes closes the digital divide.
           http://www.firstmilesolutions.com/Cambodia/pressrelease.htm

Krauss, Michael
    2005   Can linguistics be ethical? LSA Conference on Language Documen-
                tation: Theory, Practice, and Values, 10 July.

Liberman, Mark
    2001   *Concerning the Recording and Publication of Primary Language
                Materials.*   http://www.ldc.upenn.edu/exploration/expl2000/papers/
                liberman/liberman.html
Marsden, Susan
    2004   Northwest Coast *Adawx* Study. http://www.law.ualberta.ca/research/
                aboriginalculturalheritage/adawkwebversion_Oct1104.pdf
National Library of Australia
    n.d.   Submission to the Copyright Law Review Committee on Reference
                to Review and Simplify the Copyright Act 1968.
                http://www.nla.gov.au/ policy/clrc.html
Palys, Ted and John Lohman
    1999   Informed Consent, Confidentiality, and the Law: Implications of the
                Tri-Council *Policy Statement.* Simon Fraser University Research
                Ethics Policy Revision Task Force.
                http://www.sfu.ca/~palys/ Conf&Law.html
Reporters' Committee for Freedom of the Press (RCFP)
    2004   Can We Tape? A Practical Guide to Taping Phone Calls and In-
                Person Conversations in the 50 States and D.C.
                http://www.rcfp.org/taping
Rice, Keren
    2005   The Linguist's responsibility to the community of speakers. Presenta-
                tion at the conference on Language Documentation: Theory, Practice,
                Values. Harvard University, 10 July 2005.
Sullivan, Robert
    2002   Indigenous Cultural and Intellectual Property Rights: a Digital library
                context. *D-Lib Magazine.* May, Vol. 8 No 5. http://www.dlib.org/
                dlib/may02/sullivan/05sullivan.html
U.S. Copyright Office
    2004   Works Made for Hire under the 1976 Copyright Act. Circular 9.
                http://www.copyright.gov/circs/circ9.html
W. Maurice Young Centre for Applied Ethics
    1996–   Applied Ethics Resources on the WWW. http://www.ethicsweb.ca/
    2005   resources
Whalen, Doug
    2001   Report on SALSA Special Colloquium on Archiving Language Ma-
                terials in Web-Accessible Databases: Ethical Challenges, 22 April.
                http://sapir.ling.yale.edu/~elf/ethics.html

Wittenburg, Peter
    2001–05   Code of Conduct. http://www.mpi.nl/DOBES/INFOpages/applicants/
                DOBES-coc-v2.pdf
World Trade Organization (WTO)
    1994   Agreement on Trade-Related Aspects of Intellectual Property Rights.
                Annex C of the *OAS Summary Description of the Uruguay Round
                Marrakesh Agreement Establishing the World Trade Organization.*
                http://www.sice.oas.org/summary/ur_round/ur19.asp
World Intellectual Property Organization (WIPO)
    1996   Amendments to Articles 6, 7, 8, 10, 12, 13 and 14 of draft treaty No. 1.
                http://www.wipo.int/documents/en/diplconf/distrib/12dc.htm
World Intellectual Property Organization (WIPO)
    1998–99   Intellectual property needs and expectations of traditional knowl-
                edge-holders.
                http://www.wipo.int/tk/en/tk/ffm/report/final/pdf/part1.pdf
World Intellectual Property Organization International Bureau
    1886–   Berne Convention for the Protection of Literary and Artistic Works.
    1979   http://www.wipo.int/treaties/en/ip/berne/trtdocs_wo001.html
World Intellectual Property Organization International Bureau
    1998   The Protection of Expressions of Folklore: The Attempts at Inter-
                national Level. *Intellectual Property in Asia and the Pacific,* WIPO
                Publication No. 435 (E), January-June, No. 56/57.
                http://www.wipo.int/arab/en/documents/pdf/expressions_folklore.pdf

Chapter 3

Fieldwork and community language work

Ulrike Mosel

Introduction

Linguistic fieldwork, especially language documentation, relies heavily on the working relationship between the professional linguist and the indigenous language workers – a challenging relationship because except for their interest in the community language, both parties do not share much common ground in terms of background and aims. This chapter will first outline the differences between the linguist's and the community's approach to language documentation and then describe the kind of input the linguist can give into the community's linguistic training and language work. Drawing from experiences in the Primary Education Materials Project in Samoa (1997–2000) and the Language Documentation Project of Teop in Bougainville, Papua New Guinea (2000–2005), the chapter will deal with individual apprenticeship and teamwork and conclude with a short section on workshops.

1. Research aims and personal motivations

If we take a close look at why researchers and indigenous people engage in linguistic fieldwork, we can distinguish between research aims and personal motivations. In most general terms, the linguists' research aim is to contribute to our scientific knowledge of the world's languages or to linguistic theory, while the local language workers' aim is to do something for the maintenance and development of their language and culture. Thus linguists and local language workers research the same language, but take different perspectives. While the linguists ask what makes this language interesting for general linguistics, historical linguistics, linguistic typology, or linguistic anthropology, the native speakers may ask what does their language and culture contain that they want future generations to learn, or at least to remember. As a consequence, academic field researchers focus their attention on otherness, on what makes this language unique in comparison to already researched languages, whereas the community members see their language in relation to the dominant official language and their neighbors' languages.

Beyond intellectual curiosity, linguists are also motivated by academic career prospects, just as the indigenous people are concerned with their status within the community and earning money as fieldworkers. The linguists must meet the expectations of their funding institution and deliver the work they had planned in their application for funding. In many cases, this will be a PhD thesis with a focus on theory or some specialized investigation, rather than a dictionary for the speech community or a language documentation. In contrast, the objectives are less clearly defined for the indigenous people. Frequently, a dictionary ranks highest on their list of priorities, followed by educational reading materials, or translations of texts that are important for the community (e.g. religious texts).

Table 1. Linguists' and local language workers' perspectives on fieldwork projects

	Linguists	Local language workers
Aims	academic	educational, cultural
Perspective	focus on otherness	focus on identity
Motivation	intellectual curiosity academic career advancement	intellectual curiosity status, money
Products	PhD thesis, specialized investigation	dictionary, reading materials, translations

These different viewpoints, which are summarized in Table 1, can give rise to conflicts. If linguists make a strong commitment to the community's interests, they (or their supervisors) may feel that the academically relevant aspects of the fieldwork are not receiving sufficient priority. Neglecting the community's interests on the other hand may lead to feelings of guilt towards the language community, who are being exploited with no real benefit in return (see also Chapter 2). The sections below try to show that true cooperation, in which each party recognizes the other's interests, can lead to fruitful results (see also Mithun 2001). But before discussing in detail how such a cooperation can work, I'll briefly outline further differences between linguists and local language workers' interests when collaborating in compiling a language documentation.

2. The two perspectives of language documentation

Assuming that both parties have agreed on producing a documentation of the language, comprising recordings with transcriptions and translations, a dictionary and a grammar, they still do not share much common ground. On the contrary, their views differ with respect to the most relevant issues: the choice of speech genres to be recorded, the content of the recordings, the choice of orthography, the format of the texts resulting from the recordings, and the content and format of the dictionary and the grammar.

2.1. Speech genres

From the linguist's point of view, a language documentation ideally consists of a large variety of speech genres ranging from ritual language and formal speeches, to casual gossip (see Chapter 1). Local language workers take a different point of view. Gossip, for instance, generally not only appears unsuitable for school materials, but also socially inappropriate, and the knowledge of the ritual language may be restricted to the holders of chiefly titles. In order to avoid the impression of being intrusive, the linguist should be sensitive to the people's attitudes, and be content with what they are prepared to offer. For a detailed discussion on rules of conduct, see Chapter 2.

2.2. Content of recordings

The same applies to the content of the recordings. The ideas of the linguist or anthropologist may not meet with the approval of the local language workers. An additional potential complication lies in the fact that local language workers may well disagree among themselves. While some people would like to preserve the old legends because they are no longer transmitted to the younger generations, others may argue that they belong to the "dark ages", and are unsuitable for children's education. The researcher should try to avoid becoming involved in debates on such matters of principle – their outcome might be counterproductive – but simply try to convey the message that the community's oral literature will be lost forever unless it is recorded now, and that the community may well later regret its loss. A list of ethnographically interesting topics that might be suggested to the speech community is discussed in Chapter 8.

2.3. The format

Speaking and writing are conceptually different activities, and so is a language in its spoken and written form. For the scientific documentation of a language it would suffice to render all recordings utterance by utterance in a phonetic transcription with a translation, and the metadata that explain all relevant circumstances of the recording. This is, however, not necessarily what indigenous speech communities want.

For language maintenance measures and educational purposes, transcriptions are not regarded as suitable because they usually contain hesitation phenomena, speech and factual errors, repetitions, etc. They need to be edited. But these edited versions differ in many respects from oral literature in written form. In fact, they represent a quite different kind of language to the oral narrative in respect to its physical nature, its conceptualization, its discourse structure, its phraseology, its grammar, and its lexicon. Consequently, such educational materials may introduce a new form of the language (or at least type of text) into the community, hence arguably changing the language and the culture of language use. For this reason, it might be argued that their value for language maintenance and the preservation of cultural identity is doubtful, as the written form of the language will be heavily influenced by the dominant language and culture (Foley 2003). Undeniably, the written language developed for educational purposes will be different from the spoken one, but the real question is whether one should deny the community's desire to have reading materials in their language. Surely if the community expresses such a wish, it is the linguist's obligation to provide all the assistance she can. Language documentation and language maintenance do not mean preserving the language untouched like a fossil in a museum. In fact, language purism can be most harmful to endangered languages (Florey 2004). In creating an authentic literature that can be rooted in oral traditions (though this is not a prerequisite), the linguist can encourage and assist the people to find their own ways of developing new modes of expression, rather than taking the written dominant language as a model (see below the section on editing texts).

Such somewhat artificially created text editions are in fact innovative communicative events and may lead to a change of the language's structures (for a brief account of such changes, see Raible 1994). However, they are not useless for future linguistic research. Provided that the linguists do the right job, they reflect the native editor's linguistic competence, and the expressive potential of the language, and thus are a genuine object of linguistic research. Therefore, these edited versions deserve the linguist's attention and should also be archived and accompanied by metadata, translations, and comments on their language and content.

2.4. Orthography

While linguists as second language learners often prefer a phonological orthography that allows them to correctly pronounce words they do not know, native readers often want a more morphologically-based orthography that just allows them to quickly recognize the words in silent reading. Orthographical issues are often of marginal interest for linguists, but they are very important to the speech community (see Chapter 11).

2.5. Dictionary

Dictionary making is the area where the linguists and the community have the most divergent interests (Hinton and Weigel 2002). As an instrument of language maintenance and as a resource for keeping the cultural heritage in memory, the community's dictionary will contain more encyclopedic information than the linguists' dictionary, and thus also meet the interests of ethnographers (see Chapter 8). Furthermore, the linguists' dictionary contains grammatical information such as the indication of parts of speech, details on pronunciation, inflection, and derivation that are irrelevant for the speech community as long as the language is vital. As nobody can predict how long a language keeps its vitality, the community should accept the presence of this kind of information. It should, however, be presented in a way that does not impede the accessibility of the dictionary by native speakers (see Chapter 6).

3. Setting up the project team

In fieldwork manuals, you can find sections like "Selecting an informant" (Vaux and Cooper 1999: 7), or a list of qualities an ideal "informant" should have (cf. Kibrik 1977: 54–56). But most of the time, linguists cannot "select" the local language workers any more than the language community can "select" a linguist from outside. Rather, the linguist will work with people who were chosen by others or who offered themselves to work on the project. Of course, the researchers can ask their intermediaries, their hosts, or some institution like the local school or church to help them find someone with particular qualities such as being literate, bilingual, and interested in language work (see Section 3 in Chapter 2). But they do not know the people's selection criteria. Not everywhere in the world is the appointment of people for certain tasks exclusively guided by their qualifications. As much as their knowledge, experience, and skills, their social standing and relationships play a decisive role. When I lived in a Samoan village, for instance, it was only socially appropriate for me to work with members of the extended family which adopted me.

As the fieldworker is a guest in the community, she is not in a position to hire and fire (McLaughlin and Sall 2001: 195). Even if a local language worker really fails to live up to expectations due to laziness, unreliability, or whatever, she cannot just dismiss her/him because the consequences for this person, for the fieldworker's relations within the community, and eventually for the project are unpredictable. In order to avoid any disruption, it would be wise to first consult the intermediary or some respected person in the community in case such a problem arises.

Leaving social and political motivations aside, the language worker others choose is the person they considered the most suitable. If he or she does not meet the fieldworker's expectations, this means that she either could not communicate her expectations well or that her expectations were unsuitable.

As long as someone has a genuine interest in his or her language, is cooperative and can afford some time to work for the project, he or she will be capable to do some job in the project (Grinevald 2003: 67 f.). As Dimmendaal (2001: 63) puts it, "It is a truism but worth repeating that different informants have different talents. Some are truly excellent at explaining semantic subtleties, while others have deep intuitions about the sound structure of their language."

While the fieldworker is prepared for her tasks – she is a trained linguist and has designed the research plan – her local counterparts mostly start their work unprepared. They do not know what kind of activities linguistic fieldwork involves and what kind of work they may be good at. In order to avoid disappointment and frustration, some time needs to be allocated for identifying their strengths and weaknesses, and most important, they themselves need some time to overcome shyness and insecurity and discover their own talents and interests. If someone does not feel comfortable with his or her job, the fieldworker might find him or her a different one. In my experience, the main tasks that can be distributed among different people are:

- helping the linguist to learn the language;
- recording, transcribing, and translating;
- editorial work;
- helping the linguist to understand and translate the recordings;
- dictionary work.

4. Learning and teaching

Fieldwork is a mutual learning and teaching process for all people involved. The researcher will learn the language and a great deal about the culture from his local counterparts and, at the same time, teach them linguistic methods and the organization of language work. But in contrast to the re-searcher, the local language workers face a situation that is completely new to them with respect to:

- the subject matter, namely, the indigenous language that has never been taught before as a second language;
- their role as a teacher of an adult second language learner (see Ch. 5);
- the fact that their student comes from a foreign and often dominant cul-ture;
- the fact that they do not share the same culture of learning with their student.

When the researcher asks a native speaker to become her teacher, he or she will probably answer, "I don't know how to teach my language." Teaching one's native language to adult learners does not belong to any speaker's natural linguistic competence, but is a skill that requires training and expe-rience. In the fieldwork situation, the local teachers will develop this skill through the cooperation with the linguist when she helps them to become aware of the structures of their language and the various areas and methods of research (see below Section 5).

In order to achieve fruitful teamwork, the researchers must be aware of the possible difference between their and the indigenous people's teaching and learning practices. German people, for instance, teach practical and intellectual skills by explaining in detail how you do this and that, and why you do it, they may even add what would happen if you do it differently, or elaborate on alternative ways of doing it. But there are other ways. One day when I was working in Samoa, I met a German medical student who was doing his practical year in the maternity ward of the national hospital. He told me in near desperation, "They don't explain anything. They just want me to watch. Just watching, how can I learn anything?" In fact, this is precisely what Samoans and many other people expect, and are expert at: learning by observation.

Such different attitudes and practices can lead to misunderstandings. If, for example, you explain how to use a tape recorder and continue talking while showing how to insert the batteries, switch on the microphone, and press the recording button, your counterpart might have the impression that you regard him or her as stupid: Too much talk can be interpreted as patronizing. Accordingly, the learner is expected not to bother the teacher with questions, but be a silent observer (see Duranti [1997: 104 ff.] and Chapter 5).

In many fieldwork situations, the indigenous teachers will be pleased when the linguist learns to actively speak the language and they may be disappointed when she does not make the effort to learn phrases and paradigms by heart. But this is not necessarily so. There are speech communities who consider it as inappropriate or even intrusive when an outsider tries to speak their language or a particular variety of the language (see also Chapter 5). My Samoan family, for example, did not want me to speak colloquial Samoan.

Many linguists no longer see the production of annotated recordings, grammars, and dictionaries as the only goal of linguistic fieldwork. Instead, they regard it as their responsibility to train and mentor the indigenous language workers to enable them to work on the documentation themselves and thus "consider themselves genuine shareholders in the project" (Dwyer in Chapter 2, also see Grinevald 2003) So, what do the local language workers need to learn in order to eventually become independent of researchers from outside? The answer is, much of what a student of linguistics also has learned at school or at university, namely:

- handling technical tools (recorders); organizing notebooks, folders, files, etc. (see also Chapter 4);
- understanding the basic theoretical concepts of phonology, grammar, and lexicography (see further Section 5);
- making recordings, transcriptions, and translations and editing the transcriptions (see further Section 6);
- organizing the work flow (see Section 7).

5. Getting started: elicitation

In the very beginning of fieldwork, the researcher has to rely on elicitation. Elicitation means getting linguistic data from native speakers by asking questions.[1] Accordingly, some older fieldwork manuals give advice on what kind of questions to ask or not to ask, how to make the interview interesting and keep the informant attentive, etc. In this manner, such manuals quite automatically assign a passive role to the native speaker.

If we regard fieldwork as a mutual teaching-learning event, this approach is no longer acceptable. Rather, we have to develop methods that involve the speaker as an active partner who eventually becomes an independent language documenter him- or herself. In the remainder of this section, we will briefly outline how in the initial fieldwork phase the data collection can be combined with training in basic linguistics. Section 6 describes how the linguist and the local language workers can cooperate in building up a corpus of annotated recordings and edited texts.

5.1. Wordlists

In the very first sessions of fieldwork, you need to compile wordlists to investigate the phonological system and create a working orthography, or understand an existing orthography. Traditional fieldwork manuals recommend compiling wordlists by asking bilingual native speakers for the translation of wordlists in the lingua franca into their native language. Some also provide the translation terms for such wordlists (Kibrik 1977: 103–124; Vaux and Cooper 1999: 44–49). This method is questionable on both linguistic and psychological grounds. The native speakers might feel embarrassed when asked for the translation of a word they do not understand or even worse, a word that they cannot translate because they have forgotten the indigenous equivalent, or because there is a taboo about it. An alternative method works like this:

– Explain what you need the wordlists for – this is not just for studying phonology and orthography; the first wordlist of about 180 words will also serve as the starting point to build short clauses;
– discuss what semantic fields might be suitable to start with, and perhaps suggest food and cooking;

–   ask the native speaker to teach you words of this particular semantic field by dividing it into subcategories, e.g.:
    –   fruit and vegetables, edible animals
    –   dishes
    –   activities
    –   tools.

Thus you ask:
–   tell me the names of fruit and vegetables you grow and eat
    (apples, spinach, beans, potatoes ...);
–   what do you do when you make a dish with potatoes?
    (wash, peel, boil, fry ...);
–   what kind of things do you use?
    (knife, spoon, tongs, pot ...);

When eliciting words expressing activities like 'wash, cut, boil, roast,' etc., it is often useful to ask for commands because imperatives are in many languages the most simple verb forms. In order to get the simplest forms and avoid complex polite expressions which may be crucial in certain societies, establish a scenario where the mother asks her daughter to wash the vegetables, boil the water, etc.

This method of active eliciting will not only help you to learn the first words and short sentences, but also make the native speaker aware of the notion of semantic fields and different word classes, e.g. verbs and nouns.

5.2. Phonology

180 words are not enough to study the phonology of a language. But nobody is expected to do a more or less complete study of the phonology before investigating morphology or syntax. Rare sounds, sound combinations, or tonal patterns that are overseen in a preliminary phonological analysis will certainly show up in the course of later analysis and then phonology can be revised accordingly. In a fieldwork methods course I taught with a speaker of Acoli, a tonal language from Uganda, most of us had difficulties hearing the tonal patterns. Instead of spending numerous frustrating sessions on phonology, we started with syntax before we had worked out the phonology in detail. This gave us time to familiarize ourselves with other features of the language, while at the same time, our teacher became in-

creasingly aware of the tone system of his own language by observing our errors, thus putting him in a better position to identify and correct our pronunciation mistakes. A German proverb says, "You learn by your mistakes." In fieldwork, your teacher learns through your mistakes and you will profit from this yourself.

Once you have come across two or three minimal pairs, you can try to explain to your teacher what a minimal pair is. Avoid any linguistic terms, work in a playful way, you may even invent games for the children, such as finding words that nearly sound the same or finding words that rhyme, e.g. the Teop words [bon] 'day', [bo:n] 'mangrove', and [vasu] 'stone', [tasu] 'throw'.

5.3. Short clauses

The next step is to ask the native speaker to build short clauses from the wordlist. If English were the language to be researched and food preparation chosen as the semantic field, the list would probably contain the words *water, fish, boil, cook*, and *fry* and the teacher would produce clauses such as *boil the water, cook the fish, fry the fish*. When the linguist tries out other combinations like **cook the water*, the indigenous teacher will correct her and, at the same time, become aware of the notion of collocation. In addition, the existence of functional words (e.g. articles) and the first rules of word order can be learned from such short clauses. Put differently, while the linguists learn the first rules of the grammar of this particular language, the native speakers have their first lesson in grammatical analysis. This would also include morphology when, for instance, the nouns inflect for case and the verbs for gender in the imperative. Similar to phonology, the more the indigenous teacher becomes aware of the grammatical structure of his or her language and of collocation rules as in the case of *boil, cook*, and *fry*, the easier it is for her to identify mistakes and thus become a better teacher.

6. Creating a corpus of recordings with transcriptions and translations

The documentation of a language should contain recordings of a large variety of naturally spoken language. But in the beginning, such recordings would be much too difficult to transcribe and analyze. Short simple stories are more suitable for both the linguist as a language learner and the indigenous language teacher who is introduced into the techniques of recording, transcribing, and translating. If the speech community has a tradition of telling stories to children, these stories may be a good starting point because their content, sentence structure, and vocabulary will be relatively easy to understand.

Before starting with the recordings for a corpus, the linguist needs to discuss the contents of the recordings (see above Section 2.2), and explain the various tasks and the workflow. Once the teacher knows how to handle the recorder, he or she can ask other people for such stories and can record them without the outsider linguist being present. I practice this method wherever possible because my mere presence creates an unnatural situation that might influence the way the people talk. At worst, speakers may even use a kind of foreigner talk (albeit unconsciously) to make sure that I understand them. Or they might speak what they think is the purest or best language, even though nobody speaks this way. Furthermore, people just might feel uncomfortable in the presence of a foreign visitor. Because the recording of people can be felt as intrusive, many linguists and anthropologists have agreed on certain rules of conduct as further discussed in Chapter 2.

6.1. Recordings

Before advising the local language workers how to operate a recorder, it will be useful to think about the sequence of steps to be done, e.g. insert the battery into the recorder or the camera and the microphone, connect the microphone, etc., and to stick to this sequence whenever you show them how to do recordings. Explain how to hold the microphone (not too close to the mouth) and that one should avoid noisy places for the recording. Practice with them and let them practice with others so that they gain confidence. If they are not used to dealing with modern technology, they will need some time to lose their fear of doing anything wrong or breaking the equipment.

6.2. Transcriptions

If the local language workers are literate in any language, they can be asked to make transcriptions. Even if their spelling is inconsistent or neglects important distinctions (ones that linguists might consider indispensable), their transcriptions will be a great help. The most important thing to teach them is to transcribe what the speaker actually says and not to correct speech errors and other mistakes, although such editing is certainly legitimate in later stages of data collection and analysis (see Section 2.3).

In order to allow for a genuine participation of the speech community in the documentation project, it is imperative that all recordings are transcribed in a practical orthography readily accessible to literate but not linguistically-trained native speakers. For specialists interested in phonetics and phonology, only a selected corpus needs to be rendered in a phonetic transcription. The more time spent on narrow phonetic transcriptions, the smaller and the less useful the corpus of annotated recordings will be for the speech community and for researchers who are not interested in phonetics and phonology. For a detailed discussion on transcription and orthography development, see Chapters 9–11.

The local language workers may be afraid of "spelling mistakes" in their work. But as long as the orthography has not been standardized, there is no such thing as a right or a wrong spelling, and they should be encouraged to follow their intuitions, which may be relevant for the analysis of the phoneme system (Duranti 1997: 170–172). As discussions on spelling problems and standardization can be quite emotional and are often guided by sociopolitical issues, they should be postponed to a later stage when the linguist is more familiar with the speech community and the local language workers have gained more experience in writing their language.

However, for the data base of the project, especially for the lexicon, a consistent working orthography that distinguishes between norms and variants is a prerequisite, but this does not necessarily imply that the local transcribers have to learn and use it. Later, when the speech community decides on their own norms, the working orthography can be adjusted to their standard orthography.

6.3. Translations

The purpose of the translation determines whether a free and idiomatic or a more literal and, hence, non-idiomatic translation is given preference. For the linguistic analysis, the latter is more suitable, but bilingual members of the speech community and readers who are more interested in the content than the linguistic form will certainly prefer the idiomatic one (see further Chapters 8 and 9) For our Teop project, we solved this conflict by having the idiomatic translation next to the transcription and giving a literal translation in the footnotes wherever we thought it necessary for a better understanding of linguistic structures.

It might be difficult to find people in the community who feel confident to do translations on their own, but if you do, employ them even if their knowledge of the target language is not perfect and their translations cannot be directly used for the documentation. Any differences between their translation and yours can provide useful indications that some of your interpretations are misguided and need to be revised. Before they start, explain to them that this will be only a raw translation and that they need not be worried about making mistakes at this stage. If they do not know the translation equivalent of an expression, or if there is none in the target language, they can use the original expression and explain its meaning in brackets or in a footnote. To clearly show how the translation relates to the original, it is advisable to number the utterances in the transcription and ask the translator to do the translation utterance by utterance using the same numbers in his or her translation. Otherwise, there is the danger that he or she might be inclined to retell the recording, rather than translate it.

6.4. Editorial work

Since transcriptions are, as mentioned above, not a pleasant read, the local fieldworkers may want to edit them. In order to prevent that they model their editorial work in syntax, style, phraseology, or discourse structure on the written dominant language (see Foley 2003), the following guidelines may be helpful:

- as an editor, always respect the speaker's way of saying things;
- never change words and phrases for stylistic reasons, but only where the speaker makes an obvious mistake;
- do not change the sentence structure; do not, for instance, replace coordinate clauses by subordinate clauses;
- do not change direct speech into indirect speech or vice versa;
- add information only where absolutely necessary for understanding; for instance, when the speaker refers to things no longer known to the younger generation;
- do not shorten the text.

7. Work flow and time management

Efficient work presupposes a well organized work flow and good time management. It is impossible to plan everything in advance, because one does not know the talents and interests of the local language workers, and they themselves do not know them before having had some practice in linguistic work. Therefore, it is advisable to start with only two or maximally three people and allocate some time for the development of a work routine. Later on, more people can join the team.

The researcher and local language workers should always have a clear idea of what kind of work needs to be done and when it needs to be done and, therefore, jointly organize their work along the following lines:

– identify what kind of activities are required to produce a piece of documentation work;
– discuss who will do what;
– make a work plan by putting the various activities into a certain order and allocating a certain time for each;
– try to stick to the work plan; finish one thing before you do the next;
– evaluate the work plan and revise it.

As the organizer of the documentation, you will only be successful if you divide your project into small and easily manageable subprojects, and always try to finish one before you start with the next. On no account should the transcription, the translation, and the description of the circumstances of the recordings be postponed until later, because the recordings might be so context-bound that they are hardly understandable once the details of this context have been forgotten. Duranti (1994: 31) reports about his experiences in Samoa: "I found that even people in the same village would misinterpret utterances when removed from their immediate context and the fact of speaking the same language or living in the same community was no guarantee of the accuracy of transcription and interpretation."

Furthermore, with each transcription and translation you will discover exciting features of the language, and you and the other team members will become more and more motivated when you see how the drafts are completed one after the other. There are areas and circumstances where you cannot use a computer and have to revert to handwriting or a manual typewriter. If, however, the field situation allows you to use a computer, you should also have a printer in order to give your co-workers printouts to read.

One problem with time management is that local language workers may hesitate to conclude a piece of work. There is always something that can be improved so that they may insist on continuous revisions. They also might be afraid of criticism from other members of the community. And criticism will definitely come. Here strict deadlines help. When I worked with a team of Samoan teachers on the Samoan monolingual dictionary for school children (Mosel and So'o 2000), I very much appreciated the strict deadline set by the funding agency, the Australian Agency for International Development. Meeting the deadline obliged us to make compromises and refrain from perfectionism. One of the mistakes we discovered soon after publication was the definition of *koale* 'coal' that translates into English as 'coal is a black or dark-brown mineral found in the ground. It is used for making fire as well as for the production of the drink Coca-Cola'. (Mosel and So'o 2000: 150) But having a dictionary containing such a mistake is certainly better than a half-finished manuscript that will never be published.

When I was working on the Teop language in Bougainville in 2004, which was my fourth fieldtrip to the area, we established the following work flow; note that all work had to be done in handwriting:

- recordings on MDs (Enoch, Shalom, Ulrike);
- writing down the metadata of the recordings and copying the MDs on cassette tapes (Ulrike);
- transcribing the cassette tapes (Enoch, Joyce, Shalom);
- checking the transcriptions and rewriting them in legible handwriting using a consistent practical orthography (Ulrike);
- discussing the transcription with the transcribers (Ulrike with Enoch, Joyce, and Shalom);
- going through the revised transcription while again listening to the tape, trying to understand the recording, noting down new words with the explanations of a native speaker (Ulrike with Siimaa and Joyce);
- translating the transcriptions into English (Ulrike with Siimaa and Joyce);
- giving the original transcriptions back to the transcribers Joyce and Enoch for editing;
- checking the editing, discussing and revising them (Ulrike with Enoch and Joyce respectively, often in the presence of Siimaa);
- giving the revised edited versions to the translator (Naphtaly);
- checking and discussing the translation (Ulrike with Naphtaly, often in the presence of Siimaa).

At the same time, Siimaa and Vaabero worked on example sentences and monolingual definitions for the dictionary, while two graphic artists, Neville and Rodney, made illustrations for the legends and the dictionary.

8. Workshops

In so-called Third World countries, workshops are frequently conducted by foreign aid agencies and non-governmental organizations in order to disseminate information, skills, or new technologies. The community might therefore expect you to run a workshop. However, before you enthusiastically agree, carefully consider the following issues:

1. What is the purpose and the envisaged outcome of the workshop?
2. How much money do you have at your disposal? How much do you have to calculate for transport, food, and accommodation for each participant per day?
3. How many participants can be invited on the basis of this calculation, and for how many days?
4. Who decides on the selection of participants? What are the selection criteria?
5. Who will help with the organization (i.e. invite the participants; organize food, stationary, and accommodation)?
6. Who decides on the agenda?
7. Who writes a report?
8. What kind of rituals are to be observed (e.g. opening ceremony, farewell party)?

The less you are involved with organizational matters the better, because that gives you more time to concentrate on the content. On the other hand, not being involved may marginalize your professional input and be counterproductive to the original goals of the workshop.

There are several kinds of workshop that are useful in the context of language documentation projects, for example:

1. introductory workshops;
2. workshops on the standardization of the orthography;
3. workshops for the training of community language workers;
4. workshops for the training of school teachers.

Content, structure, and logistics of workshops are so much dependent on the sociocultural context and the resources in terms of money, time, and manpower, that only some very general points can be discussed here.

At the beginning of the project, a half-day or maximally a full-day workshop can be useful to introduce the researchers, to inform the community about the project and what language documentation is all about, and to discuss the expectations and wishes of the community as well as those of the researchers. This workshop can also help to recruit local language workers and may be visited by many people.

The second type of workshop is of a very different nature and needs to be planned with utmost care. As already mentioned above, orthography is a sensitive, often a political, issue as the written form of a language is literally "seen" as representative of the language and a symbol of cultural identity. Practical issues like learnability or linguistic adequacy often play an inferior role, especially when there are already two or more competing orthographies in the community; more important in decision making are the societal standing of the people involved, and perhaps rivalries between various groups in the community (see also Section 2 in Chapter 11). To avoid conflicts and disruption as far as possible, it is advisable to keep the number of participants small and leave their selection to the elders of the community.

If you have the funds, the equipment, and a team of three or more linguists, you can also run longer workshops or a series of workshops in which members of the community are trained in the linguistic and technical skills needed for language documentation and revitalization. A detailed description of workshops for community language workers is found in Florey (2004).

The fourth type of workshop is better conducted by school inspectors or senior teachers so that the linguists' role may only be to assist in the production of workshop materials and make suggestions for how they can be used.

9. Concluding remarks

Working with a team of native speakers in the community is a most fascinating enterprise, intellectually, socially, and personally. Each day you discover interesting linguistic phenomena and learn more about the people's culture. Nowhere else can you find people showing so much enthusiasm for linguistic work. During your university studies, you may often have been in doubt whether you are doing the right thing, especially when relatives and friends keep asking what linguistics might be good for. But once you have started with language documentation work, you know the answer.

Acknowledgements

I am grateful to all my Samoan and Teop colleagues with whom I had the pleasure to gain experience in community language work. Special thanks go to Ainslie So'o, Fosa Siliko, and Agafili Tuitolova'a, who were my counterparts in the Primary Education Materials Project in Samoa (1997–2000), to Ruth Saovana Spriggs, who introduced me to her people in Bougainville and works on the documentation of the Teop language, and to the team of the Teop language workers. In particular, I would like to express my gratitude to my host and teacher Siimaa Rigamu of Hiovabon in Bougainville.

Note

1. For a critical overview of elicitation techniques, see Himmelmann (1998: 186 ff.).

Chapter 4

Data and language documentation

Peter K. Austin

Introduction

The role of data in language documentation is rather different from the way that data is traditionally treated in language description. For description, the main concern is the production of grammars and dictionaries whose primary audience are linguists (Himmelmann 1998; Woodbury 2003). In these products language data serves essentially as exemplification and support for the linguist's analysis. It is typically presented as individual example sentences, often without source attribution, and often edited to remove 'irrelevant material'. There may also be a 'sample text' or two in an appendix to the grammar. Language documentation, on the other hand, places data at the center of its concerns. Woodbury (2003: 39) proposes that

> direct representation of naturally occurring discourse is the primary project, while description and analysis are contingent, emergent byproducts which grow alongside primary documentation but are always changeable and parasitic on it.

For language documentation then, data collection, representation and diffusion is the main research goal with grammars, dictionaries, and text collections as secondary, dependent products that annotate and comment on the documentary corpus. The audience for language documentation is also very wide, encompassing not only linguists and researchers from other areas such as anthropology, musicology, or oral history, but also members of the speech community whose language is being documented, as well as other interested people. A significant concern for documentation is archiving, to ensure that materials are in a format for long-term preservation and future use, and that information about intellectual property rights and protocols for access and use are recorded and represented along with the data itself. Important also is 'mobilization' of materials (cf. Chapter 15), i.e. generation of resources in support of language maintenance and/or learning, especially where the documented languages are endangered and in need of support.

Woodbury (2003: 46–47) argues that a good documentation corpus should be:

1. *diverse* – containing samples of language use across a range of genres and socio-cultural contexts, including elicited data;
2. *large* – given the storage and manipulation capabilities of modern information and communications technology (ICT), a digital corpus can be extensive and incorporate both media and text;
3. *ongoing*, *distributed*, and *opportunistic* – data can be added to the corpus from whatever sources that are available and be expanded when new materials become available;
4. *transparent* – the corpus should be structured in such as way as to be useable by people other than the researcher(s) who compiled it, including future researchers;
5. *preservable* and *portable* – prepared in a way that enables it to be archived for long-term preservation and not restricted to use in particular ICT environments;
6. *ethical* – collected and analyzed with due attention to ethical principles (see Chapter 2) and recording all relevant protocols for access and use.

This means the corpus must be stored digitally and ideally collected digitally.

In this chapter we outline the major processes involved in collecting and representing language data in a documentation framework, briefly discuss the tools that are available to assist with this work, and illustrate some of the products that documentary linguists have developed to present the results of their research. Further technical details about data structures and encoding, tools, archiving, and outputs can be found in other chapters in this volume (see Chapters 13, 14, 15).

It is important to emphasize that language documentation is a developing field that has emerged only recently and that is undergoing rapid change in terms of both theory and practice. It can be anticipated that much of what is presented in this chapter will be subject to change and development in coming years.

1. Processes in language documentation

Language documentation begins with the development of a project to work with a speech community on a language and can be seen as progressing through a series of stages, some of which are carried out in parallel. In the following we discuss the processes that involve data collection, processing, and storage. These can be identified as follows:

1. *recording* – of media (audio, video, image) and text;
2. *capture* – moving analogue materials to the digital domain;
3. *analysis* – transcription, translation, annotation, and notation of metadata;
4. *archiving* – creating archival objects, and assigning access and usage rights;
5. *mobilization* – publication, and distribution of the materials in various forms.

Note that at the time when a documentation project is being developed each of these processes should be considered and relevant procedures included in the project planning. In particular, archiving and mobilization must be considered from the beginning of the project and not left to the end of the project or as an afterthought (see further below).

A crucial aspect that must be kept in mind at all stages is backup.

Backup

It is prudent for any project, and especially one involving digital ICT, to develop a regular and effective regime of backing up the project data, ideally on a range of different media (e.g. CD-ROM, DVD, flash memory, external hard disk). Backups should be incremental and intended for full recovery, should disaster strike. One widely agreed mantra is LOCKSS "lots of copies keep stuff safe" (see http://www.lockss.stanford.edu). Remember, it is highly likely that you will lose data at some point in your project work, however, a good backup regime will ensure that such loss can be minimized.

---

2. Documentation processes – recording, metadata creation, and capturing

2.1. Recording

A good documentation corpus will include audio and/or video materials, ideally recorded in authentic settings and under good conditions. When recording outdoors, if possible attempt to minimize noise from animals, traffic, machinery and electrical equipment, wind and the environment, and non-linguistic activities (e.g. children playing in the vicinity). When recording indoors, it is important to keep away from machines and electrical equipment, hard walls (that reflect sound), and windows. For video, it is necessary to consider light conditions, use artificial lighting and reflectors as appropriate, and to learn some basic filming techniques, ideally from an ethnographic filmmaker or relevant textbook.

Note that we are often unaware of and filter out much of the noise and movement around us, however, this will appear on your recordings, sometimes over the top of the intended documentary data. There are four ways to check on and reduce unwanted noise:

1. monitor the recording through closed headphones as you make it;
2. use a good quality external microphone and never rely on the microphone built into the equipment, especially for video cameras;
3. cover the microphone with a wind shield and place it as close to the speaker's mouth as possible, using a boom or shotgun microphone if appropriate;
4. reduce all unnecessary movement and sound such as shuffling papers, audience members moving, etc.

It is imperative to use good quality equipment (the best you can afford with the project resources available) including good microphones, lighting, headphones, and consumables (tapes, discs, batteries). It is also important to divide up duties and individual researchers should not attempt to do all the recording tasks. It is better to employ and train assistants, ideally interested members of the language community, to help with microphones, recorders, cameras, lights, and interaction with the people being recorded.

The choice of recording equipment (DAT, minidisk, solid state, DVD, analogue tape) may be a compromise between quality/cost and convenience and needs to be carefully considered, taking into account such factors as the local climate (DAT recorders are notably unstable in tropic climates, for example), access to electrical power, and portability. Two basic principles, however, are **never** record in compressed format such as mp3, and **never** record direct to computer hard-disk, as such techniques risk irrecoverable data loss (on sound file formats, see below and Chapter 13). There is good advice about audio and video recording available in textbooks such as Ladefoged (2003) and on the internet (see especially David Nathan's fact sheet on microphones at http://www.hrelp.org/archive/advice/microphones.html).

Video recordings have a number of advantages: they are immediate, rich in authenticity, multi-dimensional in context, of great interest to communities, and can be produced independently by members of the community without the researcher in situ. They present several problems, however, including being more difficult to produce, harder to process (transcribe, annotate – see below), difficult to access without a time-aligned transcription, difficult to transfer and store (raw video requires large amounts of storage space), and difficult to preserve in the long term (since there are as yet no universally-agreed standards for digital video). There may also be complexities having to do with prohibitions in some communities against viewing the images of dead people appearing in video recordings (necessitating delicate treatment in terms of access and use restrictions). Note that in some communities making video recordings is not possible for cultural reasons.

Audio recordings are less difficult to produce than video and are relatively simpler to manipulate, store, and curate. Audio is also more familiar as a medium and has been in general use by linguists for more than 50 years. Several audio processing software tools exist (see below), and archiving is less problematic than video. Conversely, audio recordings contain less information than video, are difficult to access without time-aligned transcription, and changing formats (both carriers and data formats) make obsolescence a major problem, e.g. locating equipment to play the media on. This is especially true of legacy sound recordings (wax cylinders, wire, reel-to-reel tape) but will becoming increasingly the case for digital media, including DAT recordings and probably minidisk as new machines are introduced by manufacturers and older equipment and carriers are no longer available for purchase.

Before starting fieldwork

It is important to test all your equipment, including cables, connectors, and adaptors **before** you leave for fieldwork. Remember that one missing cable or connector can prejudice an expensive fieldtrip so prepare your equipment before you leave for the field and get professional advice as necessary. Make sample recordings under a range of conditions and check their quality. Transfer the recordings to your computer and be sure you know how to use the relevant processing software and how to burn CD-ROM or DVD backup copies of the data. Check the data on your backups on another computer to make sure that your writer and software are working properly. If in doubt, seek advice.

While making the audio and video recordings it can be useful to take field-notes, including rough transcriptions, translations, relevant recording meta-data, diagrams, drawings, and notes that can serve as aide memoire for later writing up or checking. Fieldnotes should be written in ball-point pen (not pencil and not washable ink!) on good quality paper (ideally in a bound notebook) using one side of the page only. As soon as possible after the recording session fieldnotes should be checked and elaborated, and trans-ferred to a digital form. It is amazing how rapidly one forgets what abbre-viated notes made while recording and interviewing mean.[1]

Digital text has a number of advantages: it is compact, stable, easy to store, access, and index, and can express hypertextual relationships (links). There are a large number of tools available to process text data (text edi-tors, word processors, databases, browsers, etc), and well established liter-acy traditions and knowledge of written text in many communities. How-ever, it is less rich than audio and video as there is always loss of information when 'reducing language to writing'. Text needs to be con-nected to richer recordings of speech events through time-aligned transcrip-tions and hyperlinks (see examples below and elsewhere in this volume). However, written documentation outputs in the form of books are highly valued in many language communities and, for those where ICT resources are not available or limited, will be the ideal form of product from a docu-mentation project.

Labelling and metadata

Whatever the recording medium, it is important to rigorously label everything, including tapes, disks, CDs, containers, fieldnote books (number all the pages!) immediately, consistently, and uniquely (e.g. using date and sequence number). Write this information with an indelible marker on the object itself, since disks and tapes can become separated from their covers. It is also im-perative that a proper record of metadata (data about the recorded data, see be-low), such as speaker name, recording location, dialect, etc., is made at the same time as the recordings are labelled. You can do this in a notebook or as a computer file (create a structured file using a spreadsheet, database or Word table, whatever is most convenient).

2.2. Metadata creation

Metadata is data about data, i.e. structured information about events, recordings, and data files. It is usually represented as text (but not always, e.g., it could be a spoken introduction track on a video or audio recording), but it is a different type of media because it is collected and used differently from other types. Typically metadata is collected and stored according to some formal specification. Metadata is needed for proper description of the data and to enable it to be found and used (see Bird and Simons 2003). There are two main competing international standards for linguistic metadata, that promoted by the Open Language Archives Community (OLAC) and that promoted by the ISLE Metadata Initiative (IMDI), the former being less detailed than the latter. The choice of metadata format should be made in consultation with the archives where the researcher intends to deposit the documentary materials (see Chapter 13).

There are several types of metadata:

1. *Cataloguing* – information useful to identify and locate data, e.g. language code, file ID number, recorder, speaker, place of recording, date of recording, etc.
2. *Descriptive* – information about the kind of data found in a file, e.g. an abstract or summary of file contents, information about the knowledge domain represented.
3. *Structural* – for files that are organized in a particular way, a specification of the file structure, e.g. that a certain text file is a bilingual dictionary.
4. *Technical* – information about the kind of software needed to view a document, details of file format, and preservation data.
5. *Administrative* – background information such as a work log (indicating when the files were last saved or backed up), records of intellectual property rights, moral rights, and any access and distribution restrictions imposed by researcher and/or community.

Note that information can be metadata for more than one purpose, depending on its nature and use, e.g. the identity of the speaker in an audio recording could be relevant for cataloguing purposes and/or also for determining access restrictions.

Table 1 provides an example of the different types of metadata associated with a computer file.

Table 1. Different types of metadata associated with a computer file

Cataloguing	Title: Sasak.dic; Collector: Peter K Austin; Speakers: Yon Mahyuni, Lalu Hasbollah; Language code: SAS
Descriptive	Trilingual Sasak-Indonesian-English dictionary, linked to finderlists, morpheme forms link to Sasak text collection
Structural	Dictionary entries with headword, part of speech, gloss in Bahasa Indonesia and English, cross-references for semantic relations; SIL FOSF record format
Technical	Shoebox 5.0 ASCII text file
Administrative	Open access to all; Last edited version dated 2004-06-25; backup 2004-06-20 on DVD 012

Some linguistically-relevant descriptive metadata that you may wish to use are: speaker (name, gender, age, place of birth, languages spoken, dialect, education level), recorder (name, experience), date of recording, location of recording, duration of recording, type (genre) of materials recorded, transcriber (especially if different from the recorder), date of transcription, location of transcription, location of all digital files, media and text (and location of archive copies).

2.3. Capturing

Capture refers to the encoding and transfer of an analogue recording (as on a cassette or reel-to-reel tape) or text written on paper to the digital domain as a computer file. In many cases, modern ICT means that audio and video recordings are "born digital" and can be transferred to computers without a separate capture process, unless transcoding is involved (see Chapter 13). When using digital capture software it is important to make sure you use appropriate settings. It is also advisable to transfer fieldnotes from notebooks to computer files, ideally as soon as possible after recording so you do not forget notes, abbreviations, and comments. As for recording, it is imperative to name your computer files consistently and clearly, making sure that you should not rely on directory structure to disambiguate file names; e.g. if you have a file called fieldnotes1.doc in one directory ("folder") (for year 2004 research, say) and another also called fieldnotes1.doc in another directory (e.g. for your 2005 notes) then any loss of directory information will result in confusion between these files. Different naming schemes can be used, but clarity and transparency is the goal – see Johnson (2004) for some suggestions. It is also essential to record the relevant metadata for the data files you create as you make them, ideally in a structured way such as a relational table using standard terminology.

3.   Processing the materials

3.1. Linguistic processing

Processing the documentary materials is a very different operation from recording and capture, and operates on a very different time scale. Thus each minute of audio can take hours to process in terms of transcription and annotation (depending on familiarity with the language and the richness of the annotation), while video is even more labor-intensive and requires much more time to process. Video may require cutting and converting to create manageable chunks and file sizes (this is done with computer software[2]). There are several tools that are useful for transcription and annotation (see below).

Linguistic analysis, that is transcription, translation, and annotation, requires decisions about representation, i.e. the levels and types of units. This should make sense within the researcher's chosen framework (theory) and needs to be made clear in the structural metadata that accompanies the relevant files.

There are good reasons for aiming at a certain degree of standardization when processing the materials, including transparency, portability, and ease of sharing and access (Bird and Simons 2003). Phonetic transcription should follow the conventions of the International Phonetic Association (IPA), and phonemic transcription should be IPA or a regionally-recognized standard. Grammatical annotation tags (i.e. the abbreviated labels for e.g. part of speech categories) should follow general linguistic practice, e.g. the recommendations of EUROTYP or E-MELD (including its GOLD ontology), with a list of relevant abbreviations and symbols provided as metadata (for further discussion, see Chapter 9 and Leech and Wilson 1996).

For processed data we need to distinguish between the following:

1. *Character encoding* – how characters are represented, e.g. Windows/ ANSI, Unicode, UTF-8, Big5, JISC.
2. *Data encoding* – how meaningful structures in the data are marked, e.g. extensible markup language (XML), Shoebox/Toolbox standard markers, MS Word table.
3. *File encoding* – how the data is packaged into a digital file, e.g. plain text, MS Word, PDF, Excel spreadsheet.
4. *Physical storage medium* – the physical form used to store the file, e.g. CD-ROM, minidisk, DAT, hard disk, flash memory stick.

As an example, certain documentary materials might be encoded as a hard disk file in plain text Unicode Toolbox format (for further discussion and examples, see Chapter 14).

When we consider file encoding it is useful to distinguish between *proprietary formats* and *non-proprietary formats*. A proprietary format is one whose structure is determined and owned by the maker of the software that stores it, e.g. MS Word, Excel, Access, FileMaker Pro, or Sony ATRAC (the audio format on minidisk). As such, this means that the data is not directly accessible, and the format is subject to change (so that attempting to open a file stored in one version of the software with a later version may not always work – see Chapter 14 for examples). As a result, proprietary formats are **not** ideal for long-term storage (i.e. the encoding is not portable and reusable). Non-proprietary formats, e.g. Unicode plain text, or wav audio, are open and transferrable between hardware and software.

When processing the data it can be useful to distinguish three kinds of contexts each requiring different data formats (see also Johnson 2004):

1. *working* context – the way the data is stored for on-going research work of annotation and analysis;
2. *archiving* context – how the materials are to be stored for long-term preservation (see below);
3. *presentation* context – the form of the data for distribution and publication.

Researchers need to develop ways to *flow* data between contexts, typically by *exporting* the data into some structured format that the software used for other contexts can read (see Thieberger 2004 for some examples). Thus, a common working format for text annotation is Shoebox/Toolbox; this can be exported into rich text format (RTF) to be read by MS Word in order to produce presentation format PDF documents for printing and distribution. Table 2 gives examples of the different format types for the three contexts.

Table 2. Data formats in different contexts

	Working	*Archiving*	*Presentation*
Text	Word, XLS, FMpro, Shoebox/Toolbox	XML	PDF, HTML
Audio	WAV	WAV, BWF	MP3, WMA, RA
Video	MPEG2	MPEG2, MPEG4	QuickTime, AVI, WMV

As an illustration, Figure 1 is a screen shot which shows Shoebox format working context data for the Australian Aboriginal Guwamu language.[3] In the window on the top left is lexical information, on the lower left is elicited sentence data with morpheme-by-morpheme glossing annotation and free translation, on the top right is descriptive metadata about the people involved in the project, and on the bottom right metadata about abbreviations used in the lexical and sentence annotations. Note that the metadata is hypertextually linked to the data in the two left-hand windows, while the lexical root is hypertextually linked from the morpheme field in the sentence window, and the sentence number links from the example field in the lexicon.

A possible presentation form of the illustrated lexical entry is the following:

> **bawurra** *n*
> male red kangaroo, *Note:* used as a generic term for kangaroos, *cf.* **gula, gumbarr, dhugandu,** [SAW, WW], e.g. Gu206, Gu255

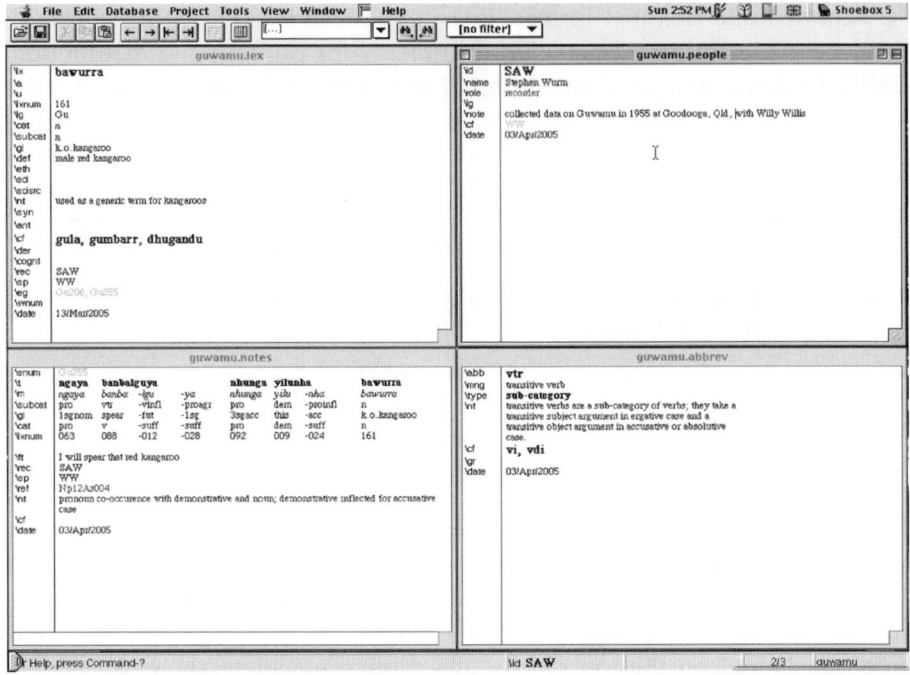

Figure 1. Working with Shoebox

Note that in the presentation format, typography (e.g. italics, bolding, font type, indentation) and dictionary literacy conventions are employed to partially represent the data structure (see Nichols and Sprouse 2003 for other examples). The sentence example can be presented as follows:

ngaya	**banbalguya**	**nhunga**	**yilunha**	**bawurra**
ngaya	*banba-lgu-ya*	*nhunga*	*yilu-nha*	*bawurra*
1sgnom	spear-fut-1sg	3sgacc	this-acc	k.o.kangaroo
pro	vtr-suff-suff	pro	dem-suff	n

'I will spear this red kangaroo'   [SAW, WW, Np12As004]

Linguists' conventions (such as the 'Leipzig Glossing Rules' – see http://www.eva.mpg.de/lingua/files/morpheme.html) have been established for annotated text so that, as in the given example, horizontal and vertical alignment on the page represents relationships between different types of data.[4]

Lost in the flow

The data structures encoded in these Shoebox files are relatively complex (see the diagram in the Appendix below, and Austin 2005) but the links between the data fields are lost in the process of export to RTF and presentation on the printed page. Note that the links could be captured in a HTML file, however, and thus be available to be viewed with a web browser. We discuss archival formats for these examples below.

3.2. Tools for linguistic analysis and processing

There are a range of computational resources that facilitate creating, viewing, querying, or otherwise using language data. They include application programs, components, fonts, style sheets, and document type definitions (DTD). Application programs can be classified into two types:

1. *general purpose software* for which the user must design the data structures and can write application programs to manipulate the data and carry out various tasks. Examples are *MS Word* and *Excel*, and *FileMaker Pro*. Such software is powerful and flexible, however, they store data in a proprietary format which is not optimal for long-term storage and access;
2. *specific purpose software* which is designed to be used for particular tasks. Examples of such software in common use by language documenters include: *Transcriber* and *EXMARaLDA* (EXtensible MARkup Language for Discourse Annotation – see Schmidt 2004) for time-aligned audio annotations, *Shoebox/Toolbox* for text and lexicon annotations, *Praat* for speech analysis and annotation, *ELAN* for audio and video annotation, and *IMDI Browser* for cataloguing and administration metadata.

Some of the specific purpose software is discussed and illustrated elsewhere in this volume.

Other useful software

In addition to the tools mentioned above, there also exist converter programs for transferring data between encoding formats, such as those developed at MPI-Nijmegen for uniting Transcriber and Shoebox encoded files, and converting them to XML for use with ELAN. Further information about available programs and computational resources can be found at the E-MELD 'School of Best Practice' website and in the list of resources at the back of this volume.

3.3. Archiving

Digital archiving involves the preparation of the recorded/captured data, metadata, and processed analysis so that the information it contains is maximally informative and explicitly expressed, encoded for long-term accessibility and safely stored with a reputable organization that can guarantee long-term curation. A number of digital language and music archives exist; the DELAMAN network created in 2003 links many of them (see resources list). Digital archiving offers opportunities to store data for communities to use, other scholars to access, and for preservation for future generations of community members, the general public, and researchers. Note that not all recorded data has to be archived (e.g. unprocessed video files) but we should aim to make our materials archivable, that is, richly structured documentations maximizing the possibilities of the digital medium. Archiving must be included as a process in our language documentation project plans, and it is advisable to seek assistance with planning for archiving from an archivist at the beginning of project conception.

Note that archiving is not publication (only those materials prepared for distribution will be published by the archive), nor is it backup (the archive will generally not accept backup copies of files alone but will expect the data and metadata to be explicitly described, often by requesting that deposit forms be completed for each archival object). Archives also commonly have systems in place to manage protocols for intellectual property rights, and for specification of access and usage rights, e.g. that a certain archival object is only available to members of the speaker community. The depositor should establish these by discussion and negotiation with the owners, and describe them via metadata and deposit protocols. Data sensitivity is **not** a reason to not archive; it is better to deposit data in an archive with restrictions than not deposit at all. Researchers should also make preparations for assigning their rights into the future by including information in your will and ensuring that your executors understand how to assign them on your death.

3.3.1. Archiving text materials

The preferred format for archiving text materials is eXtensible Markup Language (XML), a document description language used to encode the content of structured documents (see Sperberg-McQueen and Burnard 2002). XML is a subset of SGML (standard generalized markup language) and is used to explicitly describe a domain of knowledge through *markup tags* enclosed in angle brackets (see Chapter 14 with the example of a 'play structure' implicit in a published document). Each part of a structured document is described within a defined and logical structure (stored in XML schemas or DTDs 'document type definitions'). XML is a good archival format because XML documents explicitly represent data structure, and are directly readable by humans even if computer software to display the documents is not available.

XML documents are typically created by export from working context materials, rather than being directly written by the researcher, because the process of writing well-structured XML tends to be tedious and error prone (various XML editors exist and these can be used to create documents, to check markup tag syntax [well formedness], to create DTDs, and to ensure that a document complies with a schema or DTD). XML encoded documents can be transformed into various archival and presentation formats by XSLT, extensible stylesheet language transformations. Thus, an XSLT could create a concordance of an annotated text collection, or HTML files for web publication. Archivists can provide advice on possible transformations of XML documents.

The following are two examples of XML encoding. First, consider the structure of a typical bilingual lexicon (such as seen in the Guwamu example presented above):[5]

1. lexicons contain entries;
2. the attributes of entries are: form, category, subcategory, language, meaning specification (and any other additional information such as notes, speaker, recorder, sense relations, sentence examples);
3. meaning specification can be gloss (for morpheme-by-morpheme glossing and finderlist production) and definition;

4. cross-references to other lexical entries have a sequential order chosen by the lexicographer;
5. cross-references to sentences examples also have a specified sequential order.

Table 3 shows the Guwamu sample entry discussed above in XML form, which would be a possible archival representation.

Table 3. Example of an XML structure (lexicon entry)

```
<?xml version="1.0" encoding="ISO-8859-1"?>
<lexicon>
<entry id="161">
<form>bawurra</form>
<language>Gu</language>
<cat>n</cat>
<subcat>n</subcat>
<gloss>k.o.kangaroo</gloss>
<def>male red kangaroo</def>
<note>used as a generic term for kangaroos</note>
<rec>SAW</rec>
<sp>WW</sp>
<date>13/Mar/2005</date>
<xref>
<cf n="1">gula</cf>
<cf n="2">gumbarr</cf>
<cf n="3">dhugandu</cf>
</xref>
<egref>
<eg n="1">Gu206</eg>
<eg n="2">Gu255</eg>
</egref>
</entry>
</lexicon>
```

If we view this data using XML-aware software such as an XML editor[6] or a web browser such as Mozilla Firefox or the current version of MS Internet Explorer, the hierarchical relationships between the data entities are displayed as in Figure 2.

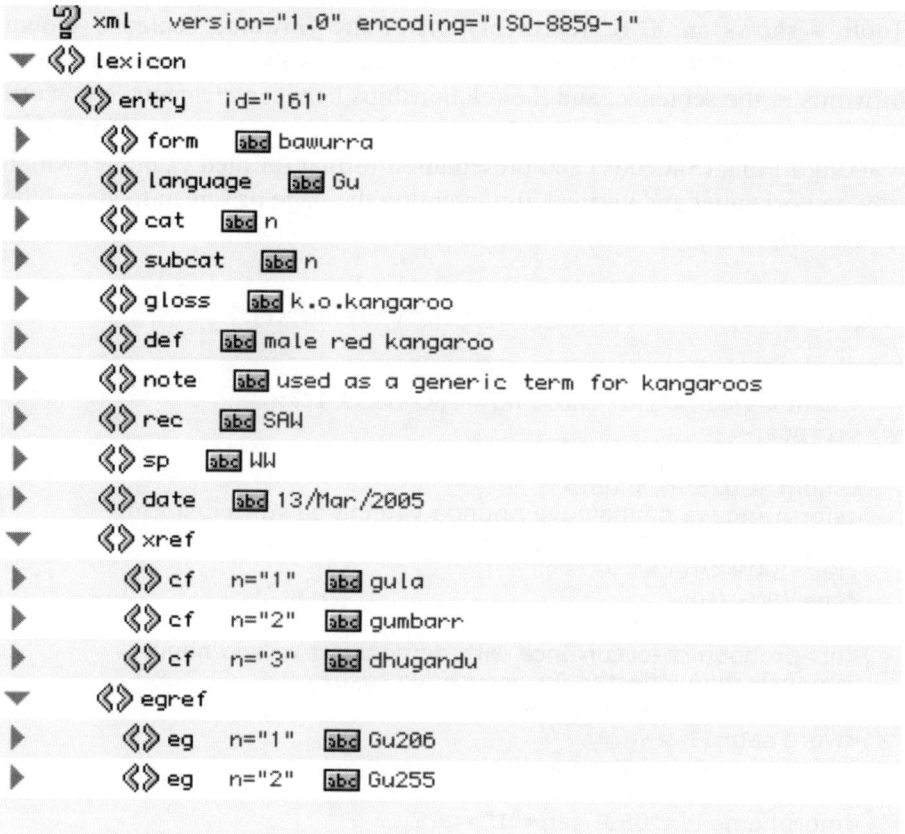

Figure 2. XML structure display (lexicon entry)

For an annotated corpus we can set up a structure where:

1. the corpus contains sentences;
2. sentence properties are: sentence number, sentence form, sentence gloss, speaker, recorder, sentence source reference, grammatical notes;
3. sentences contain words in sequential order;
4. word properties are: word form, word gloss;
5. words contain morphemes in sequential order;[7]
6. morpheme properties are morpheme form, morpheme gloss, morpheme category, morpheme subcategory.

Table 4 shows an XML representation of the Guwamu sentence shown above. Note that the XML representation makes explict the sequential order of words in the sentence, and the relationships between elements, e.g. word forms and their constituent morphemes, which are purely implicit in typical working format (Shoebox) and presentation format (printed example) which rely on horizontal and vertical alignment on the page or screen to signal the relationships.

Table 4. Example of an XML structure (Guwamu sentence)

```
<?xml version="1.0" encoding="ISO-8859-1"?>
<corpus>
<sentence>
<snum>Gu255</snum>
<sform>ngaya banbalguya nhunga yilunha bawurra</sform>
<ft>I will spear this red kangaroo</ft>
<rec>SAW</rec>
<sp>WW</sp>
<ref>Np12As004</ref>
<nt>pronoun co-occurrence with demonstrative and noun;
demonstrative inflected for accusative case</nt>
<date>03/Apr/2005</date>
<word seq="1">
<wform>ngaya</wform>
<wgloss>I</wgloss>
<morpheme id="053" seq="1">
<mform>ngaya</mform>
<cat>pro</cat>
<subcat>pro</subcat>
<gl>1sgnom</gl>
</morpheme>
</word>
<word seq="2">
<wform>banbalguya</wform>
<wgloss>will spear</wgloss>
<morpheme id="088" seq="1">
<mform>banba</mform>
<cat>v</cat>
<subcat>vtr</subcat>
<gl>spear</gl>
</morpheme>
<morpheme id="012" seq="2">
<mform>lgu</mform>
<cat>suff</cat>
<subcat>vinfl</subcat>
```

```
<gl>fut</gl>
</morpheme>
<morpheme id="028" seq="3">
<mform>ya</mform>
<cat>suff</cat>
<subcat>proagr</subcat>
<gl>1sg</gl>
</morpheme>
</word>
<word seq="3">
<wform>nhunga</wform>
<wgloss>him</wgloss>
<morpheme id="092" seq="1">
<mform>nhunga</mform>
<cat>pro</cat>
<subcat>pro</subcat>
<gl>3sgacc</gl>
</morpheme>
</word>
<word seq="4">
<wform>yilunha</wform>
<wgloss>this</wgloss>
<morpheme id="009" seq="1">
<mform>yilu</mform>
<cat>dem</cat>
<subcat>dem</subcat>
<gl>this</gl>
</morpheme>
<morpheme id="024" seq="2">
<mform>nha</mform>
<cat>suff</cat>
<subcat>proinfl</subcat>
<gl>acc</gl>
</morpheme>
</word>
<word seq="5">
<wform>bawurra</wform>
<wgloss>kangaroo</wgloss>
<morpheme id="161" seq="1">
<mform>bawurra</mform>
<cat>n</cat>
<subcat>n</subcat>
<gl>k.o.kangaroo</gl>
</morpheme>
</word>
</sentence>
</corpus>
```

Again, we can view this representation using XML-aware software and see its hierarchical structure; firstly in terms of a sentence made up of a sequence of words as in Figure 3.

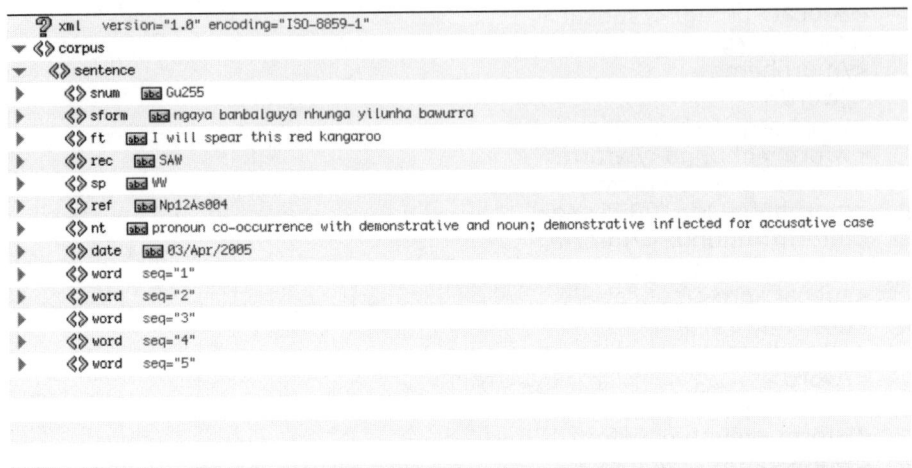

Figure 3. XML structure display (Guwamu sentence, sentence level)

Now, if we view the information about words in the sentence in detail as in Figure 4 we see that they consist of one or more morphemes in sequence (notice that the triangle icon on the left margin changes from horizontal to vertical as we move down the hierarchy).

More on archival format

Note that the information stored in the XML representation is extremely compact but is still readable by humans and the structure can be recovered, even if the software to display the data is missing; this is why XML is a good archival format. For more information on archival encoding, see the Text Encoding Initiative (http://www.tei.org) or the resources websites listed at the end of this book. There are numerous introductory textbooks for XML, though none of them explicitly deals with language documentation issues.

```
? xml   version="1.0" encoding="ISO-8859-1"
▼ <> corpus
  ▼  <> sentence
  ▶     <> snum    abc Gu255
  ▶     <> sform   abc ngaya banbalguya nhunga yilunha bawurra
  ▶     <> ft      abc I will spear this red kangaroo
  ▶     <> rec     abc SAW
  ▶     <> sp      abc WW
  ▶     <> ref     abc Np12As004
  ▶     <> nt      abc pronoun co-occurrence with demonstrative and noun; demonstrative inflected for accusative case
  ▶     <> date    abc 03/Apr/2005
  ▼     <> word   seq="1"
  ▶        <> wform    abc ngaya
  ▶        <> wgloss   abc I
  ▶        <> morpheme  id="053" seq="1"
  ▼     <> word   seq="2"
  ▶        <> wform    abc banbalguya
  ▶        <> wgloss   abc will spear
  ▶        <> morpheme  id="088" seq="1"
  ▶        <> morpheme  id="012" seq="2"
  ▶        <> morpheme  id="028" seq="3"
  ▼     <> word   seq="3"
  ▶        <> wform    abc nhunga
  ▶        <> wgloss   abc him
  ▶        <> morpheme  id="092" seq="1"
  ▼     <> word   seq="4"
  ▶        <> wform    abc yilunha
  ▶        <> wgloss   abc this
  ▶        <> morpheme  id="009" seq="1"
  ▶        <> morpheme  id="024" seq="2"
  ▼     <> word   seq="5"
  ▶        <> wform    abc bawurra
  ▶        <> wgloss   abc kangaroo
  ▶        <> morpheme  id="161" seq="1"
```

Figure 4. XML structure display (Guwamu sentence, word level)

3.3.2. Archiving sound and video

The formats for real-time media are subject to rapid technological change
and one of the major concerns of archives is to attend to refreshing files
('forward migration') so that they remain readable to the existing equipment. For video, there are two internationally-agreed compressed formats,
namely MPEG2 and MPEG4, however there is no agreement about raw
formats which in any case are extremely difficult to store due to the very
large file size. For audio recordings, archives generally use uncompressed
CD-ROM-quality (44kHz, 16 bit) encoded as WAV files; some archives
also use 48kHz and/or BWF ('broadcast wave format') where metadata is
bundled together with the audio. Note that MP3, RealAudio, or Windows

Media Player formats are all compressed in a way that loses information; they are useful for working and presentation (e.g. for publication, on web sites) but not suitable for archiving.

More on sound archiving

There are a large number of well-equipped sound archives around the world, ranging from regional, to national, to international coverage. Some, such as the Austrian National Sound Archive have been established for a long time and have extensive experience with material in older 'legacy' formats. The International Association of Sound Archives (IASA) publishes lots of valuable and up-to-date advice about archiving issues, and the Language Archives Newsletter (http://www.mpi.nl/LAN) focuses on archiving for linguistic research.

3.4. Presentation, publication, and distribution

One of the ways that the presentation, publication, and distribution of rich language documentations can be achieved currently is via multimedia which links media, annotations (time-aligned transcriptions, analysis and translations, hyperlinks) and metadata. One such format is linked files (including HTML, MP3 sound clips, QuickTime, etc.) distributed via the world wide web, but bandwidth can be problem for publication of media files – even small movies of a few minutes in a compressed format can be megabytes in size and take a long time to download via slow connections (the use of video streaming software can partially overcome this limitation). There is also SMIL ('Synchronized Multimedia Integration Language') which is an application of XML to encode mixed media, text and image information in a presentation form.

   For highly complex richly annotated and linked media currently we need to use multimedia platforms such as Macromedia Director, delivered on CD-ROM or DVD as a publication format (see Chapter 15). Unfortunately, the future of these formats and the carriers is unclear and how we can archive multimedia for the future is also currently problematic. One current major need is good multimedia players and ways for users to interact with the rich documentations; it is necessary to model and design interfaces and access formats for various audiences. An example of such a format is the *Spoken Karaim* CD, described by Csató and Nathan (2003b), which presents video and audio recordings with accompanying transcriptions, translations, glosses, lexicon, and cultural information, all of which are linked and interactive. The interface enables users to explore their own pathways through the corpus and to search, collect items of interest, backtrack, and interact with the corpus. It has a simple attractive interface that enables maximum interactivity without forcing the user to digest too much information, and has been used for Karaim language support in education, language maintenance, and revitalization (Nathan and Csató, forthc.).

Figure 5 is a screenshot from a CD-ROM of conversational documentary materials in the Sasak language of eastern Indonesia (Austin, Jukes, and Nathan 2000) which is based on the Karaim model. The top-left window shows images of the consultants who worked on the corpus, and below it a Sasak lexicon arranged alphabetically (clicking on an entry in the lexicon reveals full details of the individual item in the top left window in place of the images), and on the top right is the Sasak transcription of the conversation (colors indicate the two speakers, their voices can be heard in the left and right channels respectively of the associated time-aligned digital stereo recording). Below the transcription is a small central window displaying morpheme-by-morpheme analysis and gloss for a selected item in the text, and below that, a display of the free translation in English of the speaker turns (again color-coded). In the lower bottom left of the display there is a search facility which the user can employ to find occurrences of morphemes

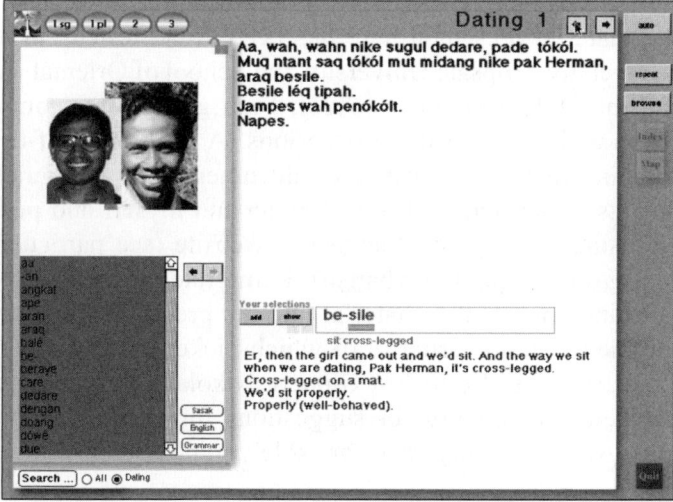

Figure 5. Screenshot from a CD-ROM presenting Sasak conversational materials

or glosses of interest throughout the corpus, and in the top left is a set of buttons that produce pronominal inflected forms of verbs (via a morphological generator) when the user moves them over a selected lexical entry in the top left window (see Chapter 15 and Nathan 2000b for further details about the morphological generator developed for the *Spoken Karaim* CD).

4. Conclusions

Language documentation is an emerging field that involves recording, analysis, annotation, archiving, and publication of rich and complex data. By properly structuring the data representations and planning methods to flow data between different formats and contexts, you can work productively with your materials, as well as publish and distribute them for others and archive your resources to preserve them for the future. It is important that all these aspects of a documentation project be incorporated in its planning and execution, in order to ensure maximally effective and useful documentation.

Acknowledgements

Most of the material presented here has been "road tested" in lectures at Frankfurt University, Uppsala University, the School of Oriental and African Studies, and the DoBeS summer school; I am grateful for comments and feedback from audiences on these occasions. A proportion of this chapter derives from information on language documentation and guidelines for grant applicants co-written by David Nathan and myself and published on the Hans Rausing Endangered Languages website (see particularly http://www.hrelp.org/documentation/whatisit). I am grateful to David Nathan for permission to incorporate this material into the present chapter, and for his detailed comments on an earlier draft which picked up a number of errors and infelicities. Thanks also to Jost Gippert, Nikolaus Himmelmann, Robert Munro, and Peter Wittenburg for suggestions for improvement of earlier presentations. Any remaining errors are solely mine.

Appendix: Guwamu data structures

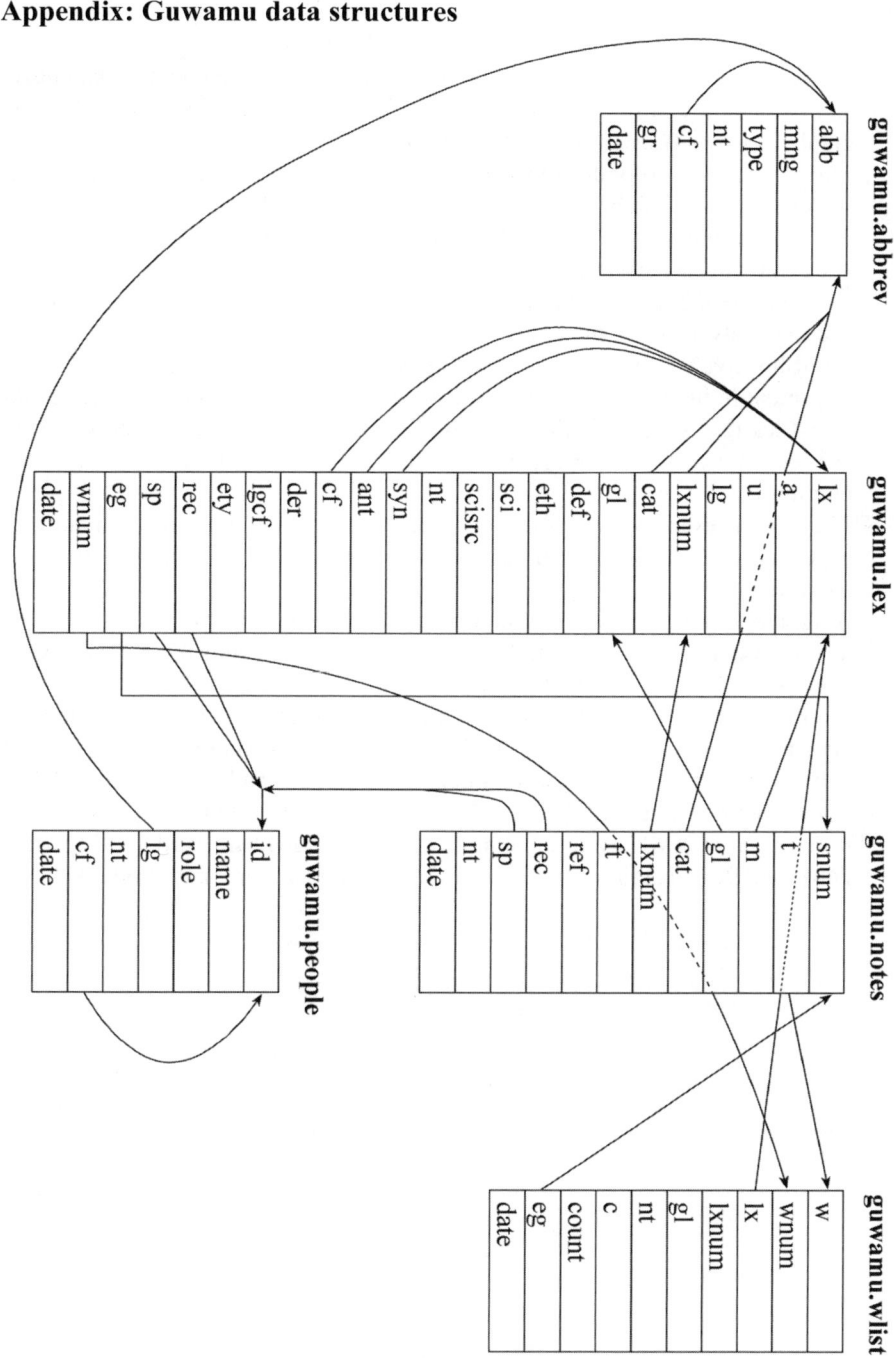

Notes

1. For further suggestions about the role of fieldnotes in documenting languages and cultures it can be useful to look at textbooks on anthropology and ethnography, such as Brewer 2000, Wolcott 2004.
2. There are a range of video editing programs, including commercially available software such as Adobe Premiere or freeware such as VirtualDub.
3. The Guwamu data was collected by the late Stephen A. Wurm in 1955 at Goodooga in Queensland from the late Willy Willis and made available to me for study in 1980. The annotations and glossing are based on Wurm's translations and my analysis of the materials.
4. The Shoebox/Toolbox tool automatically creates the *appearance* of vertical alignment in its interlinear text function, though it actually stores spaces in the data files to do so. Note that it does not store the *relationships* between the aligned information and rather relies on the user's implicit knowledge to interpret these.
5. The chosen example is deliberately simple in order to present the main concepts here; in practice lexical entries may have much more complex structures and relationships.
6. A number of commercial and freeware editors are available; cf. the list attached to this volume. The screenshots below show views within the ElfData XML editor (see http://www.elfdata.com).
7. A simple concatentative item-and-arrangement morphological model is adopted here for purposes of illustration (this is the model assumed by the Shoebox software); other morphological models could be used and represented in XML. For further discussion of the structure of interlinear text and a proposal for representing it in XML using the annotated graph formalism (Bird and Liberman 2001) see Bow, Hughes, and Bird 2003; and Hughes, Bird, and Bow 2003.

Chapter 5

The ethnography of language and language documentation

Jane H. Hill

Introduction

Documentary linguistics takes up a vision of the integration of the study of language structure, language use, and the culture of language. Documentary linguistics demands integration. If we are to succeed in sensitive documentation, which by definition requires the deep involvement of communities, we must incorporate a cultural and ethnographic understanding of language into the very foundations of our research. Indeed, documentary linguistics, because of practical necessity, may have a better chance of sustaining such an integrated project than did its predecessors.[1]

This chapter focuses on three requirements for the integration of the study of the culture of language into documentary linguistics that have an immediate practical relevance for this new discipline. The first is to move forward with the foundational idea from Hymes' (1971) formulation of the ethnography of speaking, as the study of the way that language structures and uses are diversely and locally organized in the cultures of local speech communities. Documentary linguists need to be ethnographers, because they venture into communities that may have very different forms of language use from those of the communities in which they were socialized as human beings or trained as scholars.

The second requirement is to attend to the cultural foundations of elicitation and second language learning specifically. Documentary linguists undertake to inhabit a very peculiar role, that of adult second language learner in communities that almost never encounter such a creature. Similarly, their consultants enter into relationships that are without precedent in their communities. Together, they constitute so-called communities of practice, local micro-societies that are very likely to produce emergent forms of language and interaction that evolve very rapidly. Recent work on communities of practice, specifically learning communities, provide very useful theoretical foundations for understanding what is likely to go on in these most dynamic of local systems, where goals and routines are negotiated at the level of distinct individuals.

The last requirement is attention to language ideology. One of the reasons history speeds up at the margins is that oppression and marginalization – and minority and indigenous language communities are almost by definition oppressed and marginalized – produces a special intensification of language-ideological projects. These can silence the voices of speakers, render untenable the presence of a researcher, or impede the distribution and implementation of the products of research, even within the community. Recent advances in our understanding of the semiotics of language ideologies provide very useful tools for documentary linguists, who must be able not only to identify and work among clashing ideological discourses, but assist communities with what Nora and Richard Dauenhauer (1998) have called "ideological clarification" to bring these discourses into line with what a community truly desires for endangered-language resources.

1. The ethnography of language:
Relativity and the organization of diversity

Most linguists attend almost exclusively to what Michael Silverstein (1979 and elsewhere) calls "denotational text." We can state the formal properties of declarative vs. interrogative vs. imperative sentences, for instance, without really paying much attention to the well-known fact that both assertions and questions can function as commands, or that commands can be made only under certain social conditions. But documentary linguistics on languages that are no longer taken for granted, where every construction carries a heavy political burden, really does not permit us the luxury of this particular reduction. We can find practical help in some of the foundational principles of the ethnography-of-language tradition.

The first of these principles is that speech communities will differ not only in manifesting different kinds of language structures, but in manifesting different patterns of use. An ethnography of the distribution of registers, speech-act types, and the like across the contextual landscape is critical to linguistic documentation. For instance, certain kinds of syntactic constructions may occur only in certain registers, so that even basic elicitation strategies will require ethnographic preparation. Hymes' well-known SPEAKING heuristic provides a rule of thumb to help us notice patterns of usage. The acronym "SPEAKING" abbreviates some of the major components of the speech situation: Setting/Scene, Participants, Ends, Act Sequence, Key, Instrumentalities, Norms, Genre (Hymes 1971; Saville-Troike 2003 offers a more comprehensive compilation of analytic units in the ethnography of communication). We need such heuristics, because patterns of usage are not always noticeable or easily interpretable. While we encounter some patterns as weird and jarring, others are so easily naturalized that they become invisible before we ever notice them. I have two rules I share with my own students: The first is to always assume that a difference is meaningful, not natural. The second is never to assume that a difference is due to inadequacy on the part of speakers. Indeed, for the ethnographer, the feeling that your interlocutors are rude, or stupid, or crazy, is an extremely useful signal that you probably bumped into a very interesting difference.

Let me give an example of a mistake of my own, where I assumed that a difference was natural instead of meaningful. When I was working in central Mexico and would visit my Nahuatl-speaking friends in their homes, they would greet me with a peculiar intonation contour that starts in falsetto and terminates in creaky voice. Women do a particularly exaggerated version of this "squeak-creak" contour. I simply did not pick up on this as the highly formal politeness that it was. Why? I think the reason is that most people in this population are physically rather small. It is not uncommon for older women especially to be less than 150 centimeters tall, and I often felt like Gulliver among the Lilliputians. The falsetto voice of the squeak-creak contour seemed a perfectly reasonable sound to emanate from these tiny little women, and I never stopped to think that in fact on other occasions they spoke in perfectly normal voices. I had been in and out of the field in Tlaxcala for four or five years when the Mayanist linguist Louanna Furbee asked me at a conference party if Nahuatl speakers used the same polite falsetto that she had heard among the Tojolobales, a Mayan community of the Mexican state of Chiapas. I had the sort of experience that cartoonists represent by showing a lightbulb going on in the balloon above the character's head; suddenly I could hear my friends saying, "*Coma:lehtzi:n! Ximopano:ltitzi:no! Ximotla:li:tzi:no!*" and realized that what I had been hearing was not a natural index of how small they were, but a highly meaningful message expressing social distance and hierarchical order. They meant not just "Comadrita! Come in! Sit down!" They also meant, "We are greatly honored by your presence." Fortunately my failure to understand exactly what they were doing did not, I think, have much impact on my work. But other cases of "naturalization" might have precisely such consequences. It is for this reason that one of the ethnographic arts is to "make strange," always to ask, "Why did that just happen? How might it have been different? Does it mean what I think it means? Can I find evidence in favor or to the contrary?" Staying for months on end in the hypothesis-testing mode of "making strange," rather than simply "being there," is exhausting, and we will always slip, but training in this ethnographic attitude and how to sustain it is essential for documentary linguists. And the rule of thumb – "Assume difference is meaningful, not natural" – is very helpful.

In contrast to differences in usage that are easily naturalized, some differences in usage are highly salient and even startling. These are the kinds of differences that are categorized under "cross-cultural miscommunication," that lead people from one community to conclude that those in another are uncivilized or stupid. I want to give an example that will not only show how such differences are some of the most interesting for the ethnographer, but also to show how deeply embodied in speaker habitus the differential patterns of language use are, and how departures from them will seem almost physically uncomfortable. One extremely annoying feature of my fieldwork in Mexico was working with people who treated appointments – *compromisos* – as less than fixed. When I tried to make appointments for interviews, people would smile happily and tell me to come *a una buena hora* (literally, 'at a good hour', which turns out to mean "early"), and assure me that *primero Dios* ('if God wills it'), they would be pleased to be available to help me. About 60% of the time people in fact kept such appointments. But on more than a few occasions I arrived for the appointment only to learn that the intended interviewee was far away on some errand that could have been easily predicted, such as a pilgrimage to a saint's festival that was fixed on the annual calendar or attendance at a market that occurred on the same day every week without fail. I knew better than to think of them as rude or insincere, and began to think about why this happened. Eventually I developed an account of it in terms of the theory of types of "face" from politeness theory (Lakoff 1973; Brown and Levinson 1987), which was very helpful in understanding other communicative problems as well. Put briefly, these communities were heavily biased toward attention to so-called "positive face," everybody's right to feel wanted and liked. In local terms, to make a social commitment that you could not keep was a fairly minor white lie, while to say "No" to someone's face, even very politely and with elaborate excuses, was a major threat, a threat to positive face. The threat to my negative face (the right to the autonomy that would permit me to avoid inconvenience) was practically irrelevant. I would be annoyed when I found myself 50 kilometers from my home base in front of a house compound that was deserted and locked up tight, but nobody would be there to notice. In fact, I learned that in general threats to negative face hardly counted at all in the Mexicano communities. I learned as well that when there is any possibility of a "No" in a matter where an insincerely-uttered "Yes" would create inconvenience of a kind intolerable even for these people, that intermediaries were sent to pose the question. So I did have a reasonable understanding about what was going on, and even published an article on the local culture of politeness (Hill 1980). I didn't make the mistake of thinking of local people as rude and inconsiderate. But now comes the tough part – I found it practically impossible to tell the little white lies about keeping appointments that everybody else used. If some-one said, "Next week, let's go and visit the church at Ocotlan, my daughter needs a ritual cleansing and you can take us there in your pick-up truck," and I knew that next week I was expected in Mexico City at a professional conference, I would carefully – politely, in my terms, incredibly rudely in theirs – explain that I had a previous engagement but might be able to visit the Virgin of Ocotlan another time. I knew the *Primero Dios* routine per-fectly well, understood its deep cultural foundations, and simply could not do it. In my cultural calculus, which I could not seem to set aside, the threat to negative face – the idea that someone might be inconvenienced if I didn't show up – was truly dire, while saying "No" politely to someone's face was a very minor matter. Although I attempted the *Primero Dios* routine occa-sionally when I thought the matter at hand was a fairly light one, I suspect that I acquired a reputation as a rather rude, stuck-up, and negative person, but I simply couldn't help it. The American linguist Doris Bartholomew, who worked for 40 years with Otomi speakers in a part of Mexico near my own field site, told me that she finally learned to accomplish this particular flavor of social lie with a straight face, but that it pained her every time. The lesson of this case is that diversity in usage is not merely colorful, or interesting, but that it can be very, very hard to live with, even for a person with extensive anthropological training.

A second foundational presumption of the ethnography of language is, of course, that speech communities are not linguistically homogeneous, but are "organizations of diversity." The idea of the speech community as an "organization of diversity" is a very useful one for students of minority languages who encounter communities that are at the very least bilingual. Especially important, of course, is the distribution of the linguistic resources of the minority language versus the other language or languages across the repertoire of possible speech events and acts, across genres, across the kinds of speakers and addressees, across channels, across affective keys, and the like.

This organization of diversity has very practical consequences for our work. Again, we can note the problem of "naturalization" of difference. I never really learned Nahuatl very well when I was working in Tlaxcala, the reason being that hardly anybody ever spoke it to me until I had been returning to the communities off and on for almost a decade. This seemed reasonable; I speak halfway decent Spanish, and so do they, so it was just easier for everybody to use that language and that was how I initially thought about what was going on. But in fact this was much more than just a matter of "least effort." People spoke Spanish to *any* stranger or outsider, no matter what their native language might be. It was quite astonishing to go to a public market and hear obviously indigenous sellers speaking heavily accented and even ungrammatical Spanish to equally obviously indigenous buyers throughout all the stages of the bargaining process until the very end of the event, when the deal was clinched and a few words of Nahuatl would be exchanged to express the solidarity that came in the moment of a successful transaction.

The sociolinguistic conventions that distributed Nahuatl and Spanish across the local contextual landscape would have had the most profound effect on my fieldwork had I been documenting grammar rather than language shift, since they would have made it very difficult for me to hear certain kinds of constructions or access certain lexical domains. I think it has been shown that gaining a speaking competence in a language under investigation is a prerequisite to truly sensitive description and analysis. But it was very difficult to do that in the Nahuatl communities. I did try, but without much success. I had the opportunity once to talk to a local veterinarian who had learned to speak Nahuatl, not only to facilitate his work, but because he was deeply interested in the language and its history. He discovered, however, that people did not respond well to him when he spoke it to them. He said, "When I speak it, they don't respect me." He had unwittingly run afoul of a convention of metaphorical switching that involves the use of Spanish even by Nahuatl speakers when they discuss technical topics, and, unfortunately, also of linguistic insecurity associated with Nahuatl, the idea that people who speak it are not as good as people who speak Spanish. If his interlocutors were relative strangers, he was probably even insulting them by suggesting that they did not know Spanish. Finding contexts for speaking the language in such circumstances requires the most careful analysis of how the various languages in a community are deployed, so that the face and reputation of all interlocutors are properly attended to. Indeed, any community may have certain kinds of speech events in which outsiders simply cannot successfully participate. For this reason, and also because it is both ethical and sensible to build local capacity, it is generally preferable to train local native speakers in recording techniques and have them do most of the basic recording themselves.

2. Documenting languages in a community of practice

The kinds of diversity in patterns of usage studied by ethnographers of language have often been treated as relatively stable in communities. But documentary linguists must also attend to contexts in which new conventions and forms of diversity can emerge very fast: the contexts of elicitation and adult second-language acquisition that are at the center of their work. Linguists who do field work have understood for many years that elicitation is a collaborative process that requires mutual adaptation on the part of researcher and consultant. Early attention to the problem of what happens in elicitation and in the kind of adult second-language learning that documentary linguists undertake focused mainly on problems that would emerge from different patterns about matters like asking questions. Charles Briggs' *Learning how to ask* (1986), where he argues that the acquisition of new information must be embedded in local social understandings of who is permitted to ask what kinds of questions to whom, is a classic discussion of this issue. Some anthropologists, including Briggs himself, have found that the best way to work is to undertake what is locally understood as an apprentice role. I don't think this approach is a solution to the problems faced by documentary linguists. Communities may have well-established institutions for apprenticeship in wood-carving or divination. They will certainly have very well-established patterns for first-language socialization. But it is highly unlikely that they will have well-established patterns for adult second-language learning or elicitation. And certain local patterns for adult learning may be quite inappropriate to the documentary linguist's task. A very good example is the routine of adult acquisition of ceremonial orations and creation accounts among the Tohono O'odham of Arizona described by Ruth Underhill (1946). A man (it was always a man) who wished to learn a particular oration would approach someone who knew it and present a very important gift, consistent with the significance of the target text – blankets, a rifle, a horse. If the source accepted the gift, he would then recite the oration: once. The job of the apprentice was to listen with the most intense focus, to try to master as much of the oration as possible from this single recitation. Because if he needed to hear it again, another expensive gift would be required. This particular method really would not work for most documentary linguistics – in fact, it has been tried. The linguist Bill Graves described in his dissertation (Graves 1988) encountering a Pima speaker, an immensely knowledgeable elder who had been very highly recommended by everyone, who chose to organize his role as linguistic consultant along the lines of the traditional model for learning that Underhill had described. Graves had to arrive early, because if he was even five minutes late for an appointment Mr. Brown would refuse to talk to him. Graves had to listen with the most extreme care, because Mr. Brown spoke very quietly, did not like repeating things, and refused to explain things. Mr. Brown would occasionally rise abruptly and terminate a meeting if he was annoyed. Finally, Mr. Brown required cash up front at every meeting. After a summer of this sort of thing, Graves reluctantly concluded that Mr. Brown was a bit too traditional and sought a consultant who was willing to compromise.

The absence of established routines for adult second-language learning and linguistic elicitation in most minority-language communities makes it obvious that elicitation will produce some kind of new system that emerges in collaboration. New theory in "learning how to learn" shows that such emergent systems are always produced in learning communities, even in ones that seem well-established and stable. Learning communities belong to the category of social organizations that have come to be called "communities of practice." Eckert and McConnell-Ginet (1992: 464) provided a founding definition of this entity: "A community of practice is an aggregate of people who come together around mutual engagement in an endeavor ... practices emerge in the course of this mutual endeavor." Meyerhoff (2002) has usefully summarized the theory of communities of practice, which have become an important unit of analysis in recent variationist sociolinguistics.

The key elements of Eckert and McConnell-Ginet's definition are *mutual engagement* – which may be "harmonious or conflictual," and the endeavor, which Meyerhoff defines as a *jointly negotiated enterprise*, which must be reasonably specific. Finally, a community of practice will develop a *shared repertoire* of normative practices and interactional resources that are "the cumulative result of internal negotiations" (Meyerhoff 2002: 528). These subcomponents are in dialectical relationship: mutual engagement both makes possible, and is made possible by, the negotiation of a joint enterprise, and normative practices are negotiated and in turn facilitate negotiation and mutuality. The "communities of practice" in which documentary linguists work are, then, different from the "speech communities" of the classic ethnography of language. They may be constituted only for particular purposes, they may be ephemeral, and they can form and reform, being salient at certain times and places and irrelevant in others. Furthermore, single individuals may belong to several of these, and their practices and routines may overlap to some degree.

Wenger (1998) found that successful communities of practice exhibit certain properties that are highly relevant to the documentary linguistic enterprise. These include

1. rapid propagation of innovation;
2. jargon and shortcuts to communication;
3. the development of a certain very local insider perspective on the world;
4. a repertoire of insider resources and identifying markers such as jokes, stories, and specific tools and representations.

Specifically *linguistic* variables such as phonological elements, lexical items, and routinized phrases are a very important part of the emerging normative order within communities of practice. That is, linguistic resources evolve within communities of practice and may be quite specific to these.

The problem for the documentary linguist is to be aware of these emergent properties, and to try to remain conscious not only of her own role in such emergence, but of what consultants are doing as well. To think through thoroughly the implications of the evolving theory of the community of practice for the documentary project lies beyond the scope of this chapter. But I will advance a couple of simple and suggestive examples from my fieldwork with Cupeño, undertaken more than 40 years ago when not even the tiniest ray of social-constructionist light had yet penetrated my American structuralist training. I spent nearly all of my time working with a single consultant, Roscinda Nolasquez, who was then in her mid-sixties – about the age I am as I write this. I thought of her as very old. We spent hundreds of hours together, and became very intimate, a classic community of practice of two, in which marginal members occasionally participated for brief periods.

My first example of an emergent property within our community is the fact that my fieldnotes, to my extreme embarrassment today, are very messy and often do not have glosses, in spite of the fact that I had some training in field methods. This is an excellent example of a "rapidly innovated short-cut." In 1962 I was immersed in the language and had no trouble under-standing anything in the notes, and really didn't need to systematically gloss everything, and could use ellipses for predictable (to me, then) parts of utterances. And of course this was also fine with Roscinda Nolasquez, who was very quick-witted and did not enjoy waiting while I carefully wrote things down and glossed them. We had developed a sort of rapid work rhythm and my sloppy note-taking was one of its dimensions. And I note that I'm not the only person who ever did this. Shortly before his un-timely death in 2001, Ken Hale turned over his field notes on Mountain Pima from the late 1950s and early 1960s to my graduate student, Luis Bar-ragan, who works on the language. Luis was very moved when Ken offered him the notes, and awed when he discovered that only six pages into the notes Hale, who of course was famous as a linguistic savant, stopped writing glosses. I assure you that my glosses for Cupeño are fairly dense for many more pages than six, but after two or three weeks of work they became scantier and scantier. This is exactly what we would expect from findings about communities of practice, where shortcuts emerge very rapidly, but of course what it means is that my notes (and Ken Hale's) are now very diffi-cult to use. I was so immersed in my local formation of community in the summers of 1962 and 1963 that I did not think about how, forty years down the line, there would be nobody alive to check the odd form that I really am not sure about any more. So one of the lessons is that documentary linguists really do need to keep in mind, in the face of the profound force of local social construction in the linguist-consultant relationship, that they belong to a larger community with its own needs.

    And of course consultants are contributing to the emerging structuration of the community of practice and its products. To discuss one of these con-tributions by Roscinda Nolasquez, I need to give you some background on Cupeño demonstratives. Cupeño has three demonstratives: *i'i*, a clear proximal, *axwesh*, a clear distal, and a mystery demonstrative *et*. In writing my reference grammar (Hill 2005) over the last few years, I had to figure out what on earth the mystery demonstrative meant. What I determined was that *et* and *axwesh* are contrasted as distal-proximal and distal-obviative. Part of the evidence was that only *axwesh* appeared in narrative, except for passages of reported speech, in which *et* could appear. The other bit of evi-dence was that *et* was absolutely ubiquitous in elicited sentences, where *axwesh* never appeared. For instance, in one section of field notes I was investigating which noun stems would accept locative suffixes directly, and which required relational noun constructions. I figured a fly could sit on just about anything, and put a fly in all sorts of absurd places – on the basket, on the acorns, on the string, on the berries, on the cow, etc., in sentences for Roscinda to translate. She always translated English "a fly," as *et ku'al* 'that fly' – the distal-proximal (virtual) fly to which we were both paying attention. The combination of the presence of *et* in elicitation and in reported speech in narrative suggested that its function was "distal, but within the zone of attention of discourse participants." On the other hand, *axwesh* meant "distal, but not available to discourse participants." Hence, *et ku'al*, the mutually-imagined fly of the context of elicitation, but *axwesh isily* 'that coyote,' a character of the mythic time who appears in narrative.

With my new-found understanding of the demonstratives, I am now able to more fully understand Roscinda Nolasquez's goals, and why she was willing to spend so much time with me. At the time I had completely naturalized the idea that an American Indian community should include only a few elderly speakers of a heritage language. As far as I could tell there was almost no interest in the language; Roscinda never mentioned any regrets about being one of the last speakers, and handled most of her life in English. Indeed, she positively avoided talking to a couple of other women of her age who were speakers, because she didn't like them. She called what she did with me "teaching." But, looking at my notes forty years later, I could see that she was trying to accomplish much more: She was documenting, recording an archive, although she never said as much. And the distribution of the demonstratives became one of the key pieces of evidence for this.

Roscinda really liked best of all to record stories and histories. After a couple of months of work, she said that she wanted to tell about how the Cupeño had moved from their original homeland at *Kupa, Pal Atingve*, to their reservation at Pala. This is a dreadful story, of legal machinations by greedy Whites and a desperate battle by the Cupeño to keep their lands, which included valuable hot and cold springs in an arid region of San Diego County in southern California. Roscinda was nine years old in 1903 when she and all her relatives were packed into wagons and moved out of their beautiful village with its sturdy adobe houses and inviting pools of hot and cold water and moved to Pala, to live in tents in the flea-ridden willow thickets along the San Luis Rey river designated as their place of exile. She told the story of the removal on three separate days. On the first day, she narrated almost entirely from her own point of view, using almost no reportative evidentials. When she resumed again on the second day, she began by labelling her talk as *a'alxi* 'reciting history.' In this section and in the third section, the reportative evidential appears frequently, even where she is describing scenes in which she played a role (such as the rescue of her pet cats). On the first day, narrating as a sort of conversational account of a personal experience, she uses the base *eve-*, the inflectional base of *et*, almost exclusively for the locatives. That is, even though the places being referred to are not "in the immediate discourse context," she refers to them in the voice of an interlocutor in dialogue with the listener (in this case, me, Jane Hill), who has been initiated into the world of the narrative and is taken to share her point of view. But in the second and third telling, the base *eve-* is entirely absent, and all references to place are with the base *axwa-*, *a-*, the locative bases of the obviative demonstrative *axwesh*. That is, in her second and third telling, Roscinda Nolasquez speaks in the voice of an "historian"; she animates a tradition, rather than engaging directly with me as her interlocutor. And it is clear that her descendants recognized what she was doing. One of the ways that Cupeño have always used their oral tradition is to borrow lines from it to make songs. And singers today have taken lines from my recordings of Roscinda Nolasquez's account of the removal. When I returned to the community a year and a half ago, I was treated to a performance of men singing to rattles, and was very moved to encounter a beautiful new song, composed for the 2003 centennial of the removal, that used a line that appears in her telling: *Peta'amay che'mixani chemtewa$h Kupangax* 'We lost everything from Kupa.'

In summary, the moral here is that what Roscinda Nolasquez took to be the mutual goal of the community of practice that we formed in the summers of 1962 and 1963, to document her language and its traditions, shaped even very fine details of her speech. In elicitation, where the sentences would have no historic significance, her demonstrative was *et*. In reciting texts where the sentences would have historic significance, she used obviative *axwesh*. So the notion of the community of practice teaches us that the ethnography of language in documentary linguistics must take as its site for study not only the organization of diversity in the speech community, but also organization and patterning that is emergent, including emergent in the context of elicitation and language learning itself.

3. Language ideology and documentary linguistics

The last set of ideas to be presented here involve how we can attend to the very fast-moving dynamics of language ideology in endangered language communities. Something of the significance of language ideologies has been recognized for a very long time. For instance, the early ethnographers and linguists working in indigenous North America discovered that accounts of the creation were fully performed only in the winter, and so they could not be elicited in the summertime; indeed, people thought it was dangerous to do so.

But the early ethnographers thought of this kind of ideologically-driven pattern as simply one more stable difference between them and their consultants. Today we are finding, though, that these ideological systems can evolve and spread in communities with astonishing rapidity. I will discuss an example that unfortunately I had to observe at immediate second hand – the contretemps around the publication of the Hopi Dictionary, for which my husband Kenneth C. Hill was project director. The Hopi, who live in northeastern Arizona, are the western-most of the Puebloan societies. Paul Kroskrity (1998) has shown how in the Puebloan communities of the U.S. Southwest, all indigenous language tends to be ideologically assimilated to the prototype of ritual language, the language of the kivas. Kiva knowledge is not shared with people who have not been initiated into the relevant ritual societies, and many of the pueblos have decided that their language is strictly for insiders. Indeed, one Hopi linguist, briefly employed at the University of Arizona about 30 years ago, refused to teach the language to non-Hopi students. A second point is important in understanding the dictionary controversy: During the period when public ceremonies are underway, the Hopi villages construct a sort of "anti-market" economy that extends the practice of the kiva to the entire village: nothing is sold, everything that one might need is given as a gift.

This was the background ideological context in which my husband worked for more than a decade with colleagues Emory Sekaquaptewa, Ekkehart Malotki, Mary Black, and others to compile the great dictionary of Third Mesa Hopi (Hopi Dictionary Project 1998). During the period of the research only the most minor difficulties appeared; all tribal officials were involved and participating. They all knew that the project was the brainchild and dream of a senior Hopi, Emory Sekaquaptewa. The dictionary research group was extremely careful of Hopi ritual sensitivities, and a committee of Hopi elders made sure that the dictionary would not contain anything that would be in violation of ritual prohibitions. Arrangements were made to distribute dictionaries free to schools and at a greatly reduced price to Hopis, and all royalties were to be paid to the Hopi Foundation, a non-profit foundation dedicated to Hopi education. However, when the publication date of the dictionary neared, the University of Arizona Press proudly published a handsome full-color brochure as an announcement of this major work, in which a price of $80.00 for the volume was mentioned. This announcement finally made public and unavoidable what everyone had managed to keep in the background – that the dictionary, which had been largely funded by money from the U.S. government's National Endowment for the Humanities, would be available to non-Hopis, and that it would be sold. This precipitated a difficult year during which the Hopi Director of Cultural Affairs, Leigh Kuwanwisiwma, supported by many other Hopis, argued that the dictionary should not be published at all because the Hopi language should not be bought and sold, and certainly not for the benefit of non-Hopis. Eventually the political faction that supported the dictionary prevailed and it was published, but this result was by no means guaranteed (Hill 2002 discusses this episode).

Recent theoretical work on linguistic ideologies can help us to understand this sort of episode, and perhaps to work better and more comprehendingly with community members who support documentation of their heritage language in dictionaries and development projects like language classes. Susan Gal and Judith Irvine (1995) showed that language ideologies nearly always invoke three major semiotic principles. These are "iconization," "recursiveness," and "erasure." In "iconization," elements of language are shaped to match elements "in the world" – and by erasure, any dimension of language that does not conform is ignored. By "recursiveness," "iconization" operates throughout the system, bringing elements at every level into line. Michael Silverstein (1996, 2003) has pointed out the operation of what he calls the "dialectic of indexicality," by which indexicality is reshaped as reference. Miyako Inoue (2004) has shown how certain kinds of social circumstances – episodes of rapid political economic change, in which identities are being rapidly restructured – heighten the rapidity and strength of these processes.

Using these theoretical tools, we can say something about the Hopi case, in which a language and an associated way of life that had always been taken for granted becomes the object of the most acute attention and reflection. Such attention and reflection, and the iconization principle, yields an exaggerated purism. In the Hopi case, by iconization the Hopi community itself is assimilated to the prototype of the kiva, and the language is assimilated to the language of the kiva. The words of the language become like kiva objects, which should never be seen by non-initiates. Just as ritual practice and ritual talk that occurs in the kiva is never shared with outsiders, the language should not be shared with outsiders. Just as the kiva and even public ritual is a site where nothing is bought and sold, and everything is generously shared, no price can be put on the language, so it cannot appear in artifacts that bear a price. In this case we can see the dialectic of indexicality: the language, which indexes Hopi identity, must be shaped so that it refers perfectly to that identity: it must be ritually normalized, just as the identity itself becomes the identity of a ritual participant. Thus a Hopi word in an $80.00 dictionary published by a White institution, truly makes no sense; it is, in the words of the anthropologist Mary Douglas (1966), "matter out of place," a form of pollution, and incites profound reactions in those who are offended.

Anyone who works in indigenous North America, where communities are only a few generations removed from a true genocide and continue to confront severe economic marginalization as well as racism, will be able to recount many examples like the case of the Hopi dictionary. The logic of language ideology outlined above predicts that documentary linguists will encounter similar episodes in communities that thus far have been reasonably receptive to documentary projects. The theory also predicts the general shape that such ideological projects are likely to take: they will assimilate the resources of language to some image of purity and essence, ritually validated, and will attempt to remove the language forever from history. Needless to say, such ideological projects happen everywhere. However, the community of speakers of Norwegian, or French, or German is robust enough to support the occasional outburst of purism without catastrophic results. Indeed, purism can be a positive asset if the community has the resources to do something about it; the examples of Israeli Hebrew and Catalan come to mind. But small minority-language and indigenous communities may not have such resources, and the state of the language may not give such communities time to work through such episodes and achieve positive and durable syntheses. So research specifically on such episodes, and how to handle and understand them, should be a part of our work. Leanne Hinton's work on vernacular orthographies (Hinton 2003), a focus of ideological construction that has stymied language development in some American Indian communities for decades, seems to me a perfect example of the combination of theoretical penetration and practical recommendation that we require.

4. Conclusion

Training in documentary linguistics is very demanding, requiring as it does expertise in linguistics, in anthropology, in recording technologies and data management, and in a myriad other ancillary sub-fields. What I hope to have made clear, though, is that its anthropological component needs to include training not only in the foundations of ethnographic practice – in "making strange," and in learning to notice and manage sites of miscommunication – but also in such arcana as the emergent formation of norms within a community of practice, and in the semiotics of ideology formation. The problem for us is to make these insights as straightforward for our students as is their training in phonology, morphology, and syntax. I hope that we will succeed in doing this. Just as recent advances in linguistic typology have immensely facilitated the recognition of the linguistic structures that we encounter in field work, advances in the study of cultural processes can help us organize our work and function more successfully, both as linguists and as friends, colleagues, and advocates for minority-language communities.

Note

1. Boas' (1911a) great programmatic statement in the "Introduction" to the *Handbook of North American Indian Languages* was followed by scattered work by Boas, Sapir, Whorf, and a few others on cultural dimensions of language use. But this work is barely integrated with their extensive work on the description and documentation of grammar. In the 1960s Dell Hymes, John Gumperz, and their colleagues tried to reopen the Boasian project, proposing what Hymes called an "ethnography of speaking," a "sociolinguistics" that took grammar and phonology to be simply one dimension of a pragmatics, one way that speakers actually use the material stuff of language. The diverse lines of work that Hymes enumerated as the foundations of a unified discipline exist today in over a dozen fragmented subspecialties with only occasional communication between them. Furthermore, very few people who emerged from the ethnography of speaking tradition, even those who have worked on indigenous and other minority linguistic communities, have made substantial contributions to linguistic description and documentation. Although it is a bit early to tell, the European "pragmatics" movement exhibits the same kinds of tendencies toward subspecialization, and its adherents, as far as I can tell, do not seem to be much involved in documentation of language organization at levels other than that of rhetoric and discourse.

Chapter 6

Documenting lexical knowledge

John B. Haviland

Introduction

Lexicography, the practice of documenting the meanings and uses of "words" (literally by "writing" them down), is, through its products, perhaps the most familiar branch of linguistics to the general public. It is also an ancient and much theorized activity. In the Boasian trilogy for language description of grammar, wordlist, and text, it is surely the dictionary whose compilation is most daunting. The process begins with a learner's first encounters with a language, and it ends, seemingly, never. Worse, it is an endeavor fraught with doubt, centrally about when enough is enough both for the whole – when one should assume that the basic or most common words of a linguistic variety have been captured and characterized – but also for any single putative dictionary entry, given the apparent endless variety of nuance and scope for words and forms, not to mention the idiosyncrasies of compound or derived expressions. Moreover, despite bounteous speculation, from many disparate linguistic traditions, on what metasemantic devices one might employ to capture meanings, despite multiple models and examples of the results of dictionary-making, and despite ample experience, for most of us, in the ordinary business of "explaining the meanings of words," doubt is likely to assail us on every single effort: have we said enough? have we forgotten something? did we get even this single word right?

This chapter introduces techniques and concepts relevant to producing a lexical database as part of a language documentation project. I concentrate on a series of doubt-producing obstacles for the field lexicographer, with some suggestions about how at least to address, if not to overcome them. My coverage is deliberately partial. I draw heavily on my own fieldwork in Mexico and Australia, to consider three general issues. First, I review familiar morals about the nature of word meaning – concepts from linguistic philosophy that are easy to forget in the heat of the lexicographic moment. Second I consider semantic metalanguages proposed to deal with different kinds of meaningful elements, from "functional" to lexical and from roots to stems. Third, and most centrally, I review techniques for systematically extracting lexical knowledge. I largely ignore several related and important topics: lexical variation and how to represent it (see Chapter 5), ideological issues inescapably involved in promulgating any dictionary (see again Chapter 5, and the discussions in Frawley et al. 2002), and wider issues in lexical semantic theory (about sense relations, problems of extension vs. intension, etc.), which underlie all lexicographic practice but are beyond the present scope. I begin with a highly selective review of published materials on lexical knowledge, especially as relevant to documenting endangered languages.

1. Lexicography and its products

In addition to a large theoretical literature on meaning, there is a practical tradition of dictionary-making that has spawned handbooks and histories, as well as essays on the lexicographer's craft. These rarely provide solace for the field worker.

The lexicon, in modern linguistics, has come to mean a repository for otherwise anarchic facts, an inventory of arbitrary pairings of pronunciations with bundles of features. It is where language stores its idiosyncrasies and irregularities. What systematicity there is to the lexicon so conceived derives from feature systems themselves, taken to represent syntactic and semantic patterning underlying surface lexical forms. Studying such patterning is the usual province of lexical semantics, which catalogues various relations between the senses of members of different subsets of lexical forms (Cruse 1986), systematic properties of surface word classes or "parts of speech," facts of argument structure, diathesis, and the like. The main contribution to linguistic theory of much empirical lexicography has been in elucidating semantic and syntactic interrelationships at the level of the surface word (Levin 1993).

Field linguistics, once the province of anthropological linguists, gave rise to much of the underlying conceptual apparatus of lexical semantics. Early theories pursued an analogy between phonological features and the "components" of meaning in structured sets of "folk terminology," from kinship to ethnobotany, from pronoun systems to verbal typologies. The classic studies of "ethnoscience" investigated culturally elaborated lexical systems, particularly in "natural" domains like ethnobotany. Further empirical inspiration for semantic theorizing came, for example, from the languages of

Aboriginal Australians, celebrated for their linguistic acuity and creative genius. Dyirbal verb semantics and the properties of special Dyirbal "mother-in-law" vocabulary for affinal avoidance led Dixon (1971) to postulate a fundamental difference between semantically basic or "nuclear" words, requiring some sort of decomposition into sublexical meaningful dimensions, and non-nuclear words which could be *defined* in terms of the nuclear words plus other devices of the grammar. Verbal play in ritual language games learned by Warlpiri and Lardil initiates suggested that Aboriginal ethnolinguists had developed sophisticated semantic analyses of ordinary vocabulary (Hale 1971, 1982).

The classic reference manual on lexicography is Zgusta (1971).[1] Of special interest to the field lexicographer is Frawley et al. (2002), a collection of essays by practicing lexicographers working on American Indian languages, which also considers problems in *creating* a lexicographic practice in communities without one.[2] These range over theoretical issues in lexical semantics (the nature of definition, the range of lexical knowledge that speakers possess or a dictionary might include, and the interplay between diachronic and synchronic lexical facts); to questions of representational form, to sociopolitical issues in dictionary making (for whom is a dictionary compiled and for what purposes; or, what kinds of sociolinguistic categories – specialized speech genres, gender or class specific lexical forms, for example – are to be distinguished). These works go well beyond the limited selection of topics addressed here.

The field linguist need not be a semanticist, except "for practical purposes," and lexicography in the service of documentation needs to strike a balance between opposing desiderata. For example, in what sense is "completeness" – however that might be defined for an endangered language – something to strive for? What about the mix of theoretically versus practically motivated metalanguages for representing lexical information? In the field one should avail oneself of all possible tricks: bilingual dictionaries, for example, can often start with existing word lists, in either the source or the target language, and there is no reason to stand behind strict methodological principles or purism in generating lexemes for incorporation into a lexical database.

Different lexicographic products reflect different starting points and goals for compilers of lexical databases. Zgusta (1971) dedicates separate chapters to the distinct issues involved in compiling polylingual (usually bilingual) versus monolingual dictionaries. The contrast, and the choice of which languages to include in a multilingual dictionary, raise obvious questions. For what sort of use is a lexical database produced? What knowledge on the part of the user is presupposed in its design? Why did its compiler produce it in the first place? Let me review several different kinds of field dictionaries, related to my own research in Mexico and Australia. Especially useful to me have been the introductions to two Tzotzil dictionaries by Robert M. Laughlin (1975, 1988), one modern and the other based on a sixteenth-century work.

In what I call the Colonial tradition, collecting vocabularies was always a vocation of imperialists, often an accidental byproduct of exploration and conquest. Explorers collected flora and fauna, and often they also collected words. Somewhat less innocent were the wordlists created explicitly to *aid* in conversion, conquest, and control. The friars' dictionaries of Indian languages in the New World, or vernacular vocabularies destined for colonial bureaucrats in Africa and India, represented unabashedly instrumental "documentation," often of languages whose eventual endangerment was a byproduct of colonial expansion in the first place. Such wordlists were plainly not made "for" the speakers of the languages so documented.

The missionary tradition continues to produce many field dictionaries, and reading them gives some flavor of the purposes and populations served by this particular lexicographic practice. In Chiapas, Mexico, the Summer Institute of Linguistics – a Protestant Bible-translating organization – has published many dictionaries of Indian languages from the region (Delgaty and Ruiz [1978] for Tzotzil, Aulie and Aulie [1978] for Chol, to mention just two), and they are widely used even by speakers who do not share the religious beliefs of the translators. Such dictionaries are subtly infused with cultural metacomment and religious ideology.

Here, for example, is a translation of the entry in Aulie and Aulie (1978) for the Chol word *ajaw*, reflex of a root which means "lord, master, God" in other Mayan languages. According to the Aulies, the Chol word means "*espíritu malo de la tierra*," and they go on to comment:

> They call it *lak tat* 'our father.' It is believed that a person can make a pact with it. Such a person can make requests of the spirit for or against another. The person who establishes such relations with the *ajaw* is called a "sacristán." If a man or woman offends the sacristán, the latter appeals to the spirit to curse the other, and in a short time the other person will die.

Here both the lexicographers' voice and its underlying ideological accent are plainly on display. Thus, for the Aulies there is no apparent dissonance between their proposed gloss, "evil spirit of the earth" and the alternate locution "our father" (with a first-person plural inclusive prefix). Furthermore, the 'they' of the comment is clearly someone other than the dictionary writers (though perhaps not different from the dictionary users). Note finally an interesting voicing contrast. Although the possibility of "making a pact" with *ajaw* is cited as something "believed" (presumably by 'them'), the consequences of the appeal on the part of the hypothetical *sacristán* (the term itself a Spanish loan introduced into Chol during the Catholic conversion of Chol speakers following the Conquest) are given a different epistemological status: "in a short time the other person will die." The dictionary thus incorporates different, perhaps mutually contradictory stances towards Chol beliefs and practices into the lexical entries themselves.

Slightly different is the "ethnolinguistic" lexicographic tradition, whose immediate origins are in ethnographic research. Sticking again to highland Chiapas, Laughlin's exhaustive dictionary of contemporary Zinacantec Tzotzil (1975) has the form of a traditional bilingual dictionary. The first section gives extensive glosses (in English) of Tzotzil words, both derived and simple, and arranged under their putative underlying roots. There follows an English index to the Tzotzil section. Laughlin's dictionary has over 35,000 Tzotzil to English entries, making it one of the largest dictionaries of an indigenous language of the Americas. However, it is a bilingual dictionary in Tzotzil and *English*, limiting its direct use to the handful of people who speak those two languages.[3] It is also a defiantly dialect-bound (and even gender-bound) dictionary, documenting the way middle-aged men spoke during the 1960s and 1970s in just the single municipality of Zinacantán, arguably a minority variant of what has since become a dominant Indian language in highland Chiapas with a much larger number of speakers from other dialects. Thus, the choice of language variety in the dictionary reflects accidents of the background research rather than principled lexicographic or sociolinguistic design. Moreover, grouping entries by a theoretical underlying root (a form which does not occur in speech, having only psychological rather than surface "reality"), and stripping words of all affixes – i.e. lemmatizing them – makes locating a word in this dictionary something of an analytical challenge, again, a reflection of the intellectual priorities of its producers, but with possibly inconvenient consequences for many potential Tzotzil-speaking users.

A different variant of the ethnolinguistic wordlist, from Australia, illustrates another aspect of the field lexicographer's dilemma. Many linguists have documented Australian Aboriginal languages with very few remaining speakers, often not fully fluent. My own work on the now defunct Barrow Point language (see Haviland 1998) is a minor example. In such cases, wordlists reflect serendipitous opportunity more than systematic planning, and coverage is spotty, based on happenstance and luck. Nonetheless, even haphazardly assembled lists of words may be significant when political processes – for example, "native title" claims to traditional Aboriginal territory – use linguistic evidence to establish links between land and Aboriginal culture and society (Henderson and Nash 2002). Everything from a place name to a plant name may turn out to have unsuspected relevance. Thus the issue of coverage is less a matter of scientific "completeness" than an ideological issue of clear political import, another matter to which I return fleetingly at the end of the chapter.

There is also a *pedagogical* tradition in dictionary making, source of the most common dictionaries: those used by students to look up unfamiliar words, or by tourists to translate menus. Here the question of dimension is telling. Dictionaries of Mexican Spanish (for example, Lara Ramos 1986) are explicitly graded by size: a small version meant for schoolchildren with several thousand "basic" words, a larger intermediate version with more, and so on. All celebrate Mexican Spanish, the most widely spoken variety of the language, but one relegated to a subsidiary status by the language academy of the colonial home country. The lexicon chosen and the facts of usage are drawn from a huge corpus of Mexican textual material, from letters, to newspaper articles, to popular songs. In Chiapas, the government has similarly commissioned a variety of "*diccionarios de bolsa*" or pocket dictionaries for the Indian languages of the state. These, along with a series of grammatical sketches, are meant as both pedagogical tools and political trophies, evidence of government concern for Indians in the wake of the Zapatista uprising of 1994. Of a similar design but with an opposite ideological thrust are the illustrated school primers, or basic wordlists, designed as literacy aids by Zapatista community schools which resist all government aid and standardized school materials.

2. Referential indeterminacy and other pitfalls of fieldwork

What sorts of creatures are the "meanings" of words we wish to set down in a lexical database? It is hard to escape the weight of many centuries of Western philosophizing on the subject (although there are useful antidotes in J. L. Austin's early essay "The meaning of a word" in Austin 1961).

Following Frege (1892) it is customary to begin with the notion that words (characteristically nouns) can typically be used by speakers to pick out entities in the world – the words' "referents" – by virtue of their "sense" or "denotation" independent of any instance of their use for referring or predicating about a specific state of affairs. Words, on this view, are a kind of instruction from speaker to hearer, grounded in some shared understanding of the "meanings" of expressions, and typically designed to achieve common reference.

Even with apparently simple cases, of course, the conundrums of reference as a theory of meaning immediately surface. Suppose someone wants to refer to me as I am lecturing. Consider the following expressions she might use:

(1)   Expressions referring to the same referent

    a. That guy (with a pointing gesture)
    b. The linguistics professor from Oregon.
    c. The tall guy with a black moustache at the front of the room.
    d. The Mexican with a black moustache at the front of the room.

The speaker's "instructions" if successful – that is, if they induce the interlocutor to pick me out as the person to whom she refers – rely on quite different sorts of relations to the "meanings" of the words she uses. The first relies on some sort of categorial understanding of what we can use 'guy' to refer to, combined with two direct indexical devices, the deictic *that* and the pointing gesture. At the other extreme, (b) picks out a presupposably identifiable individual from the intersection of sets of denotata generated compositionally from the constituent words (along perhaps with presuppositions of existence and uniqueness built into the definite article *the*). Expression (c) combines such a compositional strategy with some implied deixis (calculating *which* room and where its *front* is), and (d) paradoxically is likely to succeed as well as (c) despite the fact that, though I live and teach in Mexico and possibly even look Mexican, I am *not* a Mexican at all – therefore, the "meanings" of the constituent words cannot add up to a true denotation.

So reference, although it is where we start in field linguistics, cannot be where we want to end up. Quine's famous *gavagai* example (Quine 1960) – in which a hypothetical and ontologically challenged linguist, in a parodied setting of monolingual fieldwork, hears the word *gavagai* in the presence of rabbits, but cannot decide whether the word means 'rabbit' or 'rabbit part' or 'rabbit essence,' etc. – underscores the profound referential indeterminacy of linguistic behavior. Perhaps more to the point is Zgusta's analogy (Zgusta 1971: 25–26) with trying to discover the meanings of traffic signs (in a system like the European one), but only on the basis of observing the regularities in drivers' behavior. Perhaps, speculates Zgusta, one could in time decipher the meanings of, say, the red, yellow, and green signals of a traffic light by direct observation; but the meaning of a "great capital H on a rectangular shield (which means in many countries that there is a hospital not far away)" would be much harder to divine, since such signs stand in many different kinds of locations and "a uniform effect on the behaviour of other drivers is hardly observable."

Here is a less fanciful example from the annals of real field lexicography. In 1770, Lt. James Cook and his crew collected wordlists from the Guugu Yimithirr language, spoken near what is now called Cooktown, in north-eastern Australia. (One word was *gangurru*, the name for a particular species of what the world now calls kangaroos). Collating the shared entries of different observers, one can see precisely that referential indeterminacy of the *gavagai* variety plagued these early lexicographers. Thus, under the gloss 'branch (with buds or stalk)', the ship's illustrator Parkinson has *maiye*, Banks the botanist writes *maye butai* (adding the annotation 'with leaves') or *mayi bambier*. Based on the modern language, I assume that these expressions are based on the word *mayi* 'edible plant' – so not just any old branch is involved – and more specifically *mayi bambiir* 'the (edible) fruit of the mangrove species called *bambiir*'. The other "name" Banks records is plainly the expression *mayi buday* which is really an entire sentence that means "the edible part has been eaten" or "someone ate the fruit."[4] Cook's journal entry shows he was painfully aware of such Quinean problems of lexical elicitation.

> ...the list of words I have given could be got by no other manner than by signs enquiring of them what in their Language signified such a thing, a method obnoxious to many mistakes: for instance a man holds in his hand a stone and asks the name of [it]: the Indian may return him for answer either the real name of a stone, one of the properties of it as hardness, roughness, smoothness &c, one of its uses or the name peculiar to some particular species of stone, which name the enquirer immediately sets down as that of a stone.   (Cook's journal, see Cook 1955)

Part of the problem, clearly, is in a primitive model of both reference and ostension: what you can pick out by pointing, or what you can show "the Indian."

A very different model of "exemplification" is advocated by J. L. Austin in "A plea for excuses" (Austin 1961). Faced with a pair of expressions (famously, in Austin's case, the apparently similar *by mistake* vs. *by accident*) one elucidates the difference in their meanings by constructing a careful example of when you would use the first expression but not the second, and vice versa. In such a method one points not at *things* but at contexts of use.

Contexts themselves can be crucial in accessing lexical knowledge. In trying to recover words from the native Barrow Point language of the late Roger Hart, he and I worked largely through Guugu Yimithirr, a second language for both of us (see Haviland 1998). We would often search – sometimes quite naively – for the Barrow Point equivalent of a Guugu Yimithirr word. Even looking for the names of plant or animal species, however, we were often stymied, partly because the flora and fauna of Barrow Point were frequently different from those of Cape Bedford, more than a hundred kilometers to the south, but partly because the environment in general was just wrong. Roger had learned his tribal language before he was removed from his family around the age of six. I first heard him speak the language without hesitation, however, sixty years later. After a long trek back overland, he and I stumbled out onto the beach where he had been born. The country he had not seen for sixty years, its trees, rocks, and animals, seemed to speak to him in his childhood tongue, and he was only there able to respond fluently.

Reference – or more precisely those aspects of linguistic expressions that render them useful for achieving reference – though the staple of most modern formal semantics, is of course an inadequate basis for understanding meaning in an ordinary sense. The traditional notion of "connotation," for example, is based on the intuition that different words can in some sense "refer to the same thing" without, thereby, "having the same meaning." This is not the same as Frege's classic distinction between sense (what an expression means) and reference (what it just happens to refer to, as a function of what it means) where two different expressions, with different senses, can happen to refer to the same individual. Zgusta's somewhat quaint example is the lexical triad 'decease', 'die', 'peg out' (the last in my own dialect of English would be something like 'check out' or perhaps 'go belly up'). Zgusta (1971: 39–40) cites Armenian as a language which has exact counterparts (*vačxanvel, mernel, satkel*) for these English words, and Chinese as another with a considerably more elaborated set covering the same referential territory. (We could, of course, add more English expressions, changing thereby the dimensions of "connotation" evoked: 'pass [away]', 'go [to a better place] or [to meet his/her maker]', 'croak', etc.) The way to capture the difference between the terms in question, presumably, is to specify not truth conditions on the states of affairs they are used to describe (which are stipulated to be identical) but appropriateness conditions[5] on the indexical circumstances of their use: who can use which expression, to whom, speaking about which sorts of deceased entities, and in what sorts of situations, among other things.

Zgusta likens the lexicographer's problem with connotation to others related to ranges of meaning, selectional restrictions, and collocational specificity. One of Quine's examples was 'addled': "used only of eggs and brains" (see McIntosh 1961). Zgusta cites Černý on two Georgian words meaning 'to have': *makvs* (applied to things one has) vs. *mqavs* (applied to persons and animals), "but motorcars are treated not as things but as animals because one says *mankana mqavs* 'I have a motorcar'" (Zgusta 1971: 44).[6] Berlin's (1967) study of Tseltal[7] verbs of eating in which different kinds of foods require one of six different verbs of eating exemplifies a parallel phenomenon. There are conceptual muddles here which there is no space in this chapter to untangle: whereas words with different connotations seem to be appropriate to different contexts of use, or different speaker attitudes, can we distinguish selectional restrictions from denotational limitations? Perhaps *makvs* denotes a different state of affairs from *mqavs*, not merely 'the same concept' applied to different kinds of objects. Perhaps Tseltal *we`* 'eat (tortillas, for example)' is "really" a different action from *k'ux* 'eat (crunchy things, for example).' Whatever our semiotic theory, such systematic meaning distinctions clearly belong in a documenting lexicon: recording them is part of the lexicographer's "duty" and a task to which methodological attention must be directed.

Here, the problem of negative evidence (or rather the lack of it in naturally occurring talk) is critical in compiling a lexical database for an imperiled language. Evidence about limits on the range of meaning of a word or phrase, or about restrictions on its use or appropriateness in different intertextual and cultural contexts, may simply be non existent in a textual corpus, and systematic elicitation of specific lexicographic intuitions may be impossible. In the Colonial Tzotzil dictionary, for *pesar el negocio con cordura o diligencia* "treat a matter prudently or diligently" (Laughlin 1988), the friars gave an inflected version of the Tzotzil expression *-a`i ta-olonton*, literally "hear (or feel, or understand) in the heart." The Tzotzil phrase re-quires morpho-syntactic completion: the transitive verb *-a`i* needs both a syntactic subject (the one who presumably "treats" some matter) and object (the "matter" treated). Moreover, the word *-olonton* 'heart' also requires an obligatory possessor, which judging by the modern language must be coreferential with the subject of the verb, thus "x hears with his/her OWN heart" – not, with someone else's. These morphosyntactic restrictions are not obvious from the original usage. Nor is it clear that the expression is limited to the sort of referential context suggested by the English (or original Spanish) gloss: it seems instead simply to suggest careful consideration of anything, whether a *"negocio"* 'matter, business' or something less specific or concrete. Without access to fully fluent native speakers it is impossible to supply more lexical detail. More problematic, and perhaps more relevant to documenting an endangered language, is the case of an archaic word, or one in limited use in a speech community. Again, Colonial Tzotzil provides an instructive example. The ritual language of modern Tzotzil uses the ex-pression *tza-uk*, evidently formed from a (non-attested) nominal root *tza* plus an irealis or subjunctive suffix *-uk*. Laughlin (1975) suggests as a meaning for *tzauk* 'take heed' – a translation suggested by knowledgeable modern speakers. However, somewhat arbitrarily it seems, in the modern dictionary he lists the word under the root *tzak* 'catch, grab'. Only the dis-covery of the Colonial dictionary (Laughlin 1988) revealed an archaic root *tza* which has entirely fallen out of existence in Zinacantec Tzotzil except for its surviving ritual use. The Colonial lexicographers recorded it with the meanings "cleverness, cognizance, craftsmanship, guess, industriousness, intelligence, opinion, prudence, skill, speculation, talent, thought," but no evidence is provided by modern usage.

Perhaps the oldest chestnut of anthropological linguistics is denotational diversity in lexical mappings of "reality," captured in the slogan that "dif-ferent words" imply "different worlds." One classic domain is ethno-anatomy, the lexical (and thus, perhaps, conceptual?) slicing up of the body into discrete parts. Whereas English speakers distinguish 'hands' from 'arms', Russian and Tzotzil speakers do not. Tzotzil has the single root *k'Ab*[8] which can mean either 'hand' or 'arm'. Worse, it can also mean 'branch', 'sleeve', 'crossbar (of a cross)', 'front leg (of a cat)', and so on. Tzotzil *ni`* 'nose' denotes not only noses, but any relatively sharp-pointed protrusion, or the thin end of almost any sort of object, not necessarily a face or a head. So why privilege a 'body part' gloss like 'hand' or 'nose'? Perhaps a non-anatomical model is involved in such partinomies.

Another possibility is that a "basic meaning" is extended in various ways into a chain or continuum of derived meanings without well defined endpoints. Cruse (1986) argues that terms like 'mouth' in English participate in "sense spectra" where each "derived" or "metaphorical" meaning leads to another.

(2)   "sense spectrum" (Cruse 1986: 71 ff.)

John keeps opening and shutting his *mouth* like a fish.
This parasite attaches itself to the *mouths* of fishes, sea-squirts, etc.
The *mouth* of the sea-squirt resembles that of a bottle.
The *mouth* of the cave resembles that of a bottle.
The *mouth* of the enormous cave was also that of the underground river.

The kinds of meaningful elements one chooses for a lexical database are also inextricably linked to the whole of one's categorial analysis for a language, what "parts of speech" are postulated, and what sorts of semantic profiles are associated with them. The standard formal semantic starting point that nouns will map onto things (i.e. sets), adjectives to "properties" (i.e. subsets), and verbs to events or states of affairs (predicates over n-tuples of entities), quickly disintegrates in the face of the diverse sorts of semantic *conflation* (Talmy 1985) routinely observed in lexical items. A standard example is 'climb' in English, whose Frame Net[9] definition is: "to move vertically usually upwards, usually with effort." That is, the verb suggests, in the default case, vertical movement upward, combined with the sort of effort Fillmore called "clambering." Either of these conflated elements – upward motion, or effort – can be suspended, but not both without semantic oddness.

(3)   Conflation in *climb* (Fillmore 1982)

The snake climbed (up) the tree.
The monkey climbed (up/down) the tree.
?The snake climbed down the tree.

Another commonplace of anthropological linguistics is that languages conflate semantic domains in unexpected ways, perhaps most characteristically in verbs. For example, the following Tzotzil positional predicates all might receive a similar English gloss 'stuck'.

(4) Tzotzil words for 'stuck'

Kakal 'stuck (between two surfaces)'
Ch'ikil 'stuck (into a narrow or tight crevice)'
Katz'al 'stuck (in a jaw-like orifice)'
Xojol 'stuck (inside an enclosing hole)'
Tz'apal 'stuck (a pointed thing anchored in a surface)'

As the detailed glosses show, however, each word specifies different configurations, kinds of attachment, and different shapes, in both figure and ground.[10] The exact conflation, I believe, involves such factors as the following, taking the root *tz'ap* as an illustration.

(5) Conflation in *tz'ap*

a. the "end" of the Figure is "inside" the Ground;
b. the Ground need not have a *y-ut* 'inside' (or perhaps it must not be so structured, conceived of instead as a mere surface);
c. the Figure has a "pointed" "end" (in Tzotzil, *s-ni`* 'nose');
d. typically the Figure is "stuck" into the Ground pointed end-first, i.e., attached somehow, and self-supporting; and
e. typically it is vertically oriented.

Linguists have posited various classifications of semantic types, in different root classes, and the field lexicographer should borrow shamelessly from such typologies: from frames, to verb types (Dixon 1972), to verb classes based on patterns of diathesis (Levin 1993), and so on.

The multiplicity of "language games" – something that cannot long remain hidden from a serious field linguist – further complicates the traditional referential view of lexical meaning. We use words to refer; but also for many other things. Here is part of Wittgenstein's list:

> Giving orders, and obeying them – Describing the appearance of an object, or giving its measurements – Constructing an object from a description (a drawing) – Reporting an event – Speculating about an event – Forming and testing a hypothesis – Presenting the results of an experiment in tables and diagrams – Making up a story; and reading it – Play-acting – Singing catches – Guessing riddles – Making a joke; and telling it – Solving a problem in practical arithmetic – Translating from one language into another – Asking, thanking, cursing, greeting, praying.
>
> (Wittgenstein 1958: sect. 23)

Cruse (1986: 270 ff.) reminds us of the differences between what he calls "semantic modes," as in the contrast between the following two utterances.

(6)   "Semantic modes"

I just felt a sudden sharp pain.
Ouch!

If semantics is only about reference and predication, then it will be difficult to capture the meaning of 'ouch!' semantically, because the word involves neither reference nor predication. Instead, it will be important to understand such things as interjections (see Kockelman 2003) in terms of very different semiotic modes: indexing speaker stance, interlocutor's relationship to speaker, putative bodily and affective states, expected responses, and so on. That words like 'ouch' are hard to model in terms of denotata does not relieve us of the lexicographer's responsibility of recording them and explaining how they work – a problem which I return to below.

A broader and more appropriate conception of meaning derives from one of the well-known trichotomies of ways that signs can signify or "stand for" other things, due to C. S. Peirce (1932). The three semiotic modes are based on very different principles, although they generally co-mingle in most signs, linguistic or otherwise. Peirce pointed out that some signs stand for other things because of a resemblance between the sign vehicle and the thing signified – thus a photograph of a person can stand for that person (for example, in a directory or catalogue). The sign bears an "iconic" resemblance to what it signifies, although the nature of the "resemblance" can vary tremendously (consider diagrams, drawings, silhouettes, graphs, for example, or conventionalized but nonetheless onomatopoetic words whose sounds suggest their meanings: 'moo' or 'caw' or 'cackle', perhaps). There can also be an "indexical" relationship between sign and signified, such that physical, spatial, or direct causal relationships exist between the sign vehicle and what it signifies. A footprint, for example, may not "resemble" the person who made it (although it may, of course, "resemble" his or her foot), but it stands as an 'index' of the person by virtue of the fact that it took the person's foot to make the mark (hence, indicating, for example, that that person has been at a certain place). In language, 'ouch!' stands for (indeed, displays) sudden pain precisely because we imagine that the pain itself somehow (involuntarily?) produces the utterance. In a similar way, we know what person 'I' or 'you' refers to by observing the contextual relationship between the sign – the word – and the person uttering it or to whom it is uttered. Such words, then, rely on an indexical relationship (in a context) to convey their meanings. Finally, there are signs whose significance is essentially unmotivated by either resemblance or context: these are Peircean 'symbols' which rely on a conventional relationship between signifier and signified – Saussure's "arbitrariness" of the linguistic sign, in which 'cat' means cat only because that is what a particular linguistic tradition has legislated.

Figure 1 shows a sign which transparently combines all three Peircean semiotic modalities: the iconic resemblance between the drawing and a (stylized) smoking cigarette; the conventional meaning (at least in much of the Western world) of the shaded circle with the diagonal bar as a "prohibition"; and finally, the location of the sign itself, whose physical position signals indexically exactly *where* smoking is prohibited.

Figure 1. A semiotically trichotomous sign

An adequate description of the meaning of linguistic elements must capture all three modes of signification, although the major lexicographic traditions limit themselves largely to "conventional" or symbolic meaning, almost exclusively in referential terms.

3. Metalanguages for meanings and units of lexical knowledge

A second major set of issues for lexical databases is how to represent the meanings of lexical items, and how to delimit such items in the first place. Bilingual definitional equivalents are often manifestly inadequate, for the reasons that have always worried translators: mismatches in grammatical class, inexactness or lack of equivalence between target and source language terms, incompatible ranges of meaning, infinite regress or vicious circles, and so forth. Much depends on the available metalanguages.

My colleague Matt Pearson, trying to illustrate the interdependence of different expressive modalities in language, challenges beginning linguistics students as follows: "Can you define 'spiral' without using your hands?" (You might try it yourself before reading on.)

To repeat, everything depends on the available metalanguages. Even a novice mathematician can respond by giving a formula for a 3-dimensional graph, i.e., by defining a series of values for the (x,y,z) axes. Here are some sample formulas.

(7)   spiral

   $(\cos(t), \sin(t), t)$ [for a spring-like spiral]
   $(c\,t\cos(t), c\,t\sin(t), c\,t)$ (where c is some constant)
   [for a cone-like one]

Just to see how these formulas work, on the following page are two graphs of their results, plotted by my statistician colleague Albyn Jones.

The beauty of the mathematical metalanguage involved is its precision, parsimony, and presumed universality.[11] The drawback is its potential arcane incomprehensibility.[12] Moreover, though the formulas may describe quite precisely a class of geometric forms, and perhaps even would help define 'spiral,' we might still need recourse to some further (though perhaps equally general) non-mathematical devices to capture the meaning of the word in expressions like "Prices are spiraling out of control," or "We must control the insane spiral of nuclear proliferation."

One difficulty with presuming a language-independent semantic metalanguage (aside from prejudging the semiosis of words and limiting it to referential information – a worry of the previous section) is that it may do violence to the conceptual organization of particular languages. Here is the emic-etic dichotomy of classical anthropological linguistics: do we give priority to language-specific organization of forms and meanings, or to de-

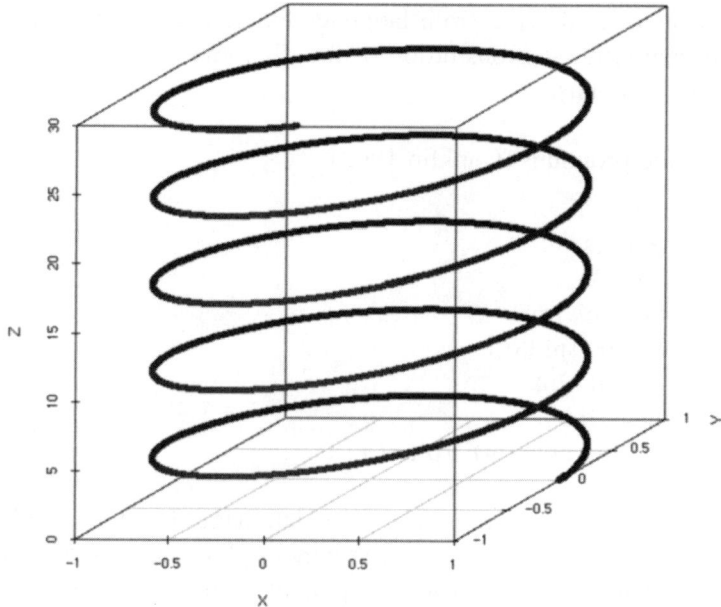

Figure 2. (cos(6t),sin(6t),t) for t in (0, pi)

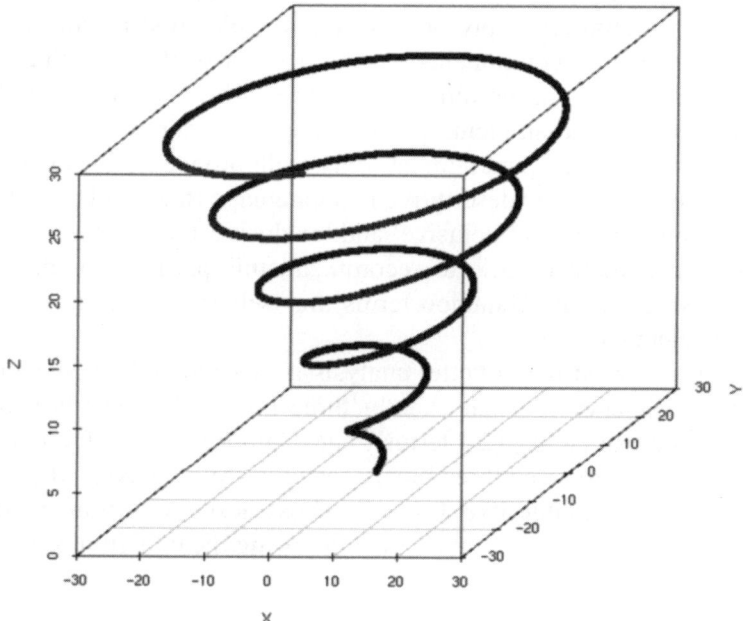

Figure 3. (t cos(t),t sin(t),t) for t in the same range

scriptive categories derived from language-external conceptualizations. An early and instructive demonstration of the dilemma is Conklin's treatment of Hanunoo pronouns.

(8)   Hanunoo pronouns (Conklin 1962)

> *kuh*   'I' 1s
> *muh*   'you' 2s
> *yah*   's/he' 3s
> *tah*   'we two' 1du
> *tam*   'we all' 1pl INCL
> *yuh*   'you all' 2pl
> *dah*   'they' 3pl
> *mih*   'we (but not you)' 1plEXCL

If we adopt the standard pronominal metalanguage, *kuh* will be glossed as "first person singular" or *tam* as "first person plural inclusive". The metalanguage thus involves a 'person' component (with possible values 1, 2, or 3), a 'number' component (with possible values, for Hanunoo, of singular, dual, or plural), and an 'inclusivity' component (with possible values inclusive or exclusive, and perhaps an unmarked value) which is defective in that it can by definition apply only to non-singular first person pronouns. Using such meaning components it should be possible to distinguish between 11–13 different pronominal forms (three different persons, with three different numbers, and an inclusive/exclusive distinction on all non-singular first-person forms). The paradigm has only eight pronouns, however. Worse, the primitive terms in the descriptive metalanguage (the number and person categories, plus the terms 'inclusive' and 'exclusive') themselves total eight, suggesting that there is little to recommend this particular metalanguage over just using the raw Hanunoo terms themselves as "primitive" or "undefinable" elements.

Conklin observed that a better analysis is possible, taking as metrics of evaluation efficiency (so that exactly three binary distinctions should be able to distinguish eight [$=2^3$] terms), and "faithfulness" to the native Hanunoo logic. His proposed three binary features are ±Speaker, ±Hearer, and ±Minimal, giving a table like Table 1, whose aesthetic symmetry inspires hope that one is discovering rather than imposing the underlying system.

Table 1. Hanunoo pronouns

	S	H	M
kuh 'I' 1s	+	–	+
muh 'you' 2s	–	+	+
yah 's/he' 3s	–	–	+
tah 'we two' 1du	+	+	+
tam 'we all' 1pl INCL	+	+	–
yuh 'you all' 2pl	–	+	–
dah 'they' 3pl	–	–	–
mih 'we (but not you)' 1plEXCL	+	–	–

Another useful descriptive paradigm widely applied to (and in fact driven by) lexicographic practice is the "frame-semantics" approach associated with Charles Fillmore (see, for example, Fillmore and Atkins 1992). Individual words, on this view, project wider, structured "frames" – configurations of elements and actions, some of which receive explicit grammatical realization and some of which remain implicit in the frame. Families of words then share frames. For example, the Framenet description of the "Commerce-buy" frame – which might be instantiated by such verbs as *buy*, *lease*, or *rent* – is

> These are words describing a basic commercial transaction involving a buyer and a seller exchanging money and goods, taking the perspective of the buyer. The words vary individually in the patterns of frame element realization they allow. For example, the typical pattern for the verb BUY: BUYER buys GOODS from SELLER for MONEY. Abby bought a car from Robin for $5,000.

Clearly, frames themselves can be interrelated. Compare the description for the "Giving" frame, which the "Commerce" frame above "inherits":

> A Donor transfers a Theme from a Donor to a Recipient.[13] This frame includes only actions that are initiated by the Donor (the one that starts out owning the Theme). Sentences (even metaphorical ones) must meet the following entailments: the Donor first has possession of the Theme. Following the transfer the Donor no longer has the Theme and the Recipient does.

In some ways related as a metasemantic device is the approach, most explicitly developed in Levin (1993), that uses various syntactic diagnostics – such as patterns of diathesis – to partition lexical sets into families or classes. Testing various diagnostic syntactic behaviors against their occurrence with specific verbs partitions the verbs into classes which can, according to this logic, be expected to display commonalities of meaning. For example, Levin proposes the following constructions as relevant tests to discover semantic classes among transitive verbs.

(9)   Diathesis diagnostics

MIDDLE: The bread cuts easily.
CONATIVE: Carla hit at the door.
BODY-PART POSSESSOR ASCENSION: Terry touched Bill on the shoulder.

Applied to specific verbs (each of which may have a variety of hyponyms, thus forming meaning families), these tests reveal different syntactic classes corresponding to putative meaning families. The meaning families can, in turn, be used to group individual lexical items, and the groupings are thus justified not simply on notional but also on syntactic grounds.

(10)   Diathesis diagnostics applied to different verbs (from Levin 1993: 6)

	touch	*hit*	*cut*	*break*
CONATIVE	No	Yes	Yes	No
BODY-PART POSS. ASC.	Yes	Yes	Yes	No
MIDDLE	No	No	Yes	Yes

4. Systematic extraction of lexical databases

After one has documented the basic structures of a grammar, and collected an ample corpus of texts, how does one supplement elicited examples and textually situated tokens of use to achieve a systematic compilation of lexical knowledge? Interlinear glossing of a large corpus can be used mechanically to generate a structured word list, whose analytical perspicacity is in direct proportion to the compiler's care and consistency in morphological and semantic tagging during the glossing procedure. Various computational tools aid lexical extraction from text corpora – not only dedicated linguistic database tools like SIL's Shoebox/Toolbox, but also both general and specialized concordance tools (written, for example, as unix shell scripts, or with programming languages like PERL or ICON[14]).

Other computer techniques can also aid in eliciting lexemes in a language, taking advantage of regular phonological patterns. A well-known example is Terry Kaufman's method for generating an exhaustive list of "potential roots" in Mayan languages, based on the observation that the root canon in Mayan is CVC or some simple variant thereof. Table 2 shows a short ICON program that begins with all the consonants and vowels[15] in the Mayan language Tseltal and produces a complete list of all permutations of the form *CV(:)(j)C*. The program produces 8820 potential roots. (The first of those beginning with *b* are shown in Table 3.) Each of these can be exhaustively (and exhaustingly) tested with native speakers to see which forms actually produce recognizable lexical items – many speakers of Mayan languages and others with similarly straightforward phonotactics have, over the years, been subjected to such a mind-numbing task.

Table 2. Tseltal root salad, in the Icon programming language

```
procedure main()
C := "`bcCjkKlmnpPrstTwxyzZ"
V := "aAeEiIoOuU"
M := "0j"
  every (c1 := !C) do {
    every (v1 := !V) do {
      every (m1 :=!M) do {
              every (c2 := !C) do {
              root := c1||v1||m1||c2
              write(root))
}}}}
end
```

Table 3. The first possible Tseltal roots beginning with *b*

ba' bab bach bach' baj bak bak' bal bam ban bap bap' bar bas bat
bat' baw bax bay bats bats' baj' bajb bajch bajch' bajj bajk bajk' bajl
bajm bajn bajp bajp' bajr bajs bajt bajt' bajw bajx bajy bajts bajts'
baa' baab baach ... etc.

Mechanically generated wordlists will inevitably reveal areas requiring further lexicographic work – phrasal lexical units, syntagmatically defined paradigms, "functional" vs. "lexical" elements, or particles, for example – and they ordinarily also expose to view especially elaborated lexical domains worthy of deeper exploration. Such domains may, on the other hand, emerge not from obvious gaps or hypertrophy in lexical sets revealed in text collections or elicited wordlists, but in clues from the communicative practices of a speech community itself: aesthetic judgments about "beautiful" or "eloquent" – if not "ugly" or "awkward" – speech, for example, especially marked and evaluated kinds of talk, or specialized speech genres or performances, on the one hand; and, on the other, cultural "preoccupations" with associated lexical expression: elaborated vocabularies for professions, activities, or other kinds of interests, or insistence on "getting the right word" or on "proper" and "accurate" expression.

Most methods for lexical elicitation are, for better or for worse, "extensional" and "referential" – that is, they are based on presenting exemplars of things or situations in the world to native speakers and asking for appropriate linguistic expressions which can be used to refer to or to characterize them. Such a method is perhaps inescapable for first-level lexical documentation, but it leaves largely unanswered difficult questions about the intensions of words: what they actually mean, what meaning distinctions they encode, what sorts of meaning relationships they enter into with other words and expressions, rather than simply what states of affairs they can be used truthfully to refer to. Such elicitation techniques are also often helpless to capture such non-referential aspects of meaning as politeness registers, specialized uses and contexts, and the like. Such issues can – and perhaps must – be ignored for the first stages of building lexical databases in language documentation, but they cannot be ignored forever.

Here is a single example from my own fieldwork on Guugu Yimithirr. I quickly learned that the everyday Guugu Yimithirr word *nambal* meant 'stone' but was also extended to mean 'money'. My primary teacher (and social father) in the community, who sometimes had occasion to borrow money from me, often instead used (or whispered) another word to me when he wanted to refer to money: *wambugan*. However, *wambugan* is really a polite equivalent for the ordinary word *nambal* in the respectful vocabulary, obligatory in speech with avoided affines and referred to in the published literature as "Brother-in-law language" (Haviland 1979). Its denotative range is in fact somewhat broader than that of *nambal* – it includes stones (including specially named grinding stones, quartz, etc., which are not normally called *nambal*) AND money. Crucially it is an over-polite word, no longer used in modern Hopevale with avoided affines nor, indeed, widely known beyond a few old men, and with them still carrying a euphemistic tone of respect. Both factors combine to make *wambugan* a perfect code word for an embarrassing task like asking one's courtesy son and pupil for a loan.

Ignoring such difficulties for the moment, let us consider techniques for supplementing the lexical information haphazardly collected through mechanical reversal of text corpora. The trick, obviously, is systematic but controlled elicitation, by presenting or simulating aspects of "external" reality so as to stimulate native speakers into using words and expressions to represent as yet unencountered states of affairs. Somewhat artificially I have divided sample methods according to what aspects of "reality" they purport to simulate: 'natural' facts, socio-cultural institutions, and in the final sections pragmatic facts of (inter)action, and ideological constructions on language and society.

4.1. 'Nature'

The tradition in anthropological linguistics, variously labeled "ethnographic semantics" or "ethnoscience," purports to display culturally specific knowledge about the natural world by detailing the semantics of lexical domains related to the corresponding natural phenomena: Hanunoo medicinal plants, Tseltal categories of firewood, ethnobotany or ethnozoology; parts of houses or bodies, taxonomies of disease, local technology, and so on. A classic example of the genre is Berlin's (1968) detailed study of Tseltal numeral classifiers, a detailed compendium of the several hundred classifiers once obligatory in Tenejapa Tseltal numeral expressions. Numeral classifiers specify countable units of different kinds of substance, often on the basis of shape. The notable feature of Berlin's study, for our purposes, is his use of carefully elaborated photographs both as stimuli (i.e. to elicit Tseltal numeral expressions from speakers) and as a vehicle for metasemantic representation: the photos accompany and illustrate his verbal characterization of the Tseltal forms so elicited. (Berlin also used Kaufman's mechanical procedure to generate potential numeral classifier roots, as described earlier.) To give an idea of both the semantic specificity of the Tseltal forms and the nature of the photographic stimuli, here are two sample pictures from Berlin's study. (Note that in Figure 5, illustrating the classifier *hiht'*, the caption suggests that a Tseltal speaker also noticed an appropriate use for *behč'* in the same stimulus photograph – a nice example of the serendipitous consequences of using such stimuli.)

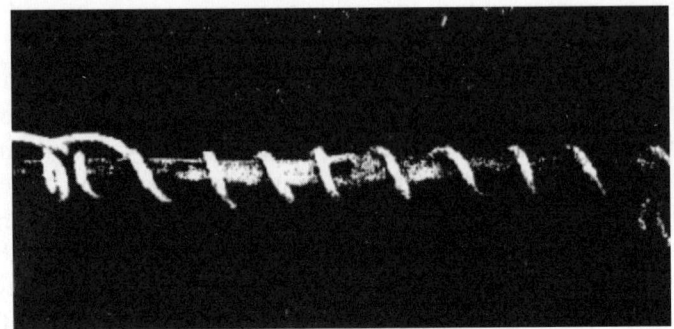

Figure 4.   Tseltal /b'ehč'/: "'individual wraps of slender-flexible objects in sequential spiral around some long non-flexible objects, as a piece of wood.' Included in photo: /lahunb'ehč' laso/ 'laso in the state of ten sequential wraps around long non-flexible object'"   (Berlin 1968: 39 Pl. I)

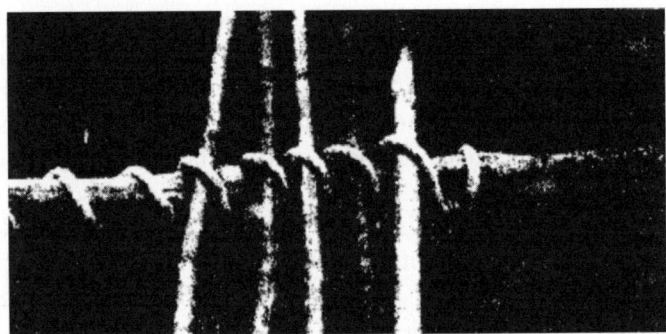

Figure 5.   Tseltal /hiht'/: "'individual wraps of slender-flexible objects in sequential lash-loops around two pieces of long non-flexible objects at 90° angles to one another, as in fence making.' Included in photo: /hoʔhiht' laso/ 'laso in five lash loops around two pieces of long non-flexible objects' [noted to the left of the photo, the rope in state of /ʔošb'ehč'/ 'three continuous wraps']"   (Berlin 1968: 39 Pl. II)

Other semantic fields with somewhat more abstract cognitive structures have been recently explored, also with the help of various artificial stimuli.

Following Talmy's typological deconstruction of motion verbs (Talmy 1985), and using a variety of "elicitation kits" involving photographs, drawings, videos, and cartoons,[16] field researchers have explored in detail linguistic systems of spatial adpositions,[17] directionals, motion verbs and other auxiliaries, and what have been called spatial "frames of reference" (Levinson 2003).

For a slightly different sort of example, just as Tzotzil speakers use a highly elaborated set of semantically specific positional roots, it is clear in practice that certain 'families' of verbs grouped by rough notional meaning categories (Dixon 1991) incorporate distinctions, often unfamiliar to speakers of other languages, that require careful lexicographic delimitation. Zgusta (1971: 89 ff.) provides a rich discussion of such families of verbs, what he calls "chains" of "near synonyms," citing as an example multiple Chinese words for 'carry'. There are many monolexemic Tzotzil transitive verbs which might most naturally be translated into English as 'carry', although it is not clear that anything justifies grouping the words together other than this fact about English translations. Thus, for example,

kuch 'to carry (a largish burden) on the back, usually with the aid of a tumpline'

pet 'to carry or hold in the arms, in front of the body (e.g. a baby)'

lik 'to carry by holding a handle from which the burden dangles (e.g. a pail)'

kach' 'to carry by gripping between two surfaces, normally in the jaws (e.g. a dog with a bone)'

jop 'to carry cupped in the hands or some other concave surface (e.g. an apron)'

tom 'to hold or carry in the hand, usually a longish thing gripped in the hand but extending above or beyond it (e.g. a torch, a rifle)'

mich' 'to carry squeezed, usually between the fingers or fist'
etc.

There is, incidentally, as far as I know no more general Tzotzil 'carry' verb that could be used to cover all of these cases.

Another such Tzotzil verb family is that of 'insert' (Haviland 1994) where – as in the case of "carry" verbs – the distinguishing criteria involve the shapes of inserted object and container, the types of contact or containment involved, the tightness of fit, the orientations of container and inserted object, etc. Both to elicit and to illustrate such distinctions I have made small films of different kind of "inserting" actions, performed with familiar objects, which speakers can view and discuss: what is the best way to describe what they see? are there other ways to describe it? and so on.[18]

It is hard to know in advance what areas of vocabulary will enjoy lexical hypertrophy in an undocumented language. The advantage of the elicitation tools developed by the Max Planck Institute for Psycholinguistics (Nijmegen) and elsewhere is that they can be used to invite speakers to exploit their full repertoire of expressive resources by describing standardized stimuli. Children's cartoons such as the *Maus* series from German television[19] are both entertaining and useful for investigating domains of motion, for example. Of course the sense in which speakers of different languages, with different sorts of cultural backgrounds and life experiences, will see these stimuli as "the same" is problematic and, in fact, a central issue to be investigated in linguistic fieldwork.

4.2. Socio-cultural reality

Of obvious interest for language documentation are lexical domains that encapsulate central aspects of society. Linguistic anthropology again provides the classic example: kinship terminologies, once a central part of comparative ethnography, are for speakers of many endangered languages an area of intense personal and conceptual concern (see also Chapter 8). In societies where the central social categories are defined by family relationships, whether genealogically or otherwise construed, the terminology denoting such categories is essential to any characterization of social life. The asymmetry in Tzotzil sibling terminology, for example, seems suggestive about family relationships. For a male Ego, Tzotzil distinguishes older and younger brothers (*bankil, itz'in*) from older and younger sisters (*vix, ixlel*). For a female Ego, however, the gender distinction is neutralized between younger brothers and sisters. Thus, a female speaker distinguishes older brother and older sister (*xibnel, vix*) and lumps together younger siblings of both genders (*muk*). Furthermore, note that the distinction between gender of Ego is neutralized precisely in the case of the term for older sister, *vix* for both men and women speakers (see Figure 6). These asymmetries suggest that the relationship between an older sister and her younger siblings of either gender is specially marked terminologically and conceptually. A plausible explanation is the expectation in many Tzotzil speaking communities that an older sister has special mother-like responsibilities for the care of her *muk* or younger siblings, regardless of their gender. This special care is terminologically matched by a reciprocal terminological projection for younger siblings that their *vix* or older sister is a kind of substitute mother.

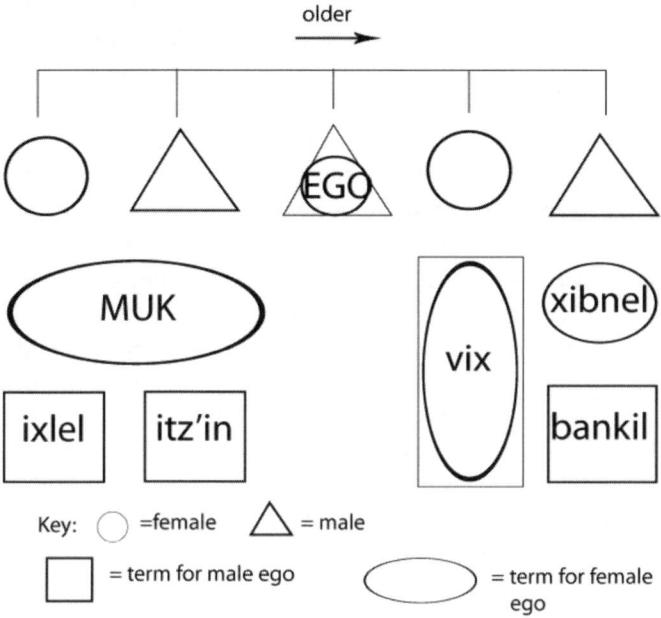

Figure 6. Tzotzil sibling terms

As the classic debates show, however, kinship "algebras" and diagrams conceal a central problem in documenting lexical knowledge, one already mentioned above: the tension between so-called "etic" metalanguages and "emic" categories. In any given language, one can justifiably question whether putatively universal descriptive terms for characterizing a particular kin relationship (in terms, say, of gender, generation, and kin-line, or with allegedly primitive relational terms like F[ather], M[other], H[usband], W[ife], or with algebraic symbols like +, −, ♂, ♂) do justice either to the meaning of a particular natural language term or to a specific relationship between two individuals. Indeed, in societies which display a clear obsession with kinship and kinship terminologies (for example, in the Australian Aboriginal communities where I have worked), a central area of dispute and conceptual wrangling is often exactly how to give the proper lexical label to a relationship, or how to explain what a particular unambiguously named relationship entails. My main Guugu Yimithirr teacher, for example, would often point out a kinsman walking past and say, "You should call that man X; because his father was your W; but then again, he turned around and married your Y, so what does that make him? your Z?" A genealogical relationship between two individuals does not uniquely determine what the relevant kin term might be, since that, in turn, may respond to considerably more complex factors about what aspects of the relationship are most important. In modern Zinacantán, in some cases a ritual relationship of *compadrazgo* or fictive-mutual-parenthood (between the parents and the godparents of a newly baptized child, for example) may actually take precedence over an immediate genealogical relationship: brothers may become *compadres* and cease to refer to each other with sibling terms.

For purposes of systematic documentation, this domain again illustrates the tension between a "corpus" of examples and systematic eliciting. No single network of actual social/genealogical relationships and the corresponding terminological distinctions can hope to capture the systematicity of the overall terminological-conceptual complex. At the same time, no extensional metalanguage (such as the genealogical primitives of kinship algebra) will be sufficient to guarantee that all socially significant variables emerge from mechanical elicitation. An adequate lexical database must combine both kinds of information.

4.3. Pragmatic reality

Methods for enriching a lexical database to include the use of indexical linguistic units inextricably bound to context are somewhat harder to find in recent literature. All linguistic behavior is, of course, tied to context and linked with action, but some of the most intractable lexical items frequently have *inherent* links to their indexical surrounds – pronouns and other deictics being the most obvious examples, since even their referents (whom they pick out) must be computed by reference to the contexts of their use. Studies of such lexical domains suggest that the only practical approach to the description of such parts of the lexicon is a kind of exhaustive observational fieldwork. Thus, Hanks (1990) gives detailed analysis of the system of demonstratives in Yucatec Maya based on extensive fieldwork in which he recorded, in detail, situated occurrences of spontaneous deictic usage, inducing from the corpus and from the linguistic forms the theoretical components of an adequate account of deictic practice.

Another exemplary domain is that of exclamations and interjections. Kockelman's extended treatment of interjections in Q'eq'chi (Kockelman

2003) involved a field methodology much like that of Hanks. He systematically recorded the circumstances when utterances categorized as interjections occurred in a Q'eq'chi speaking community in Guatemala. On the basis of such a corpus, he elaborated a theory of interjections which goes well beyond the received model of their "expressive" nature (part of an ancient tradition in Western linguistic thought, dating back to the Latin grammarians), to consider the multiple and bi-directional indexical properties of these expressions: exhibiting emotional and affective stances, explicitly inviting reciprocal exhibits from interlocutors, drawing interlocutors' attention to circumstances, requesting actions, and so on. Such studies suggest that there are few shortcuts to an adequate account of what such pragmatically charged linguistic elements mean, and that extensive ethnographic fieldwork is thus an essential part of field lexicography.

The same can be said of more prosaic vocabulary, from ordinary body part terms to specially marked polite and impolite registers, such as joking and cursing speech. I have already mentioned the residual lexical complexities produced by changed use of Guugu Yimithirr respectful or "brother-in-law" vocabulary, and such complexities are only multiplied when several more or less well regimented speech registers are in active use in a speech community. Classic anthropological descriptions of such phenomena attest to the subtlety and nuance communicated by strategic choice between alternate lexical forms in societies from Aboriginal Australia and Samoa to Bali (Duranti 1992; Errington 1985; Geertz 1960), or between address terms and personal pronouns from Europe to Japan (Brown and Gilman 1960). Laughlin (1975) proposes a series of labels to distinguish in Zinacantec Tzotzil such things as "ritual speech, joking speech, male and female speech, baby talk, polite speech, scolding, denunciatory speech, archaic [words]," etc. Whether or not a field lexicographer can give a complete account of such facts for an entire lexical database, it is important to be aware of the sorts of metalinguistic speech categories that might be relevant in a given speech community.

For self evident reasons, systematic investigation of such genres – for example, tabooed speech – may be hard for inexperienced fieldworkers. Similarly difficult are whole systems of linguistic tropes which sometimes dominate parts of a language's expressive resources. Again, the only remedy seems to be wide ranging and systematic ethnographic attention. Here are two examples from my own fieldwork. As I learned Guugu Yimithirr, I noticed that many expressions dealing with human propensities and "inner states" were transparently metaphors, based on a small set of words which seemed simply to name parts of the body. Whether or not, as anthropologists have sometimes suggested, these expressions represent an implicit theory of the anatomical distribution of emotions and mental faculties (as we might argue, for example, with English expressions like 'hard-headed' or 'hard-hearted'), or instead are simply opaque culturally conventionalized idioms (as we might argue for 'green thumb' or 'lily-livered'[20]) it was clear that Guugu Yimithirr had a semi-productive system for generating diverse expressions based on "body-part" tropes. (11) gives an example based on the Guugu Yimithirr word *miil* 'eye'. The only way I could document the system was to keep my ears open (as it were) for relevant expressions in conversation, and to try systematically to force new combinations of body-part words with adjectives and verbs, usually yielding only guffaws instead of new lexemes.

(11)   Guugu Yimithirr expressions based on *miil* 'eye'

miilgu	= (lit., eye + EMPHATIC suffix) awake
miil warnggu	= (lit., 'eye sleep') sleepy
miil nhin-gal	= (lit., eye sit) watch out, keep an eye out
miil biyal	= (lit. eye sinew) staring all the time
miil ngamba	= (lit. eye careless) unobservant, shutting one's eyes to something
miil waarril	= (lit., eye fly) feel faint, go crazy, faint, get drunk[21]
miil bagal	= (lit., eye poke) deceive, trick, become jealous
miil bathibay	= (lit., eye bone) sharp-eyed, always staring
miil biinii	= (lit., eye die) go blind
miil gulnggul	= (lit., eye heavy) sleepy
miilgu nhin-gal	= (lit., eye-EMPHATIC sit) stay awake ….

Consider, too, the language of Tzotzil ritual (Gossen 1974, 1985; Haviland 1987, 1996, 2000). In contexts from prayer and song to formal denunciation, Tzotzil speakers abandon ordinary lexicon and grammar in favor of a highly structured speech style that involves parallel lines which differ in only a single word or phrase. These parallel lines are interpreted in terms of a standard "stereoscopic" image (Fox 1977) invoked by the paired expressions. Thus, to refer to the body one can use different doublets, depending on the context. One is highly literal, using *pat, xokon* 'back, side' as a metonym for the whole. Another is considerably more opaque, and suggests an image of humility, as in the following extract from a curing prayer, where the doublet *lumal, ach'elal* 'earth, mud' (both in possessed form) refers to the patient's body or self.[22]

(12) From a Zinacantec curing prayer

ja' me ta jmala lalumale
I am waiting for your earth.

ta jmala lavach'elale
I am waiting for your mud.

A further example is the doublet in Zinacantec ritual speech to refer to liquor: *xi`obil, sk'exobil,* literally 'cause for fear, cause for shame'. Such expressions share properties with euphemism, always a problematic phenomenon for lexicography that requires careful ethnographic fieldwork. Systematic elicitation reveals little about the overall system of imagery in ritual language, although it is an essential part of the language's expressive power. Laughlin's (1975) dictionary of modern Zinacantec Tzotzil annotates and illustrates words that participate in parallel constructions under the rubric 'ritual speech'. In my own work, I have relied on exhaustive recording and transcription of prayer and other genres that employ parallelism to expand on the list of doublets.

5. Conclusion

When does documentation of the lexicon end? While the lexicon is a repository for the exceptional and the chaotic in language, it is also a site of considerable regularity and productivity. Nonetheless, field lexicographers like Laughlin express doubts about how well structured or widely-shared lexical knowledge is across a speech community, basing his skepticism on elicitation with both Zinacantec peasants and Washington D.C. university students. Notoriously difficult even for well-studied languages is distinguishing between 'literal' and 'figurative' or tropic uses of words: older Tzotzil speakers describe airplanes as *xulem k'ok',* literally (as we say) 'buzzard fire' or telephones as *ch'ojon tak'in* 'wire of metal' – enduring the giggles of younger speakers (who simply use a Spanish loan instead). Even more difficult is distinguishing obscure polysemy from simple (but formally unpalatable) homonymy. Laughlin's Tzotzil dictionary posits two homonymous roots, *jav*(2) – a positional root meaning 'belly (or face) up' –

and *jav*(1), a transitive verb root meaning 'to chop in half' because the two meanings seem divergent enough to warrant separate entries. However, Zinacantec folk etymology conjures a succinct image that connects the senses: when you split, say, a log in two (using a verb based on *jav(1)*), the two halves fall "belly up" (*jav(2)*). This is thus a case of covert polysemy,[23] or perhaps of underlying monosemy of a single root with different grammatical costumes. Such phenomena may remain intractable throughout a lexical documentation project.

Similarly, how much ought the lexicographer to include of what might be labeled "erroneous usage" – malapropisms, puns, or nonce creations? Zgusta (1971: 56–57) distinguishes "systemic" from "occasional" uses of words. An author may use 'bondage' occasionally to mean 'marriage,' without thereby changing the systemic meaning of either term. Zinacantec men, during several weeks of ribald gossip sessions in 1970, coined what was at the time a highly creative Tzotzil sexual euphemism using a loan *inyeksyon* from Spanish *inyección*, at a time when hypodermic injections were still a relatively novel foreign introduction. Some of these men still jokingly use the term almost 40 years later. The word is not in Laughlin's Tzotzil dictionary – but perhaps it should be.

Finally, questions already mentioned about aims and audience – for whom is a lexical database produced? to what ends will it be put? – complicate decisions about what words must be documented and how. The problems are especially vexed when a lexical database may serve as the basis for standardization or stabilization, especially in the form of a published dictionary.[24] When people can use a dictionary to look up a word, to see how it is spelled, and to read a definition, the speech community's authority over "proper" usage is irrevocably altered. How much belongs in the lexical database of a language documentation project is thus never simply a matter of "completeness" or "coverage" but also involves ideological decisions that may have far-reaching effects on the future of a language.

Building a lexical database is an expected part of any documentation project, perhaps the final most demanding analytical task of all. It can be aided by mechanical techniques applied to textual corpora and by familiarity with the great lexicographic traditions, which have already grappled with most of the problems a fieldworker is likely to encounter: lexical units, the nature of meaning, the vagaries of usage, and, finally, ideologies of language and social life. The end product is essential, but producing it relies on both drudgery and ethnographic inspiration, on systematic elicitation and serendipitous discovery. One inevitably (re)discovers that enough is *never* enough, and that calling a halt by declaring the database closed is simply an arbitrary rest stop on a very long journey.

Acknowledgements

This chapter, loosely based on the lecture presented at the DoBeS summer school in Frankfurt, September 2004, owes a considerable debt to experiences in lexicography shared with my Tzotzil and Guugu Yimithirr teachers, to comments by Nikolaus Himmelmann and Jost Gippert, and to the hospitality of Elena, Renato, and Lisetta Collavin during its final drafting.

Notes

1. Especially with reference to dictionaries for literate European traditions, both Landau (1984) and Svensén (1993) are useful surveys. See also the multiple volume handbook edited by Hausmann et al. (1990–1991).
2. Although languages like Nahuatl enjoy their own centuries' old dictionary traditions (Canger 2002; Amith 2002).
3. A Tzotzil-Spanish version is currently (2005) in press, to be published by the *Centro de Investigaciones y Estudios Superiores en Antropología Social* in Mexico. As Tzotzil speakers increasingly cross the border into the United States, the number of Tzotzil-English bilinguals will, of course, only grow.
4. See Haviland (1974). Nick Evans' (2002) remarks on misunderstandings of Aboriginal expressions, even in English, in hearings before the Australian Land Tribunal shows how such misunderstandings can have serious legal consequences.
5. See the notion of "rules of use" in Silverstein (1976).
6. Jost Gippert reports that "Georgian native speakers confirm that *mqavs* is applied to anything mobile, such as cars, bicycles, airplanes, or the like."
7. In Berlin's works the older spelling "Tzeltal" is used.
8. The symbol *A* denotes a hypothetical vowel that alternates between *a* and *o* in derived stems.
9. See http://framenet.icsi.berkeley.edu/index.php and Section 3 below.
10. English is interestingly different in its elaborations, as can be seen by the entries in the Framenet "being_attached" frame which include: *affixed, anchored, attached, bolted, bound, chained, fastened, fused, glued, handcuffed, lashed, manacled, moored, nailed, pasted, pinned, plastered, riveted, sewn, shackled,*

stapled, stuck, taped, tethered, tied, welded. In English the central variable seems to be the kind of material creating the attachment.

11. There are proposals from linguistics itself about a "Natural Semantic Metalanguage" through which definitions of complex notions can be framed in terms of simpler, allegedly universal (hence 'natural') semantic primes. See http://www.une.edu.au/arts/LCL/disciplines/linguistics/nsmpage.htm, where one can find a bibliography of the many publications of Anna Wierzbicka.

12. Faced with Pearson's challenge, Reed College senior Chris Haulk "promptly came up with, 'oh, you mean – wrap a string around a cylinder; versus, wrap a string around a cone'" (Albyn Jones, personal communication, March 1, 2005) – proving that mathematicians can be lexicographers, too.

13. Note that "Donor" here is a single entity, defined in Framenet as "The person that begins in possession of the Theme and causes it to be in the possession of the Recipient."

14. Visit http://www.cs.arizona.edu/icon .

15. The program symbolizes glottalized or ejective consonants and long vowels as capital letters, and a 0 is used to signal the absence of medial *j*.

16. See the descriptions of various stimulus kits developed by the Language and Cognition Group at the Max Planck Institute for Psycholinguistics at http://www.mpi.nl/world/data/fieldmanuals .

17. See Levinson et al. (2003) for an unashamedly extensional, comparative approach.

18. A short video used to elicit descriptions for Tzotzil 'inserting' actions is available on the book's website.

19. Samples of the sort of cartoon I have found useful for such tasks are available at http://www.wdrmaus.de/lachgeschichten/mausspots in streaming video format.

20. The expression is not confined to English; both Italian *pollice verde* (according to Elena Collavin) and German *grüner Daumen* (according to Nikolaus Himmelmann) have exactly the same metaphorical and literal meanings as 'green thumb', i.e., someone good at gardening. Similarly, Italian *senza fegato* 'without a liver' suggests a meaning similar to 'lily-livered.'

21. I ignore basic syntactic issues here: for example, in the expression *miil waarril* the word *miil* 'eye' is the syntactic subject of *waarril* 'fly.' In *miil bagal* 'eye' is syntactic object of *bagal* 'poke.'

22. In the Tzotzil of nearby Larraínzar, the equivalent ritual doublet is at once humble and literal: *ach'elal, takopal* 'mud, body.'

23. See Zgusta's discussion of polysemy (1971: esp. 77 ff.); also Evans and Wilkins (2000, 2001), Evans (1992).

24. See Jane Hill's discussion of the Hopi dictionary project in Chapter 5.

Chapter 7

Prosody in language documentation

Nikolaus P. Himmelmann

Introduction

Prosodic aspects of a linguistic message such as intonation and lexical accent are essential elements of its formal make-up. To date, the basics of analyzing prosodic features have not yet become an integral part of linguistic fieldwork training, and, accordingly, a reasonably detailed and comprehensive documentation and description of prosodic features is not yet part of standard linguistic fieldwork practices. This chapter is specifically concerned with the *documentation* of prosodic features, i.e. with the question of what kind of data a language documentation has to contain so that a thorough analysis of prosodic features is possible. In order to be able to productively apply the suggestions discussed in this chapter, a basic understanding of the core units and procedures of prosodic analysis is necessary. For a more comprehensive introduction to basic prosodic fieldwork focusing on issues of analysis and description, see Himmelmann and Ladd (forthcoming).

Given that a language documentation includes a large corpus of recordings of communicative events of different types, it may well be questioned whether there is any need to pay special attention to prosody when compiling it. Provided that the recordings are of a reasonable quality,[1] there can be no doubt that such a corpus can be used for prosodic analyses even when no particular attention was paid to prosodic features at the time of compiling the corpus.[2] However, there are essentially three reasons why some special attention for prosodic features is necessary when compiling a corpus of primary data so that it becomes really useful for prosodic purposes:

1. Prosodic phenomena are highly variable and susceptible to contextual influences. This makes it difficult to recognize basic distinctive patterns. Prosodic pattern recognition is much facilitated by having the same utterance produced by a number of different speakers (or at least to have multiple versions of the same utterance). See further Section 2.

2. Words produced in isolation are minimal utterances showing both lexi-cal and utterance-level (post-lexical) features. Hence, the widespread practice of recording words in isolation when recording a wordlist is of limited use for prosodic purposes. See further Section 3.

3. Acoustic and auditory data (i.e. recordings of spontaneous and elicited utterances) do not provide direct evidence with regard to the perception of native speakers, i.e. what native speakers actually perceive as rele-vant prosodic contrasts (conversational material may provide indirect evidence, though; see further below). The most straightforward way to obtain perception data is to run perception experiments, as further dis-cussed in Section 5.

Before these points are further elaborated, Section 1 provides a bit more detail on what exactly the term *prosody* is intended to refer to here. Further-more, when discussing points (1) and (2), it will be repeatedly suggested that elicitation may provide useful materials to complement the data found in recordings of spontaneous speech. However, eliciting prosodic data is not an easy task, as discussed in Section 4.

1. Prosodic phenomena

Table 1 lists the major prosodic phenomena according to the different do-mains in which they are manifest, i.e. the recordable sound wave (acoustic), the perceptual impression (auditory), and as a component of the language system (phonological category). The rightmost column lists the most widely attested functions which may be conveyed by prosodic features (but of course can also be conveyed by non-prosodic means).

Table 1. Prosodic phenomena according to domain

Acoustic	Auditory	Phonological category	Function/meaning
– fundamental frequency – duration – intensity – spectral characteristics[3] – pauses/silence	– pitch – length – loudness – stress/ prominence – rhythm/tempo – grouping – voice quality (creaky, etc.)	– tone – quantity – (lexical) accent – intonation – levels in prosodic hierarchy (syllable, foot, etc.)	– delimiting units – distinguishing lexical units – grammatical categories – speaker attitude – sentence modality – information structure – interactional tasks

In discussing prosody, it is important to keep the different domains distinct and to be aware of the fact that there is no unambiguous mapping relation between features in different domains. To take just pitch as an example, regular correspondences exist between changes of fundamental frequency (F0) observed in the acoustic signal, changes in pitch perceived by the human ear, and tonal or intonational distinctions. But these correspondences do not consist of simple and direct mapping relations between the domains. Thus, there are changes in fundamental frequency which are generally not perceived as such by the human ear. These are known as "microprosodic perturbations" and include phenomena such as the lowering of F0 regularly induced by voiced consonants.[4] Furthermore, while it is true that tonal and intonational categories are primarily marked by changes in pitch, other auditory parameters such as length, loudness, and voice quality often also play a role in the marking of these categories.

In the present chapter, the above distinctions and the corresponding terminology will be observed rather strictly. Many of the terms are widely used in the literature in the sense they are used here, but it may be worth pointing out that the strict distinction also applies to the terms *(lexical) accent* and *stress*, which are used in many different and often somewhat confusing ways in the literature. Both terms refer to the phenomenon that a given syllable is in some sense more prominent than neighboring ones, but *lexical accent* here designates this property with reference to the phonological structure of lexical items (i.e. as a phonological category), while *stress* refers to an auditory impression (which may or may not have clear acoustic or phonological correlates). In this usage, then, "lexical accents" can be realized in different ways, including "stress" or a fixed change in pitch (so-called melodic or pitch accent as found, for example, in Japanese; cf. Beckman [1986] and Gussenhoven [2004] for further discussion).

There is no space and need here to discuss in detail all the prosodic phenomena and functions listed in Table 1. The main purpose of this table is to give an extensional definition of the range of phenomena referred to with the term *prosody* in this chapter. A detailed introduction to the phonetics (both acoustic and auditory) of prosodic features can be found in Laver (1994: 431–546; see also Ladefoged 2003: 75–103). The major phonological categories are discussed in Ladd (1996), Cruttenden (1997), Hirst and di Cristo (1998), Hyman (2001), Yip (2002), Gussenhoven (2004), and Jun (2005), among others. These works also provide useful information regarding the crosslinguistic variability of prosodic features.

The discussion in this chapter in principle applies to all the prosodic features listed in Table 1. However, intonation and accent will usually be mentioned as the main examples and often be singled out for extra comment because these are the two categories that have been most widely neglected in linguistic fieldwork, as opposed to tone, for example, which is a standard topic in linguistic fieldwork.

2. The need to work with several speakers

Linguistic fieldwork often involves the close cooperation with just one or possibly two native speakers who are the main contributors or "informants" in the sense that a) they provide most of the elicited information on the language (texts are often recorded with a broader range of speakers); and b) all data provided by other speakers is processed and checked with them. This procedure is based on the fact that with regard to core grammatical features the information provided by different speakers tends not to differ (or to differ only minimally). Thus, for example, if one speaker states that the definite article has to precede the noun and cannot be postponed, this will in all likelihood be confirmed by all other speakers in the community.

While this set-up works reasonably well for the most basic structural features of a language, it becomes more and more problematic when more variable and complex linguistic features are being investigated. The phonetics of prosodic features are highly variable and depend on a complex set of factors, including speaker variables and context. There are very few, if any absolute values. What is high with regard to pitch for one speaker, may be low for another; what is loud in one context, is just normal in another; and so on. Furthermore, the perception of prosodic features tends to be heavily influenced by the investigator's own native prosodic system, which further distorts the data and complicates the analysis. In the early stages of an investigation of the prosody of a language, it thus tends to be extremely difficult to recognize a basic pattern in the recorded data. This problem is particularly pressing in the case of intonation, which for this reason serves as the major example in this section, but it may also occur with regard to lexical accent or tone.

The easiest way to solve the pattern-recognition problem is to have several speakers "do the same thing," i.e. to produce the same utterance in the same context with the same intention. Figure 1 illustrates the problem and the suggested solution. It shows fundamental frequency tracings of the segment *(was für große) Ohren du hast* '(what big) ears you have', taken from the recordings of the folktale *Little Red Riding Hood* by five German speakers.[5] All speakers produce a rise on the initial accented syllable *Oh* and then a continuous fall until the end of the utterance. Note how variable the initial rise is (shaded area of left-hand column). For speaker JH it is quite long, starts steep but then becomes flatter, while for speaker NF it is steep and short. Speaker JN's rise is very minor indeed and it could be argued that there is no rise at all in this syllable. Nevertheless, as the five speakers are doing the same thing, i.e. producing the same utterance in the same context (of reading the story aloud) with the same intention (of expressing surprise at the radical changes in the grandmother's appearance), it is also legitimate to assume that the different rise-falls in F0 seen in these tracings are in fact realizations of the same category, i.e. the nuclear fall of Northern Standard German (symbolized with $H*+L$ in ToBI notation). Or, viewed from the point of view of someone trying to detect a basic pattern, the fact that one may reasonably assume that the five performances of the utterances are "the same" on the level of the language system allows one to recognize a common pattern, rise on the accented syllable plus continuous fall until the end of the intonation unit.[6]

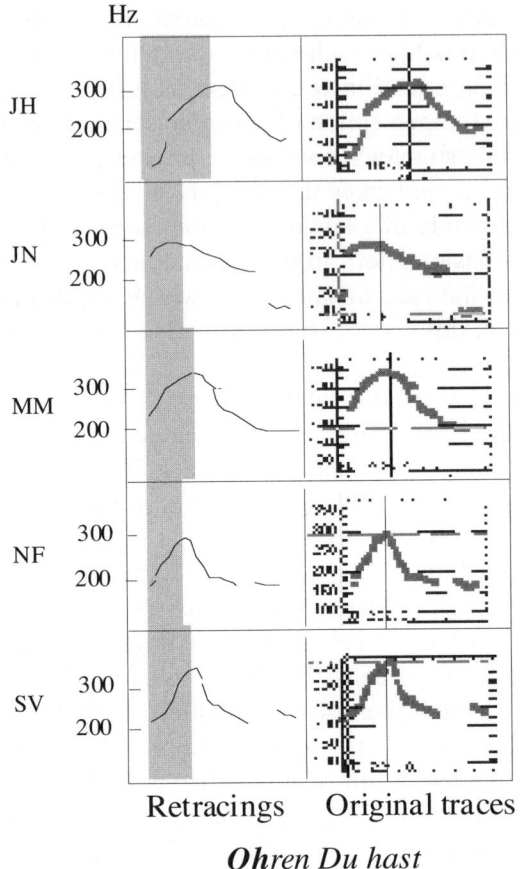

Hz

Retracings   Original traces

***Ohren** Du hast*

Figure 1. Multiple performances of the same utterance (from Grabe 1998: 245,
    Appendix C)

"Doing the same thing" here importantly involves three aspects. First, the
utterances have to be segmentally identical (or at least very similar), because different segments have different microprosodic effects and it is not a
straightforward task to filter out these effects in an attempt to recognize a
basic pattern. Second, the utterances have to convey the same meaning and,
most importantly, they have to be performed with the intention of achieving
the same illocutionary act. As is well known, segmentally identical utterances can be used to ask a question, give a command, make an ironic comment, express surprise, etc. All of these different functions affect the prosodic packaging and hence have to be controlled for when searching for

prosodically identical utterances. Third, the utterances have to be produced in identical (or very similar) circumstances, e.g. as casual remarks between adolescents, in a working environment between people of different status, etc.

With regard to the number of "same" utterances needed for a detailed prosodic analysis, there are the following rough guidelines. The absolute minimum for recognizing a pattern with some degree of reliability is three instances, because with only two versions of the same utterance it is difficult, if not impossible, to decide what is distinctive and what coincidental with regard to those aspects where they diverge. A good start with a detailed analysis can be made with four versions of the same utterance, ideally two by male speakers and two by female speakers. With eight different versions, statistical analyses become more viable and useful. With 10–12 speakers, the sample size approaches that which is found in much work on well-documented languages such as English or Japanese.

There is no principled upper limit for the sample size and, depending on the phenomena being investigated, larger samples may become necessary which also take into account variables such as age, register, and local dialect. But to repeat, in the typical field setting of a hitherto undocumented language spoken by a small number of speakers, samples of four to ten versions of the same utterance will provide a good basis for a detailed prosodic analysis and will thus greatly improve the databasis for prosodic research.

Note also that, while preferable, it is not absolutely necessary that the different versions are produced by different speakers. They could also have been produced by the same speaker(s) on different occasions. Importantly, more or less immediate repetitions of the same utterance (such as when asking the speaker to repeat something she just said or to say something twice) usually do not produce multiple versions of the same utterance in the intended sense, because repetition usually has some impact on prosody.

It should be obvious that even in a very large corpus of recordings of more or less spontaneous speech it will be difficult to find a set of four to ten versions of the same utterance in the intended sense. There may be hundreds or even thousands of utterances one may reasonably safely identify as polar questions (e.g. *Is he coming tonight?*). But how many of these will be segmentally identical or at least very similar? Furthermore, the circumstances in which the question is asked may not be really comparable. All of which makes it difficult to determine those aspects in the prosodic packaging that are related to categorical distinctions. To be sure, in the case of polar questions, it may be possible to determine these aspects with a reasonable degree of certainty on the basis of a sufficiently large sample from spontaneous speech. But it is more cumbersome to do this only on the basis of such a sample and it may become more and more difficult to do it when investigating more complex issues. In particular, when investigating problems in the prosodic packaging of information structure (focus, contrast, deaccenting, etc.), the number of variables to be controlled and accounted for may become so high that all results remain speculative.

Ideally, then, a comprehensive language documentation should contain sets of different versions of the same utterance, each set representing a different major function where prosody may be of relevance (i.e. one set for polar questions, one for all-new utterances, one for polite commands, and so on). While such sets may happen to occur in a sufficiently large corpus of spontaneous recordings without paying particular attention to the topic of prosodic analysis, there are three ways to ensure that they are in fact represented in the documentation.

First, work with prompting tools such as video clips, a picture story, or matching games where one speaker instructs another to identify an object among a set of similar objects or to find a path through an imaginary landscape (the so-called "map task") will produce similar, if not truly identical utterances.[7] Particularly useful are games where speakers engage in different types of speech acts (e.g. asking a question, giving directions, confirming a suggested solution), provided that the structure of the game forces speakers to talk about the same "world" (i.e. to use the same lexical items) so that the utterances become reasonably similar with regard to their segmental make-up.

The second method to produce relevant data sets is to try direct elicitation by asking speakers to produce utterances or, more precisely, mini-discourses prepared in advance. The major problem here is how to present the target utterances in such a way that the prosody is not influenced by the prompt. We will look at the prompting problem more closely in Section 4. Here are a few examples of the kind of sentences one may want to try to elicit with an indication of the prosodic function they target given in square brackets:

(1)   Has X arrived? No, I haven't seen seen him/her/them yet.
      [polar question-answer pair]

(2)   (In the market:) What are you looking for? (I am looking for)
      vegetables. [question word – question-answer pair]

(3)   Have a seat, please! [polite command]

(4)   (Group of people standing at road side, obviously agitated.
       What happened?):
       A bus turned over!
       or: The dog killed a pig! [all-new utterances]

(5)   I like the **blue** shirt, not the **red** one. [contrastive focus]

(6)   Have you ever eaten a black snake? No, I don't eat snakes.
       [deaccenting][8]

(7)   (Surprise:) How big you are already! [speaker attitude]

This list of examples is not complete and should be expanded and adapted as required by the project setting and make-up. However, since eliciting such examples will usually not be an easy task and not something which native speakers will be very eager to do, one should plan to spend considerable time on drafting the right set of examples and to test all of them with one close collaborator before approaching a larger number of speakers for a recording.

One consideration in drafting the examples is segment structure. Examples should include as few fricatives as possible and in general should avoid voiceless consonants of all manners of articulation. The ideal example in fact consists only of like vowels and nasals, which of course is an ideal that will hardly ever be attainable when attempting to construct examples which make sense and are culturally appropriate. Having semantically and pragmatically well-formed and culturally appropriate utterances will in general be the more important concern since otherwise the elicitation will not work at all.

The third way of getting comparable data sets for prosodic analysis is to make sure that the corpus of recordings contains a sufficient number of utterances using stylized intonation. A typical example of an everyday use of stylized intonation is a calling or vocative contour (Ladd 1996: 88, 136 f.). There may be different calling contours, for example, one for calling someone ("Peter!"), one for market cries, one used by street-vendors for advertising fish, and so on. In many languages, listing items (e.g. *they had lots of cows, goats, chicken, and dogs*) also involves a special, somewhat stylized intonation ("listing intonation"; see also next section). Otherwise, stylized intonation is a common feature of many forms of ritual speech, in particular of the so-called chanted speech.

For purposes of prosodic analysis, the main advantage of stylized intonation contours consists in the fact that by its very nature, intonational contrasts are more stable and more marked than in non-stylized contours. Consequently, patterns are generally much more easily recognizable. In fact, while native speakers often do not have very clear intuitions about non-stylized intonation patterns, they often know about stylized contours and can readily imitate them.

Obviously, patterns used in stylized intonations differ from those used in non-stylized ones and similarly, it may be the case that intonation patterns in elicited examples differ quite clearly from those found in spontaneous speech (compare the phenomenon of "reading intonation" found in many European languages). In this regard, it should be clearly understood that elicited and stylized data sets have the function of allowing one to get started on prosodic, and specifically intonational, analysis. They enable the investigator to get a basic idea of what kind of contrasts are being made in the language and thus to develop hypotheses that have to be tested with the spontaneous material. A comprehensive prosodic analysis of course has to be able to account for the full range of phenomena found in a corpus of spontaneous recordings.

3. Recording words

It is a widespread practice in linguistics to record lists of elicited words in order to be able to check one's transcriptions and to document the basic sound structure of lexical items. The format usually used in such recordings is first to give the translation equivalent of the word in the contact language being used (or the number of the word in a word list) which is then followed by the word in the documented language, often repeated once or twice. In this way, words are recorded "in isolation," which is often understood to mean "in their most basic form, free from any 'contaminating' contextual influences." This, however, is a misconception, since uttering an isolated word always constitutes a minimal utterance, which is of particular import for prosody. Importantly, "words in isolation" do not only display whatever lexical prosodic features they might have (lexical tone or accent) but also features of (usually declarative) utterance prosody. This may appear to be a rather trivial point, but even in the specialist literature this distinction has not been made consistently until fairly recently.[9]

As an example, compare Figures 2 and 3. Figure 2 shows the waveform and F0 tracing for a single Waima'a word, *kaluha* 'cloud', recorded in isolation. Figure 3 shows the waveform and F0 tracing for a short Waima'a utterance, *kii baa ini* 'there are people fighting' (lit. 'people hit each other'; an all-new response to a *what's-going-on* type of question). Note that the F0 tracing is essentially identical in both figures: it starts out flat at mid-level,[10] rises and begins to fall again on the penultimate syllable, and continues to fall on the last syllable. Hence, the question arises whether the rise on the penultimate syllable in *kaluha* is part of the lexical make-up of this item, reflecting at least in part a regular lexical accent on the penultimate syllable. Alternatively, this rise-fall on the last two syllables – which can be observed for practically all Waima'a lexical items uttered in isolation – is due exclusively to the fact that uttering a Waima'a word in isolation also involves the utterance-level features of a standard Waima'a declarative utterance. (At the time of writing this chapter, I believe that the latter option is correct, but this needs further research and testing. For current purposes, it is not relevant which of the two options turns out to be correct. The point to be clearly understood is that words in isolation always and by necessity display features of utterance-level intonation.)

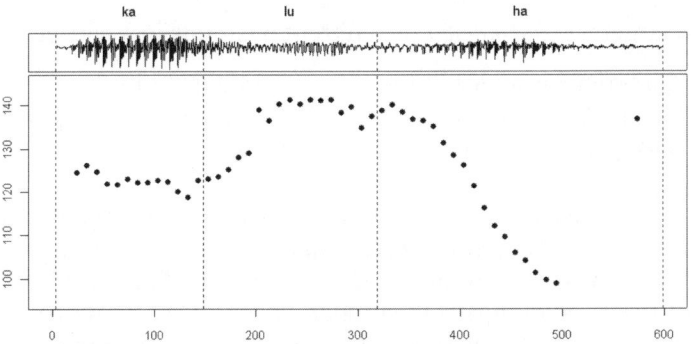

Figure 2. Waveform and F0 for Waima'a word in isolation (*kaluha* 'cloud')

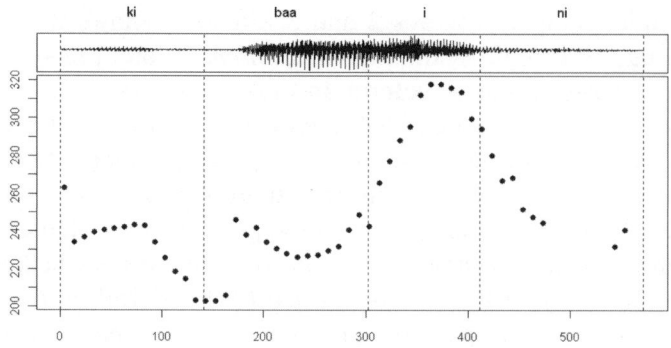

Figure 3. Waveform and F0 for Waima'a short utterance (*kii baa ini* 'there are people fighting')

In order to be able clearly to separate lexical and post-lexical (utterance-level) prosodic features, it is now a common practice in research on prosody (but also in many segmental phonetic studies) not to record words in isolation even when lexical features are the primary concern. Instead, the ideal is to record the target word(s) in different positions in a carrier phrase, as in the following English examples:

(8)   The target word *America* in different positions in a carrier phrase

    a. "America" is a word I know.   [initial position]
    b. I said "America" once.   [phrase-internal position]
    c. She said "America."   [final position]

As seen in these examples, the different position will usually involve different information structural implications, which may, but do not have to, correlate with post-lexical prosodic distinctions. Furthermore, since the purpose of these recordings is to compare characteristics of different lexical items, the carrier phrase usually involves very general items, in particular verbs such as "say", "hear", or "know (a word)" which in principle are compatible with all lexical items.

Figures 4 and 5 illustrate the effect of carrier phrase position with another example from Waima'a. Here, the target word *aboo* 'grandparent, old/respected person' occurs at the end of a carrier phrase (*ne ehe aboo* 'she said *aboo*') and at the beginning of another one (*aboo aku de nau* '[the word] *aboo* I don't know').[11] Note how the change in position correlates with a clear change in pitch (rise-fall on *boo* in final position, late rise on

boo in initial position). But note also what remains constant in both positions. Most importantly, in both instances *boo* is roughly twice as long as
the initial syllable *a*. Consequently, it may be hypothesized that *boo* contains a long vowel as part of its lexical make-up and that the fact that this
syllable is long in both recordings is not due to an utterance-level effect.

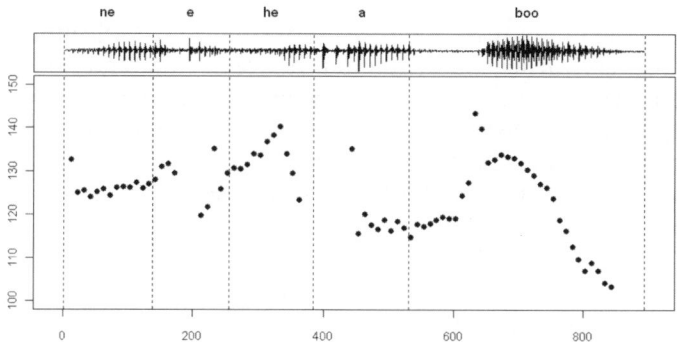

Figure 4. Waima'a carrier phrase with final target word (*ne ehe aboo* 's/he said
aboo')

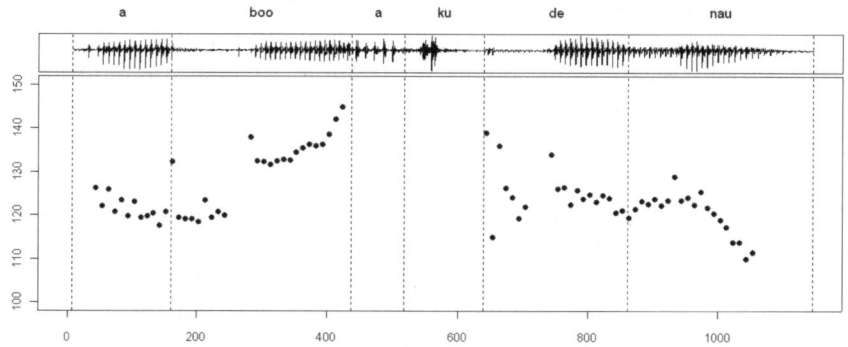

Figure 5. Waima'a carrier phrase with initial target word (*aboo aku de nau* 'aboo I
don't know')

If working with carrier phrases proves to be too cumbersome or does not
work for some other reason (see next section), one may try to record words
in mini-lists of three to four items, alternating the position of the words
contained in the list, as in (9).

(9)   Mini-lists with alternating orders

    a. *America*, Africa, Antarctica
    b. Africa, Antarctica, *America*
    c. Antarctica, *America*, Africa

    etc.

While not as useful as recordings in carrier phrases, such mini-lists often allow one to make at least a distinction between final and non-final utterance prosody, provided that the speakers actually use listing intonation and do not simply produce three isolated utterances in rapid sequence. As in the carrier-phrase example, prosodic features which remain the same across different positions in the list can be hypothesized to be lexical rather than post-lexical.

4. The prompting problem

Most of the procedures discussed in the preceding two sections involve the elicitation of prosodic data by asking speakers to produce various kinds of utterances or mini-discourses. While elicitation quite generally may involve problems with regard to the naturalness and reliability of the data thus obtained, elicitation of prosodic data is particularly prone to major distortions since prosodic features are highly susceptible to contextual influences. Thus, there is little use in presenting the items to be recorded simply by having native speakers repeat what the researcher or one of her local co-workers says. In almost all circumstances, this will produce highly distorted utterances which will largely imitate features of the presented utterance or display the prosodic characteristics of a repeated utterance.

The most widely-used procedure in prosodic research on languages with a well-established writing tradition is to have speakers *read* the target utterances. This procedure, while not directly influencing the prosody by providing a model for imitation, may encounter a number of other problems. Most importantly, the reading tasks require that the speakers actually enact the intended utterance type. Obviously, there is little use in having someone read a question or a surprised exclamation in a rather flat, non-engaged monotonous voice. Not all speakers are capable or willing to engage in such a performance. Successful reading prompts also presuppose that the speakers are reasonably fluent in reading the language. This will often not be the case even in those communities where speakers are literate in a dominant language but not used to seeing their own language written (reading in such circumstances will be slow and in a word-by-word style). Another complication may arise from the fact that reading intonation differs significantly from conversational intonation.

In non-literate societies, written prompts obviously will not work at all. The main alternative here is to try various kinds of role-playing or the experimental tasks involving video clips, etc., already mentioned above in Section 2. Role-plays may work when carefully prepared with a local team member. They involve speakers pretending to be in a given situation and reacting with an appropriate short utterance rehearsed in advance. Thus, for example, one may ask a pair of speakers to pretend meeting one another in the market, one asking *what's happening there*? and the other responding with the target utterance *people are fighting*. In the best of circumstances, the speakers engaged in this role-play will actually engage in a short conversation, continuing this imagined question-answer pair with a short sequence of further utterances. It will often not be possible to make them use exactly the target utterance prepared in advance, but minor variations in its segmental make-up will usually not cause major problems for comparability. The more realistic the role-playing is, the better the quality of the prosodic data produced in this way will be.

In preparing role-plays and experimental tasks it should be kept in mind that these will in all likelihood be very strange kinds of communicative events for native speakers who are not familiar with the basic idea of role-playing, experiments, or interviews. Thus, one has to be prepared to face quite a few obstacles when trying to collect data in this way. Continuous laughing or giggling because of the unusualness and unnaturalness of the situation is one very common problem. Speakers may also change the speech act, i.e. rather than responding with a statement ("He has gone to the market") they may produce a command ("Go to the market!"). Furthermore, it is not uncommon that speakers who are asked to retell a short action sequence in a video clip comment on the kind of dress people are wearing or the color of the sky visible in the clip instead of engaging with the given task. Considerable time and ingenuity in developing appropriate prompts may thus be required in order to make experimental tasks work or to develop useful forms of role-playing in a given community. But this effort will be well spent because the data generated in this way will be very useful not only for prosodic analyses, but often also for other types of analysis.

5. Perception experiments

The procedures presented so far in this chapter all focus on production data, i.e. sets of utterances which can be analyzed acoustically and auditorily. But production data do not provide any basis for determining which components of the complex signal are actually perceived as prosodically distinctive by native speakers. It is well known from research on European languages that not all the distinctive information available in the acoustic data is perceived as such by native speakers. Consequently, there is a need for data to answer questions such as: Is this clearly observable prominence (e.g. a change in pitch direction, or increased loudness or duration) actually perceived by native speakers? Is it perceived at the location where it is observed in the signal? Which of the major phenomena observed for lexical accents is perceived as distinctive: pitch, duration, length, or vowel quality? The most straightforward way to answer such questions is to run perception experiments. In such experiments, the prosodic parameters observed in a set of utterances are modified and sets of modified utterances (or sets of modified and unmodified utterances) are then evaluated by native speakers. For example, loudness on a lexically accented syllable could be reduced and then it could be tested whether the syllable is still perceived as prominent. Or, the final rise in a question utterance could be reduced or shifted to an earlier syllable and then tests could be run to determine whether the utterance is still perceived as a question.

It is not an easy task to prepare and run perception experiments of this type and to date, very few perception experiments have been reported for languages outside Europe and Japan.[12] In some ways, the easiest part is the preparation of stimuli since speech analysis tools such as *EMU, PRAAT, Wave Surfer,* or *Speech Analyzer* allow for a relatively easy and straightforward modification of pitch and other prosodic parameters in digitized utterances. The more difficult part is to find a way of how to run the tests, especially in societies which have little or no experience with experiments.

That is, perception experiments are also faced with the prompting problem. Problems here may already arise because speakers may refuse to put on a headset (which is the best way of ensuring that they can listen carefully to the stimuli). But the main challenge consists in defining a manageable task. It will usually not be possible to ask directly for the identification of prosodic properties with questions such as: Where is the major prominence? Is X higher than Y? etc. Instead, what may work are tasks which involve some kind of comparing and ranking two different items, asking questions such as: Which of these two items is more natural/more appropriate/more often heard? Which item would you use when speaking in public? or the like. Otherwise, general comments on the stimuli (such as: "this sounds rather odd or foreign"; "that's how people down south speak"; etc.) may also provide important clues, although they will make for a very heterogeneous and difficult to quantify dataset.

In this regard, it should be noted that non-experimental, conversational data may sometimes also provide important clues as to which prosodic features are perceived as relevant in a given speech community. A somewhat trivial, but nonetheless relevant example is the fact that a conversational corpus allows one to collect a set of examples of utterances which are treated by the interactants as questions and to compare these to utterances which are prosodically similar but are not taken up as questions by the listener. More complex are examples where a misplaced emphasis or wrong intonation contour produces a misunderstanding, leading to a repair sequence. See the contributions in Couper-Kuhlen and Selting (1996) and Couper-Kuhlen and Ford (2004) for relevant observations and examples.

Acknowledgements

I would like to thank Bruce Birch and Bob Ladd for extensive discussion of the issues and ideas presented in this chapter. They, of course, are not responsible for the use I have made of their input. Thanks also to Jan Strunk for help with plotting the figures.

Very special thanks to Maurício C.A. Belo, my Waima'a collaborator, who has patiently suffered through various trial runs of the procedures discussed in this chapter as well as some other procedures which have been found not to be productive. Further information and full acknowledgements for the Waima'a project can be found at http://www.mpi.nl/dobes/WebpageDobes1/ SubpagesTeams/SubpageWaimaa/Frameset.htm.

This work was made possible by a research professorship funded by the Volkswagen foundation and I am most grateful for this very generous support.

Notes

1. Features defining a good recording are listed in Section 2.1 of Chapter 4.
2. Examples of what can be done – and what cannot be done – in terms of prosodic analysis on the basis of a corpus of recordings alone are King's (1994) and Bishop's (2002) theses on the intonation of Dyirbal and Bininj Gun-wok, respectively. King's thesis is exclusively based on tape recordings of narrative and procedural texts made by R.M.W. Dixon in the 1960s and 70s. On the basis of this material, King is able to make a proposal for some key features of Dyirbal intonation. However, at various points she has to take note of the fact that the available genres (mostly narrative) severely limit the scope of her analysis. Furthermore, she notes that much of her analysis remains speculative as long as it is not possible to test whether the prosodic distinctions she establishes on the basis of acoustic data alone are actually also perceived as significant distinctions by Dyirbal speakers. For perception, see also Section 5 below.
3. "Spectral characteristics" here refers to those aspects of the formant structure of speech sounds which reflect prosodic features, e.g. the energy distribution across the frequency spectrum, which may be an acoustic correlate of stress.
4. Figure 3 below includes a very clear illustration of this effect in that the /b/ of *baa* causes a noticeable "dip" in the F0 contour. Laver (1994: 452–456) provides a fuller discussion of microprosodic perturbations.
5. The tracings are given in two versions, the right-hand column presenting the original F0 extractions, the left-hand column a somewhat smoothed version of these. See Grabe (1998: Chapter 2) for further information on the procedures used in collecting and processing the data. This thesis is available at http://www.phon.ox.ac.uk/~esther/thesis.html.
6. The precise details of the analysis are of no concern here. Note that Grabe (1998: Chapter 3, Section 2) makes the proposal that the nuclear fall in Northern Standard German allows for two major alternative realizations, one with a clear rise on the accented syllable and one where pitch is more or less level in the accented syllable (as with JN in Figure 1). The distinction between these two (phonetic) realizations of the same phonological category is argued to be gradual.
7. Further references and links for prompting tools can be found in Chapter 6 and on the book's website.
8. Examples (4)–(6) all target distinctions of information structure, a rather complex topic which cannot be adequately dealt with here. See Lambrecht (1994) and Jacobs (2001) for a thorough discussion of some of the basic distinctions and issues involved, Ladd (1996) for the role prosody may play in marking information structure, Drubig (2003) for a typological survey, and Dimroth (2002) for an elicitation task targeting information structure.
9. Bruce (1977) is widely considered the first modern work where the distinction is fully and consistently applied.

10. As mentioned above, the initial "dip" in Figure 3 is a microperturbation caused by the /b/ in *baa*. The utterance in Figure 2 is by a male speaker, the one in Figure 3 by a female speaker and therefore overall considerably higher. Wavefiles containing the utterances of Figures 2–5 are available at the book's website.

11. The speaker, of course, knows the word *aboo*, but putting it in initial position and not using a negation (i.e. using the equivalent of '*aboo* I know' as a prompt) was not felt to be appropriate.

12. Most recent work in this field has been done by researchers associated with the Phonetics Laboratory, Universiteit Leiden Centre for Linguistics, mostly on languages of Indonesia, in particular Malay. See Ebing (1997), Odé (1997, 2002), van Zanten et al. (2003), and Stoel (2005: 108–208) for examples and references. These works also provide detailed discussion as to how prosodic experiments can be devised and administered. There is also a fair amount of work being done on the perception of prosodic differences between Russian dialects by a group of researchers associated with the Bochum *Linguistic Lab* (http://www.ruhr-uni-bochum.de/lilab/Index.htm).

Chapter 8

Ethnography in language documentation

Bruna Franchetto

Introduction

Ethnographical information is a crucial component of any language documentation. If the wider goal is not simply to collect texts and a lexical database, but also to present and preserve the cultural heritage of the speech community, then ethnographical information must be linked to the linguistic data and its annotation and analysis. However, the integration of linguistic and ethnographic data in a comprehensive documentation stored in an electronic archive is not an easy task.

The main question to be addressed here is: What does an ethnographer look for when she or he consults a language documentation as conceived of in this book? In other words, which kind of information may be irrelevant for a linguist but highly relevant for an ethnographer? In addressing this question, I will have little to say about 'how to annotate ethnographical information' in technical terms. Instead, my main concern will be to make explicit the requirements of a demanding user of a language documentation, the ethnographer or anthropologist.

There are two main sources on which the discussion in this chapter is based. On the one hand, I have interviewed anthropologists working in Brazil and their responses have been condensed into the key topics mentioned in Section 2. On the other hand, I heavily draw on three years of experience in the project "Linguistic, historical and ethnographical documentation of the Upper Xingu Carib language or Kuikuro" (hereafter referred to as the "Kuikuro Project"), which was funded as part of the DoBeS initiative. I shall use this experience in Section 3 to illustrate one of the possible ways of managing ethnographic information in a language documentation (unless otherwise mentioned, all the examples and illustrations provided here come from this project). So although what follows undoubtedly will provoke more general questions and ideas, it should be remembered that it reflects a specific experience. As a background for the discussion in Sections 2 and 3,

Section 1 provides a few general observations regarding the role of language in ethnography.

1. A note on language and ethnography

As Bronislaw Malinowski (1935) emphasizes, we must not forget that language is the primary tool used by ethnographers who obtain much of the information comprising their knowledge of the "other" through the discourse of "their natives" (later called "informants" and nowadays referred to as "consultants"). However, the way this linguistic input is dealt with will of course differ as researchers with different theoretical backgrounds usually look for different things. For example, the prominence given to the notion of codes in structuralist theory means that linguistic data are subject to a particular form of scrutiny to provide evidence for basic structural patterns underlying language, culture, and society. For culturalists, on the other hand, direct observation, involvement, and interpretative work all form essential aspects of the ethnographic process.

Ethnographers aim to recognize genres and registers of speech, describe the contexts of speech events, and identify apparently significant terms and expressions. The latter may become key native "categories" to be widely explored in their analyses and their endeavors to explain cosmologies, social structures, ritual events, transcriptions and transformations between human and non-human worlds. As a result of their endeavors, ethnographers produce another form of discourse in their own language and that shared by their readers and listeners – the famous "ethnographic narrative" – allowing their public to share knowledge about or produced by the other. In doing so, ethnographic discourse faces the double task of introducing its audiences to a particular universe without losing its comparative horizon, turning the exotic familiar and the familiar exotic, following Claude Lévi-Strauss's theoretical and methodological agenda. Indeed, opening up the particular to comparison is an aim shared by the ethnographer and the linguist.

This entire process involves successive phases of transcription and translation. Transcription is a painstaking task which should aim to represent melodic and rhythmic units as closely as possible (see also Chapter 10 for further notes on transcribing spoken discourse). In the transcripts that follow (as well as in the overall Kuikuro documentation), I have tried to apply the ideas of ethnographers specialized in verbal art forms, such as Dell Hymes (1977, 1992), Joel Sherzer (1990) and Dennis Tedlock (1983).

Translation is a favorite theme of anthropology in general. Anthropology teaches us about the possibilities and risks of translation, continually emphasizing the importance of translation work and the skill and sensibility required to achieve a good translation – "good" in the sense of trustworthy, as Malinowski put it; "good" in the sense of competent, something only made possible by allying linguistic and ethnographic knowledge; "good", too, in the sense of respecting the meanings carried by the "source" language and thereby respecting its speakers.

The work involved in translation is most delicate. Chanted words frequently derive from special registers, the famous "words of the ancestors." Faced with their esoteric quality, many ethnographers have declared this kind of language unintelligible. Here linguists can contribute through their capacity to disclose the meanings of phrases and terms used in these formulaic and *sui generis* languages. Translation work also typically faces difficulties in turning extremely dense and elliptical metaphors into something at least minimally comprehensible.

Although translation is not approached here as a separate topic, it underlies everything else in this chapter. Translation must be understood in the widest possible sense, ranging from kinds of transcription and annotation that allow the basic characteristics of verbal performances to be recovered, especially the most elaborate examples in terms of form, rhythm, register, vocabulary and meanings, to translation properly speaking, working from a source-language to a target-language. Vast literature exists on translation, mostly found in the areas of literary criticism and poetic theory, which would be interesting to investigate further in order to understand the problems and reach of translation at all levels. Useful starting points for exploring this literature are the books edited by Swann (1992) and by Rubel and Rosman (2003), as well Bringhurst (1999).

2. Some topics an ethnographer is likely to look for

Assuming that the core of a language documentation consists of a collection of "texts" (i.e. annotated recordings of speech events) and a lexical database, there are somewhat different, but also largely overlapping topics an anthropologist may look for in each of these components. Before we take a closer look at these, it will be useful to note that most ethnographers have little interest in information on linguistic structures *per se*. That is, ethnographers, with a few exceptions, do not read grammars. Linguistic structure only becomes interesting when it can be linked directly to culture and history. Thus, for example, etymologies are one of the favorite "linguistic" exercises of ethnographers, and it is probably fair to say that, not infrequently, such etymologies are amateurish at best. Here providing an indication of morphological boundaries for lexical items, backed-up by a clear descriptive exposition of the basic morphology, will help to avoid amateur etymologies. More complex examples of when linguistic structure becomes highly relevant to anthropological concerns will be found in Section 3 below.

2.1. Consulting a lexical database

Like most other users of a lexical database, ethnographers will profit from the amount of detail provided in definitions and the care given to the wording of translations (for further discussion of the issues raised in this section, see also Chapter 6). Whenever possible, one should try to distinguish basic and derived uses when explicating the full range of a term's meanings. For example, translating Kuikuro *oto* simply as 'owner' fails to capture the dense web of its uses: these are only attainable by collating all occurrences of the expression X-*oto*, 'owner of X', which include festivals, community structures, forms of knowledge, objects, kinship, etc. *Oto* therefore designates a very particular relationship of control between a person and a culturally relevant object, and the complete set of contexts in which it occurs allows the anthropologist to consider the nature of this relationship and attain the level of abstraction needed to attempt to define it independently of any one of its specific occurrences. Another example is *tolo*, which means 'bird', 'pet', 'a song genre', and 'my lover'. This list of meanings immediately raises the question of which is the basic sense and how the derived senses are linked to it? Various kinds of evidence suggest that the basic meaning is that of 'bird', the prototypical pet of the Upper Xingu. The relation between the pet bird and its 'owner' is one between a fledgling and the person who lured and caught the young bird in order to "familiarize" it. As Fausto (1999; see also Erikson 1987) notes, the relation between a pet and its 'owner' is found throughout Amazonia and defines various thematic domains, such as shamanism, ritual, warfare, capture, hunting and so on. In the Upper Xingu, a lover is thus equivalent to a pet bird; the prototypical *tolo* songs are messages from a lover to her/his beloved one.

The search for ethnographically relevant information is facilitated by the definition of *thematic domains* in addition to the *semantic domains* used by many linguists and lexicographers. Here *semantic domain* refers to a set of features which define very general and inclusive fields of meaning, are often relevant to grammatical marking and which are associated with a large number of lexical entries. The categories used may be created by the researcher or form part of native classifications. Examples include features such as ANIMATE, BODY PART, ACTION, or PROPERTY.

Although some semantic domains may contain information useful for ethnographic purposes, the more narrowly defined thematic domains will be of greater interest in this regard. But note that the difference between the two types of semantic annotation is gradual at best, and there are some overlaps, as will be clear from the following brief review of major thematic fields, some of which (e.g. body parts or kin terms) are also often found in semantic domain classifications.

KINSHIP terminology is a key area of ethnographic inquiry. These terms, on the one hand, denote positions in a genealogical structure, but they are also inherently relational terms, associated with multiple denotata. The determination of kin relationships is influenced by many variables, such as genealogical distance or proximity, the calculations made through a third relation mediating between ego and the individual being addressed or referred to, as well as contextual and momentary variables, such as factional disputes, broken marriages, extraconjugal affairs, and so on. A systematic analysis of kinship terminology must include a precise indication of the positions covered by each term in a genealogical structure, using the vocabulary or abbreviations currently used in anthropology. An extended example, representing the Kuikuro consanguineal kinship terminology, can be found in Appendix 1.

In addition to kinship terms proper, related general and specific terms are also part of this thematic field. For example: Is there a general term for 'kin'? Possibly no equivalent of general terms such as 'kin' is found in the language under study, but we may find collective terms in generation Ø (ego's generation), such as terms for male relatives of the same generation (i.e. a cover term for 'brothers' and 'cousins'), and this is a relevant source of ethnographical information.

BODY PARTS: Here the existence of alternative terms for the same body part may prove to be an interesting source of information. In Kuikuro, lines on the palms of hands are also called *katuga etoho* 'used for (the) *mangaba* (resin ball)[1] to come', and the upper central region of the forehead and the thigh can be referred to with *katuga agitoho* 'used to throw (the) *mangaba* (resin ball);' both designations refer to an ancient and abandoned ritual game.

MATERIAL CULTURE or ARTEFACTS: The terminology relating to the building and structure of the traditional house may prove relevant, for example, if some of its parts are named after human body parts, as well as being useful from a comparative perspective. Here we can observe the fertility of symbolic analyses of the 'house' in an Amazonian context in the work of Hugh-Jones (1995) as well as Bourdieu's (1970) classic on the Kabyle 'house' in northern Africa.

TERMS RELATING TO SUBSISTENCE ACTIVITIES: These include plants, verbs denoting actions and events in the agricultural economy, often extractable from origin myths on cultivated plants. In the Amazonian context, the lexicon relating to types of swidden agriculture and phases of cultivation enables the extraction of important data on the organization of agricultural work as well as comparative observations. For example, comparison can then be made of the use of a swidden field over time among an Amazonian forest group such as the Parakanã (Tupi-Guarani) and an Upper Xingu group such as the Kuikuro, who live in an area of transition between forest and savannah. In Amazonia, different patterns of mobility and distinct conceptions of alimentary diets, based on plants or animals, are associated with a greater or lesser diversity of species of cultivated plants as well as a greater or lesser investment in agricultural production, reflected in distinct kinds of cultural ethos (Heckenberger 1998; Fausto 2001; Hugh-Jones 1995; Descola 1998).

Many more thematic fields could be named here, but they will vary with the specific cultural or geographical area. SHAMANISM is a key thematic field for many societies, in particular Amerindian people. Ideally, the lexicon would include all the terms designating supernatural beings or entities, explicating them individually and as a whole, and associating them with etiology, the classification and denomination of illnesses, cures, rituals, masks, and so on, as will be further illustrated in Section 3.5 below.

2.2. Consulting "texts"

In a language documentation as conceived of here, "texts" comprise *annotated sessions*. Usually, these are audio or video recordings of elicited or spontaneous performances of verbal genres – such as narratives, conversations, ritual discourses – which have been transcribed, translated, analyzed, and commented upon.

When consulting a corpus of "sessions", which are the most relevant ones from the viewpoint of ethnographers, especially those averse to what they call the "butterfly collector syndrome"? There is no straightforward and easy answer to such a question, among other things because of the large variation that can be observed across different cultural and geographic areas. But the following suggestions may provide a basic idea of the range of topics of interest to an ethnographer:

- STANDARD TOPICS IN ETHNOGRAPHY for which material can probably be collected in all cultures are body, conception, pregnancy, soul, ghosts, birth, female and male reclusion, first menses and menstruation.
- RITUAL WAILING and other verbal-musical genres. It should be noted, however, that recording events such as ritual wailing, as well as other songs and shamanic cures, may be prohibited. This applies to the Kuikuro project, for example.
- GREETINGS as a verbal genre with its specific formulas. This is also what the "naïve consumer" usually wants to see/read/learn.
- ONOMASTICS, i.e. the system of attributing and transmitting personal names. This needs to be documented through censuses, village maps, and genealogies.
- TOPONYMS: In the best of circumstances, the documentation would include a map of the territory with the toponyms in the indigenous language, where possible translated and analyzed morphologically and semantically, noting their associations with mythical and historical events and interpretations.
- MALE and FEMALE SPEECH in sessions which deal with topics affected by gender distinctions, such as the division of labor, sexual relations, jealousy, love affairs, marriage, menstruation, conception theories, etc.
- NATIVE METALINGUISTIC DISCOURSE: What do speakers have to say about their own language and other languages with which they are in contact? See further Section 3.1.
- TURN-TAKING RULES in different kinds of conversation; for example, those applying to interactions in domestic spaces versus those used in public spaces.
- Data on LANGUAGE ACQUISITION as seen in interactions between children of different ages and between children and adults of different ages possessing different relations to the child.
- The INDIGENOUS PERSPECTIVE ON THE FOREIGN INTERLOCUTOR, i.e. ourselves, in the form of narratives and other materials on "white people" (or other types of outsiders coming to the community for reasons such as research, trade, or politics). With regard to the interaction with a documentation team, this could include written and spoken materials

that allow an understanding of the processes involved in translating between the universe of the foreigners and the indigenous universe. Of particular interest would be the translation of foreign texts, such as legislative documents and health manuals, into the native language, enabling the analysis of loan words and their use, or the creation of terms to designate new "objects". Furthermore, a documentation should include sessions containing verbal interactions between native speakers and foreigners in other languages than the one(s) being documented, especially the dominant language (national or regional), reflecting the full range of knowledge/fluency existing in the indigenous community.

This list of topics, though far from comprehensive, is already considerable and attempting to cover them in full during fieldwork will be both impractical and unrealistic given the time and resource limits imposed on most language documentation projects – even more so when dealing with endangered languages, and above all endangered speakers. But an awareness of these key topics may at least allow the non-anthropological researcher to identify and collect culturally important data whenever possible.

Apart from topic areas, there are some other considerations in compiling a documentary corpus which may be of equal if not greater importance. Thus, it is important to be aware of the fact that mythic narratives are ethnographic works in themselves. Special attention should be given to those narratives that are useful for comparative purposes. In the Amerindian universe, relevant mythical narratives include those on the genesis or origin of the world and the different classes of beings, the origin of sex/gender distinctions, the origin of death (or short life), the origin of "white people", and the origin of language (the absence of the latter type of myth should be noted and commented upon, as well as noting where cues to a "native philosophy of language" can be found). Comparative observations on different styles are also important, such as, for example, the differences between the short and dense narratives of the Parakanã and the long, rhetorical and formal narratives, filled with repetitions, of the Kuikuro.

Another point to be noted is that the documentation of rituals is problematic since the more performative the "event" to be captured, the less adequate purely linguistic data becomes; on the other hand, the less performative the ritual, the more relevant linguistic data proves. In this regard, an observation concerning video documentation will be in order. Today, video is widely used as a means of capturing elements which – whether or not analyzed by the documenting team – can provide important data for other researchers. However, one should not overestimate the "power" of video. Vision, like any other form of perception, is always partial, and simple filming lacks a basic element of good ethnography: participant observation over an extended period, guided by specific training that enables pertinent questions to be formulated at any given instance. In addition, visual documentation to date very often involves amateurish products of dubious quality and professionalism.

In summary, ethnographers – as other researchers – are interested in sets of information that enable the formulation of questions and hypotheses as well as the corroboration of the latter. Productive questions, however, cannot be simply derived from documentary material without the prior definition of issues based on actual ethnographic field research, or without comparative aims and objects. Nothing substitutes for ethnographic field research. For this reason, the ideal scenario is to work in an interdisciplinary team. Although the Kuikuro Project is nowadays multidisciplinary, this structure evolved over time. At the beginning of the project, we had already been working for a number of years in close cooperation with an ethno-archaeologist conducting research in the Upper Xingu region and, more specifically, the Kuikuro territory. An anthropologist formally joined the team only in 2002. Although this has complexified and slowed down the documentary work well beyond initial forecasts, the experience has been and continues to be extremely productive and positive. Collected and recorded data can now be more comprehensively contextualized, deepening the knowledge of the language and the richness of its constructions and meanings. Reflecting on the relationship between language and culture has become a much less trivial operation. And, last but not least, the involvement of the Kuikuro themselves in the documentation process – the fact that they are today much more subjects-actors-guides than consultants-objects – is due in part to the interest generated by the "good" questions posed by a good ethnographer.

3. Exploring a language documentation from an ethnographic point of view

In this section, I will discuss a few examples from the Kuikuro documentation in order to exemplify ways in which an ethnographer may look through documents (i.e. sessions) in a language documentation, thereby also making it clear which kinds of resources will be of particular use in this regard. Repeatedly throughout this section we will have occasion to note that in digitally stored documentations, the perhaps major resource is a network of links between sessions and other resources included in the documentation, i.e. to make full use of the hypertext possibilities inherent in the digital design. An intelligent network of links between narratives, lexica, images, and analytic studies will help the user to navigate through a culture's twisting networks of meanings.

As a starting point, I shall look at language identity, trying to understand what the Kuikuro mean when they say that the word *tisakisü* 'our (exclusive) words/language' may be used as a synonym for *tisügühütu* 'our (exclusive) way of being' or, as they would say today, 'our culture'.[2] This naturally leads into a discussion of different speaking styles, and we will take a closer look at one of the more formalized or ritualized speaking styles, the 'chief's speech', in Section 3.2. Ritualized speech forms often abound with references to the past in a number of ways, one of which will be exemplified in a bit more detail in Section 3.3. Another major characteristic of ritual speech found in many communities throughout the world is parallelism in its linguistic and rhetorical structure. Section 3.4 provides a very brief example. Section 3.5 concludes this exploration by drawing together the different facets mentioned along the way in exemplifying one way of resolving typical translation problems in one key thematic field of Amerindian ethnography, i.e. shamanism.

The current section heavily draws on two resources which the reader should have at hand during the exploration in order to be able to make full use of the discussion. On the one hand, Appendix 2 provides an overview of the structure of the Kuikuro documentation at the time of writing. On the other hand, the website of this book provides access to the primary data discussed in this section in the form of audio and video clips.

3.1. Language and identity

Based on my experience with the Upper Xingu people in Brazil, I shall highlight here one essential point: Language is a diacritical marker of individual and collective social and political identity (Franchetto 2001).

The Upper Xingu is one of the few multilingual systems without a common lingua franca still in existence in the South American tropical lowlands. These systems seem to have been more numerous and complex in the past – that is, until the disastrous effects of European conquest took their toll (until the 18th century).

The Upper Xingu is home to groups speaking genetically distinct languages, sharing the same basic cultural traits and interacting within a dense network of ritual, trade, and matrimonial exchanges (see Map 1). The careful observance of these linguistic differences is a crucial factor in maintaining and reproducing the global system. It is unsurprising, therefore, that the Upper Xingu peoples possess a rich set of metalinguistic notions. In fact, they enjoy speaking about "the music of languages", just as they like to compare different languages and put a lot of effort into the work of translation. Not by chance, dictionaries (vocabularies) attract particular attention. They claim dictionaries rather than grammars are the best way to learn a new language.

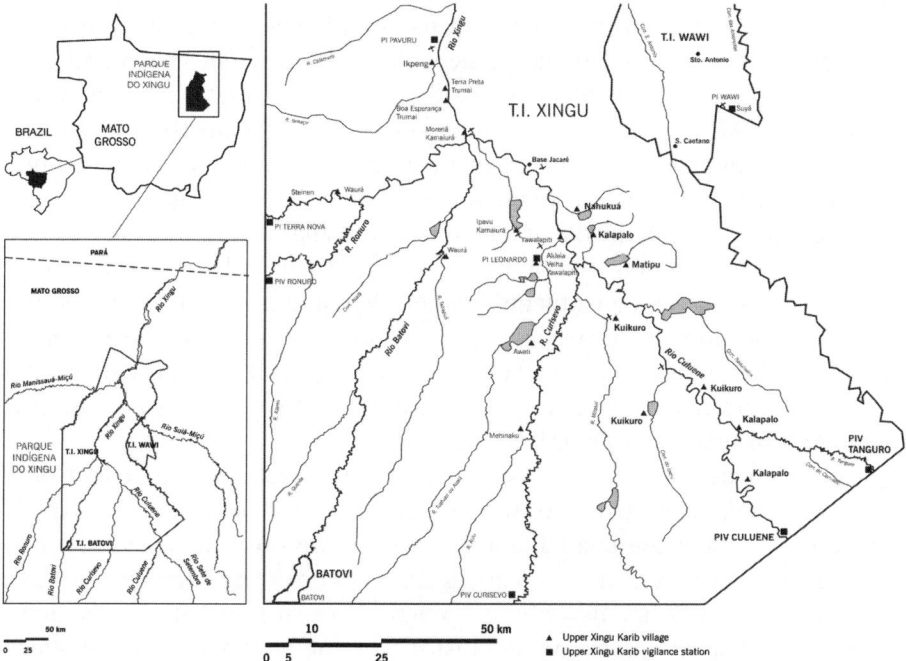

Map 1. Local groups and villages in the Upper Xingu region

The Kuikuro, speakers of a language from the Carib family, contrast themselves with those peoples speaking languages from the Arawak family as "those who speak in the throat" versus "those who speak with the tip of the teeth". This is an accurate description of the articulatory characteristics of the languages under comparison: the preponderance of dorsal and uvular articulations in the upper Xingu Carib languages and the preponderance of dental and pre-palatal articulations in Arawak languages.

But such socially functional linguistic differences also involve the distinction between dialectal variants of the same language. Kuikuro is one variant of the Upper Xingu Carib language; the other variant is spoken by the Nahukwá, Kalapalo, and Matipu. The factors differentiating these variants are not so much lexical and morphological elements, but primarily prosodic structures or distinct rhythmic patterns.

Kuikuro builds moraic troquees from right to left. The main accent of the word is generally on the penultimate syllable, but it shifts to the ultimate syllable of the word when it is related as an argument to a head. This allows us to identify prosodically phrasal constituents such as the verb with its internal argument, the postposition with its complement, or, more generally, the relation between a head and its dependent. High pitch, vowel and consonant lengthening, and intensity are the parameters that characterize the main accent. All converge on the same syllable. Consequently, speakers of the Kuikuro language say their language is spoken straight, direct, in a line.

The Kalapalo dissociate tonal pitch from intensity (loudness). Tonal pitch generally occurs on the antepenultimate syllable and intensity on the penultimate. In addition, the language's phonology, unlike Kuikuro, does not "read" syntactic constituents; rather the simple word (and not the phrase) is the domain of accent. Speakers of these variants are therefore said to speak in jumps, waves, and curves. In keeping with their culture, the metaphor preferred by Upper Xingu peoples is musical in kind: *tisakisü angunda* 'our (exclusive) words are dancing'.

To get a better idea of this basic difference between the two dialect variants, let us look at and listen to two women in two video segments (as mentioned above, these are available at the book's website). In video segment A: KUIKURO [HONEY], the woman speaks Kuikuro. The segment displays her first utterances when describing a practice lost and forgotten by younger people: the ritual of harvesting and distributing native honey. Paying attention to the melody of the speech, you will discover that it results from the interplay between rhythmic structure and pitch melody.

Video segment B: KALAPALO [TUKUTI] displays a speaker of the Kalapalo variant where melody and rhythm clearly differ from the preceding segment. Segment B is from the beginning of a description of the power of *tukuti kuegü*, the Hyper Humming Bird, whose image or representation the speaker is holding in her hand. This is the supernatural being who caused her a severe illness, and her cure meant that her husband became an "owner" of the *Hugagü* ritual. We will return to this segment further below in section 3.5.

What I would like to emphasize here is that the linguist's particular skill lies in documenting and describing the variants of a language – in our sample case, distinctions in rhythm which represent complementary oppositions at the socio-political level. Here, metrical phonology combines with native metalinguistic concepts, providing us with data crucial to the understanding of a social and cultural system.

In a language documentation, such information should be presented in the metadata through which a session is accessed. Obviously, users of a documentation will profit even more if this aspect is also dealt with in an analytically elaborated form, i.e. in the form of phonological and comparative studies, which should be cross-linked to the relevant sessions.

3.2. Ways of speaking (genres)

In the previous section we saw the importance of musicality in understanding the sociolinguistics, and more generally the sociopolitics, of the Upper Xingu people. Musicality interconnects three domains: (i) the study of rhythm in phonology; (ii) the speakers' metalinguistic awareness and categories; and (iii) the identification of speech genres (speeches) since these are in part identifiable by differences in rhythm and melody, as we shall see in this section.

In the Upper Xingu, the identifiable verbal speech genres are distributed in a continuum whose poles are formed at one end by everyday speech, dominated by the metric pattern proper to the dialect variant (as exemplified above), and at the other end by songs where the rhythm of the everyday language is subject to, or transfigured by, another metric pattern, another beat, another rhythm. Along this continuum between prosaic speech and song we find genres where a patterned, fixed rhythm transfigures the prosaic musicality into another style, a psalm-like succession of monotonal lines. This is the case with the chanted speech characterizing *anetü itaginhu*, the 'chief's speech', a verbal performance which marks the apex of the large inter-tribal rituals in the Upper Xingu. Here, local identities and the global society are celebrated simultaneously, giving center ground to the history of the birth of the groups along with their chiefs. These rituals are a celebration of local and regional history through the memory of the great chiefs and their descendents (Franchetto 1993, 2000).

Imagine that we are watching and listening to a small segment of the *anetü itaginhu* performed in the 2002 dry season in the run up to the *egitsü (kwaryp)* ritual celebrated in the Yawalapiti (Arawak) village. Video segment C: CHIEF'S SPEECH shows chief Tahukula welcoming three Yawalapiti messengers who have just arrived in the village to invite the Kuikuro to the festival. At the beginning of the clip, the chief is still inside his house with his brother, waiting for the moment to come out into the middle of the village and walk to the front of the men's house, where the three messengers to be officially greeted are waiting, sitting in the sun.

The chanted speech style *anetü itaginhu* is made up of a sequence of discourses. The chief summons other Kuikuro chiefs[3] in order for one or more of them to accept the task of leading the Kuikuro to the Yawalapiti village. Finally, Tahukula crouches down with the chief (or chiefs) who accepted being the leader of the Kuikuro for this event in front of the grave of the dead chiefs situated in front of the men's house, and in front of the messengers, thereby confirming acceptance of the invitation. Afterwards, chief and messengers recite another part of the 'chief's speech' in unison. Everything is "said" by *anetü itaginhu*.

The transcription and translation of a small section of the 'chief's speech' is reproduced below. The *anetü itaginhu* comprises a sequence of altogether six main speeches. There is the speech to celebrate the arrival of the messengers from another village, the speech to 'make the messengers sit' on the stools placed in front of the 'men's house' located in the middle of the village, and so forth. Each speech marks a particular phase of the ritual for welcoming those who come from outside. The sixth speech is the apical discourse, the one in which the great chiefs of the past, the founders of the Kuikuro in this case, parade in sequence, each one the central persona of a unit of the speech, here called a block, which is composed of various lines or verses. The parallelistic structure characterizes both the verses making up a block and the relationship between various blocks. In the apical speech, the effect produced is like wandering through a portrait gallery filled with the great ancestors, whose sequence consubstantiates the existence of the current chiefs and the Kuikuro as a whole. The following is the block relating to Amatuagü, one of the founder chiefs:[4]

(1)   Transcript of video segment C: CHIEF'S SPEECH

etsuhehetselüi etsuhehetsegake ngingoku
(ancient words)   messenger
it's a mistake for you to come here, messenger

ahütüha   kukuge   tühigümbükila   ngingoku
ahütü-ha   kukuge   tü-   hi   -gü -mbükila   ngingoku
NEG-AFF   our/people RFL-grand/son-REL-PASTNEG   messenger
our people have no more descendents, messenger

Amatuagü tühigümbükila ngingoku
there are no more descendents of Amatuagü, messenger

angolo   atai   hüle   **wãke**
true   when ADV distant/past
and that, by contrast, was the time of the true ones (chiefs)

üngele higümbügü   kaenga atsakuhotagü   ngingoku
üngele hi   -gü -mbügü kae -nga atsaku-ho -tagü ngingoku
AN   grand/son-REL-PAST   LOC-ALL run   -HYP-CONT messenger
you should run towards the descendents of this one (Amatuagü), messenger

isagingo   geleha   atsakugake   ngingoku
is-agingo gele-ha   atsaku-gake ngingoku
3-same   yet-AFF   run   -IMP messenger
just like him still, run, messenger!

ünago   imalüa   geleha   atsakugake ngingoku
ünago   ima -lü -a   gele-ha   atsaku-gake ngingoku
AN   trail-REL-like   yet -AFF run   -IMP messenger
as if it were along their path, run, messenger!

anetão imalüa   geleha   atsakugake ngingoku
anetão ima -lü -a   gele-ha   atsaku-gake ngingoku
chiefs trail-REL-like   yet -AFF run   -IMP messenger
as if it were still along the path of the chiefs, run, messenger!

We are dealing here not with 'words' (*aki*) but with 'speech' or 'talk' (*itaginhu*). Despite the appearance of being a monological genre, for the Kuikuro the 'chief's speech' in its highly ritualized performance is a 'conversation'. The speech is conceived of as an interaction or a dialogue – or more than this: a conversation with a polyphony of voices. The chiefs squatted in front of the messengers very often perform the formulas of *anetü itaginhu* simultaneously; on other occasions, messengers and host chiefs speak at the same time, each grouping in their own language.

There is no space here to explore the ethnographic significance of the *anetü itaginhu* in detail. It will suffice to note that it contains a condensed set of meanings, values, and attitudes which help illuminate politics, chiefdom, and social morphology. The chief links the past to the present, representing and maintaining the unity of his local group in relation to other groups, thereby allowing his own to open up to others. Although being a chief is a condition transmitted by blood lines of inheritance, this condition has to be continually constructed by the full exercise of chiefdom, by certain qualities and, last but no least, by knowing the *anetü itaginhu* speeches and how to perform them.

It can also be observed that, apart from almost untranslatable terms and dense metaphors typical for this genre, the segment contains – as in *anetü itaginhu* as a whole – the self-derogatory posture typical for interactions between affines and indicative of hierarchical relations characterized by a specific verbal and behavioral etiquette.

Note also the occurrence of the particle *wãke*, which ends the line dividing this unit of discourse into two parts. The other lines end with the word *ngingoku* 'messenger' – a term from the special lexicon of the chief's speech. *Wãke* means 'past', the truth value and authority of a speech 'above all suspicion', as a metaphor of a collectivity and the chiefdom. More precisely, *wãke* is a marker of an epistemic modality, as further discussed in the following section.

3.3. History

The previous section examined some of the general information necessary to begin to understand the 'chief's speech', which should be incorporated in the metadata directly linked to the session containing the full recording of the event. In a more complete annotation, one would have to investigate the social and political meaning of the 'chief's speech' within the intertribal system, its function within a specific ritual, the speech genre which characterizes it, the status and roles of actors and their interaction. Additionally, it will be useful to include a careful network of links to other sessions of different genres, the lexicon and non-linguistic components such as images, iconography, genealogies, studies, and so on in order to allow for a full exploration of its functions and meanings. For example, in the case of the 'chief's speech', links with sessions containing historical and personal narratives, providing access to collective and individual memories, are crucial, as briefly illustrated in this section.

The historical oral tradition contains narratives where an elder called Hopesé tells how his grandfather swapped his name with the German ethnographer Karl von den Steinen, called *Kalusi* by the Kuikuro, at the end of the 19th century (Steinen 1940, 1942). These narratives take us back to the time when the Kuikuro group was formed and the differentiation of the dialectical variants began. It was the time of the founder chief Amatuagü, a persona from the 'chief's speech' mentioned in the segment transcribed above. The following is a transcription and translation of the beginning of this story, from the session 'Kalusi' (see audio segment KALUSI). This segment also shows how linguistic and cultural commentary can be linked directly to the line it is most relevant to, with further links included in some of these commentaries.[5]

(2)   Transcript of audio segment Kalusi

\trs   isinügü **wãke** ingila Intagü Intagü ilá ande Intagü
        ilá
\te   "A long time ago he came from Intagü, Intagü is
        over there,
\ntl   *Observe the second position particle* wãke, *which*
        means 'distant past' combined with the epistemic
        value of "true statement from collective memory"
        and the authority of someone (the speaker) who
        received the story through the line of his parents
        and grand-parents; his grand-father was the one who
        saw Kalusi/Steinen (faithfully reported first hand
        experience). SEE KUIKURO STUDIES > ON LANGUAGE >
        EPISTEMIC MODALITIES
\ntc   *Intagü – name of an old Nahukwá village. Kalusi*
        came through the Nahukwá villages situated along
        the Curisevo river until the beginning of the 20th
        century. The names of the villages mentioned in
        this session correspond to those villages existing
        at the time of Steinen. SEE MAP STEINEN.[6]

\trs   **Kuhikugu imünhige Lahatua imünhige**
\te   **in the direction of Kuhikugu, in the direction of**
        Lahuatá
\ntc   *Kuhikugu – the first Kuikuro village founded after*
        a number of families departed from the Oti villages
        complex, thought to be inhabited by the Uagihütü
        people (Matipú). SEE SESSION 'KUKOPOGIPÜGÜ' (THE
        APPEARANCE OF THE KUIKURO PEOPLE). Lahatuá –
        Kuikuro village already settled in the twentieth

> *century and inhabited up to the 1950s. SEE MAPS*
> *(HISTORICAL AND PRE-HISTORICAL SITES) AND STUDIES*
> *ON CULTURE > HISTORY.*[7]

\trs   **isitühügü Kalusi etsühügüha**
\te   **it was him who arrived, it was Kalusi who arrived**
\ntc   *Kalusi is now introduced as the main protagonist of*
       the story. The name Kalusi derives from Karl, in
       Portuguese Carlos, adapted to the phonological
       structure of the upper Xingu Carib languages, where
       there are no consonantal clusters, and to their
       syllabic structure (CV).

\trs   **Maginatu hekeha ingitühügü**
\te   **Maginatu brought him**

\trs   **Maginatu akatsange ingitinhi <u>wãke</u> Kuhikugunaha**
       Kuhikuguna
\te   **a long time ago Maginatu brought him to Kuhikugu,**
       to Kuhikugu

\trs   **Maginatu Tugumai ekisei Maginatui**
\te   **Maginatu, he was a Trumai, Maginatu was**
\ntc   *In the Hopese version of the encounter, von den*
       Steinen was brought to the village of Kuhikugu by a
       Trumai Indian called Maginatu.

The particle *wãke*, an epistemic modality marker we already encountered in the chief's speech, is present here in the first and penultimate lines (and underlined). The description of so-called epistemic modalities is a theme of great interest to ethnographers. Epistemic modality markers convey information about the relationship between the speaker and his or her statements and the interlocutors. They include evidentials, hear-say particles, and other modalizers of a statement's truth value. An extensive literature exists on this topic.[8] Hence, it is important to comment in the session annotations on the presence and meanings of these elements in the language.

Many of these particles can be found in Hopesé's narrative, centered on the figure of Karl von den Steinen. The most interesting ones are those that indicate the speaker's attitude in relation to the contents of his recollections, thus indexing a sub-genre of narratives which we can define as "historical". These marks distinguish historical narratives from the narratives we call mythic, which tell of the origins of cultural goods and are located at the beginning of time, when humans or non-humans, or quasi-humans, lived and communicated with each other. The epistemic markers help us in the work of distinguishing narrative registers such as the historical and mythical, and kinds of memory – important topics in today's ethnological debates.

Along with deictics and particles carrying an aspectual value, these small words are called *tisakisü enkgutoho* by the Kuikuro, a beautiful metaphor meaning roughly 'made for our words to beach safely'. They are predicative anchors, actualizing the statement and closing its living meaning.

Links between components, sub-components and their contents help to deepen the ethnographic information. Continuing with our example, historical narratives can be connected to historical and archaeological studies. In the Kuikuro case, one of the results of the research work undertaken by Michael Heckenberger, the ethno-archaeologist collaborating with the Kuikuro project, is the reconstruction of the pre-historic villages, i.e. those preceding the first historical record written by Karl von den Steinen (Heckenberger 2005). We were thus able to reconstruct the village of Kuhikugu, the first settlement built by the Kuikuro group, still in existence at the time of von den Steinen, when the ethnographer met the grandfather of the elder Hopesé (see Map 2). The pre-historical villages were much larger and more complex than contemporary ones, linked in a more impressive way than today to a network of primary and satellite villages, connected by large 50-metre wide pathways. Above all, each archaeological site is associated with historical and mythic narratives that allow a geo-historical map to be interconnected with a cosmological map. Consequently, native oral history, ritual performances of verbal art forms, the history written by outsiders and archaeological research are combined to delineate a history in which indigenous voices play an active and determining role.

3.4. Parallelism

Like any oral performance, the narrative about Karl von den Steinen told by Hopesé contains many repetitions. The high incidence of repetitions especially applies to a culture based on primary orality. Rather than being mere repetitions, these are usually parallelistic constructions.[9] This parallelism (lexical and grammatical in kind) is a defining characteristic of verbal art genres, although, as I mentioned, it can already be found in sketchy and elementary form in prosaic and informal discourse. We can see the interweaving between parallelism and versification in the 'chief's speech', at the extreme end of chanted speech.

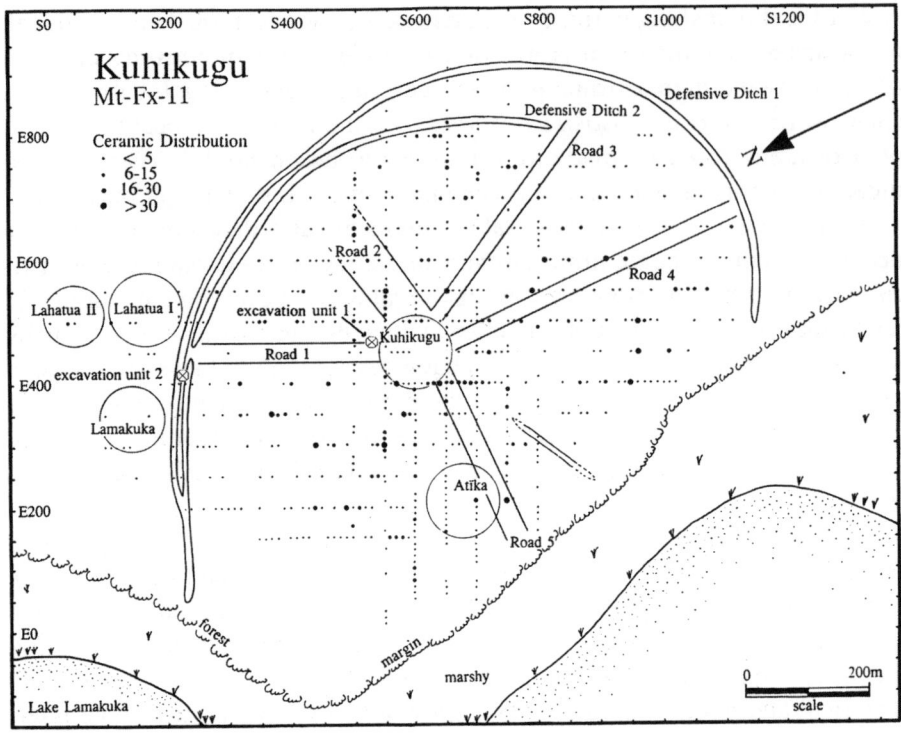

Map 2. Map of prehistoric site of Kuhikugu showing locations of the Kuikuro village occupied over the past 150 years (denoted by closed circles). Black dots represent collection units.　　　　(From Heckenberger 1998: 638)

In traditional narrative, the ability to construct micro and macro parallelisms defines the skill of a recognized *akinhá oto* 'owner/master of narrative'. The resources provided by the grammar are the object of a conscious manipulation deployed to produce 'beautiful speech' (*atütü itaginhu*). In Kuikuro, for example, the play of alternations between transitivity and intransitivity (or causativity and anti-causativity) is marvelously exploited by experienced narrators (Franchetto 2003). Let us examine just one example here, taken from the (historical) narrative on the origin of the Kuikuro people:[10]

(3)   Segment from Session Kukopogipügü: IV, d, 142–143

[tsiu] otohinhakenügü   leha
[tsiu] ot-   ohinhake   -nügü leha
[id]   3/DETR- manioc swidden/cut-PNCT CMPL

tutuhi   itu   ohinhakenügü   leha   iheke   [tsiu]
tu- tuhi   itu   ohinhake -nügü leha   i- heke [tsiu]
RFL-manioc   manioc swidden/cut-PNCT CMPL 3-ERG   [id]
      swidden place

[tsiu] he cleared the manioc swidden place
he cleared the place for his own manioc swidden field [tsiu]

In this example, the scene of the chief clearing the first swidden field for manioc in the new village is seen through the concomitant and complementary perspectives of an intransitive and a transitive action (compare lines 1 and 2).

Exploring the Kuikuro metalanguage again, we discover that there is a term designating synonymy and, obviously, the parallelistic relationship between expressions such as the one in our example. This is the term *otohongo* which means 'the same other' or 'the other same', a term used in many other (non-linguistic) domains as well, such as the differentiation of species, kinship relations (siblings) and local groups.

As we emphasized above, distinct semantic and thematic domains can be interrelated – in this instance, on the basis of formal traits pertaining to different genres of verbal art. Documentation of the latter is in fact particularly relevant in contemporary ethnology as part of an ongoing discussion about ethnopoetics and the problems of translation.

3.5. Thematic fields and untranslatable terms

Ethnographers can search the Kuikuro database for key words linked to texts, lexical entries and other components relating to *thematic fields*, which were briefly discussed in Section 2.2 above. As well as enabling the understanding of a specific culture, the topics coded in thematic fields are especially important for comparison. The ethnography thus produced contributes to anthropological theory, essentially a comparative science.

One of the key themes in the Kuikuro documentation is shamanism. This topic connects cosmology, rituals, social morphology, conceptions of sickness, death of the body, and incorporeal principles (different kinds of soul, shadow, breath, the invisible arrows of the witch, etc.), curing conceptions and practices, politics, and prestige. The shaman has been defined as a translator, mediating human and non-human worlds, a master of transformations (see, for example, Carneiro da Cunha 1999, which provides further references). Here we briefly illustrate how this very complex topic can be approached via links between relevant sections of the documentation.

In a session already mentioned above, Tapualu, a Kalapalo woman, holds in her hand the representation of the powerful and feared *tukuti kuegü*, the Hyper Being (spirit-animal) of the Humming Bird. She explains who or what *tukuti kuegü* is. She is showing the cause of her illness: the Hyper Being is associated with the pequi tree (Caryocar brasiliense) and the pequi origin myth. *Tukuti kuegü* encountered her while she was collecting pequi fruits and the Being struck her, causing her to feel terrible pains. Returning home, she spent weeks in her hammock in delirium, dreaming and shouting. In a related session, Samuagü, Tapualu's husband, recounts what happened, recollecting the myth and offering explanations (see video segment D: ITSEKE-TUKUTI1). Then, the shamans rush to diagnose the cause of the illness and cure the victim. In another session, one of the Kuikuro shamans talks about the woman's illness and the process of diagnosis and cure (video segment E: ITSEKE-TUKUTI2). *Tukuti kuegü* was "tamed" through the *hugagü* ritual which the woman's husband then "owned" for a number of years (video segment F: HUGAGÜ).

All rituals – or better, all ritual complexes – connect worlds, but they are also the core motors of productive cycles, the circulation of goods, the system of exchanges, and the maintenance of the local supra-domestic unit, the village. Rituals engender social roles, actualize relationships of kinship and alliance, and confer prestige. A ritual is a festival, dance, and song; it is beauty, it restores well being, it is joy and health. Ritual is transformation.

Every session linked to the key word 'shamanism' will obviously allow certain lexical entries to be built up more carefully, such as *kuegü* (roughly translated here as 'hyper'), an operator categorizing every 'supernatural' entity, or *itseke*. Every *kuegü* being is *itseke* (translatable in a highly equivocal fashion as 'spirit'). These are terms whose meaning cannot really be grasped without referring to the entire cosmological and shamanistic complex. How to attribute glosses, translations, and definitions to these almost untranslatable terms? The shortcut translation – or "glossing" – of core cultural categories is at once an unavoidable task and a frustrating one (Franchetto 2002). Our attempt in the Kuikuro lexicon is far from satisfactory, even though we have strived to include native definitions wherever possible. Consider the entry for *itseke*:[11]

```
\lx     itseke
\entyp  root
\lc     itseke
\ph     [i'ʦɛkɛ]
\ps     N
\ge     hyper-being
\xkk    tinegetinhüha ugei itsekeinha
\te     I am afraid of the hyper-beings
\xkk    itseke ingilüha kupehe kukapüngu igakaho
\te     we see the hyper-beings before we die
\xkk    kagamuke kaginenügü itseke heke
\te     the hyper-being frightened the child
\defkk  itseke ekisei kukengeni, kugehüngüha ekisei, inhalüha
        ingilüi; itseke kukilüha ngiko heke kukengeni heke;
        itseke ekisei kukotombani kukügünuhata.
\defe   Itseke is that which eats us, it is not a person, it
        cannot be seen; we say that itseke is something which
        eats us; itseke is that which hurts (otomba-) us with
        invisible arrows when we are sick. Itseke is a super-
        natural being, a spirit, a 'beast;' it dwells in the
        forests, rivers and lakes; it causes illness and
        death; only shamans and the sick can see them.
\cf     kuegü, otomba
```

To give an appropriate meaning explication for words such as *itseke* or *akunga* 'souls' is obviously a very demanding task. But for these words it is at least possible and useful to assume that speakers share a single concept which can be approached by combining different metalinguistic explications with a large number of textual occurrences. However, there are other cultural categories – extremely salient and apparently empty – where even this assumption does not hold and thus any single, unifying gloss or definition is misleading on a very basic level. This is the case with the notion of *kugihe*, which in first approximation we may gloss with 'witchcraft (substance)'. This term lies at the center of beliefs concerning causality, illness, death, curing, and individual capacities. People cannot say what *kugihe* is, but they can talk about the effect *kugihe* has and the social relations that surround *kugihe*. Its exact meaning seems to remain ineffable to speakers.

It would thus be a mistake to think that all categories are represented with a definition and that definitions are shared within the speech community; this is the case with many non-observational categories. As Boyer

(1990: 37) says: "A vocabulary of a natural language is not a uniform landscape." Not everything comprises a signifier with its conceptual counterpart and terms such as *kugihe* are not common shared categories. These terms should be especially marked when occurring in texts or in the lexical database (see also Chapter 6). If the lexicon forms a functional part of the text interlinearization, as in Shoebox, the use of an oversimplified and strictly speaking "wrong" gloss is unavoidable. Description, native definitions, comments as well as links defining a network of explanatory, narrative and performative pieces can, albeit partially, make up for the ethnographic poverty of our documentation tools.

4. Conclusion

The purpose of this chapter was not to answer the question of how to annotate ethnographical information in a language documentation in technical terms. This would be an impossible task, not only for practical reasons but also because of the ever shifting and evolving research interests in the field of anthropology. Instead, I have attempted to give an idea of what an ethnographer might look for in a language documentation and how she or he would make use of it. I suggested that, where relevant and necessary, metadata attached to sessions could provide more detailed and sensitive ethnographical information, i.e. contain a kind of compacted, theme-specific ethnography. Obviously, the inclusion of an ethnographic sketch in a language documentation will also be of major assistance in accessing the documentation from an anthropological point of view. While a well worked-out sketch and even session-specific mini ethnographies may well be beyond the expertise of researchers who lack a training in anthropology, a systematic collection of amateur observations will still be of some use, in particular if it includes pointers to possibly relevant sessions as well as a frank assessment of the quality of the translation of, and commentary on, mythological and other ethnographically relevant material.

But even where the expertise for including a full-fledged ethnography is available, I think that the digital format provides for perhaps an even better way to deal with the complex data needed for anthropological research. This involves designing digital architectures with multiple and multidirectional links between different sessions and qualitatively different kinds of information such as lexica, analytical papers, photos, and so on. We can thus design paths which intelligent users can follow in order to construct their own possible ethnographies or their own possible narratives on the ways of being and thinking of the people whose language, words, and talk are "crystallized" in the documentation.

Acknowledgements

I thank Eduardo B. Viveiros de Castro and Carlos Fausto for their suggestions and comments.

Notes

1. *Mangaba* is the fruit of a plant (*Hancornia speciosa*) typically found in savannah regions. The resin extracted from it went into making a small ball used in an intra- and inter-tribal ritual game in the Upper Xingu.
2. In this chapter, all the words and utterances in the Upper Xingu Carib language (in both variants, Kuikuro and Kalapalo) are transcribed in an orthography developed as a result of literacy programs. The communities decided on an orthography which is not strictly phonemic in that it represents some sub-phonemic units as well. The conventions for correspondences between phonemes/phones and graphemes which do not have their IPA values are the following: /ɨ/→ <ü>, uvular tap → <g>, /ŋ/ → <ng>, /ɲ/ → <nh>, /ʦ/ →<ts>, / ᵑg/ → <nkg>.
3. There is a multitude of chiefly roles in an Upper Xingu village: "the owner of the village," "the owner of the plaza," "the owner of the house," "the owner of the main trail," "the owner of the trail to the water." Each one is considered *anetü* (chief) by inheritance and the label of his status defines some kind of dominance or control, not just symbolic, of one of the elements of the village's social and ritual spaces. Thus, the "owner of the middle" is the person who controls the center of the village, a male public and ritual space *par excellence*; the "owner of the main path" controls the arrival and departure of the messengers who come to invite others to the inter-tribal festivals that take place periodically in the Upper Xingu villages; the "owner of the house" represents a domestic group, normally an active male adult with children and sometimes grandchildren. 'Owner' or 'master' is a rough translation of the term *oto*, whose meaning has already been discussed.
4. The abbreviations for interlinear glosses are the following: ADV – adversative; AFF – affirmative; ALL – allative; AN – anaphoric; CONT – continuative (aspect); HYP – hypothetic (mood); IMP – imperative (mood); LOC – locative; PASTNEG – negative past; REL – relational; RFL – reflexive.

5. This is a direct extract from our Shoebox file where each line is preceded by a code: \trs – orthographic transcription; \te – English translation; \ntl – linguistic notes; \ntc – cultural notes.
6. Map not included here.
7. Maps not included here.
8. Compare, for example, Chafe and Nichols 1986; Basso 1987, 1988, 1995; Silverstein 1993. See also Franchetto 2005.
9. On parallelism see, among other authors: Jakobson 1960, 1966, 1968, 1973; Lord 1985; Zumthor 1983; Tedlock 1983; Fox 1998; Finnegan 1992; Hymes 1992; Sherzer 1990; Urban 1991; Monod-Becquelin 1987.
10. The abbreviations for interlinear glosses are the following: CMPL – completive (aspectual particle); DETR – detransitivizer; ERG – ergative; id – ideophone; PNCT – punctual (aspect); RFL – reflexive.
11. The example is taken directly from the Kuikuro lexical database in Shoebox where the following line codes are used: \lx – lexeme (main entry); \entyp – entry type; \lc – citation form; \ph – phonetic transcription; \ps – part-of-speech; \ge – English gloss; \xkk – example in Kuikuro; \te – English translation of the example; \defkk – original definition in Kuikuro; \defe – English translation of the Kuikuro definition; \cf – cross-references.

Appendix 1: Kuikuro terms for consanguineal basic kin types

The tables below, extracted from the ethnographical component of the Kuikuro documentation, show the multiplicity of denotata of each term (Tables 1 and 2).*

Table 1. Kuikuro consanguineal kin terms (male ego)

Term	Denotata	English gloss
G+2		
ngaupügü	FF, MF	grandfather
ngitsü	MM, FM	grandmother
G+1		
uü	F, FB, FFB	father
ama, ata, isi	M, MZ	mother
ijogu	MB	maternal uncle
etsi, ipügü	FZ	paternal aunt
G0		
hisuügü	B, FBS, MZS	brother
hinhano	eB, FBeS, MZeS	older brother
hisü	yB, FByS, MZyS	younger brother
ingãdzu	Z, FBD, MZD	sister
hãü	MBCh, FZCh	cousin
G−1		
mugu	S, BS	son
indisü	D, BD	daughter
hatuü	ZS	nephew
hati	ZD	niece
G−2		
higü	SS, SD, DS, DD	grandson/-daughter

* The tables make use of the commonly used abbreviations for kin relations: F = father, FF = father's father, M = mother, Z = sister, B = brother, S = son, D = daughter, Ch = child, e = elder, y = younger, etc.

Table 2. Kuikuro consanguineal kin terms (female ego)

Term	Denotata	English gloss
G+2		
ngaupügü	FF, MF	grandfather
ngitsü	MM, FM	grandmother
G+1		
uü	F, FB, FFB	father
ama, ata, isi	M, MZ, MMZ	mother
sogu	MB	maternal uncle
etsi, ipügü	FZ	paternal aunt
G0		
hisuügü	B, FBS, MZS	brother
hasü	eZ, FBeD, MZeD	older sister
ikene	yZ, FByD, MZyD	younger sister
hisü	B, FBS, MZS	brother
hãü	MBCh, FZCh	cousin
G−1		
mukugu	S, ZS	son
indisü	D, ZD	daughter
hatuü	BS	nephew
hati	BD	niece
G−2		
higü	SS, SD, DS, DD	grandson/-daughter

The lexical entry of a kinship term in the lexical database should minimally be associated with the specification of the denotata and the sex of the speaker, as in the following examples:

```
\lx  uü        \gle father        \den  F, FB, FFB
\lx  ingãdzu  \gle sister        \den  Z, FBD, MZD
                                       <m.s. (= man speaking)>
\lx  hasü      \gle older sister  \den  eZ, FBeD, MZeD
                                       <w.s. (= woman speaking)>
```

Appendix 2

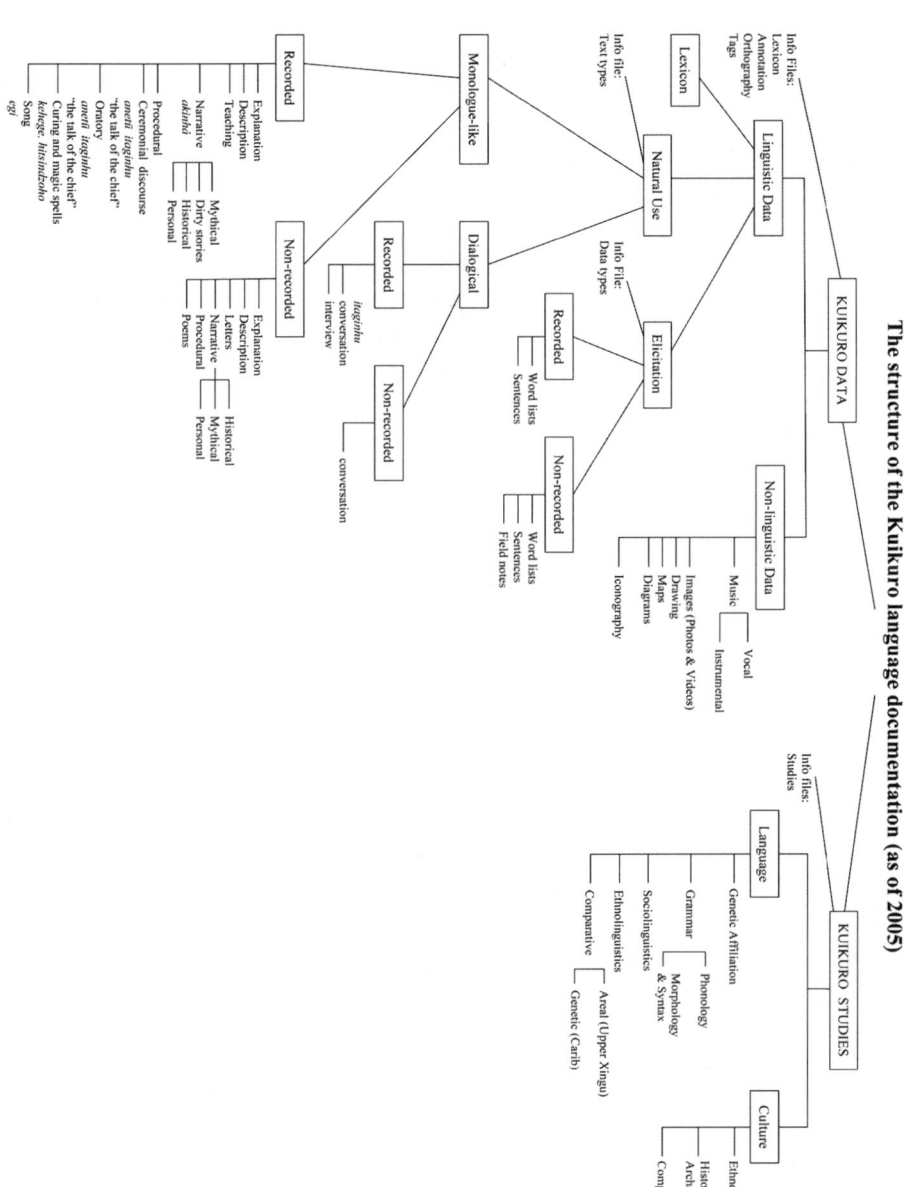

The structure of the Kuikuro language documentation (as of 2005)

Chapter 9

Linguistic annotation

Eva Schultze-Berndt

Introduction

This chapter is concerned with linguistic annotation of a documented communicative event, i.e. the annotation of its linguistic aspects – which is, at the same time, the type of annotation that is likely to be produced by, and to be of interest to, linguists. Following Bird and Liberman (2001), the term **annotation** will be used here as a cover term for all types of information (including transcriptions) that can be related to the recording of a communicative event, or that may represent aspects of a communicative event for which no recording exists. Apart from linguistic annotation, there is also a type of annotation relating to the cultural norms and practices of the speech community that form the background of a given communicative event. This type of annotation is discussed in Chapter 8. It goes without saying that especially in the area of semantics and translation (see Section 3), linguistic and ethnographic commentary overlap.

Linguistic annotation can also be distinguished from metadata or "header" information – comprising information about the language used, the time and place of the recordings, the participants including the documenter, access rights, and so on. Metadata are further discussed in Chapters 1, 4 and 13, and will not be considered any further here.

1. Basic assumptions

Let us first consider the significance of linguistic annotation for the enterprise of language documentation, in the sense in which this expression is being used throughout this volume. It should be obvious that what is documented is not "a language" but a selection of communicative events, where the communicating parties consider themselves as sharing a code or language.[1] For simplicity's sake and without an implication of homogeneity, people sharing a language will henceforth be referred to as a "speech community". The main motives for selecting certain communicative events for documentation include:

a) their accessibility to the documenter(s) – which is of course the condition for documentation,
b) their representativeness of communicative events conducted in the speech community – i.e. communicative events that are likely to take place even in the absence of any person documenting it, referred to as "observed communicative events" by Himmelmann (1998),
c) their representativeness of the structural possibilities of the language in question – this is the reason for including what Himmelmann (1998) terms "staged communicative events" and elicited utterances, elicited precisely for the purpose of elucidating some aspect of the structure of the language.

It is self-evident that the task of documenting a communicative event does not stop at simply recording it (by producing, e.g., an audio- or video-recording). Especially in the case of languages only spoken by a small group of people, such a recording would not be interpretable by the majority of people with a potential interest in the language – e.g. linguists, anthropologists, historians, or the general public. In the case of endangered languages, the recording would possibly not even be interpretable to the descendants of the speakers themselves. Therefore, a recording has to be accompanied by further information, in a format that is accessible to a wider, possibly non-specialist, audience.

For simplicity's sake, I have assumed above, and will assume in most of what follows, that the communicative event in question was spoken rather than written, that it has been captured in audio or video format, and that the annotation can indeed be related to segments of that recording. The segmentation of the recording session into smaller units – such as turns, sentences, clauses, or intonation units – as "minimal units" for the purposes of annotation, is presupposed here. Segmentation, by no means a trivial issue, is discussed in detail in the Chapter 10. It is recommended practice that the basis for segmentation is made explicit in the documentation and that, in the written transcription, intermediate units (often referred to as intonation units) are each represented on a separate line.

It is important to remember that even an audio- or video-recording is just a representation of the original communicative event – albeit an iconic (or analog) representation that preserves a great deal, but by no means all, aspects of the original communicative situation (cf. Duranti 1997: 114; Lehmann 2004b: 182, 205). Even a video recording preserves only auditory and visual information (restricted by the camera angle), but not, for example, the smell or temperature to which the original participants were subjected. Nevertheless, within the context of a language documentation, such audio- or video-recordings can be regarded as the primary data which form the basis for further annotation. Representations, e.g., of a pitch contour or amplitude, as produced by acoustic analysis, can be considered as further, derived iconic representations – these are not part of linguistic annotation proper since they can be derived at any time if the original recording is preserved, and will not be discussed any further in this chapter.

This chapter deals with three main levels of linguistic annotation. The first level, discussed under the heading of "transcription" (Section 2), comprises various types of symbolic representations of the formal or *significans* side of the linguistic expressions used in a communicative event (cf. Lehmann 2004: 205–206). The second level, termed "translation" here (Section 3), comprises any type of annotation that attempts to capture, in terms of one or more metalanguages, the *significatum* side (i.e. the meaning and function) of the communicative event. The third level, dealt with in Section 4 ("grammatical annotation"), comprises all annotation related to structural aspects of complex signs. In two further sections, I consider two further types of annotation that can in principle relate to any of the three levels mentioned above. The first of these can be termed the level of "meta-commentaries", i.e. commentaries on aspects of the annotation, for example, on its reliability (Section 5). The second type is cross-referencing (Section 6), i.e. the linking of representations of different communicative events.

It is by no means a trivial task to derive annotations comprising the different types of representations just mentioned from the "raw data" – as has already been pointed out, for the case of transcriptions at least, by Ochs (1979) in her seminal article on "Transcription as Theory". On the one hand, the representations reduce the information present in the recording, e.g. in the case of a written representation of a speech event. On the other hand, representations also enrich it, in that they incorporate an analysis of different aspects of the code underlying the communicative event, e.g. a phonological analysis (in the case of a phonological transcription), a semantic analysis – however preliminary – in the case of glossing and translation, and a grammatical analysis in the case of grammatical annotation. The interaction of annotation – as one aspect of documentation – and linguistic description and analysis will therefore be a constant theme throughout this chapter (see also Chapters 1 and 12).

For each of the main types of annotation and their subtypes, I will provide some evaluation of their potential usefulness (for different users) in language documentation, as well as pointing out existing and possibly competing conventions. Illustrations will come partly from my own annotated corpora of Jaminjung and Ngaliwurru, two closely related varieties belonging to the Northern Australian Mirndi family, one of the Non-Pama-Nyungan language groups. I will however refrain from recommending a single annotation format, since the aims and means of each documentation project will be different. Generally, in line with the scope of this volume, only those annotation formats are considered here which appear to be suitable in the actual context of the documentation of a lesser-used language. The issues arising in this context are clearly different from annotation issues for corpora of major languages, intended e.g. for research on speech recognition, speech synthesis, or discourse analysis, such as those distributed by the Linguistic Data Consortium (LDC). Only spoken language is considered here; issues of the transcription of sign languages are beyond the scope of this chapter and beyond my expertise, although much of what is said below about translation and grammatical annotation and other types of commentary will be equally applicable to the documentation of signed languages.

In language documentation, each project will have to find a balance between completeness of annotation on the one hand, and on the other hand, the time and effort involved in producing annotations, which is easily underestimated. The estimates for the time needed for the full annotation of one minute of recording vary between 1 hour and 150 hours. The differences in these estimates are essentially due to the level of detail and scrutiny that is applied to the annotation. The estimates at the higher end typically come from phoneticians who have in mind a very detailed, segment-by-segment annotation which requires listening to the recording over and over again. It will be useful to keep these figures in mind when deciding on the basics of the annotation scheme to be used within a documentation project. Taking only the level of transcription as an example, there is not much use in providing a large amount of very sloppy and superficial transcripts where lots of segments are missing or wrongly transcribed and which, even with the recording at hand, are difficult to interpret. On the other hand, the more features one includes in a transcript, the longer the transcription process takes, the more mistakes can be made and the less of the recorded materials gets transcribed. Practicability will thus be a recurring theme in the discussion of different types of annotation below. It is assumed that certain types of annotation (e.g. a detailed prosodic annotation or grammatical annotation) will usually only be undertaken by someone with a certain analytical goal in mind. For this reason, the recommendations given here differ from any recommendations made with maximal explicitness and consistency in mind, such as those outlined by Lieb and Drude (2000).

Readability and relevance for potential users should also be considered in deciding on an annotation format, since from the perspective of a user, too, an annotation burdened with too much detail – even if there are technical solutions for displaying only selected aspects of the annotation – can be cumbersome rather than helpful (an impressive demonstration of the effect of increasing detail in a transcription on readability is provided by Duranti [1997: 122–161]).

Another important point to remember is that "language documentation is an inherently ongoing process" and that annotations may be produced or corrected "multiple times by one or multiple authors" (Holton 2003: 6; cf. also Edwards 2001: 322). It is thus quite possible that, for example, an annotation consisting of a transcription in a practical orthography and a translation will be supplemented, many years later, with a prosodic annotation by a research project on prosody, and with grammatical annotation by someone working on a reference grammar of the language.

A few more notes on some basic assumptions are in order here. First, I assume that the linguistic annotation will be produced in machine-readable format or is at least convertible into machine-readable format. As a consequence, only symbolic types of annotation are considered, ruling out, for example, iconic representations of fundamental frequency (pitch contours; see Section 2.4 on prosodic annotation).

A further assumption made here is that the annotation itself will be in multi-tier or interlinear format (Edwards 2001: 327). This means that annotation of different types is displayed in different "fields" or "tiers" (e.g. phonetic transcription, orthographic transcription, interlinear gloss, translation) which represent different aspects of the same section of speech. The tiers themselves obviously have to be labelled according to the type of annotation they represent. An illustration of the use of labelled tiers is provided in example (1). The conventions employed here and in subsequent examples follow the format employed by Shoebox/Toolbox, one of the most widely used databases for linguistic analysis. The type of annotation is indicated by a label consisting of a backslash and a few letters chosen for their mnemonic value, separated by a space from the actual annotation. For example, the label \ref stands for the reference ID which serves to uniquely identify each line of the transcript, in this example, incorporating information about the year of the recording, the tape number, the section of the tape, and the line of the transcript.[2] The label \sp precedes the initials of the speaker (see further Section 2.6), the label \orth stands for an orthographic transcription, and the label \ft marks the free translation (all labels used in this chapter are included in the list of abbreviations at the end of this chapter).

(1)   Illustration of multi-tiered annotation (Jaminjung example[3])

> \ref   1999_A03_01.034
> \sp   IP
> \orth   malarabiya dibard ganunyngungam, bangawu
> \ft   the frog now is jumping away from the two, look

Again for simplicity's sake I will further assume, throughout most of the chapter, that all types of annotation in a multi-tiered format are aligned with (i.e. refer to) the same segment of audio- or video-data (and, in fact, may be linked to that segment via time codes; cf. also Edwards 2001: 328). Cases of non-alignment will be discussed in the sections dealing with overlap (Section 2.6) and with the alignment of free translation and contextual commentary (Sections 3.2 and 3.3). In addition, I will argue that annotation may also take the form of cross-reference between data sets (Section 6).

Annotation proper has to be distinguished from "markup" (cf. Edwards 2001: 322), the standardized representation of the structure and format of a text for the purpose of exchange of digitally encoded text. The current standard for markup is XML. In this chapter, I am mainly concerned with the content and structure of the annotation and not with aspects of markup or technical implementation. Aspects of technical implementation other than markup include:

– the linking of corresponding elements on different tiers, e.g., via indices or time codes (cf. also Edwards 2001: 328);
– flexibility in displaying the full annotation or hiding parts of the annotation irrelevant to the task or output at hand;
– conversion into other formats, including printable output;
– the use of characters (the current standard being Unicode compatible fonts).

There exists an ever-growing body of literature on those technical aspects (cf., e.g., Bird and Liberman 2001; Bow, Hughes, and Bird 2003; see also Chapters 4, 13, and 14 for discussion and references). For an overview of software employed in various projects as well as current encoding standards, see also Edwards (2001: 337–338, 342–343). Suggestions for annotations – including prosodic and paralinguistic annotations – in an XML-compatible format have been developed by the Text Encoding Initiative (TEI). For the latest version of the TEI recommendations, see TEI Consortium (2005) (especially Ch. 10, "Transcriptions of Speech").

2. Transcription

The label "transcription" is used here to refer to any symbolic representation of the *significans* side of documented speech events. As has already been indicated above, no transcript can be regarded as a direct, unbiased representation of a communicative event – it is by necessity filtered and influenced by the annotator's decisions, usually according to his or her "theoretical goals and definitions" (Ochs 1979: 44; Edwards 2001: 321).

Types of transcription that will be considered below are orthographic, phonemic, and phonetic transcriptions of segmental information, and transcription of prosody and of paralinguistic and non-linguistic phenomena. To these is added a section of a more general nature dealing with the representation of multi-speaker and multilingual discourse.

The issue of transcription does not arise for genuine cases of written communicative events that may be included in the documentation, such as newspaper articles, letters, or graffiti in the documented language. Written communicative events usually employ an orthographic representation (which may or may not be standardized; in the latter case, a rendition in standardized orthography could be added to the documentation). In terms of annotation other than transcription, written communicative events can be treated just like spoken communicative events.

In the process of language documentation, it will quite often happen that a spoken communicative event is not recorded, but written down at the time of speaking or immediately afterwards, e.g. overheard utterances or elicitations that were not deemed interesting enough to be recorded. The transcription of unrecorded utterances will usually be in the same format that is chosen for the transcription of recorded utterances – e.g. a phonetic transcription in the early stages of the documentation process, or an orthographic or phonemic transcription, possibly in addition to the phonetic one, or even a rudimentary rendition of the most salient prosodic features of the utterance (see Section 2.4). However, except in exceptional cases of annotators with very good phonetic memory, transcriptions of unrecorded utterances will include less information than transcriptions of recorded utterances, and have to be considered less trustworthy.

In the case that a recording is present, it is recommended that the transcription – whether on the orthographic, phonemic, or phonetic level – should represent as faithfully as possible what is being said. This includes so-called filled pauses, false starts and self-repair (see (18) for an example), and repetitions. It is also recommended that a stretch of speech which is not transcribed because it is not intelligible to the transcriber is marked in the transcript – a common convention is to use the letter 'x' for each unintelligible syllable. If a publication of some of the data is intended, speakers – understandably – often prefer an edited version which does not include such features, but which comes closer to a version in written rather than oral style (see, e.g., Mosel 2004b). If at all possible (i.e. acceptable to the speech community), such an edited version should not replace the original transcript, but either be added in the form of a further transcription tier or (especially in the case of heavy editing) be treated as a separate communicative event, linked to the original by cross-referencing (see Section 6). Likewise, independent transcriptions by native speakers, especially those with little training in linguistic conventions, could be treated as primary data and linked to a "standardized" version of the transcript. For further discussion of these points, see also Chapter 10.

2.1. Orthographic transcription

If an orthography for the language under investigation is already established and accepted by the speech community, it is virtually an obligation for a documentary linguist to provide an orthographic transcription as part of the annotation, since this greatly adds to the accessibility of the documentation for the members of the speech community themselves. This is why orthographic transcription is discussed first in this section.

In the case where no established orthography exists, or where an existing orthography is not acceptable to the current speech community for one reason or another, the documenter(s) will often be involved in devising a new orthography. The principles, decisions, and potential problems involved in this process are discussed in Chapter 11.

Two outcomes of the process of devising an orthography are of immediate relevance for the linguistic annotation. One concerns the faithfulness of the orthography to the phonological system. If the established orthography is not transparent, especially if phonemic contrasts are under-represented in the orthography, it is necessary to provide a phonemic transcription of the type discussed in Section 2.2 as well as an orthographic transcription. If the practical orthography is transparent, i.e. if it renders all distinctive segments and (if relevant) tones of the language, there is in fact no need for a phonemic transcription. It is, however, indispensable that the relationship between graphemes and phonemes is described in the grammatical sketch or the general information accompanying the documentation, e.g. in the format illustrated in (2) for some of the orthographic conventions employed in Jaminjung examples throughout this chapter.

(2) Some orthographic conventions for Jaminjung and Ngaliwurru (preliminary orthography)

    <r>   retroflex approximant /ɻ/
    <y>   palatal glide /j/
    <rd>   retroflex stop /ɖ/
               (voiced in word-medial and voiceless in word-final position)
    <ny>   palatal nasal /ɲ/
    <ng>   velar nasal /ŋ/

The second relevant question concerns the script. If the script employed in writing the language is a non-Roman script, then it is advisable, with general accessibility in mind, to provide a transliteration (i.e. a character-by-character rendition) in Roman script. Again, the conventions of transliteration will have to be stated explicitly as part of the general information provided with the language documentation. Strictly speaking, this is not necessary if a phonemic transcription in Roman script is provided, but it has to be kept in mind that the transliteration as an orthographic representation is not necessarily phonemic. For example, in Modern Greek, the letters <η> and <ι> both represent the phoneme /i/; they will therefore be distinguished in a transliteration but not in a phonemic transcription.

    The question of whether to use an orthographic transcription at all arises if the speech community does not appear to have an interest in an orthography. In this case the documenters may decide to use a phonemic transcription only. Where a transcription renders all the phonological contrasts of a language but deviates from the convention of using IPA symbols, the documenters have in effect devised a preliminary orthography that may well constitute the basis for the development of an accepted orthography later on. In actual practice, this will often be adapted from orthographies used by other speech communities in the region, or by linguists in descriptions of neighboring languages.

2.2. Phonemic transcription

A phonemic transcription is one that represents only the distinctive sounds and possibly tones of a language, i.e. those that potentially make a difference in the meaning of a word or morpheme. Therefore, the use of a phonemic transcription presupposes at least a preliminary phonological analysis of the language (and the phonemic transcription may have to be revised repeatedly in line with revisions of the phonological analysis). Procedures for working out the distinctive sound features of a language (for example, by establishing minimal pairs) are stated in all good introductory textbooks on phonology and will not be repeated here (for an example of the distinction between the phonetic and the phonemic level, see (4) in Section 2.3). The symbols used in a phonemic transcription are often based on one of the conventions for phonetic transcription discussed in Section 2.3.

A phonemic transcription (just like an orthographic transcription), moreover, includes word boundaries (indicated by spaces). In a strictly phonemic transcription, these would indeed have to be phonological words rather than grammatical words. In principle, the recognition of phonological words presupposes a phonotactic and (partial) prosodic analysis. Although word boundaries are not easily recognized in connected speech, in the actual practice of linguistic fieldwork the integrity of a lexical word is fairly easily established in most cases – words are those units that can be uttered and often also translated in isolation by native speakers. The analysis and hence representation of clitics and function words can create notorious problems, though (see Chapter 10).

A phonemic or orthographic representation should also be used in creating a lexical entry for each morpheme in the lexical database. In this way, the process of morpheme-by-morpheme gloss can be automatized (see further Section 4.1).

2.3. Phonetic transcription

We now turn to the question of whether to include a phonetic transcription in the annotations used in language documentation. A phonetic transcription is one that attempts to represent the articulatory characteristics of perceived segments as well as possibly some suprasegmental characteristics on the lexical level such as word stress and tone (for other suprasegmental characteristics, see Section 2.4), without embodying a decision as to which of these characteristics are distinctive (as in a phonemic transcription).

The most widely employed standard for segmental and tonal phonetic transcription is the IPA alphabet (devised by the International Phonetic Association), which is based on the Roman alphabet but includes many special symbols. Americanists have been using a somewhat different phonetic alphabet involving diacritics such as those employed in standard orthographies of several European languages. A good overview of the phonetic symbols used in both traditions is provided by Pullum and Ladusaw (1996).

Although with the advent of Unicode, the use of special phonetic fonts has become less of a problem for the exchange and archiving of data, the process of phonetic transcription using a standard keyboard may still prove cumbersome. The SAMPA system (Speech Assessment Methods Phonetic Alphabet) has been devised to overcome this problem, as it relies solely on characters available on a standard keyboard, e.g. by making use of capital letters and digits. For an overview of this system, see Wells et al. (1992), Wells (1997), and the online description provided by Wells (2004). As an example, consider the following phonetic transcription of two German words in both the IPA and SAMPA systems, following Gibbon (1995) and Wells (2004).

(3)   Phonetic transcription using IPA and SAMPA symbols (German)

\phonet_ipa   'pyŋkt.lıç
\phonet_sampa   'pYNkt.lIC
\orth   pünktlich
\ft   punctual

\phonet_ipa   'ʃø.nə
\phonet_sampa   'S2:.n@
\orth   schöne
\ft   beautiful (F)

Some training in the basics of phonetics and phonetic transcription can be considered essential for anybody undertaking a language documentation. Since a phonetic transcription can be undertaken without prior phonological analysis, it is often the type of transcription used in the initial stages of linguistic fieldwork. However, as all but the most phonetically gifted fieldworkers will probably confirm, these initial transcriptions are likely to be unreliable and should not be included in the annotations, or used as the sole basis for a phonemic or orthographic transcription, without subsequent checking.

Once a phonological analysis has been undertaken, it is strictly speaking not necessary to include a phonetic transcription if the original recording is provided together with the annotation. However there are several good reasons for providing a phonetic transcription for at least part of the corpus. Depending on the place of a phonetic transcription in the language documentation project at hand, the phonetic transcription employed will be "broad" or "narrow". These terms really describe a continuum with a phonemic transcription at the "broad" end, and a phonetic transcription including as much detail as possible on the "narrow" end. A fairly broad phonetic transcription of at least part of the text corpus can be used to provide information on allophones, i.e. the realization of phonemes in different phonological environments. The distribution of voiced and voiceless stops in Jaminjung may serve as a simple example. Voicing is not distinctive in Jaminjung, since voiceless and voiced stops are in complementary distribution: As in many other Australian languages, stops are always voiceless word-finally, but always voiced word-initially and medially. In the phonemic transcription illustrated in (4), only the symbols for voiced stops are employed. In an allophonic phonetic transcription, the last /g/ would have to be rendered by the symbol for the voiceless velar stop, [k]. Similarly, the second /u/ in the phonemic transcription is replaced, in the broad phonetic transcription, with the symbol for the centralized allophone which occurs in unstressed syllables, [ʊ].

(4)   Illustration of phonemic and broad phonetic transcription
       (Jaminjung example)

       \phonem   gugug
       \phonet   'gugʊk
       \ft   'in the water' (water-LOCATIVE)

Allophonic realizations like those illustrated above should be described in a grammatical sketch accompanying the language documentation (see Chapter 12). An allophonic transcription is therefore not absolutely necessary, although it can provide users of the documentation (provided they have the appropriate training) with a quick illustration of the basic allophonic principles.

For some language documenters, a phonetic analysis of the language will be one of their research goals. In this case, a narrow phonetic transcription of some parts of the textual corpus will prove crucial, but will have to be supplemented with carefully elicited materials for instrumental analysis of articulatory and acoustic characteristics of the speech sounds. Maddieson (2001) and Ladefoged (2003) are good introductory texts to phonetic analysis in fieldwork conditions. An overview of the sound systems likely to be encountered in the world's languages and their phonetic characteristics is provided by Ladefoged and Maddieson (1996).

Another possible use for a phonetic transcription tier is a faithful rendition of variation in pronunciation which may turn out to have relevance for the description of sociolects or dialects, allegro forms (fast speech forms), or forms otherwise noteworthy or deviating in pronunciation from forms used in careful speech. For example, in the common German allegro form given in (5), the nasals are assimilated in their place of articulation to the following and previous consonants, respectively, and the reduced vowel of the last syllable is replaced by a syllabic nasal.

(5)   Differentiating allegro forms and standard forms in phonetic and phonemic tier (German)

        \phonet   ʔaŋgeːbm̩
        \phonem   angebən
        \ft   indicate(INF) (or: boast(INF))

There is a good reason for both representing the actual pronunciation, e.g. in the phonetic tier, and the "standard" or careful speech form in the orthographic or phonemic tier as in (5), as the latter greatly facilitates searches for this word form. If a phonetic representation is used, it makes sense to be consistent in the level of detail (i.e. consistently use a narrower or broader transcription, cf. Rischel [1987: 62–65]) and to indicate this in the general explication of the transcription conventions.

2.4. Prosodic annotation

By prosodic transcription we mean the representation of non-lexical suprasegmental characteristics of the speech signal (as opposed to lexical characteristics such as word stress and lexical tone). Suprasegmental information that might be represented in a transcription includes the following characteristics (following Llisteri 1996):

- pitch movements, pitch direction or pitch contour, both local and global, some of them indicating prosodic boundaries;
- accent at phrase level;
- lengthening (beyond lengthening that is distinctive on a segmental level);
- pauses and pause length.

Whereas an orthographic or phonemic transcription is essential for any language documentation, and there are good reasons to include a (broad) segmental phonetic transcription with at least a part of the annotation, the relevance of a prosodic transcription seems less obvious. To be sure, prosodic information is often crucial for the analysis of the phrase structure as well as the information structure of spoken language (as there is no punctuation in spoken language!). However, prosodic transcription is very time-consuming and it is more difficult (and much less common) to undertake a prosodic analysis of a language than to arrive at a segmental phonemic analysis, and hence to produce a prosodic transcription capturing only the distinctive aspects. Moreover, there is no standard transcription system for prosody even on the "phonetic" level comparable to the IPA system for segmental phonetic transcription.[4] It is therefore to be expected that people involved in annotation and documentation will only add a prosodic transcription if one of their goals is a prosodic analysis.

Many of the transcription systems for prosody that have been developed in modern linguistics are not compatible with the demands of machine-readable annotation. A few of those that are compatible will be introduced very briefly below. One important issue that one has to address in the case of prosodic transcription is whether this will be superimposed on a segmental transcription in one of the formats described above (e.g. the orthographic or the phonetic transcription), or whether suprasegmental characteristics will be annotated in a tier that does not include information on segmental characteristics. The latter option facilitates searches for prosodic patterns, but necessitates some link between the units on the segmental and the suprasegmental tier (e.g. via time codes).

The various prosodic transcription conventions employed in linguistic discourse analysis are all examples of prosodic annotation superimposed on the segmental – usually orthographic – annotation. The annotation systems described in DuBois et al. (1993), Ochs, Schegloff, and Thompson (1996), Selting et al. (1998), and Couper-Kuhlen (2001), and also those employed in the CHAT conventions (see McWhinney 1991 and the CHAT website) and the TEI conventions, all belong to this type. Many of them share features such as:

- the use of capital letters or diacritics for accented syllables;
- the use of punctuation marks for boundary intonation, e.g. period (.) for falling intonation and question mark (?) for rising intonation;[5]
- the use of arrows for salient changes of pitch.

An advantage of the discourse analysis formats is that they have been developed for an annotation on the phonetic level which can be undertaken prior to decisions regarding the prosodic analysis. Moreover, just as with segmental phonetic annotation, the transcription can be more or less detailed (i.e. broader or narrower). An example of a fairly broad prosodic transcription in this tradition is provided in (6). Phrasal accent is represented by capitalizing the accented syllable; the semicolon indicates non-final boundary intonation (slightly falling or level), the slash and backslash, rising and falling boundary intonation, respectively, and the equals sign, interlacing of intonation units without a pause. This type of prosodic annotation – indicating only phrasal accent and boundary intonation – is relatively easy to produce and can be very helpful for an assessment of the syntactic structure of the units in question. Pause measurements are also provided in this example, but since these are very time-consuming, this practice is not necessarily recommended for a general-purpose annotation.

(6) Prosodic transcription in the discourse-analytic tradition (German example)[6]

\pros	wir ALbern im KORB; (0.8)
\pros	NEKken uns; (4.1)
\pros	SCHERzen / (=)
\pros	dass wir uns hinAUSschmeissen ; (=)
\pros	gegenseitig \
\ft	we laugh around in the basket, tease each other, joking that we will throw each other out
\cc	account of a balloon ride

Another transcription system that is explicitly designed with crosslinguistic applicability in mind (hence a system on the phonetic level) is INTSINT (INternational Transcription System for INTonation; see, e.g., Hirst and Di Cristo 1998; Hirst, Di Cristo, and Espesser 2000). In this system, absolute pitch with respect to the frequency range of the speaker can be indicated, as well as relative pitch at a turning point in the intonation contour and iterative relative pitch (upstep and downstep); the symbols used are either capital letters or different arrow symbols (Hirst and di Cristo 1998: 15). However, neither word level stress nor phrasal accent nor lengthening are explicitly marked. The advantage of this system is that the prosodic contour can be transcribed on a separate tier from the segmental transcript.

A system of prosodic annotation which is popular in prosodic research is called ToBI (Tones and Breaks Index), following from the work of Pierrehumbert (1980) and subsequent revisions (see, e.g., Silvermann et al. 1992). This system relies on the decomposition of prosodic contours in tones of two pitch levels, high (H) and low (L), which can be linked to stressed syllables and intonational phrase boundaries. The main problem with this system – from the point of view of language documentation – is that it presupposes a phonological analysis of the prosodic system in question. Prosodic annotation in ToBI style can therefore only be undertaken by annotators who are seriously concerned with the prosody of the language in question.

2.5. Transcription of paralinguistic and non-linguistic aspects of the interaction

In Sections 2.1 to 2.4, we have been concerned exclusively with the transcription of spoken language in the narrow sense, i.e. the linguistic component of speech events. As anybody with any experience with the transcription of natural (rather than read) speech knows, speech events have other features which are usually not captured by writing systems (even modified ones such as the IPA notation).

Following the classic paper by Trager (1958), non-linguistic aspects of speech events can be divided into paralanguage on the one hand, comprising voice quality and vocal events such as coughing, whistling, laughing, or the so-called "filled pauses", and non-vocal or kinesic events on the other hand. Non-vocal events, in turn, can be divided into speech-accompanying gestures and any other events that may occur during or in conjunction with a speech event, such as the slamming of a door – which may or may not have a communicative impact. Shifts or changes in vocal quality (e.g. whispering or shouting) or speech tempo are referred to as paralinguistic features since they cannot be separated from the linguistic features of the communicative event.

For some time, linguists involved in discourse analysis (including conversation analysis) have been aware of the importance of paralinguistic and non-linguistic aspects of communicative events, and have, accordingly, developed conventions for transcribing these. Just as for the transcription of prosody, many earlier systems are not compatible with the demands of digital processing (cf., e.g., Ehlich and Rehbein 1979; Halwachs 1994). Currently emerging standards tend to be based on transcription conventions where the transcription of paralinguistic and non-linguistic features is superimposed on a segmental transcription. Some examples of relatively recent, and fairly similar, suggestions resulting from this tradition can be found in Selting et al. (1998) and in the Appendix of Ochs, Schegloff, and Thompson (1996: 461–465), as well as in the conventions employed by CHAT and those recommended by the TEI (TEI Consortium 2005: esp. Ch. 10.1).

For the purposes of most language documentation projects, it will prove too time-consuming to produce a detailed transcription of non-linguistic and paralinguistic aspects of all documented speech events. However, some of these aspects can be transcribed relatively easily and can greatly facilitate the understanding of the interaction. These include hesitations and filled pauses (e.g. *uhm*), laughter (which can be represented by *L*), and significant changes of vocal quality, such as whispering. Non-linguistic events can often be considered part of the contextual information and may be described in the tier devoted to the contextual commentary (see Section 3.3).

While many paralinguistic and non-linguistic vocal events can be transcribed relatively easily, the transcription of gesture – although often a very important part of the interaction – is difficult and extremely time-consuming, and no standard transcription conventions exist. Obviously, the possibility of annotating gesture also depends on the availability of video recordings. For the purposes of a language documentation project not specifically devoted to the annotation of gesture, it is nevertheless recommended that gestures (mainly pointing gestures) accompanying deictic expressions are annotated and treated as contextual information (e.g. "speaker points to the top of the tree"); these can be noted during the event by an observant fieldworker even in the absence of a video recording.

2.6. Transcription of multi-speaker and multilingual discourse

So far, the examples of annotation given in this chapter were of a monological nature, i.e. they involved only one speaker. Naturally occurring
communicative events, however, are rarely monologues, but rather involve
at least two participants. It is fairly obvious that any annotation has to indicate changes of speaker (also termed "turns"). In transcripts of interactions
in discourse analysis frameworks, each turn starts on a new line and begins
with a representation of the speaker, e.g. by capital letters or initials, as
illustrated in (7).

(7)   Representation of multi-speaker discourse in the discourse-analytic
      tradition (DuBois et al. 1993: 49)

      A: now that we have the [side door] fixed,
      B: [That's kind of] –
      A: he could.
      B: Yeah,
      C: Yeah.

As also seen in this example, it is common to indicate overlapping speech,
which frequently occurs in multi-speaker discourse, by enclosing overlapping segments in angled brackets and arranging them in parallel with each
other. This works reasonably well in print, but is not easily transferred into
a machine-readable format. Furthermore, consistent marking of overlap can
be a very time consuming and difficult affair (see DuBois et al. 1993: 50–
52, for examples and discussion). For the purposes of providing a base
transcript in a language documentation, one may well leave this task to a
later user who is actually interested in analyzing the structure of conversational exchanges.

   In a multi-tiered annotation format, speaker information will appear in a
separate tier rather than being included with the transcript, as illustrated in
version (a) of example (8), and in (9) below. Alternatively, different labels
can be employed for transcript tiers of different speakers as shown in version (b) of example (8); this is the solution implemented in the CHAT and
ELAN annotation conventions.

(8)   Representation of multi-speaker discourse in a multi-tiered format
      (adapted from (7))

   a. \sp   A
      \orth   now that we have the [side door] fixed,
      \sp   B
      \orth   [That's kind of] –

   b. \orth_A   now that we have the [side door] fixed,
      \orth_B   [That's kind of] –

Presenting the utterances of different speakers on consecutive lines is the
most widely used, but not the only option of representing multiparty discourse. Alternatively, one could also arrange the utterances of different
speakers in different parallel columns (see Ochs 1979 for an example and
discussion), or present them like different voices in a musical score, i.e. in
blocks of parallel lines running across the full width of the page (see Ehlich
1993 for exemplification). The latter option is actually the one implemented
in time-linking software such as ELAN which provides the possibility to
link a segment of a transcript to the corresponding segment in the original
recording. In ELAN, participants are distinguished by different labels not
only for the transcript tiers, but also for all other annotation tiers that are
aligned with the transcript tier. The advantage of this type of notation is
that overlaps are easier to represent. The disadvantage is that in multi-party
interactions, the transcript becomes rather difficult to read.

   The interaction with a researcher who is not a member of the speech
community can be treated as a special type of multi-speaker discourse. This
implies that the researcher's part of the interaction also be documented (cf.
Samarin 1966: 125), even if this is done in a more cursory fashion. Documenting the researcher's questions and comments may help to uncover
misunderstandings and mistakes in the translation later on.

   An even more complicated annotation format is needed in the case –
which is the rule rather than the exception in the case of speakers of endangered languages – that speech events tend to be multilingual rather than
monolingual. Reserving one tier in a multi-tiered annotation format for the
language name will be sufficient if there is no code-switching within units.
In the latter case, however, some indication in the transcript itself is required (leaving aside the notorious problem of deciding between code-
switching and borrowing in this case). In example (9), the dominant language (or matrix language) for each intonation unit is indicated in a sepa-

rate tier; the languages involved are the Australian languages Ngarinyman –
the dominant language for speaker ER, Jaminjung – the dominant language
for speaker DB, and Kriol, an English-lexified creole which is the lingua
franca of the area and often features in utterance-internal code-switching. In
this example, Kriol insertions, being the "unmarked" case, are indicated by
angular brackets without any further marking (as in lines (9b) and (9c)),
whereas insertions in another language, as in line (9d), are marked by additional characters (here *Ng* for Ngarinyman).

(9)   Example of a multi-speaker and multilingual discourse

    a. \sp   ER
       \lg   Ngarinyman
       \mo   yanarnin=barnalu   gani::ny,
       \it   come:PST=1PL.EXCL   ??
       \ft   we came here
       \cc   account of work on cattle station when speakers were young

    b. \sp   ER
       \lg   Ngarinyman
       \mo   <wilbarra>-yawung,   mangarri-yawung \
       \it   wheelbarrow-PROPR   plant.food-PROPR
       \ft   with a wheelbarrow, with food

    c. \sp   DB
       \lg   Jaminjung
       \mo   <wilbarra>   ya gan-anthama!
       \it   wheelbarrow ?? 3SG.A:3SG.P-bring.IMPF
       \ft   she used to bring a wheelbarrow

    d. \sp   ER
       \lg   Kriol
       \mo   ya, gatta wilbarra   wi bin   pushim, <Ng mangarri>,
       \it   yes with wheelbarrow we AUX.PST push:TR plant.food
       \ft   yes, we pushed food with a wheelbarrow

3. Translation

A free translation of the transcribed speech events into a widely accessible
language is essential in the documentation of a less widely known language.
This is one feature that distinguishes language documentation as envisaged

in this volume from the compilation of corpora for widely spoken languages such as English or Japanese, for which often no translation is made available.

The first problem to be addressed in this context is the choice of the language(s) to be translated into (Section 3.1). Different styles of translation are discussed in Section 3.2, while in Section 3.3 it is argued that information on the non-linguistic context of the utterance should not be incorporated into the translation, but provided in a separate tier as contextual commentary. Morpheme-by-morpheme glosses (interlinear glosses), while obviously involving the process of translation, also involve morphological analysis and are intimately linked to other types of grammatical annotation; they are therefore treated together with these, in Section 4.1.

3.1. Metalanguage(s) used in glossing and translating

One major decision to be made in the process of translation in language documentation is the choice of the metalanguage(s) (or target languages) for the translation, keeping in mind the aim of making the documentation accessible to a varied group of users. Possibilities for the choice of a target language include the following:

- The second/dominant language(s) for speakers of the documented language – typically, but not always, also a regional lingua franca or an official state language;
- A language of official status in the country where the language documentation is undertaken, which could be one of the national language(s) or the language primarily used in education – e.g. Hindi in large parts of India, Indonesian in Sulawesi, Turkish in Turkey, and often a colonial language such as English in Nigeria or Spanish in Guatemala;
- A standard language in case of the documentation of nonstandard varieties or dialects of a language for which a written standard exists;
- The native or dominant language of the person undertaking the translation – e.g. Spanish in the case of a Mexican researcher with Spanish as the first language;
- The language of academic affiliation of the person undertaking the translation – e.g. French if the person in question undertakes language documentation as part of obtaining a degree at a French university;
- An academic *lingua franca* or "world language".

It is of course quite possible to combine translations into more than one language – although the cost in terms of the additional time involved in annotation is immediately obvious. Criteria for deciding between the different possibilities include, obviously, the abilities of the person undertaking the translation and/or the possibility of employing additional translators. A further essential criterion is the accessibility to members of the speech community and, importantly, their descendants who may not speak the documented language anymore. The most sensible (though somewhat ironic) choice in this case is a translation into the language that is most likely to be the target of language shift, generally the dominant regional language or an official language of the country in question. Often the institution funding the research will have requirements for the language of translation. If the funding comes from a regional institution, this is likely to be an official language of the country where the documentation is undertaken; for academic institutions outside this country, it is more likely to be the language of education used in that institution. Today it seems to be assumed by most academic advocators of language documentation that English should be at least one of the metalanguages employed not only for the translation, but also the other descriptive components of a language documentation, with the aim of making the documentation accessible to the international academic community.

3.2. Free translation

Translation is a skill (many will say, an art) which, if undertaken to professional standard, usually requires a lot of training, and is fraught with methodological problems. It seems highly unrealistic to burden documenters or annotators with the expectation that they ought to provide translations that meet the standards of professional literary or scientific translation. This is all the more so as the translation is often undertaken by someone who is not a member of the speech community and, moreover, is only just beginning to learn the language to be documented and to understand its structure as well as its cultural background. In addition, often a documenting linguist will translate into a language which is not his or her native language (e.g. English, Spanish, or Indonesian). Therefore, all users and potential users of language documentations should be discouraged in the strongest possible terms from using the free translations which are provided as part of the annotation as more than a clue to the meaning and analysis of the documented utterances.

Apart from the choice of language, one choice to be made in translating is the choice between a free translation and a more literal translation – although the boundaries are gradual and nothing much hinges on a consistent decision in this respect. A literal translation remains closer to the source language and is therefore more helpful in the understanding of the structure of the language, and less likely to be misleading. A free translation is idiomatic in the target language and therefore more readable especially for people fluent in this language. It may also be richer in that it incorporates the pragmatic effect of the original utterance, and in this respect, the translator has of course to be careful in order not to give a misleading impression of a pragmatic effect.

Of course it is possible to provide both a free and a literal translation, either in different labelled tiers or by adding, for example, the literal translation in brackets to the free translation. The first possibility is illustrated in (10); the free translation is labelled \ft and the literal translation \lit. This example illustrates the difficulty of translating the complex predicate consisting of the non-verbal element *dibard* 'jump' and the inflecting verb *-(ng)unga* 'leave' in Jaminjung. Note also that if an interlinear (morpheme-by-morpheme) translation is provided (see further Section 4.1), as in the line labelled \it in the following example, this in itself already provides an extremely "literal" kind of translation.

(10)   Interlinear, free, and literal translation (Jaminjung example)

\orth	malarabiya	dibard	ganunyngungam,	bangawu
\mo	malara=biya	dibard	ganuny-ngunga-m,	ba-ngawu
\it	frog=SEQ	jump	3SG.A:3DU.P-leave-PRS	IMP.SG-see
\ft	the frog now is jumping away from the two, look!			
\lit	the frog now is jump-leaving the two, look!			

If a free rather than a literal translation is chosen, a common practice is to provide a translation for larger units of segmentation such as paragraphs, as illustrated in (11), instead of translating each intonation unit. This, however, is only recommended if an interlinear translation is also provided, since otherwise it becomes too difficult to relate the translation to the transcript.

(11) Free translation relating to more than one intonation unit (Jaminjung
    example)

    a. \orth   a: ya:,   ngiyinthuni barrajjung ngayiny
       \mo   a: ya:,   ngiyinthu-ni barrajjung ngayiny
       \it   INTERJ INTERJ DEM-LOC   further   animal

    b. \orth   ganunyma   jarndang
       \mo   ganuny-ma   jarndang
       \it   3SG.A:3DU.P-hit.PST go.down.completely?

    c. \orth   gugubina
       \mo   gugu-bina
       \it   water-ALL

    d. \orth   wiribmijjung
       \mo   wirib-mij-jung
       \it   dog-COMIT=CLITIC
       \ft   ah yeah, this animal then pushed the two all the way down
               into the water, (the boy) together with the dog.

Example (11) above – again from a Jaminjung retelling of the Frog Story –
also illustrates two further issues in translating. The first is that a free translation, especially when the translation is that of a whole paragraph, tends to
assume the stylistic features of written as opposed to spoken language. This
is not a major issue if the translator is aware of it and if the translation is
regarded as an aid for the interpretation of the original utterance by later
users, not as a faithful rendition of the original. In special cases however,
e.g. when translating ritual speech events or verbal art, the translator may
well strive to represent aspects of the original discourse structure (for discussion of this issue, see e.g. Sammons and Sherzer 2000).

   The second issue is that of adding information not present in the original,
illustrated by the addition of the noun phrase *the boy* in brackets in the free
translation of (11), the omission of which would result in an ungrammatical
sentence in English. In Jaminjung, on the other hand, the information about
the referent is only indicated by the second person dual object prefix in line
(11b) and the comitative case in line (11d), together with the preceding
context. It is recommended that additional information of this kind is
marked by brackets or some other means, since this greatly helps later users
of the documentation to assess immediately where the translation deviates
from the original.

In addition to providing a more idiomatic as well as a more literal translation where appropriate, I have found it good practice to include the literal, rather than edited, version of any translation into a contact language provided by native speakers. (Alternatively, this can be done by cross-referencing – see Section 6 – if such translations are documented as communicative events in their own right.) In example (12) below, the translation into Kriol, labelled \ot, provides a much closer rendition of the Jaminjung utterance than the free English translation because it is basically a calque of the former: first, the causal interrogative expression *nganthan-nyunga* 'what-ORIG' is translated literally as 'what from' (the 'Origin' case, apart from acquiring a causal function, also functions as a marker of origin, as in 'the man from Bulla'). Second, the lexeme *mangarra* is translated as *taka* (< Engl. *tucker*); both Jaminjung *mangarra* and Kriol *taka* are generic terms used for any edible plant or food made from this plant. Thus, an original translation can often provide important cues to the structure of the original utterance.

(12) Original translation by a native speaker (Jaminjung example with Kriol translation)

\mo	nganthan-nyunga	nganth-unga-m	mangarra?
\it	what-ORIG	2SG.A:3SG.P-leave-PRS	plant.food
\ft	why are you leaving your food (rather than eating it up)?		
\ot	wat from yu livim taka		

3.3. Contextual commentary

During the process of translation for the purpose of annotating recorded speech events, the annotator should remember to add contextual information where it is crucial for an interpretation of the utterance by anybody who was not present during the original speech event. Relevant information of this kind may pertain to the entity, event, or "stimulus" referred to by the speaker, to the addressee and the intended pragmatic effect of the utterance, or to an action of the speaker or other participants accompanying the speech event. This information may overlap with, complement or partly replace a transcription of non-linguistic aspects of the interaction (see Section 2.5) and also overlap with ethnographic commentary, discussed in Chapter 8. Contextual information can consist of a prose description of the context, but also of links to photographs of some aspect of the speech situation (e.g. an artefact under discussion), or of stimuli used in elicitation.

Providing contextual information is particularly important when an utterance is not embedded in a longer text which would aid its interpretation. In example (13), again from Jaminjung, the tier labeled \cc provides the contextual information without which the utterance – even with the translation – could hardly be interpreted. In the case of transcribing an unrecorded, overheard utterance such as (13), it is important to immediately note as much detail as possible about the circumstances of the communicative event, since there is no recording to assist in the recovery of such information.

(13)   Contextual information about the event referred to
         (Jaminjung example)

       \mo   juwurlab   ga-rna-ya   ngayin
       \it   swell.up   3SG-burn-PRS   meat
       \ft   the meat is "swelling up" because of the heat
       \cc   tinned meat on the fire rising out of the can

Rather than in an additional tier, contextual information could be included with the free translation (see Section 3.2), e.g. (in the case of example (13)) 'the (tinned) meat is swelling up (i.e. rising out of the can) because of the heat (on the fire)'. While this saves space, it makes the translation less readable and obscures its relationship to the original utterance. It is therefore recommended to provide contextual information in a separate tier.

As in the case of the free translation, a contextual commentary will often relate to more than one line in the transcript (i.e. to more than one intonation unit). This can be represented in a straightforward manner if each tier is linked to a segment of a recording via time-codes; another method is to explicitly link a contextual commentary with the reference numbers (see example (1)) of several units.

4.   Grammatical annotation

4.1. Interlinear glossing

It has become standard practice in the linguistic literature to provide data from languages other than the most widely known languages in a three-tiered format: a (phonemic or orthographic) representation is combined with morpheme-by-morpheme glosses, commonly referred to as interlinear glosses, and a free translation. In an annotated corpus, it is also recommended practice to include interlinear glosses for all or at least part of the transcriptions. Done manually, interlinear glossing is very time-consuming; if, however, the text database is linked to a dictionary database listing individual morphemes, glossing can be done largely automatically by dictionary lookup, as implemented by the CLAN and Shoebox/Toolbox software.

Interlinear glossing involves the addition of two additional tiers. The first is derived from the phonemic or orthographic transcription tier, but with the addition of morpheme and clitic breaks which are standardly indicated by a hyphen and an equals sign, respectively; the second tier contains the morpheme-by-morpheme glosses. Some of the conventions employed in interlinear glossing (at least among linguists) are illustrated in the tiers labelled \mo and \it in (14), repeated from (10) above.

(14)   Illustration of interlinear glossing (Jaminjung example)

\orth	malarabiya	dibard	ganunyngungam,	bangawu
\mo	malara=biya	dibard	ganuny-ngunga-m,	ba-ngawu
\it	frog=SEQ	jump	3SG.A:3DU.P-leave-PRS	IMP.SG-see
\ft	the frog now is jumping away leaving the two, look!			

The most important conventions include:
- The use of corresponding boundary symbols (space, hyphen, equals sign) in both the morpheme break tier and the gloss tier;
- The use of lower case for glosses of lexical morphemes and of upper case (or rather, small capitals) for glosses of grammatical morphemes;
- The use of dots to separate the grammatical components of portmanteau morphemes in fusional languages (e.g. IMP.SG as the glossing for the single prefix *ba-* above), and of colons to separate glosses where a segmentation in the morpheme tier is possible in principle but not applied because of convenience, or because of unclarities in the exact position of the morpheme boundary (e.g. 3SG.A:3DU.P in example (14) – here the prefix *ganuny-* could be further segmented as *gan-uny-*, but since the boundary is not always clear with other transitive pronominal prefixes, I have chosen to generally gloss them in the format illustrated here);
- The consistent use of a single gloss as translation equivalent of any given morpheme, even though this may not be the closest translation equivalent in the free translation (for example, the verb *-ngawu-* is glossed as 'see' throughout my annotated corpus even though the closest

translation equivalent in examples such as (14) is 'look'). This not only avoids arbitrary decisions regarding the polysemy of a given morpheme, but also greatly facilitates automatic searches.[7]

For a more detailed discussion of these conventions, the reader is referred to the pinoneering paper on interlinear glossing by Lehmann (1983), the revised version (Lehmann 2005) as well as the versions published in König et al. (1994) and Bickel, Comrie, and Haspelmath (2004). These recommendations also include abbreviations for common grammatical morphemes. While the adherence to such standards facilitates the use of a documentation for linguists, it is more important that an explanation of all abbreviations used in the glossing is included with the documentation. Ideally, also, the function of all grammatical morphemes will be discussed in the sketch grammar accompanying the documentation (see Chapter 12).

Interlinear glossing presupposes that a morphological analysis and some degree of semantic analysis of the language has already been undertaken, since the indication of morpheme breaks involves a decision on what the smallest meaning-bearing units are, and the glosses provided for the grammatical and lexical morphemes – even if they are considered preliminary – involve some degree of grammatical and lexical semantic analysis, respectively. The principles of morphological segmentation are outlined in all textbooks on morphology, see e.g. Matthews (1991) or Haspelmath (2002), and will not be repeated here, with one exception: A problem frequently arises in the morphological segmentation of languages where morpheme boundaries tend to be blurred by morphophonemic processes. Apart from the use of colons as illustrated above, it is possible and often practiced in these cases to include the "underlying forms" of the morphemes in question in the morpheme tier, and use these as the basis for glossing, as illustrated in (15).[8]

(15)   The representation of underlying forms in the morphological tier
(Tagalog example, Nikolaus Himmelmann, p.c.)

\orth	mamulot	nung		manga	bunga
\mo	maN-pulot	noón=ng		mangá	bunga
\it	AV-pick_up	DIST.GEN=LK	PL		flower
\ft	(their means of living was) to pick fruit,				

One disadvantage of interlinear glossing as recommended by linguists is that it is often difficult to read for non-linguists. In some cases, the annotator may therefore opt for not glossing some grammatical morphemes, or for using the closest translation equivalent in the metalanguage for any grammatical morpheme where this is possible (for example 'me' instead of '1SG.ACC', 'for' instead of 'BEN' (benefactive) or 'now' instead of 'SEQ' as in example (14)). If employed consistently, glosses of this kind may still be converted by global change into standard linguistic interlinear glossing. A more radical departure from the principles of interlinear glossing is the glossing of whole word forms instead of morphemes, bordering onto a very literal translation (see Section 3.2). If glosses of this kind are expected to be of value to some potential users of the documentation, it is probably best to add them as a separate tier. This is illustrated in (14):

(16) Illustration of "non-linguistic" interlinear glossing
(Kwakw'ala example, from Boas 1911b: 554)[9]

\orth	lá:'lai	Gí:x̣dən
\mo	la:-'la-i	Gí:x̣dən
\it	go-RPRT-DIST	PN
\it2	then_it_is_said	Gixden

\orth	dəx'ʷuɬt'á:lis		la:q.
\mo	dəxʷ-u:ɬt'a-giɬ-i:s		la:-q
\it	jump-out_of_enclosed_space-MOTION-beach		go-3.OBJ
\it2	jumped_out_of_woods_on_beach		to_them

\ft	Then Gixden jumped out of the woods.

4.2. Grammatical tagging

The grammatical information provided by interlinear glossing is obviously limited: it does not show grammatical analysis of constituency or dependency for structures beyond word level. While the coding of this kind of information is often an important feature of published corpora of widely spoken languages, in the practice of language documentation it is only rarely attempted, first because of its time-consuming nature, second, because a grammatical analysis will only be developing in the course of the annotation. Some possibilities of adding grammatical information to the annotation are nevertheless mentioned here and in the following section on grammatical notes (Section 4.3). Any grammatical regularities that can be observed early on in the documentation process, such as (for many languages) word order, should be included in the grammatical sketch (see Chapter 13).

The type of grammatical information that is most often being provided in corpora of less widely spoken languages is that on the part-of-speech membership of individual morphemes or of word forms (as illustrated in the tiers labelled \ps_mo and \ps_w, respectively, in (17)). This is often referred to as "morphosyntactic tagging" in the corpus linguistics literature.

(17)   Part-of-speech tagging on morpheme and word level
       (Jaminjung example)

\mo	thanthu=biya	wajgany	wirib-ni..
\it	that=SEQ	sugarbag	dog-ERG
\ps_mo	dem=clitic	n	n-case
\ps_w	dem=clitic	n	n
\ft	that honey, the dog		

\mo	mu-mirrang	gani-ngayi-m=ngarndi
\it	FS- look.up	3SG.A:3SG.P-see-PRS=FOC
\ps_mo	pv	bpron-vtr-tense=clitic
\ps_w	pv	vinfl_tr
\ft	is looking up at it	

The tier indicating the part of speech category can be used to search for patterns of distribution and can therefore assist in grammatical analysis. Technically speaking, at least part of speech assignment on a morpheme-by-morpheme-basis can easily be done automatically in conjunction with automatic interlinear glossing, e.g. by the Shoebox/Toolbox software. It should always be borne in mind, however, that the assignment of parts of speech to lexical items in a language which has not been well described is by no means a trivial task and should not rely on semantic criteria (see, e.g., Schachter 1985; Sasse 1993; Broschart 1997; and references there). Unless the language under consideration has straightforward criteria for word-class assignment (usually morphological criteria, e.g. clearly different inflectional paradigms for the major parts of speech such as nouns and verbs), it is perhaps advisable not to add part-of-speech tagging until at a later stage in the documentation process.

A next possible step in grammatical annotation is the coding of constituency in the form of reduced tree diagrams (e.g. by bracketing). An illustration is provided in (18), where NP stands for noun phrase and CP for complex predicate, consisting of a preverb and an inflecting verb (there is no evidence for a verb phrase level including a noun phrase in Jaminjung).

(18)   Grammatical tagging of constituency (Jaminjung example)

\mo	thanthu=biya	wajgany	wirib-ni..
\it	that=SEQ	sugarbag	dog-ERG
\gr	[dem=clitic	n]NP	[n]NP
\ft	that honey, the dog		

\mo	mu-mirrang	gani-ngayi-m=ngarndi
\it	FS- look.up	3SG.A:3SG.P-see-PRS=FOC
\gr	[pv	vinfl_tr]CP
\ft	is looking up at it	

As pointed out above, this type of grammatical annotation presupposes a good understanding of the grammar, as well as the adherence to a particular model of constituency. Note also that it is rather difficult to change following a change in either the grammatical analysis or the model adopted, unlike a change in grammatical glosses or part of speech tags which can be done in a (semi-)automatic fashion. It is therefore not necessarily recommended for the purpose of language documentation and certainly should not be undertaken in the early stages of a documentation project.[10]

4.3. Grammatical notes

While a consistent annotation of grammatical structure will prove impractical for many if not most documentation projects, the annotator may well wish to highlight particularly good or relevant (or indeed, problematic) examples of certain constructions by adding keywords or even a more full-fledged commentary on the structure in question (see also Section 3.2 of Chapter 12). If keywords are used, it is advisable to apply these consistently (i.e. to employ a controlled vocabulary) in order to facilitate later searches; ideally, the items in the list will also be commented on in the sketch grammar, or at least in a glossary accompanying the documentation. Grammatical notes of this nature greatly aid the production of a sketch grammar and/or a comprehensive reference grammar, either by the original annotators or by later users of the documentation.

In the examples below, the tier labelled \grn contains grammatical notes of the nature discussed above. In (19), the description "case marking: ablative agent" is intended to alert the user to the (rare) phenomenon of agent marking with the ablative (rather than ergative) case. If the user had to rely on a search for "Ablative" (e.g. by looking for the gloss 'ABL'), one would have to go through at least 95% of examples where the ablative has its more common function of indicating a spatial source.

(19) Use of grammatical descriptors (Jaminjung example)

\mo	mugmug-ngunyi	ngayirr	gan-arra-m
\it	owl-ABL	peep	3SG.A:3SG.P-put-PRS
\ft	the owl is looking down at him		
\grn	case marking: ablative agent		

The use of a grammatical notes tier can be extended to "semantic notes", i.e. highlighting examples that are of particular relevance for the semantic description and lexicographic treatment of a given lexical item (see also Chapter 6). In some cases, like that illustrated in (20), this may border on ethnographic commentary, as discussed in Chapter 8.

(20) Use of grammatical descriptors for semantic description (Waima'a example, Waima'a DoBeS team)

\mo	tou	hile	**thunu**	la	udo-wai	gai/
\it	PTL	again	bake	at	rain	maybe
\ft	(let me know) when you again make a sacrifice for (calling) rain					
\grn	/thunu/ "bake" is also widely used for ceremonies and festivities of all kinds, including making a sacrifice or having a party. Malay *bakar* 'bake' is used in the same way in local usage.					

A tier dedicated to grammatical notes can further be used to document grammaticality judgments elicited by means of variations of the utterance in question, e.g. when the fieldworker deliberately changes the word order, case inflection, or other aspects of an attested utterance in order to ascertain whether this will or will not be accepted by native speakers. For example, in (21) the descriptor tier indicates that I have inquired about the possibility of using the verb -*inama* 'do with foot' in the context of closing a car door with one's foot (described using a different verb in the attested example) but that this was not accepted by the speaker whose initials are given in brackets.

(21)   Use of grammatical descriptors for grammaticality judgments (Jaminjung example)

\mo	jubard	gan-arra-m	wirlga-ni
\it	shut	3SG.A:3SG.P-put-PRS	foot-ERG/INSTR
\ft	she shuts it with her foot		
\cc	car door		
\grn	verb: * -*inama* 'do with foot' (JM)		

5. Metacommentaries (notes and questions)

In the actual practice of annotating a recorded speech event, the annotator
will often wish to add notes or "metacommentaries" on some aspects of the
annotation. Often, these will appear in the form of questions – e.g. when a
certain lexeme is expected on the basis of the translation and the context
but can only be imperfectly recognized in the acoustic signal, or when the
annotator is unsure of the contextual relevance of the utterance. Such questions may or may not be resolved in later stages of the annotation process.
Their inclusion in the annotation greatly helps the annotator(s) to systematically check for open questions at a later stage. If the problems cannot be
solved, the existence of a note to this effect also helps later users of the
documentation to interpret the annotation. In the most systematic annotation format imaginable, one would probably employ a separate "metacommentary" tier accompanying every single annotation tier. In actual practice
though, a single tier for such metacommentaries will be sufficient and more
practicable, since the target of the commentary is usually clear. In example
(22), both the note in the metacommentary tier (labelled \qu) and the question marks in the interlinear gloss (\it) and translation (\ft) tiers point to an
uncertainty in the transcription of the verb – the expected imperfective form
of the verb would be *ganngarnanyi,* but the transcribed form is *gannginyi.*

(22)   Use of metacommentary tier (Jaminjung example)

\mo	thanthiya=biya	gan-nginyi=yirrag
\it	DEM=SEQ	3SG.A-1.P-give?:IMPF?=1PL.EXCL.OBL
\ft	that one she gave to me (?)	
\qu	ganngarnanyi??	

Example (23) illustrates the use of a metacommentary tier for noting metalinguistic commentaries of speakers on an utterance. Strictly speaking, this

would not be necessary if the whole discussion had been recorded and transcribed (see also Section 6).

(23)   Metalinguistic information as metacommentary (Jaminjung example)

    \mo   ning   nga-jga-ny nganju
    \it   break.off 1SG-go-PST tendon
    \ft   I tore my tendon
    \qu   some dispute as to whether *ning* or *bag* 'break' was correct;
              MW said *ning* spontaneously but eventually agreed to *bag*

Notes may also include any commentary on an aspect of the recording that is not systematically incorporated into the annotation – for example, when prosodic information (see Section 2.4) is not generally transcribed but the annotator wishes to indicate that a particular word was spoken with extra high pitch.

6. Cross-referencing

One further type of annotation that can greatly enhance the value of a documentation is the use of cross-referencing. Cross-referencing can be employed to indicate the relationship between an original utterance and a metalinguistic comment related to this utterance, as may arise when a recording is played back to native speakers for clarification. This is illustrated in (24); the utterance in (24b) is the paraphrase given by a different speaker during playback of the recording of utterance (24a). Cross-referencing is achieved here by including the unique reference number of each utterance in the tier labeled \cf of the corresponding utterance (see also the extensive illustration of cross-referencing in Chapter 9).

(24)   Cross-referencing to the paraphrase of an utterance
     (Jaminjung examples)

    a. \ref   99_v01_06_756
       \sp   VP
       \mo   burnduma-ny=biya jirrama maja=yirram=in=ung
       \it   2DU:come-PST=SEQ two   thus=two=ERG=CLITIC
       \ft   the two (crocodiles) came now, both of them like that
       \cf   99_FN_433

b. \ref   99_FN_433
   \sp   IP
   \mo   burnduma-ny,   bunyju-bu-wa
   \it   2DU:come-PST   2DU.A:3SG.P-POT-bite
   \ft   the two (crocodiles) came, and were about to bite it (the dog)
   \cf   99_v01_06_756

The question of whether or not to include such metalinguistic communicative events in the documentation arises, in particular, when they involve a contact language, i.e. a language other than the language to be documented. If they are not included in the documentation, such original translations and discussions can instead be incorporated into the annotation in a separate tier, in the manner discussed in Section 3.2.

Cross-referencing can also be employed to link written, edited versions of an utterance or text to a transcription of the spoken version (cf. Mosel 2004b). Sometimes it may be preferable to provide a link between two annotated texts or sessions on the level of metadata rather than utterance-by-utterance (although both could be combined). Cross-referencing can further be employed to link utterances referring to the same event or referent, e.g. comments on the same picture or video scene.

One further use of cross-referencing is more akin to grammatical notes (see Section 4.3) in that it allows the annotator to link examples that display interesting contrasts in a grammatical or semantic feature, i.e. which constitute "syntactic minimal pairs" in some sense. In this case, it makes sense to combine cross-referencing with a comment in the grammatical notes tier, as illustrated in (25). The utterances in (25a) and (25b) are both from the same text (on hunting echidnas), by the same speaker. They contrast in two respects, first, the word order between the inflecting verb and the uninflected "preverb" (in both examples, *thawaya* 'eat'), and in the choice of the inflecting verb employed with this preverb.

(25) Use of cross-referencing between contrasting examples
      (Jaminjung example)

a. \ref   1997_a02_01_014
   \mo   ngalanymuwa   ga-ngga=mang   thawaya   muyu
   \it   echidna   3SG-go.PRS=SUBORD   eat   ant
   \ft   since the echidna eats ants
   \grn   word order, verb use
   \cf   1997_a02_01_023

b. \ref   1997_a02_01_023
   \mo   thawaya=biyang ga-yu=ndi
   \it   eat=SEQ   3SG-be=FOC
   \ft   … (and) is eating them now
   \grn   word order, verb use
   \cf   1997_a02_01_014

7. Summary

This chapter has provided an overview of the main types of linguistic annotation that may be employed in the documentation of a language which is
not widely spoken and that meet the demands of machine-readable and
multi-tiered annotation formats (see Section 1). As has been pointed out
repeatedly throughout the chapter, when deciding on an annotation format,
it is important to keep in mind that there is a trade-off between the amount
of information that is included and the time spent on the annotation, and that
some types of annotation can be added later by annotators with specialist
interests, provided a minimal annotation and the original recording are
available. The annotation format chosen should therefore be one that can be
implemented within the time frame and with the personnel available for the
project.

   As a rule of thumb, an annotation should serve to make the actual recording accessible to potential users including members of the speech
community, point to interesting aspects of the recorded speech event, and
serve the annotators' particular interests (if any). The minimal annotation
format to be recommended comprises at least an orthographic transcription
(Section 2.1), a free translation into one or more widely accessible languages (of which one should be accessible to members of the speech community under documentation; see Sections 3.1 and 3.2), and any contextual
commentary that is essential for an interpretation of the communicative
event in question by outsiders (Section 3.3). If a phonemic transcription
(Section 2.2) cannot be derived from the orthographic transcription, this
will have to be added as well. It is moreover essential that the annotation
format allows for an adequate representation of multi-speaker discourse,
and in many cases also multilingual discourse (Section 2.6). It is also recommended that rudimentary suprasegmental features such as the unit-final
prosodic contour or unusually high pitch, and paralinguistic and non-
linguistic features such as whispering, laughter, filled pauses, and pointing
gestures are included in the annotation (see Sections 2.4 and 2.5).

Less essential but potentially useful types of annotation are interlinear glossing (morpheme-by-morpheme translation; see Section 4.1), grammatical notes (Section 4.3), metacommentaries (e.g. commentaries on the reliability of some aspect of the annotation; Section 5), and cross-referencing between annotated utterances that are related or contrastive in content (Section 6).

More specialist types of annotation that will generally only be undertaken by people with specific research goals in mind are phonetic transcription (although a phonetic transcription of a small subset of the corpus is recommended; see Section 2.3), a narrow transcription of prosodic, paralinguistic, and non-linguistic features including gesture (Sections 2.4 and 2.5), and grammatical tagging (Section 4.2).

It is worth repeating here that every documentation should be accompanied by explicit statements of all conventions employed in transcription and glossing, such as the general annotation format, the orthography, symbols employed to represent prosodic and paralinguistic features, and any abbreviations. Conventions may of course change in the course of decisions made at later stages of the documentation project because of new insights, or in response to the wishes of the speech community. Care should therefore be taken to ensure consistency in the conventions employed, and their meticulous documentation.

Acknowledgements

For very valuable detailed comments on previous drafts of this chapter and further examples, I would like to thank Nikolaus Himmelmann and Ulrike Mosel.

Abbreviations

\cc	contextual information and comments tier	\it	interlinear glosses tier
\cf	cross-reference tier	\lg	language information tier
\ft	free translation tier	\lit	literal translation tier
\gr	grammatical analysis tier	\mo	morphological analysis tier
\grn	grammatical notes tier	\orth	orthographic transcription tier
		\ot	original translation tier

\phonem	phonemic transcription tier	GEN	genitive
\phonet	phonetic transcription tier	IMP	imperative
\pros	prosodic transcription tier	IMPF	imperfective
\ps	part of speech tier	INF	infinitive
\ps_mo	part of speech tier, morpheme level	INSTR	instrumental case
		INTERJ	interjection
\ps_w	part of speech tier, word level	LK	linker
		LOC	locative
\qu	question and meta-commentary tier	M	masculine
		N/n	noun
\ref	reference ID tier	NP	noun phrase
\sp	speaker information tier	OBJ	object
1, 2, 3	1st, 2nd, 3rd person	OBL	oblique case
A	Agent	ORIG	origin case
ABL	ablative case	P	Patient
ACC	accusative case	PL	plural
ALL	allative	PN	proper name
AUX	auxiliary	POT	potential mood
AV	actor voice	PROPR	proprietive ('having')
bpron	bound pronoun	PRS	present tense
COMIT	comitative	PST	past tense
CP	complex predicate	PTL	particle
DEM/dem	demonstrative	pv	"preverb" / "coverb"
DIST	distal demonstrative	RPRT	reportative (evidential)
DU	dual	SEQ	sequentiality marker
ERG	ergative case	SG	singular
EXCL	exclusive 1st person	SUBORD	subordinator
F	feminine	TR	transitive marker
FOC	focus marker	vinfl	inflected verb
FS	false start	vtr	transitive verb

Notes

1. This does of course not exclude the possibility that the communicating parties share more than one code, or that their knowledge of the other's code is only a passive one.
2. This tier is omitted in subsequent examples for reasons of space.
3. This example is from a Jaminjung version of the Frog Story based on a picture book by Mayer (1969); cf. Berman and Slobin (1994).
4. The IPA conventions only include symbols for a few suprasegmental charac-teristics such as word level stress and vowel length, superimposed on the seg-

mental level. Conventions for prosodic annotation – termed SAMPROSA – have also been developed as part of the SAMPA conventions (see Wells et al. 1992) but do not seem to have become a standard in prosodic annotation.

5. This use of punctuation marks does not correspond to their use in written language and therefore is potentially confusing to the inexperienced reader (and annotator). Alternatively, the slash (/) and the backslash symbols (\) may be used for rising and falling boundary intonation, respectively (see Edwards 2001: 325 and example (6)). Although it works well for the human reader, the use of capitals is also not the best solution with machine-readability in mind.

6. The example comes from the "Kölnkorpus", a corpus of colloquial spoken narratives recorded at the University of Cologne. The annotation is by Carmen Dawuda.

7. Homophonous morphemes should of course receive distinct glosses.

8. The use of underlying forms is also implemented in the *Shoebox/Toolbox* software.

9. I am grateful to Nikolaus Himmelmann for providing this example. Boas' phonetic spelling has been adapted to phonemic spelling; the annotations included in the tiers \it2 and \ft are by Boas, those in \mo and \it by Himmelmann.

10. Lieb and Drude (2000) provide a very detailed framework for grammatical annotation (including not only constituency but also dependency analysis); however, the authors themselves concede that an implementation of their framework is too time-consuming to actually put in practice for more than a fraction of the documented texts.

Chapter 10

The challenges of segmenting spoken language

Nikolaus P. Himmelmann

Introduction

The core of a language documentation as conceived of in this book consists of a corpus of audio or video recordings of more or less naturally occurring communicative events with annotations and commentary. As already discussed in Chapter 9, the most basic form of annotation is a transcription of the linguistic utterances contained in the recording. Transcriptions of spoken language involve a number of decisions regarding the representation of relevant features of the speech event (e.g. the question of whether to use a narrow phonetic transcription or a practical orthography to represent phonological segments). One major decision pertains to the units into which the continuous flow of spoken language is to be segmented.

There are four major segmentation levels for spoken language, two of which are dealt with at length in Chapter 9 and will not be further discussed here. These are (phonetic or phonological) segments and speaker turns, i.e. utterances produced by different speakers (see Sections 2.1–2.3 and 2.6 in Chapter 9, respectively). The present chapter is concerned with the following two segmentation issues:

1. a middle-sized transcription unit, delimited by empty spaces, which represents a basic unit in terms of meaning, grammatical function, or sound structure, typically a morphosyntactic or phonological word.
2. higher-level transcription units, indicated by various kinds of punctuation marks and by the spatial arrangement of larger units on a page (lines, indentation for a new paragraph, etc.), representing a stretch of discourse that coheres in terms of intonation and/or pragmatic import and/or syntactic structure. Typical units of this type include intonation units, clauses, sentences, and paragraphs.

The first level is addressed in the literature on morphology and orthography. Major issues relevant for documentary linguistics are summarized in

Section 1. Our main concern, however, will be with level 2 units because there is very little agreement and much confusion as to how to proceed on this level of segmentation. Section 2 will be devoted to this issue.

Before we take a closer look at level 1 and 2 transcription units, two general remarks are in order. First, transcription practice on all segmentation levels is very strongly influenced by the writing systems for European languages, which evolved over more than two millennia. In reflecting on transcription practices, it will thus be instructive to take a look at writing practices at earlier stages of the development of the modern European systems as well as at the major writing traditions outside Europe (see, for example, Daniels and Bright 1996 or Coulmas 2003). In a classic paper, Ochs (1979) reviews some biases inherent in the European writing tradition which may adversely affect the analysis when uncritically adopted in transcribing spoken interactions.

Second, if you happen to be able to work with native speakers who are literate in a dominant language and may thus be able to work independently on transcriptions, it will be very instructive to document such independent transcriptions as primary data. In the initial phase, the transcripts may often be difficult to interpret because they appear to be full of inconsistencies and lack the indication of higher level units (transcripts can go on for pages without a single punctuation mark or indentation to show the beginning of a new unit). Over time and usually influenced strongly by the practices of the researcher(s) or the dominant writing culture, a more consistent and "orderly" set of transcription practices may emerge which in turn may feed directly into an emerging literacy in the speech community. Documenting this process will be of great interest for many reasons, including the fact that such transcripts may provide independent evidence for native speaker intuitions about segmentation units such as words or sentences.

1. Segmenting 'words'

It is a matter of controversy whether and to what extent the 'word' is a basic structural unit in all languages. There are also differing reports as to whether native speakers have intuitive knowledge regarding word boundaries. In many literate societies, native speakers have relatively clear ideas about wordhood, but their perception of word boundaries is largely based on the orthographic conventions familiar to them (a word is 'what one writes between spaces'). In many non-literate societies, speakers are also able to segment utterances into form-meaning pairings of word-like sizes (as when asked to 'dictate' an utterance to a researcher not yet familiar with the language). The consistency with which such segmentation is performed, however, varies greatly between individual speakers and speech communities, depending in part at least on the overall structure of the language. Thus, segment size in 'dictation' (i.e. speaking slowly and very articulately for the benefit of an outsider) may vary between a syllable or a (metrical) foot and a phrase. In a similar way, historically evolved conventional orthographies often show considerable variation and inconsistency in indicating word boundaries (compare, for example, English *blackfish* with *black snake* (with initial stress) or *cannot* with *may not*).

However, it would be wrong to conclude from the inconsistencies observed in many orthographies as well as in native speaker behavior that variation here is totally arbitrary and that 'word' is not a useful unit, having no cognitive validity whatsoever for speakers in non-literate communities. Instead, it is important to note that variation and inconsistency in delimiting word boundaries pertains to a well-known set of phenomena, most importantly compounds such as *blackfish* and *black snake*, clitics (e.g. /nt/ in English *shouldn't*), particle constructions such as English *put off*, and lexicalized phrases (e.g. *forget-me-not, whatsoever, kick the bucket*). Disregarding these problem areas, it probably holds true that speakers of all languages have clear intuitions about "smallest, completely satisfying bits of isolated 'meaning' into which the sentence resolves itself," as Sapir (1921: 34) put it. Thus, there never seems to be any doubt about the fact that clear affixes such as *-ing* in English *sing-ing* are part of a single word form *singing*. And conversely, there is no doubt about the fact that a unit such as *book on the table* is phrasal, consisting at least of two words (*book* and *table*), while the wordhood of *on* and *the* may be less clear.

Consequently, native speaker input will provide the major source for segmenting continuous discourse into word-sized chunks. In the problem areas, however, it will in general not be possible to rely exclusively on this input. Rather, it will be necessary to devise a set of criteria to be adhered to when segmenting units involving clitics, compounds, and the like. Before we turn to these, it will be worth emphasizing a point already made at the end of the preceding section. A documentation should include clear evidence as to how native speakers handle word boundaries, both in the clear and the unclear cases. This may be done by including recordings of acts of 'dictation' (for example, recording a transcription session where the native speaker listens to a previously made recording and dictates it in workable chunks to the transcriber) or by including specimens of unedited transcriptions in those instances where speakers are able to provide these themselves (usually based on the literary skills acquired for a dominant language).

As for the problem areas, it will be useful to distinguish two separate, though clearly interrelated issues: problems of analysis and questions of orthographic representation. Problems of analysis are widely discussed in the morphological literature, both in textbooks and specialist work (see, for example, Matthews 1991: 206–222; Basbøll 2000; Haspelmath 2002: 148–162; and the contributions in Dixon and Aikhenvald 2002). Here it will suffice briefly to introduce the basic issue and some useful terminology.

In most languages, there are different criteria for defining words and these criteria can be in conflict with each other. Major conflicts often arise between phonological and morphosyntactic criteria for defining words, giving rise to two different 'types' of words, i.e. the *phonological word* and the *morphosyntactic* (or *grammatical*) *word (form)*. Thus, for example, English *shouldn't* is clearly a single phonological word as seen by the fact that it carries only one stress and /nt/ does not fulfill the phonotactic requirements of a minimal word form in English (among other things, an English word has to have at least one vowel). But *shouldn't* clearly also comprises two morphosyntactic words as seen by the fact that it consists of two constituents which are separable from each other (as in *Why should you not apply?*).

In those instances where the phonological and morphosyntactic criteria define units of different sizes – a common but by no means universal occurrence – all possible interrelationships of the units thus defined are attested: A phonological word may comprise two or more morphosyntactic words (as in the case of English *should=n't*). Conversely, a morphosyntactic word may comprise two or more phonological words. Apart from the long morphosyntactic words found in polysynthetic languages, this is also common in some types of reduplication which involve the complete lexical base (or a significant part of it) as in Malay *rumah-rumah* 'houses'. One reason for considering this form as two phonological words is that /hr/ is a consonant cluster otherwise not attested in Malay phonological words. Finally, Dixon and Aikhenvald (2002: 29f.) report two instances where some phonological words consists of one morphosyntactic word plus part of a second morphosyntactic word, that is, the formation of phonological words here "ignores" morphosyntactic word boundaries.

While best known, conflicts in determining wordhood do not only arise from the application of criteria at two different levels, phonological and morphosyntactic. They may also arise by the application of different criteria at the same level. That is, two phonological features or rules may not target the same unit, giving rise to two types of phonologically defined words (and similarly for morphosyntactic words). Woodbury (2002: 91–97) provides an example from Cup'ik.[1]

Turning now briefly to the issue of orthographic representation, it is a widely accepted and used practice to write items which clearly are single words as separate items delimited by spaces on either side and not to use any further means of orthographically indicating wordhood. As for problematic items such as compounds, clitics, and lexicalized phrases, the western writing tradition offers essentially three options for representing these orthographically. One may write problematic items as single units as in *shouldn't, blackfish,* or *whatsoever,* thus emphasizing their wordhood but obscuring their constituency. Or one may write them separately as in *black snake* and *kick the bucket,* thus making their constituents and original phrasal structure more easily recognizable but also rendering them orthographically indistinguishable from productively formed (compositional) phrases. Finally, one may write them with a hyphen as in *forget-me-not* in an attempt to convey both word-like coherence and phrasal transparency.[2]

No widely accepted principles or practices exist as to how to represent the typical problem cases. Both conventional writing systems and practical orthographies developed by descriptive linguists differ widely in this regard. Thus, while in English noun-noun compounds such as *clothes peg* are often written apart, in German they are regularly written as a unit (*Wäscheklammer*). Similarly, in the Northern Philippine language Iloko enclitics are regularly written together with the preceding word as in *Surátemon!* (suráten=mo=en 'write =2SG=now') 'Write it!' (Rubino 2005: 334), while in Tagalog, a Central Philippine language, clitics are generally written as separate items, hence *Isulat mo na!* 'Write it!'.

Sometimes there are good reasons for either option. In the Philippine case, for example, Iloko clitics tend to fuse with their hosts to a much larger extent than Tagalog clitics, which mostly appear in the same shape regardless of the host. Hence, writing the Iloko clitics together with their hosts provides for an orthographic representation of (phonological) words which is close to their actual articulation. But very often there are conflicting motivations for both options which are difficult, if not impossible, to resolve in a totally consistent and systematic fashion. A good example for this state of affairs is provided by the lively debate concerning the principles of orthographic wordhood in German which has accompanied the development of the modern German writing system from its beginnings and continues to be a matter of considerable controversy. Thus, this issue is, once again, one of the most contested aspects of the last orthography reform in German writing countries (see Jacobs 2005 for a recent attempt to resolve the problems in a principled manner).

In dealing with cases of problematic orthographic wordhood, it will be useful to keep the following considerations in mind:

– Issues of orthographic representation usually have to be resolved by taking into account non-linguistic factors such as learnability or already established neighboring orthographies, as discussed in detail in Chapter 11. Of course, the (practical) orthography used in transcriptions does not have to be identical to the practical orthography used in, or developed for, the community. But in most instances it will not be feasible to use two practical orthographies in parallel. Hence, the non-linguistic factors will also play a role for the orthography used in transcription.
– While in writing no major difference exists, in reading it appears to be easier to process shorter simplex units which have to be combined into a larger unit (as when one has to determine that *clothes peg* is a compound and not a phrase) than to break down longer complex units into their constituent parts (as in the case of Iloko *surátemon*). Note that this 'principle' is contravened by the principle that whatever clearly forms a single, phonological *and* grammatical word should be written together. Hence, there are no orthographies which write clear affixes consistently as separate items.³
– It is a widespread, though by no means universal, practice to base orthographic wordhood on the criteria for the grammatical word wherever phonological and grammatical wordhood are in conflict. For example, clitics are widely represented as orthographically independent items. However, there may be indications for the opposite option, e.g. when clitics show fusional tendencies (as in the Iloko example above) or when particles are separable from the verb with which they form a grammatical unit (cp. *to put off the meeting* vs. *to put it off*).

2. Intonation units, 'paragraphs' and more

The segmentation of continuous spoken discourse at levels higher than the orthographic word is rarely, if ever explicitly, addressed in descriptive linguistics. That is, it usually remains a mystery as to how exactly the author(s) arrived at the format of a transcript published in a text collection or in the appendix of a grammar. Most transcripts are presented with sentence and paragraph structure, with standard punctuation (commas, full stops, indenting) indicating major units. But with few exceptions (for example, Heath 1980: 2–5 [see also Heath 1984: 589–619] or Himmelmann and Wolff 1999: 83, 98f.), the authors usually remain silent as to how the various boundaries implied by these marks have actually been determined.

If one happens to have access to the original recording underlying the published transcript, one will almost immediately notice that in fact quite a lot of editing and interpretation is involved in arriving at the "clean" published form. False starts, repetitions, and hesitations ('uhm' and the like) are usually edited out. Decisions as to what to include in a single clause and sentence are usually based on semantics and, if available, morphosyntactic evidence. But more often than not, such decisions are also influenced by what a sentence in written English looks like (or whatever written language the editor is most familiar with). Given this mixture of variables, many of which are difficult to handle in a consistent manner, it is almost unavoidable that decisions regarding sentence and paragraph structure become almost arbitrary. It is thus highly unlikely that two editors working in this way with the same recording and the same speaker would arrive at a reasonably similar "clean" transcript for publication (to my knowledge, no experiment along these lines has been conducted so far, but it seems reasonably safe to predict this outcome).[4]

The importance of the (edited) transcript resides in the fact that for most analytical procedures (in particular in morphosyntax and semantics but also in phonology) it is the transcript (and not the original recording) which serves as the basis for further analyses. Obviously, whatever mistakes or inconsistencies have been included in the transcript will be carried on to these other levels of analysis, perhaps not always causing major harm but clearly introducing unknown variables into these further analyses. This problem may become somewhat less important in the near future inasmuch as it will become standard practice to link transcripts line by line (or some other unit) to the recordings, which allows direct and fast access to the original recording whenever use is made of a given segment in the transcript.

Nevertheless, even with transcripts linked to the recording, one still has to decide on some higher-level unit into which the flow of spoken discourse is to be segmented. As opposed to descriptive linguistics, such segmentation has been a major concern in anthropological linguistics and in (some variants of) discourse analysis, and we will heavily draw on this work in the remainder of this section.[5]

Work in anthropological linguistics such as Tedlock (1983) or Sherzer (1990, 1992) has focused on verbal art where segmentation units above the word such as verse/line, couplet, or stanza tend to be indicated by a host of prosodic, lexical, and grammatical features. The variants of discourse analysis of interest here have mostly been based on everyday speech, mostly narratives and conversation. The basic higher-level segmentation unit identified in most of this work is the *intonation unit* (also known as *tone group, breath group, intonational phrase*, and the like).[6] The intonation unit roughly corresponds to the line (or verse) in verbal art genres. It is widely held to be the basic unit into which native speakers themselves chunk their utterances, i.e. it is seen as a unit of speech production which in some sense has a psychological reality for the speakers (as opposed to a purely analytic construct "invented" by linguists). In this section, we will first take a closer look at how intonation units can be identified and then briefly discuss the possibilities of identifying even larger units above the intonation unit.

2.1. Identifying intonation units

In most languages, evidence for intonation unit boundaries is provided by changes in pitch and rhythm. Evidence from pitch is of three kinds: a) the occurrence of a boundary tone at the end of an intonation unit, i.e. a clearly perceptible change in pitch on the last syllable(s) of a unit; b) a new onset at the beginning of the next unit, i.e. typically a jump in pitch between the offset of one unit and the beginning of the next one; and c) a reset of the baseline which is most clearly visible in the fact that early pitch peaks in the new unit are higher than the final pitch peaks in the preceding one. Major rhythmic evidence is also of three kinds: a) a pause in between two units; b) lengthening of the final segment of a given unit; c) anacrusis, i.e. an accelerated delivery of the unstressed syllables at the beginning of the new unit.[7]

It is rarely the case that all the diagnostics for a boundary listed above can actually be observed at a given boundary in spontaneous speech. In fact, most of the diagnostics are optional, i.e. they do not have to occur at every boundary. Only two diagnostics, i.e. the final boundary tone and the new onset, are, in theory at least, obligatory in many languages.[8] But in spontaneous speech, there are various factors which may make it difficult or impossible to identify relevant phenomena in a given instance (more on these shortly). Nevertheless, at least two or three of the diagnostics will be present at a given boundary in most instances. That is, between 80–90% of the intonation unit boundaries occurring in spontaneous speech are relatively easily and clearly identifiable, although there may be considerable variation across speakers and genres (boundaries in monological speech are generally easier to identify, in part simply because there is only minimal interference from other speakers).

In practical terms, the two most common and useful diagnostics for boundaries are the final boundary tone and pauses, both of which, however, are not always straightforwardly identifiable. As for pauses, the major problem lies in the fact that not all pauses occur at the boundary of an intonation unit but some types of pauses – widely known as *hesitation pauses* – also occur within intonation units. Some hesitation pauses are easily distinguished from boundary marking pauses by the fact that they involve a rather abrupt stoppage in the stream of speech which often ends in a glottal stop. They often also include some kind of filler (*uhm* and the like) and may be followed by further disfluencies as in *but uhm (0.2) the the sound*. Pauses at intonation unit boundaries, on the other hand, are characterized by complete silence, the audible relaxation of the vocal organs, audible exhalation, and/or an audible breath intake. Apart from hesitation pauses and boundary pauses, a third type of pause needs to be distinguished, namely rhetorical pauses. These may occur as part of a package of features used to put particular emphasis on a given item, as in *That is the most* [pause] *ludicrous idea I have ever heard*. These are much rarer than the other types of pauses and usually are easily distinguishable from them because of other contextual features which signal special emphasis.

As for final boundary tones, these are often only clearly identifiable if the unit ends on one or more unstressed syllables. If the unit ends on a stressed syllable, it may be difficult to distinguish between a pitch change related to stress and a pitch change related to the boundary. A second problem regarding final boundary tones pertains to the fact that more often than not, the inventory of boundary tones in a given language contains a default member which is characterized by the lack of a major pitch excursion, the unit typically ending somewhere in the non-descript middle of a speaker's pitch range. Such instances may be difficult to distinguish from hesitations. And finally, the voice at the end of a unit may become creaky and/or very low in intensity so that actually occurring pitch changes may become hardly perceptible (this, of course, is also the case when actually occurring pitch changes are masked by co-occurring noise such as overlap from another speaker, laughter, etc.).

The following example from a spontaneous English narrative[9] illustrates some of the features of intonation units mentioned above (see also Figure 1). In the first unit, you can hear a brief hesitation pause where the speaker audibly does not release the vocal organs right after the initial *and*, which is a very typical place for hesitation pauses to occur. With regard to pitch, the unit ends somewhere in mid range without a clear rise or fall, which is indicated here with a semicolon (;). The second unit ends on a clear rise which, however, occurs on a stressed syllable and hence combines characteristics of an accentual tone and a rising boundary tone (rising boundary tones are marked by a slash /). In the last unit, on the other hand, the final (rising) accent tone is on *strong*, which is followed by a clear fall to the lower bottom of the speaker's pitch range (170–180 Hz in this story), a very clear example of a falling final boundary tone (final falls are indicated by a backslash). The numbers in parentheses indicate pause length in seconds.[10] In contrast to the hesitation pause at the beginning of the first unit, these pauses are completely silent. Note, finally, that the speaker starts each unit in the lower mid of her pitch range (around 230 Hz), which in each instance involves a jump up or down from the pitch target reached at the end of the preceding unit (new onset).

(1)   PEAR-L-36FF

    36.   and (0.4) you see his hand sometimes at close up ; (1.1)
    37.   uh snatching the pears from the tree / (0.8)
    38.   and you hear the sound really: strongly \ (0.8)

The following example is a bit more complicated and illustrates two of the most common difficulties that may occur in determining intonation unit boundaries. These are false starts/self-repairs, as in units 49–51 of the following example, and latching, i.e. two units occur in immediate succession, without an audible break intervening, which is indicated by an equal sign in parentheses (=) instead of a pause duration at the end of lines 49–51:

(2)   PEAR-L-48FF

    48.   he climbs down the ladder / (0.5)
    49.   and he puts a couple of the pears– (=)
    50.   well: (=)
    51.   as he's standing there ; (=)
    52.   couple of the pears fall \ (0.4)

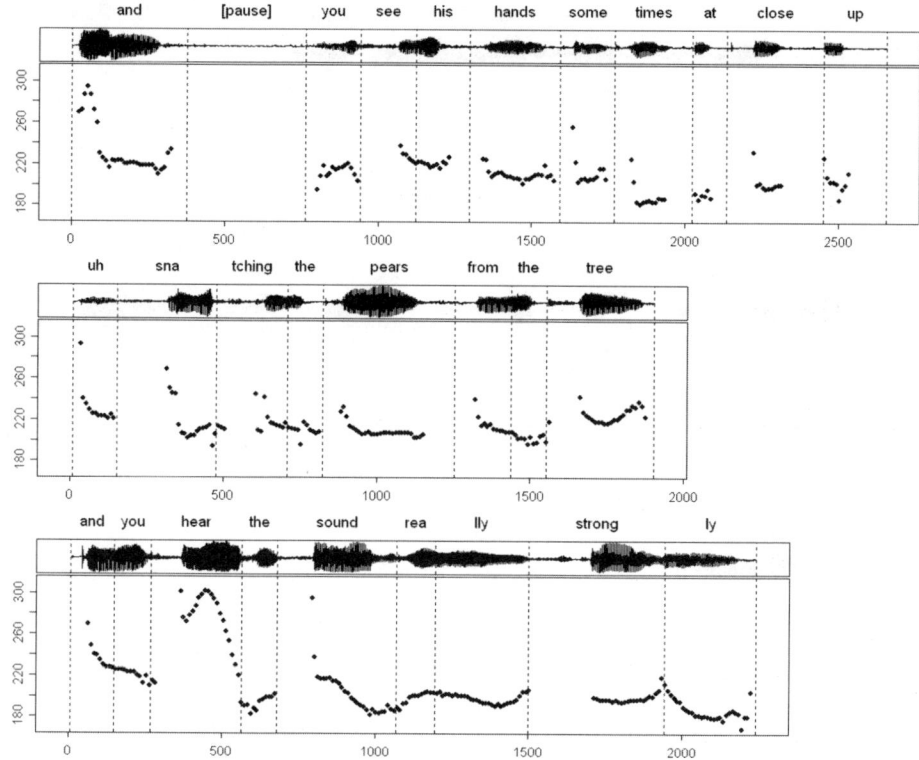

Figure 1. Waveform and fundamental frequency[11] for example (1)

Going briefly through this example line by line (see Figure 2), the intonation unit in line 48 is very easily identifiable since it ends on a clearly identifiable boundary tone (strong rise on the final unstressed syllable of *ladder* followed by a boundary pause with audible breath intake). Unit 49 illustrates the phenomenon of self-repair where the speaker interrupts herself as she starts pronouncing the final fricative of *pears*, breaks off before finishing this segment (signaled by a dash –), and immediately restarts in mid range with a slightly lengthened *well* (lengthening is indicated by the colon :), which here functions as a lexical repair marker. Then she immediately starts the repair unit (51) which ends on a clear fall across the final two syllables (*ing there*). This fall, however, does not reach the bottom of her range (it ends around 195 Hz) and is therefore marked here by a semicolon. The final unit again starts without an audible pause preceding it. This unit ends on a fall on the final (stressed) syllable to the bottom of her pitch range.

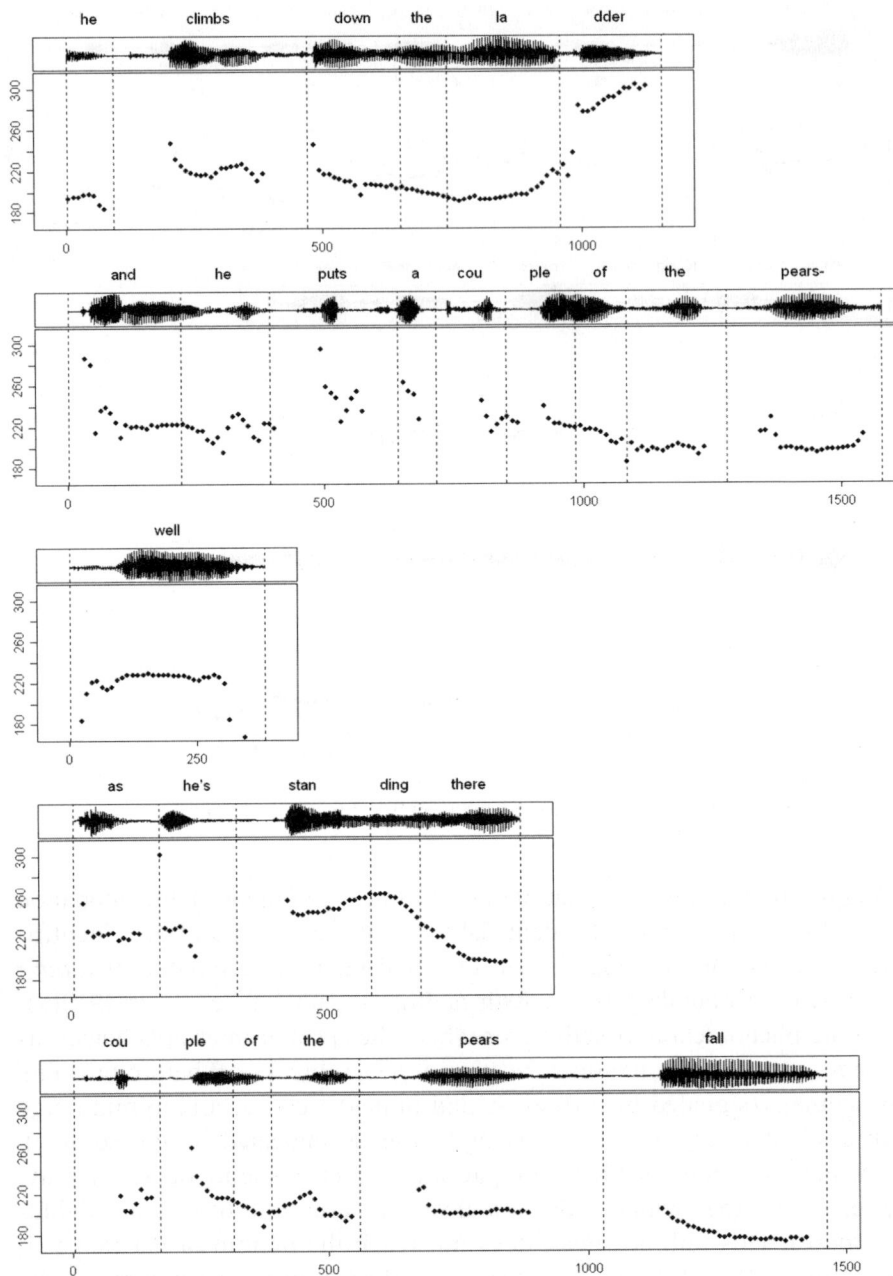

Figure 2. Waveform and fundamental frequency for example (2)

Latching as in units 49–51 often causes some problems in that the other indicators for intonation unit boundaries become then all important. Thus, e.g., at the end of unit 51 there is a clear fall across two unstressed syllables, which is interpreted here as a boundary tone. But, importantly, unit 52 does not start with a clearly new onset of pitch. Instead, the pitch continues without any audible interruption. Hence, the only reason for assuming a boundary between 51 and 52 is the fall at the end of 51.

Self-repairs are often easily recognizable by the abrupt break-off of the word under way. They are more difficult to identify when the break-off occurs after the word or construction currently under way has been finished. In such instances they may be difficult to distinguish from intonation units that do not end on a clearly identifiable boundary tone.

Lexical repair markers such as *well* in unit 50 and other kinds of so-called discourse markers such as *and then, you know, I think, let me see* pose a minor practical problem in that it is often not clear whether they should be considered intonation units of their own (as in unit 50 above) or whether they are part of the preceding or following unit (that is, in the example above units 50 and 51 could also be combined into a single unit: *well: as he is standing there*). The prosodic evidence for either option is often not very clear. In the case of tags as in *and he sort of slips, you know* the prosody can actually be somewhat complicated in that there may be clear indications for the end of an intonation unit before the tag but no evidence for a new onset on the tag. However, for the practical purposes of a base transcript in a language documentation nothing much depends on how these elements are represented. As usual, the main concern here should be with consistency, i.e. to put them all in units of their own or to include them in the unit they appear to belong to (in a few instances it may not be a straightforward exercise to determine whether this is the preceding or following unit).

In this regard, it may also be noted that coordinating and subordinating conjunctions in many languages allow three options of prosodic packaging. They may either occur together with the second conjunct (see unit 49 in (2) above) or the subordinate clause they introduce, as in:

(3)　he didn't notice / (0.3)
　　　because he was busy picking pears \

Or they may occur at the end of the first conjunct or the matrix clause, as in:

(4)　he didn't notice *because* / (0.3)
　　　he was busy picking pears \

The third alternative is to have them form an intonation unit of their own:

(5)   he didn't notice / (0.3)
       because ; (0.7)
       he was busy picking pears \

In this last case, there will often be no clear-cut boundary tone at the end of the intermediate intonation unit. Arguably, instances such as (5) can often also be analyzed as instances of (3), i.e. as a single intonation unit with a hesitation pause following the initial word or phrase: *because (0.7) he was busy picking pears*.

As a general rule of thumb, it may be of help to remember that intonation units are in some sense planning units for the speaker and rarely include more than 5–7 content words (2–3 words in highly polysynthetic languages). In fact, it has been suggested by Chafe (1994; see also Pawley and Syder 2000) that each intonation unit contains only a single bit of new information (which is also known as the *one-new-idea-at-a-time hypothesis*). Thus, with regard to spontaneous speech, overly long intonation units making reference to several new participants or activities not mentioned before should be regarded with some suspicion. This rule of thumb, however, does *not* hold true for more ritualized forms of speech which often contain large formulaic chunks that have been memorized. Similarly, units containing quoted direct speech are often significantly longer than the average intonation unit in a given speech event.

The planning load to be managed by the speaker also manifests itself in the following phenomenon widely observed in spontaneous monologic speech (in particular narratives of various types but also procedural texts). At the beginning of a narrative or similar genre, there tend to be lots of hesitations and false starts as well as a mixture of longish and very short intonation units, while later on, the delivery will become more fluent and rhythmically spaced. This is probably due to the fact that at the beginning of an extended monologue speakers have to deal with a higher planning load, since apart from putting together individual intonation units, they also have to develop and implement an overall plan for the delivery of their story. In terms of transcription and segmentation, this means that identifying intonation units at the beginning of a monologue is often more difficult and cumbersome than later on, and it may be a good idea to start the segmentation of a narrative a minute or two into the telling and turn to the beginning only after the rest of the recording has been dealt with.

A somewhat different problem pertains to the fact that when transcribing spontaneous speech in a language one understands very well, there is a strong tendency for semantic and syntactic factors to interfere with one's perception of prosodic boundaries. That is, indications for prosodic boundaries within clauses or noun phrases tend to be missed and, conversely, there is a tendency to hear prosodic boundary signals at, e.g., clause boundaries when in fact there are none. A well-known example for these tendencies is the fact that clause-internal pauses are often not perceived and at the same time, pauses are "heard" at clause boundaries when according to the instrumental evidence there aren't any. It is, therefore, important to control for these interferences by instrumentally crosschecking a sample of the boundaries marked auditorily (checking all boundaries acoustically will normally not be feasible because it would be too time consuming). Otherwise, one ends up with boundaries based on a mixture of prosodic, semantic, and syntactic criteria which tend to lead to irresolvable inconsistencies.

Note in this regard that the diagnostics listed above in part pertain to offset phenomena and in part to onset phenomena. In almost all instances, these two align in the sense that where there is an offset, there is also an onset. However, this need not be the case. Speakers may choose to start a new unit, providing all the evidence for new units (most importantly, a new onset), without having properly finished the preceding one (which then remains a fragment). Furthermore, and this is even less common, they may also construct a new unit as a continuation of the preceding one although the preceding unit was in fact "properly closed". This latter case is illustrated in the following example from the same Pear Story:

(6)   PEAR-L-88FF

> 88. because he looks Hispanic \ (0.7)
> 89. probably a Mexican: ; (1.3)
> 90. worker being exploited by some landlord / (1.5) ((laughs))

The unit of interest here begins with line 89. While there is no clear final boundary tone at the end of this line, the final *n* of *Mexican* is lengthened (about 200 ms) and followed by a long pause with audible breath intake, both being clear indications of an intonation unit boundary. However, the first word of line 90, *worker*, is produced as if it were a direct continuation of the preceding unit. There are no indications whatsoever for a new onset. On the contrary, the pitch of the first syllable continues very precisely the pitch of the final *n* of *Mexican*, which is quite remarkable given the long

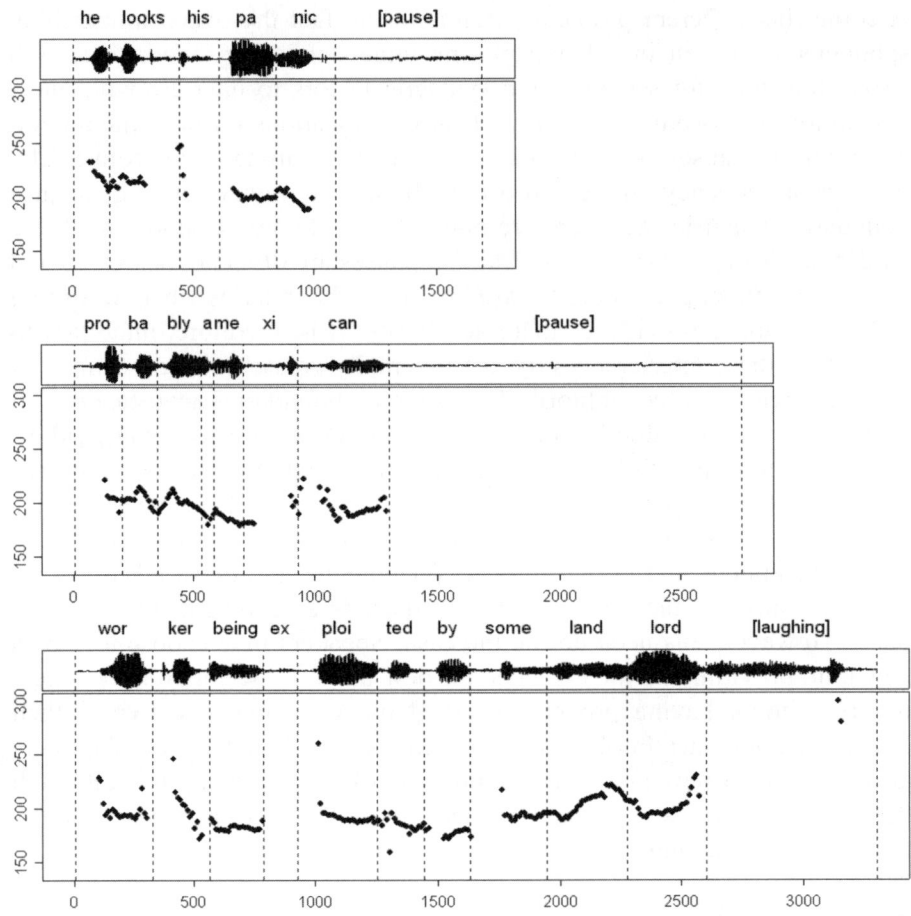

Figure 3. Waveform and fundamental frequency for example (6)

pause in between.[12] Note that in the transcript in (6), no attempt has been made to capture this very special relation between the two units, which arguably could also be considered a single intonation unit. It would appear to be of such rare occurrence that it is not feasible to introduce special conventions for this case.

The ability to identify intonation unit boundaries auditorily needs some practice, and it is a highly recommended exercise for anyone planning to undertake a language documentation to transcribe a number of recordings of spontaneous speech in his or her own language (both monologues and conversations) in order to get a "feeling" for working with spoken language and also for the amount of work and time involved in transcribing it. The level of detail to which features of spoken language are included in a transcript varies significantly across various transcriptions conventions (see Edwards and Lampert 1993 for a survey). The conventions used in the transcription examples given above are loosely based on the ones proposed by DuBois et al. (1993), which are fairly simple and widely used in spoken discourse research.

Since the transcripts included in a language documentation are only intended to provide a starting point for further analysis in different frameworks, it is recommended to be rather sparse with regard to the inclusion of such features as voice quality, speech tempo, laughter, and so on. Pauses will in general not be measured instrumentally but simply indicated by some convention such as a (.) = short pause and (..) = longer pause. The number of boundary tones distinguished should also be restricted to an easily manageable number. In the conventions used above, the only differences indicated are: clear rise (/), clear final fall to the bottom of the speaker's range (\), and everything else (;), which includes falls to lower mid range as well as level ending units. More detailed annotation schemes will inevitably increase the number of problematic decisions to be made and, in the case of boundary tones, a more detailed schema will normally only make sense when the phonological structure of the intonation unit has been analyzed in detail.

While the conventions used in spoken discourse research may thus be a bit too detailed and cumbersome for the amount of transcription involved in a language documentation and should be further simplified along the lines just indicated, it is highly recommended to include all kinds of hesitations and false starts in a base transcript since these may prove to be crucial for various interpretative and analytical tasks. Omitting hesitations and false starts from transcripts can in fact lead to major errors of analysis. In Tolai, for example,[13] one may get the impression from heavily edited transcripts that the form of the article is *a* for subjects and *ra* for objects, thus involving a case-like distinction in grammatical relation marking. However, listening closely to spontaneous speech and preparing adequate transcripts makes it clear that this alternation has nothing to do with grammatical relation marking but pertains to pausing: *a* is the form of the article after a pause (and at sentence boundaries) while *ra* is used when no pause precedes. This becomes obvious when transcripts include all pauses, making it clear that *a* is also used before objects provided a pause precedes.

Furthermore, repair strategies may yield important evidence for morpho-syntactic structure in that they generally target morphosyntactic units rather than some arbitrary number of syllables or segments. Thus, e.g., some types of self-repair recycle the complete word, phrase, or clause that the speaker abandoned before completing it and thus provide evidence for the viability of these structural units, as seen in the following example (again from the Pear Story):

(7)   I assume <this take pla-> this is taking place in California ; (0.3)

Here the speaker begins a complement clause (*this take pla-*), breaks off half-way into the word *place* and then restarts at the beginning of the complement clause. See Marandin and de Fornel (1996), Fox et al. (1996), and Apothéloz and Zay (1999) for further discussion and exemplification.

2.2. Evidence for paragraphs/episodes

Spoken discourse does not simply consist of a sequence of intonation units. Instead, when listening to a coherent stretch of spoken discourse, it is quite clear that some intonation units "belong closer together" than others, form-ing units larger than a single intonation units. The nature of these units and the boundaries separating them is not yet well understood, and there is a large variety of terms in use for referring to them, including *paragraph, (spoken* or *prosodic) sentence, episode, utterance, intonation unit complex*, etc. (these terms have various readings and, depending on the framework, may refer to units of different sizes).

To date it remains unclear as to whether speakers of unwritten lan-guages have strong and clear intuitions about these units. I am not aware of any reports concerning such intuitions in the literature, and the issue does not seem to have been investigated systematically. Reports by experienced fieldworkers provide conflicting evidence. According to some reports, there are native speakers who are very consistent in marking something which can be called a 'sentence boundary'. Other fieldworkers have quite the oppo-site experience of speakers producing transcripts and written texts which go on for pages without a single indication of sentence or paragraph structure (I myself belong to the latter group).

Note that the issue here is not 'clausehood'. Speakers often have reason-ably clear and consistent intuitions about the fact that a (finite) verb forms some sort of unit with its arguments and at least some of the more peripheral adjuncts.[14] The issue here pertains to intuitions about which clauses together form larger sentence-like units, including both what from a grammarian's point of view are main and subordinate clauses. To give just one example for possibly conflicting evidence in this regard, in languages which allow for extended chains of subordinated or nominalized clause constructions such as the converb constructions found in Turkic or Papuan languages, some speakers will accept or even propose major boundaries at points within the chain which grammatically speaking are sentence-medial forms.

It may thus be the case that with regard to higher-level segmentation, in at least some languages the native speaker's position is not very different from that of a non-native researcher. It is in fact likely that both draw on the same kind of evidence when attempting to determine the boundaries of higher-level units. In the rare instances where it is explicitly discussed, the evidence for such boundaries usually involves a mixture of semantic, pragmatic, and prosodic factors. Semantic-pragmatic criteria include, for example, changes relating to time and space of the setting (*the next morning, arriving at the river*) and a change of topic or subject. The most important prosodic phenomena occurring at such higher-level boundaries are: a) a boundary tone signaling finality (usually a strong fall to the lower bottom of the speaker's range); b) long pauses, i.e. pauses that are distinctly longer than the pauses occurring at the end of a paragraph-internal boundary (this appears to hold statistically when comparing pause lengths across a suffi-ciently large corpus, but is of little help in making decisions in individual instances); c) reset in declination, i.e. the baseline reaches its absolute minimum at the end of a paragraph and the new paragraph starts with a higher baseline as seen in the level of onsets and low and high tonal targets; d) a particular pitch pattern at the beginning of the unit, often associated with some special lexical expression introducing a new paragraph (some-thing like *after this happened ...*).

As usual when applying a fairly heterogeneous set of diagnostics, there are many instances where these diagnostics provide conflicting evidence, some (a final fall and a long pause, for example) indicating a major boundary, others (no topic change, continued declination) indicating continuity. To date, there is no agreement as to how to resolve such conflicts.

In working on transcripts, there are three points to keep in mind. First, for many analytical procedures higher level boundaries are irrelevant (ob-viously, they are not irrelevant when looking at conjunctions, discourse markers, and the like). Hence, in many instances it may be preferable not to indicate any such boundaries rather than marking them in a haphazard and unsystematic way. Second, if one decides to indicate such boundaries, consistency is of paramount importance which is usually helped by explicitly listing the diagnostics and their relative rank. Finally, it is important to keep in mind that units in spoken language are often quite different from those in written language. For example, taking final falls as a major diagnostic, it is not uncommon that units thus delimited in German or English narrative are of extremely varied size. That is, a very long paragraph consisting of 37 intonation units may be followed by another one which consists just of one intonation unit, the next one comprising ten intonation units, and so on.

From these remarks and observations, it follows that for reasons of time economy it will in general not be feasible to attempt a systematic segmentation into higher level units of all recordings when working on transcriptions within a language documentation project. Obviously, whenever there are clear indications for such higher-level structure, these should be explicitly noted and commented upon. Furthermore, it will be useful to document the various segmentation stages applied to those texts which have been chosen for publication and are edited both by native speakers and researchers in the process.

3. Conclusion

This chapter has surveyed two major segmentation issues in transcribing spoken discourse. With regard to segmenting words, the primary source of information will be native speaker intuition which, however, has to be supplemented by an explicit convention for transcribing problematic items such as clitics, compounds, and lexicalized phrases. This convention will be based on phonological and morphosyntactic criteria for wordhood, but will also have to take into account non-linguistic factors in deciding on the representation of problematic items. The segmentation into intonation units, on the other hand, will be based primarily on auditory impression, listening for the boundary signals produced by the speaker. The auditory impression should be repeatedly checked acoustically (instrumentally) in order to contravene biases introduced by the semantics and pragmatics of the utterances transcribed or, in the case of a non-native speaker doing the transcription, by one's native prosodic system, which may be tuned to a somewhat different set of boundary signals. Depending on the amount of recordings to be processed within a documentation project, segmentation at levels higher than the intonation unit will often not be feasible for reasons of time economy. However, inasmuch as native speakers themselves indicate such higher-level segments, these should of course be preserved as part of the annotations stored with the recording of a given event.

Acknowledgements

I am grateful to my co-editors and Eva Schultze-Berndt for useful discussion and comments on an earlier version of this chapter. Special thanks to Jan Strunk for preparing the figures and to Louisa Schaefer for help with the Pear Story data.

Notes

1. See also the work on word domains done in the AUTOTYP framework (http://www.uni-leipzig.de/~autotyp).
2. In principle there is an almost limitless number of further possibilities for indicating different types of words (word-like coherence) by using additional symbols in place of a hyphen, thus having complex words with '&' (*fair&play*), ones with '=' (*should=nt*), ones with '_' (*tittle_tattle*), and so on. But there are severe limits on how many of such extra symbols can be used consistently by writers and parsed by readers without constantly checking the conventions. It is probably not by chance that there are few, if any, practical orthographies which have gone beyond the three ways of dealing with wordhood orthographically just mentioned (written together, written with a hyphen, written separately).
3. A possible exception is the Japanese writing system, where lexical elements are represented in Chinese characters (Kanji) while morphological elements which arguably can be considered suffixes are consistently written as orthographically separate items (in Hiragana, one of the two syllabaries). This distinction is often reflected even in Roman transcriptions (using spaces or hyphens).
4. Often native speakers are also involved in the process of editing transcripts of spontaneous speech for publication. They usually tend to prefer very clean forms which are similar in structure and appearance to the forms of written language they are familiar with. See Mosel (2004b) for discussion.
5. See Serzisko (1992) for a thorough review and discussion of the discourse analysis literature on segmenting spoken language.

6. The major alternative is the *turn constructional unit* used in Conversation Analysis which, however, is not easily identifiable on the basis of a simple, all-purpose operational procedure. See Ford et al. (1996) for some discussion.
7. See Chafe (1994), Schuetze-Coburn (1994), Ladd (1996), Cruttenden (1997), or Wennerstrom (2001) for a more detailed discussion of the intonation unit and its boundaries.
8. The major exception here are prototypical lexical tone languages, i.e. languages where (almost) every syllable inherently carries a lexical tone. In such languages, there may be either no boundary tone (as has been claimed, for example, for Yoruba) or the boundary tones interact with the lexical tone of the unit-final syllable, resulting in a modification of this lexical tone (e.g. Chinese or Thai).
9. This and the following segments are from a Pear Story (Chafe 1980) by a female speaker of American English recorded by the author. Thanks to Wallace Chafe for the permission to use the pear film. Wave files containing the segments are available at this book's website.
10. In documentary work, it will in general be neither feasible nor necessary to measure the length of pauses instrumentally. See further below.
11. Fundamental frequency (also known as "F zero") is the acoustic measure for the rate of vibration of the vocal cords when producing voiced sounds. It corresponds quite closely to pitch, which is an auditory/perceptual category. But fundamental frequency and pitch perception may diverge and hence need to be distinguished (see Laver 1994: 450ff., for discussion and exemplification).
12. As noted with regard to the transition from unit 51 to 52 in example (2), continuation of pitch level also occurs in latching. But as soon as there is even just a very short boundary pause, there is typically also a clearly new onset of pitch.
13. Thanks to Ulrike Mosel for providing this example (cp. Mosel 1984: 17).
14. Obviously, the consistency and strength of such intuitions depends in part on the typological profile of a language. In so-called non-configurational and, in particular, in polysynthetic languages, intuitions about which words together form a clause may be less clear and rather similar to the vague ideas about 'sentencehood' reported for some languages with relatively tight and hierarchically organized clause structure.

Chapter 11

Orthography development

Frank Seifart

Introduction

Written records, such as transcriptions of video-recorded speech events, are essential components of language documentations. Much of the success of a language documentation depends on casting these records in an orthography that appeals to the speech community. As a matter of fact, if it is accepted that the documentation has to be accessible to the speech community, the development and implementation of a practical orthography in the speech community is an absolutely necessary task in an early phase of a documentation project. Nevertheless, orthography development is usually not given much attention by linguists. The idea persists that a good orthography is simply one that represents all phonological contrasts. However, orthography development is in fact a highly complex issue, which involves not only phonological, prosodic, grammatical, and semantic aspects of the language to be written, but also a wide variety of non-linguistic issues, among them pedagogical and psycholinguistic aspects of reading and writing and the sociolinguistic situation.

Given the variety of language structures and sociopolitical situations found throughout the world, it is neither feasible nor desirable to propose a step-by-step model, which would lead to an optimal orthography. The aim of this chapter is rather to give an outline of the most important general issues involved in orthography development. It does so primarily by identifying a number of "factors" that are relevant when making decisions about orthographic design and by discussing the application of these factors to examples of various languages with special reference to situations of language endangerment. The focus is exclusively on the practical decisions that have to be made in the process of developing an orthography or in reforming an existing one. Wider issues of the impact of introducing literacy to oral cultures (see, e.g., Fishman 1991; Mühlhäusler 1996) or the differences between written and spoken communication (see, e.g., Ong 1982) are not considered here. The scope of this chapter is further limited in that its main focus is on alphabetical writing systems.

The basic procedure for developing an orthography outlined in this chapter begins with the analysis of the structure of a given language which will typically reveal a number of options for its orthographic representation. E.g., word-final devoicing could be represented in an orthography or not. These options are then evaluated with respect to factors that are independent of the linguistic structure, e.g. the learnability of certain types of orthographies for beginners. These non-linguistic factors will be decisive in choosing one option over the other. However, these factors are often conflicting. For instance, an orthography that represents word-final devoicing may be easier to learn for beginners, since the written form corresponds more closely to the pronunciation. However, an advanced reader may benefit from an orthography that maintains a constant written form of a morpheme, regardless of whether or not its final consonant is devoiced in some context. Thus, an essential task in developing orthographies is balancing the advantages and disadvantages of the different options and making compromises. It should be noted that these basic principles apply not only in situations where new orthographies are developed from scratch, but also in the reform of existing orthographies.

This chapter is organized as follows: Section 1 introduces the basic concepts in orthography development. Building on these concepts, Section 2 identifies a number of non-linguistic factors for making decisions in orthography development, among them psycholinguistic, sociopolitical, and technical issues. How these factors apply in specific instances is illustrated with a number of case studies in Section 3. Throughout the chapter, the following well-established conventions are used for the different kinds of representation of linguistic data: [ ] – phonetic representation; / / – phonemic representation; ⟨ ⟩ – orthographic representation.

1. Basic concepts

In this section, the term *orthography* is defined and a brief overview of the typology of writing systems is given. Then the terms *orthographic depth*, *functional load*, and *underrepresentation* are introduced. These basic concepts will be further elaborated and exemplified in the sections further below.

Writing systems are systems that allow readers to reconstruct a linguistic message on the basis of written signs. Orthographies are writing systems that are standardized with respect to

a. a set of graphic symbols (*graphemes*), such as signs, characters, letters, as well as diacritics, punctuation marks, etc.; and
b. a set of rules/conventions, such as orthographic rules and pronunciation rules, rules for writing word boundaries, punctuation rules, capitalization rules, etc. (Coulmas 2003: 35; see also Coulmas 1996: 1380; Rogers 2005: 2ff.).

Importantly, then, an orthography is defined as the *conjunction* of a set of graphemes, such as an alphabet, and a set of accompanying rules regulating their use. The third defining feature is that both the symbols and their usage are standardized and codified. The actual visual shape of the graphemes that a writing system uses, e.g. the Latin or the Arabic letters, is called its script.

As a starting point to the following discussion, it is useful to take a brief look at the typology of writing systems. Most typologies of writing systems are based on the smallest unit of a system, i.e. its basic graphemes (Coulmas 1996: 1381; Rogers 2005: 269ff.). Different types are distinguished according to what kind of linguistic unit the basic graphemes correspond to.[1] Following this principle, a first type recognized in the typology of writing systems are morphographic writing systems. The basic set of graphemes of morphographic systems correspond to morphemes, i.e. linguistic elements that have a meaning.[2] A prototypical example of a morphographic writing system is Chinese. Each grapheme (i.e. character) of Chinese stands for a morpheme of the language.

The second main type of writing systems are phonographic writing systems. The basic units of these systems refer to elements of the sound structure of a language. Phonographic writing systems in turn fall into two main subtypes: syllabic writing systems and alphabetical writing systems. A prototypical example of a syllabic writing system is the Japanese Kana writing system. The graphemes of this system each refer to a syllable of the language. In alphabetical systems, the basic set of graphemes are letters that correspond (more or less directly) to the phonemes of the language. Well-known examples are the Greek and Latin writing systems.

It is important to note that within alphabetical writing systems "the range of correspondences between phonemes and graphemes varies both in consistency and in completeness" (Katz and Frost 1992: 67): A single phoneme may be represented by combinations of graphemes, such as di- or trigraphs (e.g. German ⟨sch⟩ – /ʃ/) or by combining letters with diacritics (e.g. French ⟨a⟩ – /a/ vs. ⟨â⟩ – /ɑː/). There may also be phonemic distinctions that are not represented by letters (e.g. vowel length in Latin). Finally, a single phoneme may be represented by a number of graphemes (e.g. English /f/ – ⟨**f**un⟩, ⟨**ph**oto⟩, ⟨lau**gh**⟩) and a single grapheme may represent a number of phonemes (e.g. English ⟨b**u**ll⟩ – /bʊl/ vs. ⟨b**u**lk⟩ – /bʌlk/).

The two main types of writing systems, morphographic and phonographic writing systems, hardly ever occur in a pure form. Rather, most if not all writing systems combine phonographic and morphographic aspects. For instance, the English writing system is basically phonographic, i.e. the letters of the English alphabet represent phonemes (even though the correspondences of letters and phonemes are quite complex, as just mentioned). However, it can also be observed in English that the same morphemes are written with the same sequences of letters, even though they may be pronounced differently in different contexts. The constant written form vs. the variable pronunciation of the stems *wild* and *reduc-* and of the plural suffix *-s* are illustrated in the following examples.

(1) a. [ˈwaɪld]   ⟨**wild**⟩
     b. [bɪˈwɪldəmənt] ⟨be**wild**erment⟩

(2) a. [ɹɪˈdjuːs]   ⟨**reduc**e⟩
     b. [ɹɪˈdʌkʃən]   ⟨**reduc**tion⟩

(3) a. [hæt**s**]   ⟨hat**s**⟩
     b. [hɛd**z**]   ⟨head**s**⟩

Despite the pronunciation differences, the graphic representation of the morphemes highlighted in boldface in examples (1)–(3) is preserved. This is an example of a morphographic principle that is at work within a basically phonographic writing system.[3] Likewise, phonographic features are usually observable in primarily morphographic systems. For instance, each sign of the Chinese writing system corresponds not only to a (meaning-bearing) morpheme, but also to a syllable of the spoken language. Thus, these signs also have a phonetic value each. As such, they can be used to write words of foreign languages, such as *Frankfurt* (example (4)).[4] In this use, their correspondence to a meaning-bearing morpheme (represented in the first line of example (4)) becomes irrelevant.

(4)   'law'   'flower'   'gram'   'luck'
      fǎ   *lán*   *ke*   *fú*
      法   兰   克   福

Thus the terms "morphographic" and "phonographic" can be viewed as principles that are at work within one and the same writing system, rather than describing writing systems as a whole. Understood as such, the distinction between phonographic and morphographic writing systems is closely related to a first basic distinction that is of central importance for orthography development, namely that between "deep" and "shallow" orthographies (Katz and Frost 1992; Bird 1999b; Ellis et al. 2004). The metaphor of the "depth" of an orthography refers to the level of linguistic structure at which forms are orthographically represented. Shallow orthographies approximate a correspondence between an orthographic representation and the surface realization of linguistic forms to the extent that they may specify the phonetic realization of these forms as they are pronounced in a given context. Examples of such orthographies are Serbian and Croatian, which use the same writing system, but different scripts, Cyrillic and Roman (Feldman and Barac-Cikoja 1996). In these orthographies, allomorphy and even regional pronunciations are represented (see Katz and Frost 1992: 69f.), and a close relation between the written form and its pronunciation is thus maintained. A deep orthography, on the other hand, approximates a correspondence between orthographic representation and underlying forms. Deep orthographies thus typically represent each morpheme of the language with one, invariable written form, and do not specify the morphophonological changes that these morphemes undergo in context. Deep orthographies are thus typically less specific with respect to the phonetic realization of a given form. A tendency towards such an orthography can be observed in the English examples (1)–(3), above.

Deep orthographies are widely in use for languages with many morphophonological changes, i.e. languages where the morphophonological representation is quite distinct to the phonetic representation, such as in English (Liberman et al. 1980; Katz and Frost 1992: 69ff.). A deep orthography for such languages can be understood as a technique for preserving the visual image of morphemes, which would be blurred in a shallow orthography. Shallow orthographies, on the other hand, tend to be used for languages with relatively few morphophonological changes, e.g. Serbian and Croatian. In these languages, the morphophonological representation is close to the phonetic representation. Consequently, a shallow orthography of such a language may preserve the graphic identity of morphemes to the same degree as a deep orthography of a language with many morphophonological changes.

The term *orthographic depth* thus refers – broadly speaking – to the level of linguistic structure at which the features represented in the orthography are located. Another important question is which of the manifold features present in a spoken message should be represented in an orthography at all. Linguistic analysis is crucial here since it reveals the distinctive features of the language, e.g. phonological contrasts. From a strictly structural point of view, a single minimal pair is enough for a given feature to count as distinctive. However, some features are clearly more important than others in the sense of "the extent to which users of the orthography rely on that feature in reading and writing the language" (Bird 1999b: 14). This is referred to as the *functional load* of a linguistic feature. For the development of an orthography it is important to evaluate the functional load of a linguistic feature in order to decide whether or not it should be represented in the orthography.

Functional load can be approximated by assessing how many words or utterances a given feature differentiates. For instance, in English some words are distinguished by stress, e.g. *cónvert* vs. *convért*, *prótest* vs. *protést*. These words are homographs in English, and in a list of isolated words there would indeed be ambiguity (and these words could count as minimal pairs in such a context). However, these words are not many, which is already indicative of the relatively low functional load of stress in English, at least with regard to distinguishing basic lexical items. In addition, the members of these pairs belong to different parts of speech (nouns vs. verbs) and thus they are easily disambiguated in context. Hence, it is clear that the functional load of stress in English is in fact very low in the sense that readers do not rely on it for disambiguating lexical items in a written message. Thus, while for the phonologist one minimal pair in a list of isolated words may be sufficient to identify a certain feature as contrastive, for the purpose of developing a practical orthography it is crucial additionally to evaluate the functional load of a potentially contrastive feature in connected texts. And if there are no, or only very few, instances where a given feature (e.g. stress) in fact disambiguates utterances in a sufficiently large text corpus, then the need to represent the distinction is highly diminished. This is particularly important if it would be cumbersome consistently to represent the feature in the orthography, as the writing of stress, e.g. by accent marks, in English would be.

This leads to a final concept to be introduced here, that of *underrepresenta-tion*. While it is true that orthographies should reduce potential ambiguity of a written message, they should also be simple. And in order to achieve this simplicity, it may be justified not to represent features that do not have a high functional load, even if they are contrastive from a strictly structural point of view. Underrepresentation in an orthography leads to homographs, i.e. more than one word is orthographically represented in the same way, and may thus lead to ambiguity. However, readers can in fact tolerate a considerable amount of ambiguity caused by homographs because they can make use of many cues when decoding a written message. Among these are syntactic cues, such as word classes (as in the case of English *prótest* vs. *protést*, mentioned above),[5] semantic cues (e.g. selectional restrictions), and contextual cues from the surrounding discourse. All this is to say that an orthographic representation may differ substantially from a phonological transcription in that a practical orthography may systematically underrepresent distinctive features for the sake of simplicity.

2. Non-linguistic factors in orthography development

This section identifies a number of factors that may be decisive in choosing one option for orthographic representation over another. These options are determined by the linguistic structure of the language to be written. The factors covered in this section, on the other hand, are independent of this structure and may therefore be called non-linguistic factors in orthography development. The basis of these factors is that different orthographic options have particular advantages and disadvantages for different potential users of the orthographies. These advantages and disadvantages are related to a wide range of issues, including pedagogical, sociopolitical, and mechanical or technical aspects of orthographies. Non-linguistic factors of orthography development are discussed in four sections: psycholinguistic and pedagogical issues (Section 2.1), existing orthographies (Section 2.2), dialect varieties (Section 2.3), and technical issues (Section 2.4).

2.1. Psycholinguistic and pedagogical issues

Psycholinguistic research has shown that different kinds of orthographies favor different kinds of users (Venezky 1970). Different user groups from the point of view of psycholinguistics are readers vs. writers, beginning readers/writers vs. advanced readers/writers, and mother-tongue speakers vs. non-fluent speakers. To make definitive statements about the learnability and usability of a given orthography for a given language, it is necessary to do extensive testing. However, drawing on results reported in the literature, some general statements can be made here.

A first, probably obvious point is that orthographies that reflect the particular structure of the language to be written facilitate the acquisition of the orthography. They do so because they build on speakers' implicit knowledge of the language, which is explicit in its grammatical description. The importance of this point is that conventions used in existing orthographies of surrounding languages, e.g. a dominant language, may be inappropriate to represent the particular structure of the language to be written, and reproducing them in a newly developed orthography may thus lead to problems (see Section 3.1 below for a case study).

The requirement of adhering to language-specific structures is particularly important for the orthographic representation of word boundaries, because words are the basic units for language processing in reading (Reicher 1969). It is well known that languages vary drastically with respect to word boundaries and that the definition of words can be a highly complex issue because there may be conflicting criteria. Careful examination of a wide variety of issues, including prosodic, morphosyntactic, and semantic factors, is thus a precondition for proposing orthographic rules concerning word boundaries (for discussion of some factors, see Dyken and Kutsch Lojenga 1993; see also Chapter 10).[6]

A second, more substantial point to be made here is that from the perspective of psycholinguistics, "the optimal orthography for a beginning reader is not the same as for a fluent reader" (Dawson 1989: 1). This general statement derives from the finding that advanced readers heavily rely on what is called a "sight vocabulary", i.e. written words are recognized as entire units and processed as such, without breaking them down into units of the sound structure. For that reason, advanced readers benefit from orthographies that preserve the graphic identity of morphemes. A sight vocabulary allows readers to quickly recognize words in written messages without much specification of phonetic details. A high reading competence also allows to make full use of contextual cues, which may require some going back and forth in a written message to disambiguate homographs. Because of the relative importance of a sight vocabulary and the relative unimportance of phonetic detail, advanced readers benefit from deep orthographies rather than shallow ones.

For beginning readers, however, things are different. The acquisition of a deep orthography at first exposure is relatively difficult because the written form may differ significantly from the actual pronunciation and may have to be memorized in a first phase. Compared to these, shallow orthographies, i.e. orthographies that represent linguistic forms in a way that is close to their actual pronunciation in each context, are considerably easier to learn for a beginning reader (and writer), including second language learners. Wherever languages display heavy morphophonological processes, orthography developers face the problem of either choosing a shallow orthography for the beginning reader or a deep orthography for the advanced one.

A further issue is that the process of reading is different from the process of writing. Again, the difference is between shallow and deep orthographies. A sight vocabulary is most helpful in the process of reading in that it allows quickly to retrieve a morpheme from the mental lexicon independent of its phonetic realization. In the process of writing, the advantages of a sight vocabulary are not as clear. In writing, it may be as easy to spell a form according to its pronunciation as to retrieve the underlying form. When making a compromise between an orthography that suits readers vs. writers, it should be taken into account that reading is far more frequent than writing (ideally, a text is written only once but read many times), so the needs of readers are somewhat more important.

A final point on pedagogical and psycholinguistic issues of orthographies concerns the particularities of endangered languages at an advanced stage of language shift. In such a situation, younger members of the speech community, who have not learned the endangered language themselves (at least not as a first language), may make up an important proportion of the potential users of the orthography. This group may be interested in writing the ancestral languages in the context of "third generation pursuit" (Dorian 1993), i.e. in an effort to revalue or revitalize the language that their parents had abandoned. They are thus in the situation of a second language learner, and they may benefit from a relatively shallow orthography that does not make heavy use of underrepresentation. Such an orthography allows them to correctly write a word from its pronunciation and to correctly pronounce a word from its written form without knowing the word. This is particularly important if the orthography is likely to be used primarily for documenting ancestral knowledge (e.g. narratives, ethno-biological terminology), rather than for everyday written communication.

2.2. Existing orthographies

Already existing orthographies – be they of the language for which the orthography is being developed or of surrounding languages – tend to be an extremely influential factor in orthography development or reform. Dealing with existing orthographies can be a highly delicate sociopolitical matter, since the emblematic function of an orthography emerges most clearly in its visual contrast to surrounding orthographies.

With respect to orthography reform, it cannot be stressed enough that reforming an established orthography may have an enormous sociopolitical impact, in particular if a substantial number of speakers are already acquainted with that orthography and if printed materials that use this orthography already exist. Thus, it may be better to live with an inconsistent orthography – even if inappropriate from a linguistic or psycholinguistic perspective – unless the speech community is really determined to change it.

How a newly developed orthography relates to existing orthographies of neighboring languages depends primarily on the sociopolitical relation of the speech community to the speakers of those languages. In a typical situation of language endangerment, an increasing number of members of the speech community acquire a dominant language to an increasing degree of proficiency. Often, they acquire literacy for the first time in that language or they are keen to do so in order to gain access to institutions of the national society, e.g. higher education. In these cases, an orthography that resembles the orthography of the dominant language may be advantageous in order to facilitate acquisition of the orthography of the endangered language for those who are already acquainted with the one of the dominant language, and to facilitate the acquisition of the orthography of the dominant language for those who acquire the one of the endangered language first.

On the other hand, it is a recurrent phenomenon that speech communities want their newly developed orthography to have a visual appearance that is decidedly different from that of dominant or other neighboring, possibly closely related languages. However, the wish for an emblematic orthography is often satisfied by choosing graphemes with a particular visual shape. These choices do not affect the overall functionality of the orthography, and

this issue is thus often relatively easily resolved when compared to the difficult choices that may be necessary when choosing between a deep or shallow
orthography, or whether to represent a given feature at all.

If literacy in the dominant language is already on the way or desired in
the future, and if it is accepted that a newly developed orthography is to
borrow elements from the orthography of the dominant language, then the
question arises how to deal with internal inconsistencies of this orthography. These are difficult to acquire in the dominant language, and would
also be difficult to acquire in the endangered language. Thus, idiosyncratic
spelling conventions that have come about for purely historical reasons,
such as Spanish /k/ – ⟨k, c, qu⟩, should in general not be replicated in newly
developed orthographies.

2.3. Dialect varieties

Dialect varieties exist in every speech community. A characteristic often
found in speech communities without a written standard is that there is no
widely accepted standard variety among the different dialects. This obviously poses a problem for developing an orthography since an orthography
by definition involves standardization. There are limited possibilities to
represent various dialects using a single orthography, as further discussed
in Section 3.4 below. Multidialectal orthographies are more feasible in case
of relatively deep orthographies, which may not represent the features that
distinguish the dialects, e.g. vowel distinctions that are contrastive in one
dialect but not in another. In any case, it is likely that a standardized, new
orthography will have to disregard at least some features of one or more of
the dialect varieties. Which ones these will be depends again largely on
non-linguistic factors, namely the sociopolitical relations among the dialect
groups.

2.4. Technical production issues

At a time when typewriters were the main tools for producing written texts
(other than handwriting, of course), the limited set of symbols available on
a typewriter keyboard as well as the ease with which they could be produced were of major practical import in designing practical orthographies.
Creating graphemes that required the use of two or more diacritics on one

base letter resulted in an extremely cumbersome typing process and thus were very rarely adopted. While modern word processors in principle allow for much greater variety and comfortable shortcuts in producing unusual graphemes, technical production and reproducibility remains a major issue.

The main point here concerns the electronic representation of characters other than those used in the Latin alphabet. This issue has unfortunately still not been satisfactorily resolved in our highly computerized age. Special fonts that contain non-Latin characters often have certain software requirements (e.g. they can only be used under a particular version of a particular system) and are thus not safe options in the long run. The newly developed Unicode character encoding standard comprises thousands of graphemes (including those of the Latin alphabet), independent of special fonts (see Chapter 14). However, Unicode is still not yet fully established (e.g. most commonly available fonts only support a small subset of these characters). Furthermore, even if computers are available, the access to special fonts and the technical know-how to install and run them may not be available to the speech community. Thus, the safest option – to ensure usability of the orthography without access to sophisticated software and computer know-how, as well as for safe long-term archiving of digital files containing text written in that orthography – is still to use only characters that can be found on the keyboard of a mechanical typewriter or combinations of these (e.g. digraphs or combinations of letters with diacritics).

2.5. Summary

Most of the factors discussed in the preceding sections relate to decisions about orthographies that vary according to two parameters: orthographic depth and the similarity of a given orthography to the orthography of dominant or other neighboring languages, which is particularly important in the case of endangered languages. The advantages and disadvantages of choosing orthographies towards one end or the other of these two parameters are summarized in Table 1.

Table 1. Advantages and disadvantages relating to non-linguistic factors for orthography development

Parameter	Advantages	Disadvantages
shallow orthography (close to pronunciation)	– easier to learn for beginning readers/writers – easier to learn for non-(fluent) speakers	– may blur graphic identity of morphemes – more difficult to encompass various dialects in one written form
deep orthography (preserves graphic identity of meaningful elements)	– easier for reading in general – easier to handle for fluent readers – easier to encompass various dialects	– harder to learn for beginners – harder to learn for non-(fluent) speakers
using conventions of the orthography of the dominant language	– easier to learn for speakers that are literate in dominant language – facilitates subsequent literacy in dominant language – facilitates technical text (re)production	– may have to live with inconsistencies in the orthography of dominant language – potentially less emblematic
using conventions different from those of the orthography of the dominant language	– highly emblematic	– potential problems with technical text (re)production

3. Case studies: Options and choices

The following sections (3.1–3.5) discuss selected aspects of a number of linguistic systems and the options that these offer for orthographic representation as well as the choices that have been made based on non-linguistic factors.

3.1. Morphemic nasality in Eastern Tucanoan languages

The reform of the orthographies of the Eastern Tucanoan languages is a good example of the need for a thorough linguistic analysis as a basis for orthography development and for the advantage of an orthography that respects the particular structure of the languages as opposed to one that uses conventions of orthographies of surrounding languages with established orthographies.

The Eastern Tucanoan languages are a group of closely related languages spoken in the Vaupés, a region on both sides of the Colombian-Brazilian border in the North West Amazon. Nasality is a pervasive feature in these languages. All oral, voiced phonemes, i.e. the six consonants *b, d, y, g, w, r* and the six vowels, have a nasal counterpart. Nasality used to be spelled out on each segment in the orthographies, as in the following examples (5a)–(5g).[7]

(5) a. ⟨ãmũmã⟩   [ãmũmã]   'neck'
     b. ⟨gnãmõrõ⟩   [ŋãmõrõ]   'ear'
     c. ⟨jĩnõ⟩   [hĩnõ]   'anaconda'
     d. ⟨gudamĩsĩ⟩   [gudamĩsĩ]   'stomach'
     e. ⟨ojoño⟩   [ohoɲõ]   'banana plant'
     f. ⟨baamĩ⟩   [baːmĩ]   '(s)he eats'
     g. ⟨ĩãbeco⟩   [ĩãbeko]   'he who does not look'

Recent research on Eastern Tucanoan languages has shown that nasality in these languages is a feature of morphemes, in particular lexical roots, rather than a feature of phonological segments. Thus, all simple (i.e. not compound) verbs and nouns are entirely oral or entirely nasal, i.e. the voiced phonemes of these forms are either all oral or all nasal. This characteristic is represented in the new orthographies of the Eastern Tucanoan languages (Gomez-Imbert and Buchillet 1986; Gomez-Imbert 1998), in which nasal morphemes are preceded by "~" (compare examples (6a)–(6g) with (5a)–(5g)). In case of polymorphemic words that begin with an oral morpheme and end with a nasal one, "~" is inserted before the nasal morpheme (examples (6e)–(6f)). In case of polymorphemic words that begin with a nasal morpheme and end with an oral one, "~" is marked at the beginning of the word and "-" is inserted before the oral morpheme (example (6g)).[8]

(6) a. ⟨~abuba⟩   [ãmũmã]   'neck'
     b. ⟨~gaboro⟩   [ŋãmõrõ]   'ear'
     c. ⟨~hido⟩   [hĩnõ]   'anaconda'
     d. ⟨guda~bisi⟩   [gudamĩsĩ]   'stomach'
     e. ⟨oho~yo⟩   [ohoɲõ]   'banana plant'
     f. ⟨baa~bi⟩   [ba:mĩ]   '(s)he eats'
     g. ⟨~ia-beko⟩   [ĩãbeko]   'he who does not look'

According to Gomez–Imbert (1998) speakers are considerably more comfortable with the new orthographies than with the old ones, presumably because the new orthography builds on their implicit knowledge of the structure of the languages. This example thus shows the importance of modeling orthographies as closely to the linguistic structure as possible, rather than taking over conventions of orthographies of better-known languages.

3.2. Palatalization in Miraña

The examples in this section come from Miraña, an endangered Amazonian language spoken in Colombia, to the South of the Vaupés region (Seifart 2002, 2005). Miraña has a linguistically very close variant called Bora, which is spoken mainly in Peru (Thiesen 1996; Thiesen and Thiesen 1998). Today, Miraña has only about 50 speakers out of ca. 400 ethnic Mirañas. All speakers are bilingual in Spanish and most are also literate in Spanish. Palatalization in Miraña will serve as an example for non-linguistic factors being responsible for the choice of a shallow orthography over a deep one.

   Miraña has a set of six palatal consonants. Most of their occurrences are easily recognizable as phonetic realizations of their alveolar counterparts in the context of a preceding /i/, such as [n, ɲ] (examples (7a)–(7b)). However, palatal consonants occur not only after /i/, but also after /a/ (example (7c)).

(7) a. [nàʔbɛ̀]
        'brother'

     b. [íɲàʔbɛ̀]
        'his/her/their brother'

     c. [táɲàʔbɛ̀]
        'my brother'

Further analysis of Miraña revealed that what is causing palatalization of alveolar consonants after /a/ is the underlying phoneme /aʲ/, whose palatal component is realized as [j] before vowels (example (8a)), spreads to alveolar consonants, which are palatalized (example (8b), see also example (7c)), and is suppressed before bilabial consonants, where the distinction /aʲ/ vs. /a/ is neutralized (example (8c)) (note that tone alternation has no effect on palatalization in Miraña).

(8)   a.   [àjɯ́hɯ̀]
             /àʲɯ́hɯ̀/
             'okay'

       b.   [tátʲá?dì]
             /táʲ-tá?dì/
             1ST_PERSON_POSSESSOR-grandfather
             'my grandfather'

       c.   [tàmámìbà]
             /tàʲ-mámìbà/
             1ST_PERSON_POSSESSOR-trunk
             'my trunk'

This phonological analysis results in a fairly simple, symmetric, and parsimonious inventory of consonant phonemes, while the vowel inventory has to be augmented by the complex unit /aʲ/ (Seifart 2002: 23–30).

The phonological system allows for the options of representing palatalization in a deep orthography, i.e. phonemically, or in a shallow orthography, i.e. phonetically. A deep orthography has the advantage of preserving the graphic identity of morphemes that begin with alveolar consonants, be they lexical roots (see examples (7b)–(7c) and (8b), above), or suffixes such as the inanimate marker (examples (9a)–(9b)) and the restrictive marker (examples (9c)–(9d)). This advantage is particularly important because a large proportion of roots begin with alveolar consonants and the most frequent suffixes also begin with these consonants, including the markers in examples (9a)–(9d) as well as the plural marker.

(9)   a.   [tsànɛ̀]
             /tsà-nɛ̀/
             one-INANIMATE
             'one (inanimate)'

    b. [tsì:ɲὲ]
        /tsi:-nὲ/
        other-INANIMATE
        'another (inanimate)'

    c. [ɯ́hɨ́ʔɔ̀ɾὲ]
        /ɯ́hɨ́ʔɔ̀-ɾὲ/
        banana-RESTRICTIVE
        'just a banana'

    d. [ɯ́βɨ́:bàɾʲὲ]
        /ɯ́βɨ́:bàʲ-ɾὲ/
        basket-RESTRICTIVE
        'just a basket'

However, from the point of view of orthography development there are two major disadvantages of writing palatalization phonemically. Firstly, it differs significantly from actual pronunciation in some instances, e.g. when palatalization spreads across glottal consonants in coda position and is realized in the onset of the following syllable, as in examples (10a)–(10b). Secondly, features that are neutralized have to be written, e.g. when /aʲ/ is followed by a bilabial consonant (see example (8c), above) or when it occurs word-finally (compare example (10c) with (9d)).

(10) a. [tsàhtʲὲ]
        /tsàʲhtὲ/
        'Take!'

      b. [tɯ́hpaʔjὲ]
         /tɯ́hpaʲʔὲ/
         proper name

      c. [ɯ́βì:bà]
         /ɯ́βì:bàʲ/
         'basket'

A delicate choice thus has to be made between orthographically representing palatalization in Miraña phonemically, i.e. as a complex vowel, or phonetically, i.e. in six additional consonants. The phonemic writing ensures an invariant graphic image of a large proportion of morphemes and may thus help to build a sight vocabulary, from which advanced readers may benefit.

However, the palatalization process as a whole is rather complex in that palatalization may be neutralized or it may spread across various segments. The phonetic writing, on the other hand, requires no knowledge of the palatalization process. Its disadvantages are that it requires six additional units (the palatal consonants) and that it introduces a lot of redundancy, in particular by writing palatal consonants after /i/, where they are easily recognizable as palatalized realizations (see examples (7b) and (9b)).

A shallow orthography with respect to palatalization was nevertheless proposed (and adopted) for Miraña. An important reason for this decision is that nowadays, many of the younger Mirañas, who are the main users of the orthography, did not learn Miraña as their first language, and many of them hardly speak it at all. Thus, they do not have an implicit knowledge of the structure of the language to the same degree as, e.g., most users of the orthographies of Eastern Tucanoan languages have about their languages. The main use of the Miraña orthography is to document myths, songs, and ethno-biological terminology, which younger speakers elicit from older ones. The proposed orthography serves these purposes well in that it provides an intuitive system for spelling and pronouncing Miraña words unknown to non-fluent speakers.

3.3. Writing tone

All languages make use of pitch in some way. However, while pitch is used in some languages, e.g. Chinese, to differentiate a vast amount of lexical items, its function in other languages is mostly limited to conveying intonational distinctions. From the point of view of orthography development, pitch is thus a feature that varies drastically from language to language with respect to its functional load in distinguishing lexical items. In languages where it is either very high or very low, the question whether or not to represent it in an orthography does not arise, but there are many intermediate cases that require careful analysis and possibly creative solutions. These issues are discussed in Bird (1999b), from which the examples presented in this section are taken.

Typical characteristics of such "intermediate" systems, which are found in many African, Papuan, and Amazonian languages, are that pitch is widely used to mark grammatical functions and that pitch patterns can only be described in terms of sometimes quite complicated sets of spreading and truncation rules. The processes that underlie the resulting surface tones may thus be extremely complex and their marking may be very difficult to handle even for experienced writers. This is the case in Dschang, a Grassfield Bantu language spoken in Cameroon. Bird (1999b: 7) reports that in this language, experienced writers attain an accuracy score of only 83.5% correct tone marks and inexperienced ones, only 53% correct tone marks when marking surface tones. Tone writing thus poses a serious problem for the orthography of this language and the question arises to what extent tone actually carries a functional load, i.e. whether it is necessary to write tones at all.

An interesting solution to a similar problem was found in Komo, a Bantu language, which is spoken in the Democratic Republic of Congo (formally Zaïre). In this language, tone is used to distinguish lexical items as well as for marking grammatical functions. With respect to lexical tones, it was found that about 28 minimal pairs are distinguished by their tonal pattern in a representative list of over 3000 words. More than half of these, however, can be easily distinguished in context, either because they belong to different word classes or because of their meaning. Thus, it was decided not to mark lexical tone in this language, even though this creates ambiguity through homographs in a few cases. On the other hand, a considerable amount of inflected and derived word forms in Komo are distinguished by grammatical tones on their first syllable and these can often not be disambiguated by context. Thus, it was decided to mark only grammatical tones on the first syllable in the Komo orthography. Example (11) (data from Paul Thomas, as reported in Bird 1999b: 23) illustrates how this tone marking disambiguates inflected or derived forms (examples (11a) vs. (11c), (11b) vs. (11d), etc.), but fails to disambiguate lexical items in some cases (examples (11a) vs. (11b), (11c) vs. (11d), etc.).

(11) a. ⟨bebhomi⟩   [bèbhòmí]   'we insulted him'
      b. ⟨bebhomi⟩   [bèbhómí]   'we did surgery on it'
      c. ⟨bĕbhomi⟩   [bĕbhòmí]   'we insulted them'
      d. ⟨bĕbhomi⟩   [bĕbhómí]   'we did surgery on them'
      e. ⟨babhomigi⟩   [bàbhòmìgì]   'insulters'
      f. ⟨babhomigi⟩   [bàbhómìgì]   'surgeons'
      g. ⟨bábhomigi⟩   [bábhòmìgì]   'they insulted habitually'
      h. ⟨bábhomigi⟩   [bábhómìgì]   'they did surgery habitually'

The Komo orthography illustrates the importance of carefully assessing the functional load of a given feature in order to decide whether it should be represented orthographically or not, in particular if writing this feature creates major difficulties for the users of the orthography. The solution found in Komo also shows that a given feature – in this case tone – may not have the same functional load in all of its contexts, and, consequently, the possibility of representing a feature such as tone only in those contexts where it effectively helps readers to disambiguate a given form, without overburdening the orthography with tone marking on (almost) every syllable.

3.4. Multidialectal orthographies

The two examples of multidialectal orthographies discussed in this section provide further illustrations of the interaction between linguistic systems and non-linguistic factors in orthography development, in particular, the concept of underrepresentation and the different needs of readers vs. writers.

Sasak is an Austronesian language spoken on the island of Lombok in Nusa Tenggara Barat, Indonesia (Austin 2000). Across the five dialects of Sasak, there are eight phonological vowels, which contrast with each other in different ways in the different dialects. The practical orthography that was established for all Sasak dialects represents only those vowels that are contrastive in all of the dialects and it conflates those that are conflated in the phonological systems of one or more of them (Table 2).[9] The disadvantage of this orthography is that it creates ambiguity through homographs in individual dialects, but it has the great advantage of offering a unified orthography for all dialect groups, and this has apparently been the overriding reason for adopting it.

Table 2. Vowels in the Sasak orthography (Peter Austin, p.c. 2004)

Phonemes	Orthography
a	a
e	
ə	e
ɛ	
i	i
o	
ɔ	o
u	u

A different solution for representing a number of dialects in one orthography was chosen for Biliau, another Austronesian language, which is spoken in Papua New Guinea (Simons 1994). The phonemic inventories of the dialects of Biliau differ in that in the western dialect /d/ and /z/ are separate phonemes, while in the eastern dialect only /d/ occurs. In this case, an orthography was established (and presumably accepted by all speakers, including those of the eastern dialect) that represents the more complex phonology of the western dialect (example (12)) (Simons 1994: 12).

(12)		western dialect	eastern dialect	
a.	⟨damom⟩	/damom/	/damom/	'my forehead'
b.	⟨zamom⟩	/zamom/	/damom/	'rotten'
c.	⟨der⟩	/der/	/der/	'a cold wind'
d.	⟨zer⟩	/zer/	/der/	'grass skirt'
e.	⟨badi⟩	/badi/	/badi/	'get up'
f.	⟨bazi⟩	/bazi/	/badi/	'feather'

In the multidialectal orthography of Biliau, speakers of the eastern dialect have to write a distinction that is not present in their phonemic system and have to memorize spellings of these words (examples (12b), (12d), (12f)). Reading will not be difficult, however. Every time speakers of the eastern dialect see a ⟨z⟩, they are taught to pronounce a /d/. Thus, the overall advantage of this orthographic solution is toward the reader. This is a good reason for giving preference to the western dialect in the multidialectal orthography, but this would probably not have been possible if it did not also have "true ascendancy in terms of prestige" (Simons 1994: 20).

A comparison of Sasak and Biliau nicely illustrates that non-linguistic factors are decisive in making choices in the development of an orthography. The phonemic systems of the dialects of Biliau and Sasak offer in principle the same two options for multidialectal orthographies: either representing distinctions that are *not* contrastive in some dialects or neglecting distinctions that *are* contrastive in some dialects. Which of these two options was actually chosen depends crucially on the sociolinguistic situation. In Biliau, one of the dialect groups has a sufficiently high status such that the other dialect group accepts its variant as the basis for a common orthography. This is apparently not the case in Sasak.

Table 3. Some graphemes of the Miraña orthography

Spanish orthography	Miraña orthography	Bora orthography	IPA	Motivation
(u)	ʉ	u	ɯ	making a difference to Spanish and Bora, local conventions
(i)	ɨ	ɨ	ɨ	new grapheme based on Spanish
qu (before e and i) c (other contexts) k (in loanwords)	k	k (before e and i) c (other contexts)	k	avoiding inconsistencies of Spanish and Bora
v, b (intervocalic pronunciation)	v	v	β	two Spanish graphemes that stand for the same phoneme in Spanish are used for two phonemes in Miraña
v, b (word-initial pronunciation)	b	b	b	
ll, y	ll	ll	d͡ʒ	two Spanish graphemes that stand for the same phoneme in Spanish are used for two phonemes in Miraña
	y	y	j	
j	j	j	h	local Spanish pronunciation
	'	h	ʔ	making a difference to Bora
(g, w)	gw	w	gʷ	making a difference to Bora
(t, d), (y)	ty, dy	ty, dy	tʲ, dʲ	digraphs based on Spanish graphemes (only two examples included here)

3.5. Choosing graphemes

This section briefly discusses the issue of choosing graphemes, using again the example of the Miraña orthography, some aspects of which were discussed in Section 3.2 above. In Miraña, these choices were determined by the Mirañas' sociopolitical relations to two other speech communities which have established orthographies: The Colombian national society, whose language is Spanish, and the Boras, who speak a linguistically very close variant of Miraña (Thiesen 1996: 11, 20; Seifart 2005: 22f.). A first noteworthy characteristic of Miraña orthography is that all of its graphemes are based on Spanish letters. Some of the Miraña graphemes are modified versions of Spanish graphemes, either in their visual graphic form or their phonetic value, as can be observed in Table 3. Miraña speakers also decided to modify the visual appearance of some (Spanish-based) graphemes used in Bora. This can be understood when taking into account that the Mirañas have long struggled to be recognized as a separate ethnic group with respect to the more numerous Boras. Table 3 gives a good impression of the two main conflicting factors that are at work when choosing graphemes: that of adhering to conventions of already known and established orthographies of surrounding languages, and that of giving an orthography a decidedly different appearance in order to fulfill an emblematic function for the speech community.

4. Conclusion

The previous sections have shown that orthography development involves a rich interaction of the characteristics of linguistic systems and a variety of non-linguistic factors. Structural properties of languages often allow for a number of alternative options of orthographic representation of a given feature. These options may correspond to a phonemic representation, but they may as well correspond to a more abstract representation (morphophonemic) or to a more superficial representation (phonetic). These alternative options may favor different potential users of the orthography. The task of the orthography developer is to balance the advantages and disadvantages of these options and find a workable compromise.

Acknowledgements

I am grateful for comments from Mandana Seyfeddinipur, Ulrike Mosel, Nikolaus Himmelmann, Julia Borchert, Jost Gippert, and the audiences at the *DoBeS* summer school in Frankfurt in 2004 and at the *Instituto Caro y Cuervo* in Bogotá in 2005, where much of the contents of this chapter was presented in seminars. I am also grateful to Peter Austin, Natalia Eraso, Doris Fagua, Elsa Gomez-Imbert, Camilo Robayo, and Maria Trillos for providing examples (along with discussion), not all of which are represented in this chapter. Thanks also to Falk Grollmus for providing the Chinese example.

Notes

1. Further theoretical possibilities to typologize writing systems, such as direction (left, right), axis (horizontal, perpendicular), or lining (top to bottom, bottom to top), are usually disregarded since they yield no insightful classifications.
2. Morphographic systems are sometimes also called "logographic" or "ideographic". Both terms are inappropriate because the units represented in these writing systems are always morphemes, and not words in the sense of units that could be modified by inflection, as the term "logographic" suggests. As a matter of fact, there are no writing systems that represent words in this sense, even though in case of highly isolating languages, such as Chinese, words tend to be monomorphemic. Furthermore, graphemes always refer to linguistic units and never directly to extra-linguistic concepts, as the term "ideographic" suggests.
3. In many cases, the spelling of morphemes is constant in different contexts despite pronunciation differences because the spelling represents an older stage of the language, when these forms were in fact pronounced in the same way. Because such spelling conventions make explicit the etymology of words, phenomena such as the English examples 1–3 can be called "etymological writing". The French orthography – which displays very complex correspondences to pronunciation – also contains many examples of etymological writing.
4. Additionally, for many Chinese signs it may be claimed that they include components with an exclusively phonetic value (Coulmas 2003: 56ff.). This is a further phonographic aspect of this writing system.
5. Note that information about word classes can also be directly represented in an orthography, for instance by capitalization of nouns, as in German.
6. Similar issues apply to the orthographic representation of syntactic units, such as phrases and sentences, which are often orthographically represented with punctuation.

7. I adapted examples 5 and 6 from a report on a workshop on the reform of the orthographies of Eastern Tucanoan languages (Eraso 2003). Examples 5a–f and 6a–f are from Makuna, examples 5g and 6g are from Barasano.

8. Note that in the new orthographies, the representation of /k/ was changed from ⟨c, qu⟩ to ⟨k⟩ and /h/ from ⟨j⟩ to ⟨h⟩ in order to facilitate the use of a single orthography in Spanish-dominated Colombia and Portuguese-dominated Brazil, where these graphemes have different phonetic values.

9. It may be of interest to note here that the writing system of Indonesian, the main contact language of Sasak, conflates the two phonemes /ə/ and /e/ in the grapheme ⟨e⟩ in most publications (although the distinction is maintained in many dictionaries by representing /e/ with ⟨é⟩).

Chapter 12

Sketch grammar

Ulrike Mosel

Introduction

The role of the sketch grammar in a language documentation project has not been investigated yet so that this chapter is based on general considerations, discussions with colleagues, and the experiences I made when working on the documentation of the Teop[1] language on Bougainville in Papua New Guinea. The chapter starts with a typology of sketch grammars, showing how the various types of sketch grammars differ from fully-fledged reference grammars, and then in Section 2 describes which demands language documentation sketch grammars (LDSGs) should meet in terms of comprehensiveness, accuracy, and user-friendliness. The content of LDSGs and its relation to the lexical database and the annotated recordings is discussed in Section 3 Theoretical issues such as the role of grammatical analysis and description in language documentation projects, or the relationship between grammaticography and lexicography will not be touched.[2]

1. Types of sketch grammars

There are at least five types of sketch grammars:

1. the preliminary grammar that presents the very first account of a language's structure on the basis of a small corpus;
2. the introductory grammar chapter that accompanies the treatise of a specific research topic;
3. the summary of a large reference grammar;
4. the grammar in the front matter of a dictionary (dictionary grammar);
5. the sketch grammar of a language documentation.

While the content of the preliminary grammar heavily depends on what kind of data the authors were able to collect and analyze[3], the author of an introductory grammar chapter faces the problem of identifying the kind of information the reader needs in order to understand the specialized investigation in question. Since a specialized investigation focuses on a certain type of linguistic phenomenon, the introductory grammar chapter can be selective and concentrate on those aspects of grammar that are essential for understanding the data presented in the main part of the book, but are not its topic. Consequently, a book on tense and aspect may lack information on the derivation of nominals because it is irrelevant, whereas a book on morphology would not deal with derivation in the introductory grammar chapter, because this constitutes an important part of the body of the book.[4]

The main difference between these first two types is that in practice the linguist starts writing the preliminary grammar as soon as he or she puts the first analyses of paradigms and constructions into words, whereas the introductory grammar chapter is written after the research on the specialized area in question has been concluded. Only then can the author identify which grammatical information the reader will need to understand the investigation. Similarly, the summary or concise version of a reference grammar only contains a selection of an already existing analysis of the language. However, the selection criteria are different. Here the grammatical phenomena to be described are not chosen with regard to the presentation of some other research areas. Rather, the author selects what she or he considers as essential features of the language from a more general perspective (see Quirk et al. 1985: 37–91, Mosel and Hovdhaugen 1992: 49–65, for an example).

The fourth type of sketch grammar, the dictionary grammar "brings together elements of the language that are separated by the alphabetical order of the headwords – typical examples are a list of numerals or an overview of derivational means of expression" (Mugdan 1989: 732, translation U.M.). Such informations can help to save space within the main body of the dictionary. For example, if the language has a regular and productive affix to derive diminutives from nouns, it is more economic to describe this affix and its use in the grammar than listing all diminutives as headwords or subentries (see Mugdan 1989 for a detailed discussion on dictionary grammars).

The sketch grammar of a language documentation is a bit of everything. Through most stages of the process of documenting the language, it is a preliminary grammar that needs constant revising. Similar to introductory grammar chapters and dictionary grammars, it is closely related to some other major piece of linguistic work, in this case the corpus of annotated recordings and a lexical database. And it also resembles the summary of a reference grammar and the dictionary grammar in that it enhances the accessibility of the work for a more general readership.

2. The aims of a sketch grammar in language documentation

The LDSG is not a so-called "short grammar" as it does not aim at describing the language as a system but at facilitating the access of the documentation. Though not being an integral component of the main body of the documentation, the LDSG is, as a kind of user's guide, essential for the utility value of the language documentation and therefore should be taken seriously from the very beginning. In particular, the sketch grammar should

- contain all the grammatical information that the reader needs to make use of the lexical database and understand how in the corpus of annotated recordings the translations relate to the transcriptions;
- at any stage accurately reflect the author's current knowledge of the language;
- be user-friendly.

2.1. Comprehensiveness

As a documentation should contain a fair amount of recordings that are annotated by interlinear morphemic glosses, the amount of information given in the sketch grammar partly depends on how much of this information is provided by the annotations (for a detailed account of annotations see Chapter 9).

For example, the Teop language has a very complex system of articles that indicate noun class, number, specificity, and grammatical relations. There are in principle two options to inform the reader about the use of Teop articles. Firstly, all the grammatical properties of articles can be explained in the sketch grammar by giving the full paradigm, in which case it is sufficient to gloss the articles in the text corpus simply as ART, e.g.

(1) *bona moon*
     ART   woman

so that ART only denotes the word/morpheme class of the glossed morpheme, but not its particular grammatical features.

Secondly, one can indicate all grammatical features in the gloss, e.g.

(2)   *bona*   *moon*
       ART: A-CLASS.SPEC.SG.OBJ woman:A-CLASS
       'specific singular object article agreeing with a noun belonging to the
       A.class'

in which case the explanations in the grammar can be confined to explaining the abbreviations. For three reasons we preferred the first solution in the Teop project. Firstly, after we had done the analysis which was necessary in any case, writing down the paradigm did not take much time; secondly, the paradigm represents the grammatical features of all articles comprising the category ART in a systematic way, and thirdly, long glosses as in (2) are not userfriendly. They take so much space that only a few words fit into one line and thus make it difficult to capture the form-meaning relations of a sentence at a quick glance.

2.2. Accuracy

The sketch grammar of a language documentation cannot provide an absolutely accurate description of linguistic facts because this would presuppose a comprehensive grammatical analysis of the entire corpus and presumably additional research on particular grammatical phenomena that are not fully covered by the corpus (see Chapter 1). However, as the following example illustrates, the sketch grammar should aim at accuracy in the sense of explicitly accounting for the assumptions that underlie the grammatical annotations in the corpus.

When starting with the annotation of Teop recordings, we found hundreds of examples where the particle *paa* seemed to be a tense/aspect/mood (TAM) marker locating the reported event in the past, e.g.

(3)   ... *me   iaa   paa gigo   anaa Solomon*
             and mum TAM pregnant me   Solomons
       '... and mum got pregnant with me in the Solomon Islands.'

                                                        (Sii 2.114–116 R)

Accordingly we glossed *paa* as PAST, ignoring a very few exceptions. Further on, however, we discovered more and more examples like

(4) *Be-an rake tea nao, ean* **paa** *nao papahiana.*
    if- 2SG want COMPL go 2SG TAM go alone
    'If you want to go, you go by yourself.'   (Aro 5.142R)

where *paa* evidently does not mark past tense, and came to realize that from the very beginning the exceptions should have been taken seriously. Our current analysis suggests that *paa* does not locate an event in time, but indicates a change of situation be it in the past or the future. Since this finding also questions the glossing of other TAM markers, we now gloss all TAM markers simply as 'TAM' and compensate for this underspecified glossing by a short description of each TAM marker in the sketch grammar. There we precisely state our hypotheses and mention open questions such as the compatibility of TAM markers with negations or temporal adverbs.

An alternative solution would be to give the TAM markers specific, but semantically neutral glosses such as T1, T2, etc. which can be easily searched for and be replaced by more meaningful glosses once their functions are better understood. But also in this case, the LDSG should explicitly explain the meanings of the glosses and describe the relevant grammatical phenomena in a way that accounts for the preliminary status of the analysis and thus minimizes the danger of misinterpretations.

2.3. User-friendliness

To be user-friendly, a LDSG must meet the user's needs, i.e. to quickly get an overview of the essential features of the language and all the information necessary for using the annotated recordings in further linguistic and related research. Therefore the LDSG should be short and the grammatical facts be clearly presented in a format that follows common practice, for instance one that presents the description in an ascending manner with the chapter on phonology first and that on complex sentences last.

All terms whose meaning is vague or variable in the linguistic literature, e.g. adverb, particle, or is presumably only known to specialists, e.g. applicative, should be defined, and all abbreviations be explained. The definitions should, however, be short and only briefly state which language specific properties have been relevant for the selection of the terms in question.

3. Content

The content of the LDSG of a previously unresearched language depends on

- the structure of the language;
- the state of analysis;
- how much and what kind of information is provided in the annotations and the lexical database.

However varied these things are, a number of characteristics of the language should be described in the LDSG in addition to the list of abbreviations used in grammatical glossing. These are

- charts of the consonant and the vowel system; a note on syllable structure, and the most important phonological processes; and a statement on how the orthography and/or transcription used in the documentation relates to these phonological characteristics (see Chapters 9 and 11);
- an overview of the word classes and the grammatical categories (tense/ aspect, number, person, gender, case etc.) in order to facilitate a better understanding of the glosses;
- inflectional paradigms as these are very difficult to extract from text corpora and are hardly ever fully represented there;
- word and constituent order rules that would help the user to quickly understand utterances.

In addition, it might be useful for linguists, especially typologists, to include a list of important typological features and for ethnographers to add a section with notes on lexical and phraseological characteristics (see Chapter 8). Strictly speaking, the latter do not belong into a grammar but unless they are dealt with in a different part of the language documentation, they may be accommodated here.

3.1. The LDSG and the lexical data base

Since the entries in a lexical database contain information on word classes and subclasses, the sketch grammar only needs to explain the principles of word classification and briefly characterize each class to facilitate the understanding of the abbreviations used in the lexical database and the annotations. For instance, in the Teop sketch grammar it is sufficient to say that causatives are derived by the prefix *vaa-* from intransitive and transitive verbs, but it is not necessary to investigate and describe which semantic types of lexemes have causative counterparts and what kind of argument or role structure they have. Any typologist interested in causativization can find out the rules by checking the lexical database and the text corpus for causatives.

Another example is the semantic motivation of noun class assignment to one of the three noun classes in Teop, the a-class, the e-class and the o-class. Since each noun in the dictionary is classified as *n.a.*, *n.e.*, or *n.o.*, the sketch grammar only needs to describe which role the noun classes play in syntactic constructions and give a rough idea of their semantics. A thorough analysis can wait until there is time for a specialist investigation.

3.2. The LDSG and the corpus of annotated recordings

To quickly find and understand interesting grammatical constructions, a large corpus of recordings with interlinear glossings and a free translation is not sufficient or at least not always practical. Imagine you are interested in a very frequent conjunction like *that* in English. Your search gives you over 1000 examples, but 98% are uninteresting, you need the 20 exceptional ones to find evidence for your hypothesis or falsify it (for a similar example see Chapter 9).

Searching can be made easier when the annotation is accompanied by notes on conspicuous grammatical phenomena and they are given easily searchable names like COMPLEMENT CLAUSE. In this manner you can even make notes on constructions that are not characterized by a particular linguistic unit, e.g. a particle or bound morpheme, and for example note down "juxtaposed/asyndetic COMPLEMENT CLAUSE." Apart from creating a useful tool for research on typological phenomena or the compilation of a reference grammar, making such notes is intellectually stimulating and helps to cope with the sometimes boring task of transcribing and translating. Furthermore, these notes give linguists the chance to document their insights into the grammatical structure that they or others can make use of later. As futher dicussed in Chapters 1 and 9, a language documentation requires a thorough analysis of the language, but it does not necessarily leave room for writing up a comprehensive reference grammar. A well-planned combination of a sketch grammar and grammatical notes in the annotated corpus of recordings can to some extent compensate for this.

Grammatical notes also help to keep the sketch grammar to a small size and, at the same time, enhance accuracy. To give another example from the Teop project, at the time of writing this chapter we only have a vague idea of the meaning and use of most demonstratives, especially when two demonstratives occur together in a single noun phrase. Consequently, we state in the sketch grammar that we have not fully analyzed the demonstratives yet and refer to the corpus where the interesting cases are identified in the notes by the label DEMONSTRATIVE.

In order to make this division of labour between the sketch grammar and the notes most efficient, the sketch grammar needs to list all the grammatical category labels used in the notes so that the users know which grammatical categories they can search for. This list of labels can be combined with the list of abbreviations used in the annotated corpus, the sketch grammar, and the lexical database, and with the glossary of terms referred to above, as illustrated in Table 1.

Table 1. Example from the index of the Teop sketch grammar

adjunct	optional constituent of the clause that refers to the particular circumstances of the state of affairs expressed by the verb complex and its arguments
ADV	prefix that derives adverbs from verbs > adverb
adverb	word that typically functions as a modifier within the verb complex
AP	> adjectival phrase
APP	> applicative
applicative	particle within the verb complex that changes the valence of a verb complex

4. Conclusion

The sketch grammar evolves in the course of the documentation work. Starting off as a preliminary sketch that is based on the very first elicitation sessions, it needs to be constantly revised as the documentary work proceeds so that the final version should be written close to the end of the project.

This process of continuous revision helps to keep a record of changes in the grammatical analysis and the usage of grammatical terms and their abbreviations. Furthermore, it allows to successively replace or complement the elicited examples of earlier versions by more natural examples from the growing corpus.

Notes

1. Teop is classified as Austronesian, Oceanic, Western Oceanic, Meso-Melanesian, Nehan-North-Bougainville (Ross 1988: 251–253).
2. For discussions on these issues see, among others, Himmelmann 1998 and Chapter 1; Lehmann 2001; Pawley 1986, 1993).
3. An example is Mosel's grammar of Saliba (1994), which, on 48 pages, summarizes the results of a one-semester fieldwork methods course at the Australian National University.
4. Typical examples of introductory grammar chapters are found in PhD theses that analyse grammatical phenomena in previously unresearched languages, e.g. Seifart 2005.

Chapter 13

Archiving challenges

Paul Trilsbeek and Peter Wittenburg

Introduction

For many years, linguists and ethnologists have collected materials on different cultures and languages in the form of recordings, photos, observational notes, and the like. Traditionally, a part of this material was made available via books and articles in which examples or, in some cases, extensive descriptions were presented. The original recordings and notes were usually not published but remained in the private cupboards of the researchers. Only a small fraction of the original material was handed over to institutions specialized in storing and preserving it. According to an estimate by D. Schüller (2004), about 80% of the material concerning endangered cultures and languages which is currently available is in the hands of individuals or people working in projects with a limited duration, who treat this material like books on shelves, storing it on inadequate storage media and in bad environmental conditions. We can thus speak of the great risk of major parts of our cultural memory getting lost. Furthermore, materials stored in individual researchers' cupboards are hardly accessible for others.

The emergence of digital technology has changed our views about storing, sharing, and accessing this type of information about cultural heritage completely. The modern state-of-the-art is indeed revolutionizing our preservation and access strategies. We understand that

- it is easy to create and distribute copies of digital material;
- it is relatively easy to give access to digital material;
- it is not relevant anymore to store the physical container such as an original tape as the incarnation of the content and that we should store the digital stream of information instead.

Copying content thus is the key to modern preservation. Based on this view, there is an increasing understanding in various disciplines that it is a good idea to hand over original materials gathered in the field or in complex experiments to institutions that have special facilities and expertise for the long-term preservation of data and providing advanced access possibilities for them. It is thus not a coincidence that one of the key elements of the DoBeS program for documenting endangered languages was the setting up of a central archive for all materials collected within this program. This was also based on the fact that the area of digital archiving is comparatively new, that even traditional archives have to consider the new requirements and adapt their strategies accordingly, and that in direct collaboration between documentation teams collecting new digitally archivable materials and the archivist appropriate strategies for a close and mutually fruitful collaboration have to be established.

While not all parties involved in the process of documenting languages such as community members, researchers, funding agencies, etc., have to be fully acquainted with the details of digital archiving, it is important for an efficient and productive cooperation in this work that all parties understand the basic issues and challenges involved in the archiving process and take these into account with respect to their mutual expectations. The purpose of the current chapter is to provide an overview of the basic challenges associated with digital archiving, focusing on three major players in the process: the depositors of the material, the potential users, and the archivists. As we will try to show, these three types of players have different goals, motivations, and preferences which may easily lead to conflicting demands. First, we will briefly describe the characteristics of modern digital archives in relation to more traditional ones and then discuss the expectations of the different players with respect to digital archives. In Sections 3 and 4, we will treat in more detail the conflicting requirements of long-term preservation and short-term access. We will then look at how these requirements influence the interaction between depositors, users, and archivists. In the last two sections, we will discuss aspects of access management and give an outlook to future developments.

1. Modern digital archives

Traditionally, archives are focused on storing original physical objects – be it sculptures, artifacts used in daily life, or information engraved in clay tablets or on "old" paper. Generally speaking, not many people are allowed to have access to these physical objects, and creating copies – if at all possible – is an expensive and time-consuming process. But the nature of the material was such that it made sense to make the preservation of the original objects the highest priority. Consequently, special environments were created in order to meet preservation goals.

For modern digital archives, the survival of the physical object – the storage medium – is in most cases not relevant. It is the information on the carrier that we have to preserve independently, whether it represents texts, sounds, videos, three-dimensional representations of artifacts, etc. However, digital archives have to meet new requirements:

– The objects stored in the archive can be subject to change. For example, a lexicon that was created by a documentation team will be further extended or new linguistic insights require modifications of the existing structure;
– Users of the archive may want to add information about resources based on their specific expertise. For example, a member of the speech community may notice that a rare bird can be heard on a certain recording and may want to add the name of that bird. Or, a researcher may want to draw relations between two or more objects in the archive and to share this added information with others;
– The objects in the archive need to be accessible and searchable for different purposes. For example, people still speaking an endangered language may decide to undertake language maintenance efforts involving the training of young people and want to access archived objects for creating course material. Or researchers may want to study the way in which languages influence each other and therefore search for sets of words or structures that provide evidence for contact phenomena.

These are only a few of the many possible scenarios in which different groups of people want to gain access to material in an archive for different purposes. In general we can say that modern archives for language resources not only have to store data, but also grant easy access to these data and, in certain cases, even allow modifications. The latter, in particular, forms a big problem from the traditional archiving point of view.

A modern language archive thus has two main functions: long-term preservation and short-term access. In the following section, we will see that the requirements for these two functions are partly conflicting. As a consequence, strategies have to be identified and agreed upon which allow for a workable compromise between these conflicting requirements.

Before turning to these requirements, let us briefly review the different types of data and media digital archives that store language documentations

are confronted with. These include the following types of documents: annotated recordings, lexica, sketch grammars, field notes, phonetic descriptions, metadata, ontologies, and geographical information. Furthermore,
they will include a number of typical media types such as text, audio, video,
and image files. But there can also be other, more specialized data types such
as laryngographic or data glove recordings that document movements of the
vocal cords and the hands, respectively. Modern digital archives have to
accommodate all these different types of information. It should also be obvious that archives containing language materials can become very large, in
particular because storing digital video recordings requires much storage
capacity.

2. Demands on language archives

Among others, we can distinguish the following three key players involved
in language documentations:

- The **depositors**, who make recordings and notes, create different sorts
  of derived material, and hand this over to the archivist. Questions that
  have to be addressed here include: In what form do the depositors deliver the material to the archive? Will the archive accept everything the
  depositors deliver? What kinds of interactions are needed between the
  depositors and the archive?
- The **users**, who want to use archived materials for various purposes.
  Questions that have to be addressed here include: Who are the users? Do
  they all have the same expectations? For what purpose will they use the
  archived material? In what form do they need to access the archived material?
- The **archivists**, who need to solve long-term preservation problems, organize the material in a consistent way, and grant access to resources to
  those users who have access privileges. Questions that need to be addressed here include: What are workable backup strategies? How can one
  automate updates to new formats and media? How can one regulate access? How can one make changes to already stored materials tractable?

These key players have somewhat differing views of the tasks of an archive
and the problems it poses (see also Figure 1), as we will show in the following subsections.

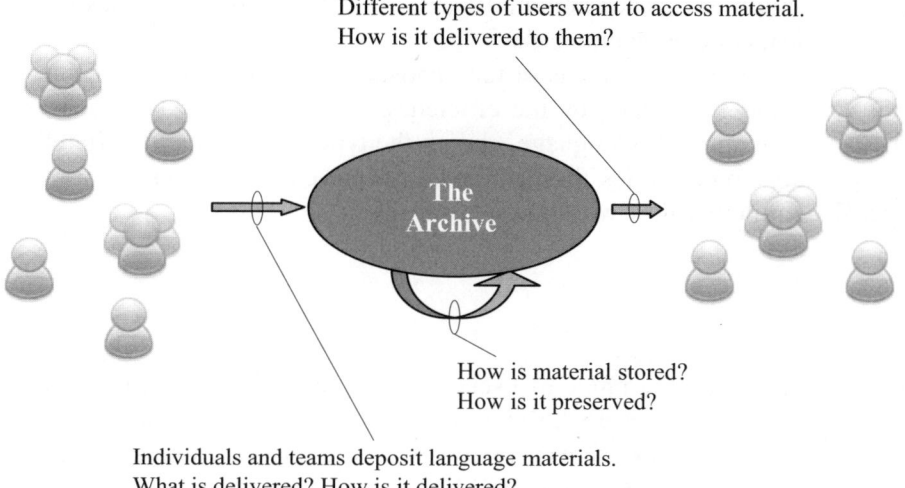

Figure 1. Different kinds of interactions with the archive

2.1. Depositors

Primarily, depositors will be researchers that work individually or in teams to gather and analyze linguistic materials. However, we can also imagine that members of the speech community or other people interested in language matters may want to contribute to a language archive.

Depositors of all types usually have their preferences for certain tools and, consequently, for certain formats used in collecting and processing language materials. Their choices are based on what they are familiar with and usually guided by criteria such as user-friendliness and efficiency, including the quality of the user interface. Field workers often have to deal with difficult field work circumstances, i.e. they have to be flexible and react quickly, which will also influence their choices, e.g. for certain types of equipment that is optimized towards size and not towards the quality of the recorded signal. For researchers, time is a major consideration, making them unwilling to use tools they are not familiar with unless these significantly increase their research productivity.

The depositors themselves are also potential users of the material they deposit, i.e. they may have specific uses in mind when creating and depositing materials. For example, they may plan to produce a printed lexicon to be used within the speech community. As researchers, they often also have specific academic publication plans.

In short, the primary focus of the depositor is on the nature of the creation tools and equipment, on the efficiency with which they can carry out the documentation of a language, and on the type of presentation offered to the primary communities they address – the research community and the speech community they work in.

2.2. Users

Unlike depositors, the range of users of a language documentation can be very broad. Among those who may want to use the material stored in language archives are researchers, members of the speech communities, students and teachers, journalists, and the general public. These groups have very heterogeneous requirements with respect to the way in which the material needs to be available and presented. For example, a researcher who wants to carry out a structured search to look for a linguistic phenomenon in some language will need a different kind of interface than a member of a speech community who wants to find recordings of a certain ceremony and listen to or look at the recordings. Researchers from different disciplines may have completely different requirements with respect to the way they want to search, browse, or view data in the archive. It is next to impossible to say anything about possible usages in a few hundreds years. We cannot know what next generations of users may want to look at.

Being faced with such a heterogeneity of possible wishes and major uncertainties regarding future uses, we can only establish a number of criteria for the way in which archived material should be gathered and stored in order to cover as many usage scenarios as possible:

–   The material should be of the highest possible quality given the current state of technology;
–   The material should be organized according to clear and documented principles;
–   All objects should be accessible as individual resources as the most neutral form of representation, leaving it to the users to combine them the way they need or like to;
–   All decisions about encoding standards, file formats, etc., have to be documented.

2.3. Archivists

The main concern of the archivist is the long-term perspective: How can we make sure that all the information on linguistic and cultural practices and structures compiled in a language documentation will still be available and accessible hundreds of years from now? In addition, an archivist has to deal appropriately with depositors and users now.

Of primary importance for the functioning of an archive is a stable and well-documented organization scheme, e.g. a metadata catalogue system such as IMDI (ISLE Metadata Initiative), which is the basis for all deposit, preservation management, and access operations. In general, the archivist must have a neutral position and should not choose formats that are biased towards certain usages. Nevertheless, almost inevitably there will be a certain bias towards certain core players – in the case of language archives, documenting researchers, and speech communities.

2.4. Possible conflicts resulting from differing demands on a language archive

The following examples demonstrate potential conflicts that can arise from the differing demands of the three different players mentioned above.

1. Many field workers appreciate MiniDisc recorders since they are small and easy to use. However, MiniDisc recordings come in a compressed format which deletes parts of the original signal. Therefore, archivists recommend making high quality and uncompressed audio recordings, arguing that while for most current uses MiniDisc recordings are good enough despite their compression algorithms, we do not know whether this will indeed be true for future uses that we do not yet know about.

2. The archivist needs to store video sequences in the format most faithful to the original (currently MPEG2), while users want to visualize video streams via the web, which currently requires the use of formats such as MPEG4 which make use of a higher compression rate.

3. Some depositors like to work with commercial spreadsheet programs such as MS Excel when creating metadata. Archivists do not appreciate this too much, since such programs produce a proprietary document format which can be changed at any moment in time and which is not openly documented. Also, data are not constrained with respect to struc-

ture and content, therefore users can easily make errors when entering data, which leads to inconsistencies in the archive and difficulties in finding certain resources.

4. Many users are used to HTML-based web pages and like to see material presented in this way. Archivists avoid storing material in an HTML representation format since it is limited with respect to structural expressiveness and it mixes representation and presentation issues, i.e. it is biased towards certain users (see Chapter 14).

There is a basic difference that underlies most of these possible conflicts. This is the difference between the preservation requirements for the long-term uses of the information stored in the archive and the more short-term exigencies of depositors and users. There is a concomitant difference between presentation and storage (or re-presentation) formats. The term "presentation" here refers to the way data are presented to users, i.e. it addresses the surface form. The storage format pertains to the way data are stored. This should be as neutral as possible with regard to different presentation formats. That is, it should be coherently structured, its different information types should be tagged explicitly, and it should make use of open, well-documented, and widely accepted standards.

Storage formats address long-term preservation needs, while presentation formats play a role in short term access issues. We will now look more closely at what is involved in this basic difference.

3. Long-term preservation requirements

Digital long-term archiving has to address two fundamental tasks:

– to ensure the survival of bit streams which is threatened by the limited life span of media carriers (tape, CD-ROM, etc.) and all kinds of possible disasters affecting such carriers;
– to ensure the interpretability of the information represented as bit streams, including the preservation of the structure of the material.

The survival of bit streams, i.e. the basic binary patterns stored on a medium, is of course crucial for the second problem. Given that a bit stream is preserved, one could speculate that "data archeologists" will be able to develop methods to interpret the data, even if the basic information on how to decode the bit stream and how to reshape it into resources is lost.

3.1. Preserving bit streams

In contrast to the cuneiform characters on the clay tables of the Sumerians, the patterns stored on our current magnetic and opto-magnetic storage media have a comparatively short life span. An average hard disk has a media life span of four years, for CD-ROMs we see specifications of up to 30 years for the accessibility of the stored patterns, and for other storage media the expectations are of similar order. This is all very short and cannot be satisfying when we speak about long-term preservation. With regard to language archives covering several terabytes of data, however, there are no other options at this point than to rely on the classical magnetic tape and disk technologies, for practical and financial reasons.

Another factor that reduces the life span of the stored patterns on such storage media can be found in the technological innovation cycle. In 30 years time, only specialized institutions will be able to support old devices and read today's CD-ROMs, for example, since new technologies will be on the market and old devices will not be supported anymore by the industry. Given a heavily reduced amount of devices, some resources will no longer be readable for the very simple reason that access to these devices will be limited.

The current solution to counter problems relating to storage media is to continuously and automatically migrate data to new storage media and widely distribute these data. Copying data to newer technology helps to overcome the limited media life span and can be done largely automatically if planned very carefully. Importantly, the copying process has to start some time before the old technology becomes instable.

It is common knowledge that all kinds of disasters may occur: a disk can become unreadable, a fire can destroy an entire computer center, etc. To overcome these uncertainties we have to distribute copies of the data – a strategy that was already applied to preserve books. However, in the digital era it is easier to automatically create these copies and distribute them. Any archive will apply both techniques within the archive as well as beyond. Tests have to be carried out regularly to check whether the data exchange protocols work correctly.

With regard to the DoBeS data, there are currently seven copies available in four different locations (Nijmegen: 2, Munich: 2, Göttingen: 2, Leipzig: 1). Within the framework of the DELAMAN network (Digital Endangered Language and Music Archive Network) it is intended to distribute the data on a worldwide level.

3.2.   Preserving interpretability

Even when we have assured that the bit streams will survive, we will be faced with the problem of readability and interpretability of the information contained in the bit stream. We can distinguish four layers that are relevant here:

–   the technical encoding of signals such as characters, images, sounds, and videos;
–   the encoding of text structure;
–   the packaging and structuring of encoded streams into files;
–   information regarding the bundling of resources, i.e. the organizational structure of a given documentation.

3.2.1. Technical encoding

We are used to being able to perceive signals of different types via displays and loudspeakers. However, on computers these signals are all stored as bit patterns and packaged into files. Hence, the question arises how to ensure that people 20 or even 500 years from now will still be able to tell what kind of signal a given bit stream represents. The problem is visualized in Figure 2. Does the shown bit stream encode a video sequence, does it encode Chinese characters, or does it encode some other type of information? The bit stream itself does not reveal this.

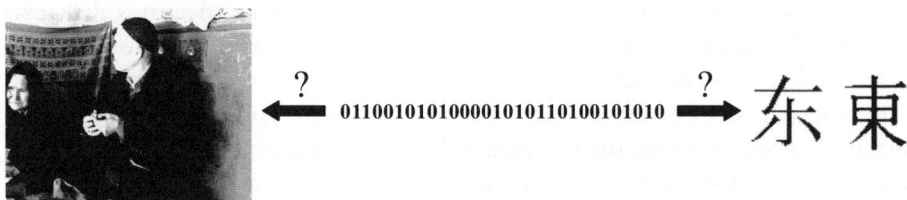

Figure 2. The basic bit stream interpretation problem: What type of signal is encoded in a given stream?

In digital form, characters have to be stored in chunks of bits, video images have to be digitized to represent the spatial and temporal information in suitable ways, and sound files have to be encoded so that the relevant information is captured. For a resource to be well-documented, it must be defined what kind of character encoding is used so that software that understands the format can select certain algorithms for the correct interpretation (see Chapter 14 for details).

For sound digitization, one major encoding format is linear PCM (Pulse Code Modulation) which is widely used for high quality material sampled at 44.1/48 kHz (or higher) with a resolution of 16 bits (or higher). Alternative formats such as MP3 and ATRAC (MiniDisc) involve highly compressed encodings. While principles for compressed encoding may change over time dependent on technology, the direct digital linear PCM encoding will not change. The interpretation of the corresponding bit streams is very straightforward, which makes it the perfect choice for archiving. For further discussion, see Wittenburg, Skiba et al. (2004).

For digital images, JPEG encoding is widely used nowadays, which however performs a lossy compression on the original material. A high compression factor here leads to a blurring of sharp lines or contrasts. TIFF is an uncompressed digital image representation format, but not yet fully standardized. JPEG is openly documented and we can expect that the algorithm and the knowledge will be available for many years to come. For the future, we expect that more devices will provide direct digitized formats or formats such as PNG that apply lossless compression.

For a number of years to come, compressed formats will be the only feasible choice for moving images. Currently, MPEG2 is a commonly used backend format for archiving. It can be derived from the DV format that is currently the most common format for digital video cameras on the consumer and low-end professional market. Due to its wide distribution and its open documentation, we can expect that MPEG2 knowledge will be available for many years. Nevertheless, new encoding ways will emerge with the steady increase in available storage capacity and network bandwidth.

In general, we can state that for long-term preservation purposes it is important (1) to rely on uncompressed and high quality data representation wherever possible; (2) to make sure that the encoding principles are simple and well-documented, and (3) that the encoding standard is under non-proprietary control. There are many such widely-accepted standards available today and current trends show that more of them will be developed in the near future.

3.2.2. Text structures and file formats

When looking at multi-layered annotations or lexica, we can find that characters are embedded in structures and form interpretational units such as words, glosses, part-of-speech indicators, and others. Not only for computational reasons it makes sense to identify the structural components explicitly by means of tags and a structure description language such as XML. A complete documentation will require that the structure of textual documents has to be made explicit and that all tags that are used to indicate structure are documented. An XML schema, a RelaxNG schema, or a DTD is the best way to define the structure of documents and to control the correctness of the files. Yet we lack generic schemas with a wide acceptance for highly structured linguistic document types such as annotations and lexica. Until organizations such as ISO finish their proposals for standards, archives have to rely on a number of XML formats that are widely used (see Chapters 4 and 14 for details).

Closely related to the issue of text structure is the file format issue. File formats define the way in which information is packaged. In general, the file extension says something about the format of a file, but this is not very reliable. Many file formats encode some format information in the header, i.e. the first number of bytes of a file. But in order to secure future interpretability, file formats have to be explicitly documented.

3.2.3. Organizational aspects

In a language archive relations of various kinds can be found between various resources. The most relevant relations from an organizational point of view are:

- resources documenting a certain language
- resources that were created during a certain field trip
- resources that share a certain genre
- resources covering different media (sound, video, etc.) pertaining to the same recording
- transcriptions and other annotations that relate to a certain sound file
- a lexicon which was extracted from a number of annotations.

These relations may be obvious for the researcher who created the documentation, but in an archive these relations have to be made explicit to make the archive manageable and the information accessible to users. Only explicit metadata descriptions accompanying each resource will be able to provide the necessary information. Currently, there are two widely used metadata sets for language resources which serve somewhat different purposes. The OLAC set (an extension of the Dublin Core set) was designed to facilitate searching in integrated metadata domains. Its function thus is quite similar to that of a catalogue in a large library. The IMDI metadata tool already mentioned above is a result of intensive bottom-up discussions within the language engineering and field linguist communities. It was designed to cover all the relations mentioned above, to support browsing and searching and the management of resources. It thus combines the cataloguing function of metadata with the function of a corpus management tool. It includes an extended set of metadata elements and enables the creation of hierarchies and bundles. It is based on an XML schema comprising definitions of the semantics of the elements used, and it has controlled vocabularies associated with it so that a high degree of consistency can be achieved. This is crucial for retrieval.

Figure 3 gives an example of a simplified IMDI corpus structure from the DoBeS archive, showing how resources such as field notes can be linked to corpus nodes. The resource metadata descriptions can be used to bundle related resources such as a video and a sound file with all associated annotations.

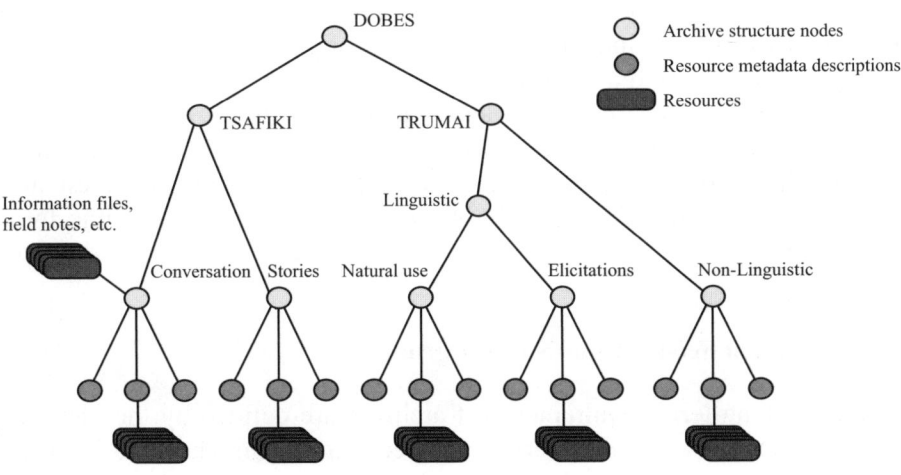

Figure 3. Example of a hierarchical organization of resources

3.3. Archive coherence

There are two diverging archiving strategies: (1) some digital archives follow the principle of taking all digital material that is donated independent of its format and store the material in the way in which it was delivered; (2) others rely on a few well-supported open formats and require that all archival objects are presented in these formats. It is obvious that a coherent archive, i.e. an archive relying on a few open formats, is more attractive for users since it is easier to use. Despite the fact that it possibly imposes requirements on them, it is also attractive for depositors in that coherence increases the chance of preservation. It is easier and less costly to transform a coherent archive into new formats as they will emerge in the coming decades. Maintaining an extremely incoherent archive and making its objects accessible to users will always be more problematic and cost intensive. In actual practice, most archives for endangered language resources will apply a mixed strategy with different foci.

The optimal way for creating and maintaining a coherent archive is to specify format requirements that have to be adhered to by depositors. However, such requirements may pose a problem for the depositors, as they may be unwilling or unable to follow them (see Section 2.1 above). A way out of this problem also practiced in the DoBeS programme is for the archive to accept materials in a broader range of formats and to convert them before ingestion as extensively as possible. The original formats need to be stored as well, since conversions do not always preserve the full content of the original. However, as indicated before, some original formats lack the necessary explicitness and are not very well documented, making a conversion expensive and prone to errors. Hence, depositors and archivists have to agree on a selection of formats acceptable for the archive. Obviously, there are also limits on the resources that an archive can afford to invest into conversions, which may further limit the range of formats workable for a given archive.

4. Short-term needs of known user groups

While the long-term requirements of archives are defined by the idea that future generations will be interested in accessing comprehensive information regarding cultures and languages of their ancestors, the short-term needs are mainly defined by current usage scenarios. Technologically speaking, their focus will be less on the storage side and more on the presentation side. The presentation of material is determined by the available technology on the one hand, and the interests of users on the other. In this section, we briefly characterize some typical usage scenarios.

4.1. Internet access vs. local copying

Current technology advocates the use of online representation because via the Internet, all media can be presented jointly, e.g. a transcription can be viewed while listening to the corresponding audio file, a lexical entry can be explained by a video clip, ritual ceremonies can be viewed in their complex organization by using textual descriptions, listening to the voice of the shaman and watching concomitant activities. The Internet will be more and more preferred since it brings all digital information to the desk of the user without having to worry about local storage capabilities, etc. However, the presentation of high-quality videos is still a demanding task for networks. For some users, including remote speech community centers, even the transfer requirements of highly-compressed video formats such as MPEG4 may still be too much. So for some years to come, it will still be necessary to provide local copies of archival materials for some users. Setting up such local copies with all the components necessary for an optimal use, however, is not a trivial task and needs to be planned ahead at the time when the basic architecture of the archive is determined. Similarly, some users may not have computers at their disposal so that, for example, a hardcopy version of a resource such as a lexicon or a compilation of texts has to be provided. Again, the basic architecture has to allow for such printed output.

4.2. What different user groups may be looking for

Researchers generally will want to discover suitable material by posing complex metadata and/or content questions. They may, for example, want to analyze the rich linguistic encoding contained in a lexicon in conjunction with ethnographic notes. Based on new insights obtained by browsing archival materials, they may want to add new types of annotations or draw relations between elements within a lexicon or even across documents. In short, a language archive is seen as a multi-dimensional and multi-medial space in which they want to navigate easily, view fragments, combine information, and create extensions of various sorts. This requires that each resource contained in the archive can be discovered and accessed separately and that it is stored as neutrally as possible. Web-based analysis and annotation frameworks with stereotypic viewers and major functionality may be of help here for researchers who are not computer specialists. For specialists, open and well-documented formats are essential to allow them to write their own software.

Indigenous community members may want to use the material for entertainment, self-reflection, or educational purposes. They often will be interested primarily in audio and video recordings, i.e. the raw material. But we also expect community members to indicate errors of various sorts and to fill in missing information, i.e. they too may want to extend and enrich the archive.

In collaboration with educators or documenting researchers, community members may want to create school material that can be used to teach community members. This may require the combination of different media into one single multimedia presentation. Alternatively, the goal may be a book that combines text and images. To prepare such a resource, one needs to have a good overview of all material available and to have access to every single object or even fragments of objects, such as short video clips extracted from lengthy recordings. In both cases, the archive has to offer atomic objects in their original form.

For many indigenous communities it will be important to have easy and direct access to methods and presentation styles that are adapted to their own culture (cf. the concept of "mobilized data" discussed in Chapter 15). It is unlikely that archives will be able to offer such highly-customized data access, because they generally will lack the necessary resources and expertise. This is also true for the creation of educational materials. However, archives can facilitate the creation of both types of data presentations as much as possible by offering the resources in a neutral and open form so that specialists can combine them in a flexible way.

Material contained in language resource archives can be expected to be used as educational resources at **universities** and **schools**. Undergraduate students, for example, may be asked to search for a specific phenomenon in an archive or to carry out certain extensions of the material by adding annotations, lexical attributes, comments, relations, etc. Education at the level of primary and secondary schools, however, will probably require simpler and more attractive discovery and presentation methods than the ones provided by a multipurpose archive.

Journalists working on a broad variety of topics ranging from general interest topics relating to language and culture, to specific issues pertaining to a community documented in the archive may need quick access to relevant multimedia material. Among other things, they may be looking for a nice example or unusual fact or observation which provides the starting point for a story or report. Their preferred ways of access will include geographical browsing or registers listing interesting phenomena of various kinds.

In summary, we can state that we cannot identify just one type of usage, but very different usage scenarios with different types of users must be envisaged. The discovery and presentation of the archived material thus has to meet a number of diverging expectations. Discovery ideally has to cover flexible and powerful structured search capabilities on metadata and content, simple Google-like full-text retrieval possibilities, and hierarchical and geographical browsing and navigation in virtual spaces created for specific communities adapted to their cultural and sociological contexts.

Presentation covers a whole range of possibilities, starting with simple access to individual objects, such as structured texts or media files. Of course, linguists and other users will not be interested in seeing an XML tag structure. Instead, they will want a presentation that comes close to what they are used to in written resources such as lexica or storybooks. Furthermore, users will want to access the objects together with their contexts – annotations together with lexica, annotations together with the underlying media fragments, house building explanations together with photos, the comparison of two annotated media fragments, etc. A combined presentation layer should allow the support of flexible, user-defined layouts. In addition, guided tours should be created to provide easy access for users with limited experience in handling digital databases.

As we have seen, a number of usage scenarios include the active enrichment and extension of archival materials. For obvious reasons, modifying archival contents is a dangerous concept. Special care has to be taken not to lose earlier versions and to separate "original" data from add-ons. Two of the most basic principles of archiving are that deletion operations are forbidden and that modifications of original data can only lead to new versions but do not replace the original version. In digital archives it is technologically very easy to manipulate content, but it is still an unresolved issue as to how to keep additions tractable while at the same time maintaining simple and straightforward discovery and presentation options.

While the demands of different users may thus be almost limitless, it should be kept in mind that for the archivist, workable resource discovery options and easy access to individual resources in open and well-documented formats has to be the primary concern.

5.   Interaction aspects

Due to the differences between the interests and priorities of archivists, depositors, and users, it will be useful to take a closer look at the interaction between these players. The main concern here is the ways in which the gap between the differing interests and priorities can be bridged without creating new problems.

5.1. Depositor–archivist interaction

To create an archive that is easily exploitable by the different user groups and that also meets the long-term preservation requirements, depositors and archivists have to find a good way of interacting. This is a challenge indeed, since the primary intentions, the working styles, and part of the terminology used are different. Figure 4 indicates the topics to be addressed in the interaction between depositors and archivists in a schematic way. It also indicates the methods that are involved in resolving these issues.

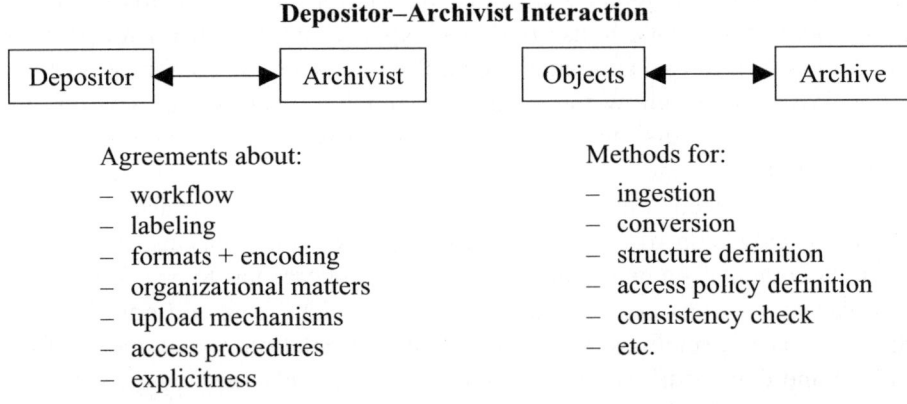

Figure 4. Topics to be resolved in the interaction between depositors and archivists

Workflow agreements describe the pattern of interaction, i.e. which addresses have to be used, what the responsibilities are, what the best channels are for exchanging valuable material, what the general timing will be, etc. For financial and sometimes for technical reasons, it is impossible for an archivist to carry out all sorts of conversions. Therefore, if possible, one has to agree on a number of formats and encoding standards for the tools that are used in collecting and processing data. Using a completely outdated program version for annotations or creating arbitrary and undocumented keyboard-character mappings may lead to unsolvable problems (cf. Chapter 14). Teams sometimes have old materials that they want to deposit as well. All this has to be made explicit at an early stage so that the archivist can anticipate the problems that may arise and can look for suitable solutions.

The labeling of any object that is exchanged is essential to enable the archivist to identify the relations. The metadata descriptions have to be created by the depositors according to an agreed-upon scheme since they will define the relations between the objects and form the basis for all discovery. In the near future it will become more common for depositors to upload resources themselves into the archive. The necessary steps to be taken here have to be made very clear since misunderstandings leading to an inconsistent archive have to be avoided.

The archivist should provide methods for structure definition that are in line with the data models, tools to build content that fit in with the agreed standards, conversion routines that allow one to convert data into a limited number of archiving formats, and mechanisms to define access policies and carry out a number of consistency checks on the archived material. With regard to the last point, archivists can only employ formal criteria. They cannot verify the correctness of linguistic content and, more specifically, they cannot detect whether an annotation is associated with the correct media file and the like. The basic principle must be that the depositor is responsible for all linguistic encoding aspects and for all relations that are difficult to trace. Since conversions are often associated with a loss of information, the depositor has to make time for checking the results of conversion processes.

The interaction between archivists and depositors also has interpersonal aspects that should not be ignored. Regular interactions initiated by the archivist, for example, can easily be interpreted as an attempt to control the documentation process. On the other hand, documentation teams may hesitate to confront archivists with "stupid questions."

Different formal channels have to be used for this interaction. Web-based bulletin boards, e-mail exchange, telephone calls, video conferences and, most importantly, bilateral face-to-face meetings all form part of an interaction process that has a potential for many problems. Training courses offered by an archive may help to increase awareness of the basic problems involved in digital archiving and in unifying different approaches. Short guides, electronic newspaper articles, and conference contributions will also help in spreading relevant information.

5.2. Archivist–user interaction

To date, there is only limited experience regarding the interaction with different user groups of an archive. The following is almost exclusively based on the many discussions with various DoBeS teams. In addition, we had some interactions with journalists working on stories about language endangerment and cultural heritage preservation.

Figure 5 summarizes major topics in the interaction between archivists and users, and major methods used in complying with user requests.

Archivist–User Interaction

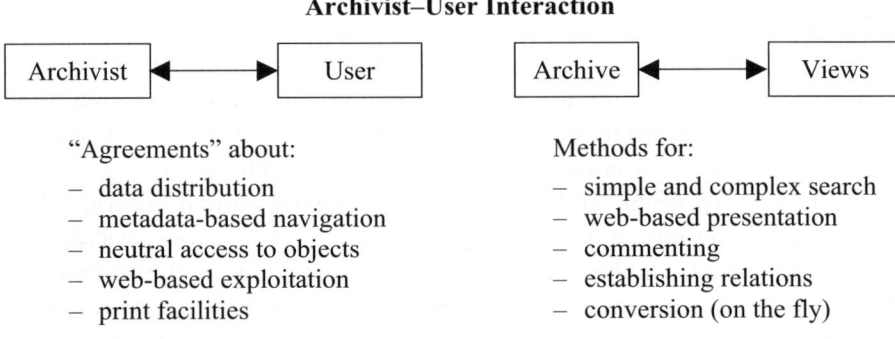

"Agreements" about:
– data distribution
– metadata-based navigation
– neutral access to objects
– web-based exploitation
– print facilities

Methods for:
– simple and complex search
– web-based presentation
– commenting
– establishing relations
– conversion (on the fly)

Figure 5. Topics in the interaction between users and archivists

Various demands on discovery procedures were discussed in Section 4.2 above and will not be repeated here. Once a user has found some interesting resources, he or she must be able to download or copy them. It should be possible to copy whole subcorpora, including the metadata descriptions and the resources. As already mentioned in Section 4.1, it should not be too difficult to install a fully operational copy on another computer, for example, in a local community center.

When a single resource, such as an annotation, a simple lexicon, or a media file, is found with the help of metadata, it should also be possible to play or visualize it directly using the usual web-browser plug-ins. However, for complex linguistic data types, such as annotated media files that consist of various media streams and several layers of annotations, this will not work with standard browsers. Here, more specialized browsers are required which can exploit the bundling of different media types. ELAN and LEXUS, developed at the MPI for Psycholinguistics, are such tools. Another approach is used by SMIL (Synchronized Multimedia Integration Language), which is a World Wide Web consortium standard for integrating multimedia files. It can be used, e.g., for adding subtitles to a video recording. A SMIL file does not contain the actual media themselves, but contains links referring to them. A media player supporting the SMIL standard is needed in order to display the combined media files.

In general, we can expect more tools to be developed that support complex operations using web access as a basis. LEXUS is such a framework that allows one to create new lexica and manipulate existing ones via the web. ANNEX is a framework for operating with a set of annotated multimedia files via the web. ANNEX and LEXUS allow the user to collect various annotated media files or lexica from different subarchives with the clear intention to support crosslanguage work. Mechanisms to solve structural and semantic interoperability problems are in the process of being designed. The selection of the resources is done based on metadata browsing and/or searching.

A functionality that is often requested by researchers is the possibility to create printouts of the materials deposited in an archive. While this may seem to be a simple task, it involves many decisions that a developer has to make on how to generate paper layouts for computer-based material. Different researchers may also have different requirements in this respect. To date, there is no standard technology that can be used by inexperienced users to associate their own layout with richly structured XML documents, although the basic technology (XSLT) is available.

6. Access management

As long as individual researchers or projects were responsible for the recorded data and stored them in their offices, the legal and ethical problems involved with holding and using such data did not become apparent. Due to some cases of misuse, the availability of data via the Internet, a greater general awareness regarding the relevance of ethical issues, and the introduction of language archives as a new abstract type of institution between the researcher and the consultants, legal and ethical issues have recently received much more attention. Any archive will be faced with a number of legal and ethical issues and has to treat them with great sensitivity.

6.1. Legal and ethical issues

The legal situation of an archive tends to be very complex, since usually different legal systems are involved. The speech community may be located in one country, the researcher in another country, and the archivist even in a third, all with potentially different legal systems. There are great differences, e.g., between Australia, Europe, and the U.S. with respect to copyright laws, which is one of the legal aspects of potential relevance for the resources that archives store. For further details and problems, see Liberman (2000) and Chapter 2.

Given the complexity and relative newness of all legal matters relating to language archives, it is currently difficult if not impossible to get formal legal advice. Nevertheless, it is necessary that an archive defines the legal basis for its activity and comes to workable agreements with depositors and users. Among other things, it has to claim the right to archive the deposited material and it has to reserve all rights on the materials for the creators. It also has to claim the right to give access to the resources, based on an informed consent achieved by researcher(s) and speaker(s) with regard to possible uses of the collected materials. Documents detailing these claims and agreements should be made available to everyone via the web site so that everyone is informed about the rules that apply in accessing and using the archive.

Since many legal aspects remain uncertain and probably will remain uncertain for some time to come, it is of crucial importance to develop a relationship based on mutual trust among all participants. In this regard, it will be useful to develop an explicit code of conduct (see the DoBeS website for an example) which has to be accepted by everyone involved in building, maintaining, and using the archive as their principle guideline of behavior. The material stored in a language archive, in particular the recordings, have to be generated with the consent of the speech community. This consent should be explicit with regard to expectations about its usage by others. Note that statements regarding the openness of resources may change over time.

The main burden with regard to regulating access to resources has to be carried by the main depositor, who often will also be a researcher. In general, archivists will assume that the depositor/researcher knows the expectations of the speakers and that he/she has a deep understanding of the ethical aspects involved. The depositor has to translate his or her knowledge in this regard into access policies, i.e. to define the type of protocol that has to be followed by users of the resource and the guidelines on how to use it.

In addition, an archive has to take measures for the time when the main depositor who knows the local situation and expectations is not available anymore. Here an advisory board consisting of experienced field workers and archivists may be of help. Alternatively, archives may require depositors to identify substitutes in case they themselves are no longer able to determine (changes in) access policies.

6.2. Access management systems

"Access management" refers to a system that implements the above mentioned access policies. It should be obvious that an elaborated access management system is needed which, however, has to be tractable even when confronted with an increasing number of access requests. Also from the users' point of view, the bureaucratic effort for granting access to selected material has to be minimal, otherwise many potential users will be turned away (for example, journalists seeking fast and easy access to materials of use in writing a piece on linguistic or cultural heritage). What we need, then, are efficient electronic ways of dealing with access requests. Currently, the first steps are being undertaken in exploring how this can be achieved.

In the DoBeS program a web-based access management system was developed which allows the delegation of rights to grant access permissions to other people, such as the responsible researchers or depositors. Authorized persons such as the archivist and the depositor can define rights together by selecting a node in the linked metadata hierarchy and a resource type. In this way, only one single command is necessary to indicate that all textual materials of a given documentation project are open to the public. The system also allows one to demand the acceptance of declarations and to indicate the intended use of the material being accessed.

Clearly, though, no access system can fully enforce the proper usage of archival materials. Only social control within the community of users can prevent that material is being used for purposes other than requested.

7. Outlook

It is highly desirable that the metadata descriptions contained in different archives be included in worldwide accessible browse and search domains so that all users can inform themselves about the types of resources that are available, irrespective of the archive they are used to dealing with. It is a widely accepted principle that the metadata descriptions have to be open to the general public. Projects in Europe, the U.S., and Australia are presently working on such an integration. The integrated IMDI and OLAC metadata domain now covers about 80 institutions worldwide, which is a promising start.

One of the goals of the DELAMAN initiative, in which a number of major archives are collaborating, is to virtually integrate the archives such that users can work with a unique identity and sign-on on all resources to which access has been granted. The individual archives that house the original copy of the resource will remain the access granting authority. It is expected that such collaborations will not only radically simplify the archives' access management, but also make it possible for interested users to navigate in these new virtual archives without bureaucratic limitations. Within the DELAMAN initiative, copies of data will be distributed among the different participating archives to increase the probability of long-term survival. Projects implementing this form of archive integration which goes far beyond the metadata integration have started recently, i.e. results can be expected within a few years.

For the utilization of complete language archives (or larger segments of an archive, involving data from different documentation projects) the lack of interoperability on various levels may create major problems. As was already indicated above, at the technical encoding and format level a high degree of coherence within an archive can and should be achieved. However, at the level of linguistic annotation we will continue to be faced with different terminologies. Depending on the language, differing descriptive traditions, and preferences with regard to linguistic theory, linguists will continue to define their layers of annotations, their lexical attributes, and the values these may take. The resulting differences in terminology and annotation schemes will, e.g., limit the scope of searches. The new web-based utilization frameworks mentioned in Section 5.2 above have to address this problem. Various initiatives exist for developing flexible frameworks that will make use of ontologies that are either generated in a bottom-up fashion, i.e. driven by the actual resource selection, or created by top-down methods determined by linguistic theory. With respect to the latter, we can mention initiatives such as ISO TC37/SC4 and GOLD. While ISO proposes a central data category registry that is an almost flat and comprehensive list of linguistic concepts, the GOLD project wants to develop an ontology covering both definitions and relations.

Chapter 14

Linguistic documentation and the encoding of textual materials

Jost Gippert

Introduction

In the documentation of languages, the notation of textual materials in written form has always played a significant role, even after the development of audiovisual means of storage. The digital age has brought about but a minor change in this respect in that we can now expect our written data to be usable by many people and for many centuries without necessarily being printed and distributed as books. To reach this aim, a few preliminaries must be kept in mind, however, which will be addressed in this chapter.

Writing down textual materials in digital form is different from using a pencil and a sheet of paper as it presupposes the adaptation of clearly defined **codes** in a twofold sense: the encoding of characters, i.e., of the letters in the words to be written down, and the encoding of the elements of textual structure, i.e., of headlines, examples, vocabulary lists, etc. Both kinds of encoding are crucial for the exchange of data with other people: A future user who has no information on what encoding schemes you may have applied will probably have great difficulties in trying to re-decode (and read) what you wrote – in the worst case, your data will be totally irretrievable. In the following pages, I shall briefly explain why this is to be expected and what can be done to avoid it. We will start with the encoding of the smallest units of text, i.e. characters, and proceed to larger elements such as words, phrases, and syntagms. Other types of encoding that may be at issue here (esp. file encoding; cf. Chapter 4) will be addressed en passant.

1. The encoding of characters: From 7-bit to 32-bit

1.1. Mainframe computers: The ASCII age

In all modern digital equipment, the encoding of characters is based on a given set of correspondences of characters with numerical values, every character being represented by one unique value. To encode the two times 26 letters (lower and upper case) of the Latin alphabet plus the digits from 0 to 9, the punctuation marks, parentheses, and the like, a set of less than 100 unique values is necessary, and this is why the "stone age" mainframe computers of the 1960s to 1970s were based on a so-called 7-bit encoding: With 7 bits, $2^7 = 128$ characters can be encoded uniquely. The most popular standard developed on this basis is the so-called ASCII standard ("American Standard Code for Information Interchange"), cf. Table 1.

Table 1. Standardized 7-bit encoding (ASCII)

	0										1									
	0	1	2	3	4	5	6	7	8	9	0	1	2	3	4	5	6	7	8	9
000																				
020												!	"	#	$	%	&	'		
040	(	)	*	+	,	-	.	/	0	1	2	3	4	5	6	7	8	9	:	;
060	<	=	>	?	@	A	B	C	D	E	F	G	H	I	J	K	L	M	N	O
080	P	Q	R	S	T	U	V	W	X	Y	Z	[	\	]	^	_	`	a	b	c
100	d	e	f	g	h	i	j	k	l	m	n	o	p	q	r	s	t	u	v	w
120	x	y	z	{			}	~													
	0	1	2	3	4	5	6	7	8	9	0	1	2	3	4	5	6	7	8	9
	0										1									

It is clear that on the basis of this encoding scheme, English texts could easily be digitized, but German, French, or Spanish texts could not, let alone Greek, Russian, or Chinese texts in their original scripts. This does not mean, however, that it was impossible then to process texts in "exotic" languages. What was necessary was the invention of encoding schemes that used more than one digital unit to represent certain characters. Cf. Table 2 which shows the 7-bit adaptation of a Sanskrit text, the Rigveda, which was produced in the 1970s on a mainframe computer, with the "traditional" transcription added for comparison. It is clear that this encoding had at least two disadvantages: It was hardly possible to visualize the text as it should be on a computer screen, which resulted in lots of inputting errors, and the encoding was not transparent (or "self-explaining") in the sense that the individual items (letters, diacritics, accent marks) could have been easily determined by someone who was not involved in the encoding process themselves. It is true that this encoding met the condition of being consistent in that a given sequence of codes always represented the same character, and this is why these texts can be used and analyzed even today. Nevertheless, it was too clumsy to be maintainable for a longer period.

Table 2. Non-standard 7-bit encoding (Rigveda 7,1)

R700123011	AGNI!M+ NA!RO DI:!D)ITIB)IR ARA!N\YOR HA!STACYUTI: JANAYANTA PRAS=ASTA
R700123012	!M / DU:RED9!S=AM+ G9HA!PATIM AT)ARYU!M
R700123021	TA!M AGNI!M A!STE VA!SAVO NY 9&N\VAN SUPRATICA!KS\AM A!VASE KU!TAS= CI
R700123022	T / DAKS\A:!YYO YO! DA!MA A:!SA NI!TYAH-
R700123031	PRE!DD)O AGNE DI:DIHI PURO! NO! 'JASRAYA: SU:RMYA:& YAVIS\T\)A / TVA:!
R700123032	M+ S=A!S=VANTA U!PA YANTI VA:!JA:H-

1	*agním náro dīdhitibhir aráṇyor hástacyutī janayanta praśastám / dūredŕśaṃ gṛhápatim atharyúm*
2	*tám agním áste vásavo ny ṛnvan supraticákṣam ávase kútaś cit / dakṣā́yyo yó dáma ása nítyaḥ*
3	*préddho agne dīdihi puró nó 'jasrayā sūrmyā̀ yaviṣṭha / tvā́ṃ śáśvanta úpa yanti vájāḥ*

1.2. PCs, Macs, DOS, and MS Windows: 8-bit based standards and non-standards

With the extension of the ASCII encoding basis to 8 bits, this problem was at least partially overcome. On an 8-bit (= 1-byte) basis, $2^8 = 256$ characters can be encoded uniquely, and since the early 1980s, many 8-bit encoding schemes were developed and applied, adding "special" characters such as those representing the German "umlaut vowels" *ä, ö, ü,* the accented vowels *é, à, ô,* etc. of French, or the Spanish palatal nasal *ñ* to the inventory. Unfortunately, this was not done in an equal, "standardized" way right from the beginning; instead, several leading computer companies developed their own individual schemes, which resulted in serious problems whenever data were to be exchanged between systems. Compare Tables 3–5 which show the encoding systems used in IBM/DOS computers, Mac computers, and MS Windows – only the latter one is more or less identical with the 8-bit

Table 3. Non-standard 8-bit encoding ("DOS/IBM", "Extended ASCII", "Code-page 437")

	0	1	2	3	4	5	6	7	8	9	0	1	2	3	4	5	6	7	8	9
000		☺	●	♥	♦	♣	♠	·	□	○	◙	♂	♀	♪	♫	☼	►	◄	↕	‼
020	¶	§	■	‡	↑	↓	→	←	∟	↔	▲	▼		!	"	#	$	%	&	'
040	(	)	*	+	,	-	.	/	0	1	2	3	4	5	6	7	8	9	:	;
060	<	=	>	?	@	A	B	C	D	E	F	G	H	I	J	K	L	M	N	O
080	P	Q	R	S	T	U	V	W	X	Y	Z	[	\	]	^	_	`	a	b	c
100	d	e	f	g	h	i	j	k	l	m	n	o	p	q	r	s	t	u	v	w
120	x	y	z	{	|	}	~	⌂	Ç	ü	é	â	ä	à	å	ç	ê	ë	è	ï
140	î	ì	Ä	Å	É	æ	Æ	ô	ö	ò	û	ù	ÿ	Ö	Ü	¢	£	¥	₧	ƒ
160	á	í	ó	ú	ñ	Ñ	ª	º	¿	⌐	¬	½	¼	¡	«	»	░	▒	▓	│
180	┤	╡	╢	╖	╕	╣	║	╗	╝	╜	╛	┐	└	┴	┬	├	─	┼	╞	╟
200	╚	╔	╩	╦	╠	═	╬	╧	╨	╤	╥	╙	╘	╒	╓	╫	╪	┘	┌	█
220	▄	▌	▐	▀	α	ß	Γ	π	Σ	σ	µ	τ	Φ	Θ	Ω	δ	∞	∅	∈	∩
240	≡	±	≥	≤	⌠	⌡	÷	≈	°	·	·	√	ⁿ	²	■					
	0	1	2	3	4	5	6	7	8	9	0	1	2	3	4	5	6	7	8	9

Table 4. Non-standard 8-bit encoding (Mac OS)

	0	1	2	3	4	5	6	7	8	9	0	1	2	3	4	5	6	7	8	9
000																				
020														!	"	#	$	%	&	´
040	(	)	*	+	,	-	.	/	0	1	2	3	4	5	6	7	8	9	:	;
060	<	=	>	?	@	A	B	C	D	E	F	G	H	I	J	K	L	M	N	O
080	P	Q	R	S	T	U	V	W	X	Y	Z	[	\	]	^	_	`	a	b	c
100	d	e	f	g	h	i	j	k	l	m	n	o	p	q	r	s	t	u	v	w
120	x	y	z	{	|	}	~		Ä	Å	Ç	É	Ñ	Ö	Ü	á	à	â	ä	ã
140	å	ç	é	è	ê	ë	í	ì	î	ï	ñ	ó	ò	ô	ö	õ	ú	ù	û	ü
160	†	°	¢	£	§	•	¶	ß	®	©	™	´	¨	≠	Æ	Ø	∞	±	≤	≥
180	¥	µ	∂	Σ	∏	π	∫	ª	º	Ω	æ	ø	¿	¡	¬	√	ƒ	≈	∆	«
200	»	…		À	Ã	Õ	Œ	œ	–	—	"	"	'	'	÷	◊	ÿ	Ÿ	/	¤
220	‹	›	fi	fl	‡	·	,	„	‰	Â	Ê	Á	Ë	È	Í	Î	Ï	Ì	Ó	Ô
240		Ò	Ú	Û	Ù	ı	^	~	¯	˘	·	˚	¸	˝	˛	ˇ				
	0	1	2	3	4	5	6	7	8	9	0	1	2	3	4	5	6	7	8	9

standard used in web environments up till now, the ANSI standard ("American National Standards Institute") also known as ISO standard no. 8859-1 (the special MS-Windows characters are displayed on a grey background within Table 5).

Table 5. Standardized 8-bit encoding (ANSI, ISO-8859-1, MS-Windows, Codepage 1252)

					0										1					
	0	1	2	3	4	5	6	7	8	9	0	1	2	3	4	5	6	7	8	9
000																				
020													!	"	#	$	%	&	´	
040	(	)	*	+	,	-	.	/	0	1	2	3	4	5	6	7	8	9	:	;
060	<	=	>	?	@	A	B	C	D	E	F	G	H	I	J	K	L	M	N	O
080	P	Q	R	S	T	U	V	W	X	Y	Z	[	\	]	^	_	`	a	b	c
100	d	e	f	g	h	i	j	k	l	m	n	o	p	q	r	s	t	u	v	w
120	x	y	z	{	|	}	~					‚	ƒ	„	…	†	‡	ˆ	‰	Š	‹
140	Œ					'	'	"	"	•	—	–	˜	™	š	›	œ			Ÿ
160		¡	¢	£	¤	¥	¦	§	¨	©	ª	«	¬	-	®	¯	°	±	²	³
180	´	µ	¶	·	¸	¹	º	»	¼	½	¾	¿	À	Á	Â	Ã	Ä	Å	Æ	Ç
200	È	É	Ê	Ë	Ì	Í	Î	Ï	Ð	Ñ	Ò	Ó	Ô	Õ	Ö	×	Ø	Ù	Ú	Û
220	Ü	Ý	Þ	ß	à	á	â	ã	ä	å	æ	ç	è	é	ê	ë	ì	í	î	ï
240	ð	ñ	ò	ó	ô	õ	ö	÷	ø	ù	ú	û	ü	ý	þ	ÿ				
	0	1	2	3	4	5	6	7	8	9	0	1	2	3	4	5	6	7	8	9
					0											1					

Still, these encoding systems were not sufficient for the immediate encoding of other scripts such as Greek, Cyrillic, or Chinese. This is why from the middle of the 1980s on, so-called "code pages" were developed for 8-bit based computers, in which, just as in the examples shown above, the "upper" area exceeding the basic ASCII plain (values above 128) was used to encode various other character sets. Some of these code pages have been standardized within the ISO standard 8859; cf., e.g., Table 6 contrasting the Cyrillic code page ISO 8859-5 with the ANSI standard, ISO 8859-1.

Table 6 a/b. Standardized 8-bit mapping: ISO-8859-1 vs. ISO-8859-5.

a.

32	! " # $ % & ' ( ) * + , - . /	47
48	0 1 2 3 4 5 6 7 8 9 : ; < = > ?	63
64	@ A B C D E F G H I J K L M N O	79
80	P Q R S T U V W X Y Z [\ ] ^ _	95
96	` a b c d e f g h i j k l m n o	111
112	p q r s t u v w x y z {	} ~	127
160	¡ ¢ £ ¤ ¥ ¦ § ¨ © ª « ¬ ® ¯	175
176	° ± ² ³ ´ µ ¶ · ¸ ¹ º » ¼ ½ ¾ ¿	191
192	À Á Â Ã Ä Å Æ Ç È É Ê Ë Ì Í Î Ï	207
208	Ð Ñ Ò Ó Ô Õ Ö × Ø Ù Ú Û Ü Ý Þ ß	223
224	à á â ã ä å æ ç è é ê ë ì í î ï	239
240	ð ñ ò ó ô õ ö ÷ ø ù ú û ü ý þ ÿ	255

b.

32	! " # $ % & ' ( ) * + , - . /	47
48	0 1 2 3 4 5 6 7 8 9 : ; < = > ?	63
64	@ A B C D E F G H I J K L M N O	79
80	P Q R S T U V W X Y Z [\ ] ^ _	95
96	` a b c d e f g h i j k l m n o	111
112	p q r s t u v w x y z {	} ~	127
160	Ё Ђ Ѓ Є Ѕ І Ї Ј Љ Њ Ћ Ќ · Ў Џ	175
176	А Б В Г Д Е Ж З И Й К Л М Н О П	191
192	Р С Т У Ф Х Ц Ч Ш Щ Ъ Ы Ь Э Ю Я	207
208	а б в г д е ж з и й к л м н о п	223
224	р с т у ф х ц ч ш щ ъ ы ь э ю я	239
240	№ ё ђ ѓ є ѕ і ї ј љ њ ћ ќ § ў џ	255

Apart from these "official" extensions, an unknown amount of local or even personal 8-bit encoding systems were developed since the early 1980s to meet the needs of languages and linguists. As a matter of fact, whenever someone developed and applied a certain font, the encoding of which did not match one of the standardized code pages, a new encoding system was created from scratch. Applying the method of "font mapping", we could thus meet, e.g., the requirements of Ancient ("Polytonic") Greek to be noted in original characters as well as Iranian languages to be rendered in a scholarly Latin transcription (cf. Tables 7–8).

The problem about all this is that whenever "font mapping" is applied, the basic requirement of documentation, viz. the persistence and recoverability of data, cannot be guaranteed as there is no unique one-to-one-relation between the character to be encoded and a given digitized value. If, e.g., we applied the Greek 8-bit font illustrated in Table 8, the value of 231 would represent a Greek lower case letter *pi* (π); the same value would stand for a Cyrillic *cha* (ч), however, if we used a font matching the standard codepage ISO 8859-5, and it would represent a Latin *c* with cedilla (ç) if we used the plain ANSI standard. This means that whenever an 8-bit encoding is applied in the encoding of textual materials, additional information must be stored as to what code page or font encoding is valid for a given character – this information, however, is not encodable as such in a

Table 7. Non-standard 8-bit encoding: Ancient ("polytonic") Greek

	0	1	2	3	4	5	6	7	8	9	0	1	2	3	4	5	6	7	8	9
000		᾽	῎	῀	᾿	῏	῍				°							.		
020		§			᾽	᾽	᾽	`		.	Ϝ	ϟ	ϡ			!	"	ἤ	ή	ῂ	ῄ	'
040	(	)	*	†	,	-	.	/	0	1	2	3	4	5	6	7	8	9	:	;
060	ή	ἤ	ῂ	?	ς	A	B	C	D	E	F	G	H	I	J	K	L	M	N	O
080	P	Q	R	S	T	U	V	W	X	Y	Z	[	ἠ	]	ἤ	·	`	a	b	c
100	d	e	f	g	h	i	j	k	l	m	n	o	p	q	r	s	t	u	v	w
120	x	y	z	ἠ	|	ή	ῆ	ἄ	ἅ	ü	έ	ᾶ	ä	ὰ	ᾱ	ῐ	ἒ	ἔ	ἐ	ῐ
140	ῐ	ῐ	Ä	ῐ	ö	ῠ	ἔ	ô	ö	ὸ	ῠ	ὺ	ü	Ö	Ü	ᾶ	ἒ	ῐ	ö	ῠ
160	ά	ῐ	ó	ύ	ῴ	ῳ	ῶ	ῴ	ῴ	ῴ	ῷ	ῷ	ῑ	ῠ	ᾴ	ῄ	ῄ	Γ	Δ	ᾔ
180	ῇ	ῇ	Θ	ώ	ὼ	Λ	ῶ	ὼ	Ξ	ὼ	Π	ὤ	Σ	ὤ	ῶ	Φ	ὤ	Ψ	Ω	ᾆ
200	ῑ	ῠ	ᾅ	ᾇ	ῇ	ῇ	ῇ	ά	έ	ί	ό	ύ	ᾴ	ᾅ	ᾶ	α	ὤ	γ	δ	ε
220	ζ	η	ϑ	ι	ϰ	β	λ	μ	ν	ξ	ὤ	π	ϱ	σ	τ	υ	φ	χ	ψ	ω
240	ϱ	ῑ	ῠ	ᾅ	ᾆ	η	ῳ	ᾳ	ά	έ	ί	ό	ύ	ῦ	ὄ					
	0	1	2	3	4	5	6	7	8	9	0	1	2	3	4	5	6	7	8	9

Table 8. Non-standard 8-bit encoding: Latin font with diacritics

	0	1	2	3	4	5	6	7	8	9	0	1	2	3	4	5	6	7	8	9
000		.	ˉ	˘	ˇ	´	`	¨	^	˝			.		ˇ	˘	´	`	¨	ˮ
020	ˮ	§	ˆ	ˎ	ˏ	Ł	Þ	ʰ	ᵘ	˙	ʻ	ʼ		!	"	#	†	°	+	'
040	(	)	*	+	,	-	.	/	0	1	2	3	4	5	6	7	8	9	:	;
060	<	=	>	?	√	A	B	C	D	E	F	G	H	I	J	K	L	M	N	O
080	P	Q	R	S	T	U	V	W	X	Y	Z	[	\	]	^	¯	`	a	b	c
100	d	e	f	g	h	i	j	k	l	m	n	o	p	q	r	s	t	u	v	w
120	x	y	z	{	|	}	~	≈	ż	ü	é	â	ä	à	å	ç	ê	ë	è	ï
140	î	ì	Ä	ø	é	æ	œ	ô	ö	ò	û	ù	ý	Ö	Ü	ā	ē	ī	ō	ū
160	á	í	ó	ú	ñ	ŋ	ā	ē	ī	ō	ū	ą́	j̇	í	ł	ú	å	ě	ì	ı
180	ů	ą	ą̊	x́	xᵘ	ž	ŋᵘ	ṛ	ī	r̄	ŭ	ą	ę	į	ǫ	ų	j̨	ų	ə	ə̄
200	ə	ą̄	ą́	ę̄	ę́	ē̦	é̦	ị	į̇	ų̦	ų́	ű	ȳ	ý	β	ƀ	č	ḍ	đ	δ
220	ǵ	ġ	ɡ	γ	ḥ	ß	ḧ	ƕ	ƙ	ḷ	ḹ	ḻ	ḷ	ṃ	m̄	m̊	m̨	ṅ	ń	ń
240	ṇ	ŗ	ŕ	r̄	ŗ̄	r̃	ś	ṣ	š	ŝ	ṣ̌	ṭ	t̨	ϑ	þ					
	0	1	2	3	4	5	6	7	8	9	0	1	2	3	4	5	6	7	8	9

standardized way, and it gets lost all too easily when data are transferred across systems. One example may suffice to illustrate this effect which would be hazardous for a long-term storage of textual materials.

1.3. Conversion and the loss of data: An example

Table 9a shows the first ten lines of a Svan folk song, digitized in the early 1980s in a DOS environment with a special font covering the requirements of the Latin transcription of South Caucasian languages. Encoded as a plain text, with no additional information whatsoever on the font, i.e., the encoding used, the text would have appeared as displayed in Table 9b on the DOS "system" screen, and the recovery of what symbol stands for what character would have been a hard task indeed. Imagine a linguist working in 200 years time who would not have any other information on the language in question (which may well have died out by then – Svan is among the languages dealt with in the DoBeS project "Endangered Caucasian Languages in Georgia"),[1] he or she would have no chance to restore the "values" of the crucial "characters" and thus to reestablish the text itself.

Table 9 a/b. Font mapping in 8-bit encoding: Svan sample text

	a.		b.
1	*vož ǧal sabirelo Nuarsala!*	1	vo■ ╠al sabirelo Nuarsala!
2	*Mušvraši ṭubas esǧəri,*	2	MuΩvraΩi ∩ubas es╠╩ri,
3	*sgobin lažxvidax Čolšare,*	3	sgobin la■xvidax ⌐olΩare,
4	*min žixaldax si moḳtare,*	4	min ■ixaldax si moⲅtare,
5	*esran irix min amxvare.*	5	esran irix min amxvare.
6	*ka lažšədax ečxän-amxän,*	6	ka la■Ω╩dax e─xaΩn-amxaΩn,
7	*meqrär šəǵasuǵv ežlažix,*	7	meqraΩr Ω╩ɹasu╠v e■la■ix,
8	*ču lažṭəxix Mušvra ṭubas.*	8	─u la■∩╩xix MuΩvra ∩ubas.
9	*Davberxo lekva esǵadäs,*	9	Davberxo lekva esɹadaΩs,
10	*Davbrar q̇ōrars xocǵanalix:*	10	Davbrar ⲅrars xocɹanalix:
11	*ləmšare sgožix mušgvriša.*	11	l╩mΩare sgo■ix muΩgvriΩa.

1.4. Unicode: Towards a worldwide standard

What, then, is the way out of this problem? The answer is clear: To be able to uniquely encode all characters that have been used in writing down human languages (including both "national" scripts and alphabets, and linguistic "metascripts" such as the International Phonetic Alphabet), the basis of encoding must be extended far beyond the 1-byte (8-bit) standard. This is exactly what has been undertaken since the early 1990s when the so-called "Unicode" standard was created: Based on 16 bits (or 2 bytes), this standard comprises $2^{16} = 65536$ basic "code points" used for the "unique" encoding of characters. Considering that for the Chinese script alone, far more than 65,000 different characters have been used throughout history, it is clear that even this standard is not yet sufficient to cover all characters used by mankind at all times. A further extension is envisaged, however, in the 32-bit standard ISO 10646 which provides a total of (2^{32} =) 4,294,967,296 code points; as a matter of fact, the Unicode standard is but one subset of this "infinite" inventory, just as the ANSI standard (ISO 8859-1) is a subset of Unicode and the ASCII standard, a subset of ANSI (cf. Figure 1).

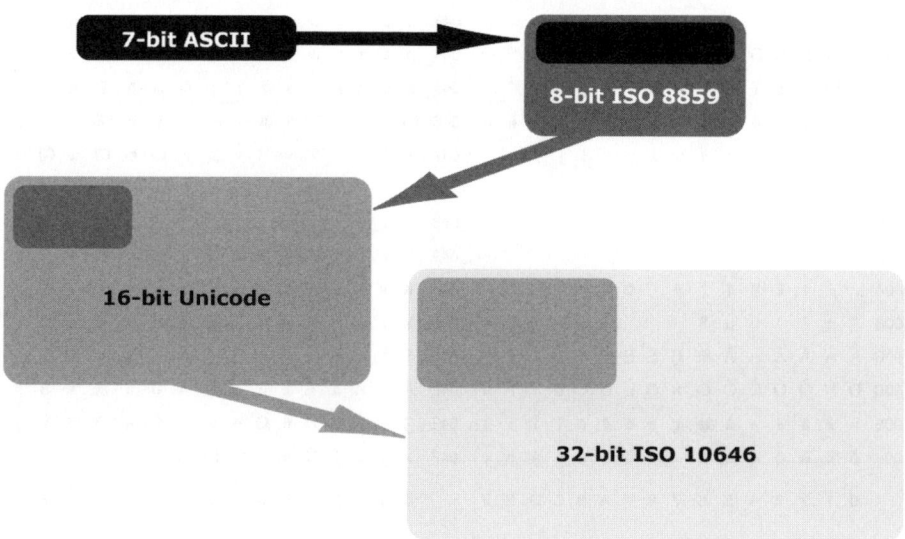

Figure 1. From 8-bit to 32-bit encoding

Along with the expansion of the World Wide Web, Unicode encoding has become more and more prominent since the late 1990s, and it is the encoding basis of more and more up-to-date operating systems and word processors. There can be no doubt that this is a huge advantage for the purposes of linguistic documentation. Cf., e.g., Tables 10a and 10b which show a few of the "blocks" of Unicode characters: The distinction of a Cyrillic *cha* (ч) and a Latin *c* with cedilla (ç) is now guaranteed by their different code points (hexadecimal number 0447 = decimal 1095 vs. hexadecimal 00E7 = decimal 231), and various Latin-based characters used in transcription systems can now as well be encoded as characters of the Greek, Georgian, or Chinese scripts.

Table 10 a/b. 16-bit encoding: Unicode blocks Latin and Cyrillic

a.

	0	1	2	3	4	5	6	7	8	9	A	B	C	D	E	F
000																
001																
002		?	!	"	#	$	%	&	'	(	)	*	+	,	-	.	/
003	0	1	2	3	4	5	6	7	8	9	:	;	<	=	>	?
004	@	A	B	C	D	E	F	G	H	I	J	K	L	M	N	O
005	P	Q	R	S	T	U	V	W	X	Y	Z	[	\	]	^	_
006	`	a	b	c	d	e	f	g	h	i	j	k	l	m	n	o
007	p	q	r	s	t	u	v	w	x	y	z	{	|	}	~	
008																
009																
00A		¡	¢	£	¤	¥	¦	§	¨	©	ª	«	¬		®	¯
00B	°	±	²	³	´	µ	¶	·	¸	¹	º	»	¼	½	¾	¿
00C	À	Á	Â	Ã	Ä	Å	Æ	Ç	È	É	Ê	Ë	Ì	Í	Î	Ï
00D	Ð	Ñ	Ò	Ó	Ô	Õ	Ö	×	Ø	Ù	Ú	Û	Ü	Ý	Þ	ß
00E	à	á	â	ã	ä	å	æ	ç	è	é	ê	ë	ì	í	î	ï
00F	ð	ñ	ò	ó	ô	õ	ö	÷	ø	ù	ú	û	ü	ý	þ	ÿ
	0	1	2	3	4	5	6	7	8	9	A	B	C	D	E	F

b.

	0	1	2	3	4	5	6	7	8	9	A	B	C	D	E	F
040	È	Ë	Ђ	Ѓ	Є	Ѕ	І	Ї	Ј	Љ	Њ	Ћ	Ќ	Ѝ	Ў	Џ
041	А	Б	В	Г	Д	Е	Ж	З	И	Й	К	Л	М	Н	О	П
042	Р	С	Т	У	Ф	Х	Ц	Ч	Ш	Щ	Ъ	Ы	Ь	Э	Ю	Я
043	а	б	в	г	д	е	ж	з	и	й	к	л	м	н	о	п
044	р	с	т	у	ф	х	ц	ч	ш	щ	ъ	ы	ь	э	ю	я
045	è	ё	ђ	ѓ	є	ѕ	і	ї	ј	љ	њ	ћ	ќ	ѝ	ў	џ
046	Ѡ	ѡ	Ѣ	ѣ	Ѥ	ѥ	Ѧ	ѧ	Ѩ	ѩ	Ѫ	ѫ	Ѭ	ѭ	Ѯ	ѯ
047	Ѱ	ѱ	Ѳ	ѳ	Ѵ	ѵ	Ѷ	ѷ	Ѹ	ѹ	Ѻ	ѻ	Ѽ	ѽ	Ѿ	ѿ
048	Ҁ	ҁ	҂	҃	҄	҅	҆	҇	҈	҉	Ҋ	ҋ	Ҍ	ҍ	Ҏ	ҏ
049	Ґ	ґ	Ғ	ғ	Ҕ	ҕ	Җ	җ	Ҙ	ҙ	Қ	қ	Ҝ	ҝ	Ҟ	ҟ
04A	Ҡ	ҡ	Ң	ң	Ҥ	ҥ	Ҧ	ҧ	Ҩ	ҩ	Ҫ	ҫ	Ҭ	ҭ	Ү	ү
04B	Ұ	ұ	Ҳ	ҳ	Ҵ	ҵ	Ҷ	ҷ	Ҹ	ҹ	Һ	һ	Ҽ	ҽ	Ҿ	ҿ
04C	Ӏ	Ж	ӂ	Ҟ	ӄ	Л	л	Ӈ	ӈ	Н	н	Ч	ч	Ӎ	ӎ	
04D	Ӑ	ӑ	Ӓ	ӓ	Ӕ	ӕ	Ӗ	ӗ	Ә	ә	Ӛ	ӛ	Ж	ж	Ӟ	ӟ
04E	Ӡ	ӡ	Й	й	Ӥ	ӥ	Ö	ö	Ө	ө	Ӫ	ӫ	Э	э	Ӯ	ӯ
04F	Ӱ	ӱ	Ӳ	ӳ	Ӵ	ӵ			Ы	ы						
	0	1	2	3	4	5	6	7	8	9	A	B	C	D	E	F

In passing it may be noted that Unicode was not the first attempt to prevent the chaos of 8-bit font mapping by 16-bit encoding. As early as 1988, the word processor WordPerfect 5.0 was introduced which comprised a set of 1632 uniquely encodable characters, among them Greek, Cyrillic, and

Japanese (*hiragana* and *katakana*) sets, plus a block of 255 "user definable" entities. In this way, WP 5 encoded texts may meet the requirements of unique character encoding even today, and it should be possible to keep the information they contain intact when transferring these texts into the Unicode standard. Unfortunately, the WP encoding system was not widely used and the opportunities it offered were mostly ignored; thus we cannot expect the automatic conversion routines for WP 5 texts offered by, e.g., MS Word 2000 to correctly interpret and re-encode any one of the nonstandard characters that may be contained in them. Cf. Table 11, which illustrates what happens when the Svan folk song we have dealt with above (cf. Table 9) is consistently encoded in WP 5 and then automatically converted into an MS Word text. It is especially the replacement of "unidentified" characters by an undifferentiated underline score (_) which makes the conversion result unusable and irreparable. The same holds true for the automatic conversion provided by later versions of WordPerfect itself (e.g., WP 9); here, we find a replacement of, e.g., ə by B, which is at least confusing. This all means that a correct conversion of WordPerfect 5 encoded texts (or, at least, of the characters contained in them) into Unicode encoding is possible, but it still requires special programming.

Table 11 a/b. Automatic text "conversion": Svan example

	a.		b.
1	*vo_ Ẏal sabirelo Nuarsala!*	1	*voǍ ġal sabirelo Nuarsala!*
2	*Mušvraši _ubas esẎ_ri,*	2	*Mušvraši Mubas esġBri,*
3	*sgobin la_xvidax _olšare,*	3	*sgobin laǍxvidax volšare,*
4	*min _ixaldax si mo_tare,*	4	*min Ǎixaldax si moåtare,*
5	*esran irix min amxvare.*	5	*esran irix min amxvare.*
6	*ka la_š_dax e...xän-amxän,*	6	*ka laǍšBdax ečxän-amxän,*
7	*meqrär š__asuẎv e_la_ix,*	7	*meqrär šBïasuġv eǍlaǍix,*
8	*...u la___xix Mušvra _ubas.*	8	*ču laǍMBxix Mušvra Mubas.*
9	*Davberxo lekva es_adäs,*	9	*Davberxo lekva esïadäs,*
10	*Davbrar _Çrars xoc_analix:*	10	*Davbrar ïörars xocïanalix:*
11	*l_mšare sgo_ix mušgvriša.*	11	*lBmšare sgoǍix mušgvriša.*

1.5. Coexisting standards: The worst case scenario

The question now is, are we really on the safe side after Unicode has become the worldwide basis of character encoding? To be honest, there are
still quite a lot of puzzling problems to be solved, not only with respect to
the conversion of older material. The major problem lies in the fact that for
the time being, digital word processing is characterized by the actual co-
existence of 16-bit and 8-bit encoding systems. Just as the 8-bit ANSI standard was integrated into the 16-bit Unicode standard as one of its "blocks",
all Unicode-based word processors such as MS Word 2000 have been designed to be ready to handle 8-bit encoded texts alongside 16-bit encoded
ones. In the same way, Unicode-based operating systems such as MS Windows 2000 have been designed to be able to incorporate 8-bit encoded fonts
side by side with 16-bit encoded ones. A few examples may suffice to show
what confusion this may bring about.

Table 12a displays the fragment of a Georgian verb list which was typed
in MS Word 6, using a plain 8-bit based Georgian font mapped onto the 8-
bit ANSI encoding scheme. When I received this text file from a colleague
in Georgia via e-mail two years ago, I tried to open it in MS Word 2002
(XP Office). The result was funny, to say the least: What appeared on the
screen was a text in Japanese *katakana* script instead (cf. Table 12b). When
I opened the text in Open Office 1 instead, another result appeared: The
Georgian characters were now replaced by Latin characters with diacritics
(cf. Table 12c), which was a foreseeable result bearing in mind that the
original encoding was 8-bit based. After applying the correct Georgian font
to this text within Open Office, the intended look (as in Table 12a) reap-
peared, and the text could even be re-mapped onto a transcriptional font
which used the same 8-bit code points (cf. Table 12d). Trying to apply the
Georgian font to the "Japanese" looking output of MS Word 2002 changed
nothing, however; the *katakana* characters remained *katakana* characters
(as displayed in Table 12b).

Table 12 a–d. Automatic text "conversion": Georgian example (wordlist)

a. Original text (MS Word 6)

0020010M გაადვილება (გაადვილებ-ისა)   0020020M გააზნაურება (გააზნაურებ-ისა)

0020030M გაბმა (გაბმ-ისა)   0020040N გაგა-ჲ (გაგ-ისა)

0020050M გაგება (გაგებ-ისა)   0020060P გაგებულ-ი (გაგებულ-ისა)

0020070M გაგზავნა (გაგზავნ-ისა)   0020080N გაგზავნა-ჲ (გაგზავნ-ისა)

b. Same text after cross-version transfer (MS Word 6 > MS Word 2002)

0020010M ツタタテナノヒトチタ (ツタタテナノヒトチ - ノ乇タ)   0020020M ツタタニヘタヨメトチタ (ツタタニヘタヨメトチ - ノ乇タ)

0020030M ツタチフタ (ツタチフ - ノ乇タ)   0020040N ツタツタ - ホ (ツタツ - ノ乇タ)

0020050M ツタツトチタ (ツタツトチ - ノ乇タ)   0020060P ツタツトチヨヒ - ノ (ツタツトチヨヒ - ノ乇タ)

0020070M ツタツニタナヘタ (ツタツニタナヘ - ノ乇タ)   0020080N ツタツニタナヘタ - ホ (ツタツニタナヘ - ノ乇タ)

c. Same text after cross-program transfer (MS Word 6 > Open Office 1)

0020010M ÂÀÀÃÁÉËÄÁÀ   0020020M ÂÀÀÆÍÀÖÖÄÁÀ
          (ÂÀÀÃÁÉËÄÁÁ-ÉÓÀ)   (ÂÀÀÆÍÀÖÖÄÁ-ÉÓÀ)

0020030M ÂÀÁÌÀ (ÂÀÁÍ-ÉÓÀ)   0020040N ÂÀÂÀ-Î (ÂÀÂ-ÉÓÀ)

0020050M ÂÀÂÂÁÄÁÁ (ÂÀÂÂÁÄÁ-ÉÓÀ)   0020060P ÂÀÂÂÄÁÖË-É (ÂÀÂÂÄÁÖË-ÉÓÀ)

0020070M ÂÀÂÂÆÀÁÍÁ (ÂÀÂÂÆÀÁÍ-ÉÓÀ) 0020080N ÂÀÂÂÆÀÁÍÀ-Î (ÂÀÂÂÆÀÁÍ-ÉÓÀ)

d. Same with different font-assignment (within Open Office 1)

0020010M gaadvileba (gaadvileb-isa)   0020020M gaaznaureba (gaaznaureb-isa)

0020030M gabma (gabm-isa)   0020040N gaga-j (gag-isa)

0020050M gageba (gageb-isa)   0020060P gagebul-i (gagebul-isa)

0020070M gagzavna   0020080N gagzavna-j
          (gagzavn-isa)   (gagzavn-isa)

How can this odd behavior of MS Word be explained? Obviously, the program executes a five-step strategy when it encounters texts encoded by other (older) versions:

- it first checks whether the document is Unicode-encoded;
- if not, it checks whether the character distribution might meet the "typical" distribution of one of the known code pages;
- if yes, it assumes that code page to be represented;
- it converts the 8-bit characters of the assumed code page into the equivalent characters of Unicode;
- it stores the Unicode characters in memory.

Reapplying the original 8-bit fonts can then be no remedy if they do not meet the Unicode encoding assumed, as in the given case where a "Japanese" code page was assumed to be present.

1.6. Persisting non-standards: The "Private Use Area"

One other problem that may be crucial even in Unicode times is the persistence of at least one area that is designed for font mapping. This is the so-called "Private Use Area" (PUA) which comprises 6144 non-predefined characters in the blocks E000-EFFF and F000-F7FF. Quite like the "user definable area" of WordPerfect 5, it can be assigned *ad libitum* by companies, user groups, or individuals, with the result that additional information is necessary to distinguish the characters "encoded" in it. Table 13 shows what can happen when the wrong font is applied to visualize PUA encoded characters; in the worst case, the intended information will again be lost.

Table 13a/b. 16-bit font mapping: The "Private Use Area"

1.7. Suggestions and recommendations

As far as character encoding is concerned, all this leads to a few general recommendations that may be helpful with respect to both data exchange and long-term archiving of textual materials:

- Wherever possible, be sure to use 16-bit encoding, not 8-bit encoding;
- if using 16-bit encoding, avoid addressing the Private Use Area;
- If 8-bit encoding is required, try not to mix up several fonts with a different encoding in one and the same document;
- always keep track of what font-and-encoding you are using;
- always inform the receivers about all this and provide the fonts (if legally possible).

Archivers should be even more rigid:

- They should convert all 8-bit documents into 16-bit Unicode documents and
- they should not use the Private Use Area for the encoding of characters.

But how to produce 16-bit encoded texts? As we have seen, the most common word processors of today are designed to handle both 8-bit and 16-bit encodings. Using MS Word 2002 under MS Windows XP and typing with a "national" keyboard as provided by the operating system, you can be quite sure that what you type will be stored in 16-bit encoding. If, however, you want to add some characters from, e.g., an IPA font, by using the symbol insertion menu, you should check whether the Unicode value given for the character in question matches the respective code point of Unicode or not – if not, the font you intend to use is most probably 8-bit encoded. As a matter of fact, MS Word 2002 does allow for mixtures of 8-bit and 16-bit encodings within a given text document – which may turn out to be the worst case as far as data exchange and storage is concerned. Problems may also occur when you use special keyboard drivers supplied by third parties such as Tavultesoft Keyman: These may have been designed for 8-bit encoding alone, giving you no chance to enter 16-bit encoded text with them. If you intend to design your own keyboard driver with Keyman or with the MS Keyboard Layout Creator, be sure to use Unicode encoding as its basis. Note, by the way, that the SIL Shoebox program was exclusively 8-bit based; it interacted well with Keyman drivers, but also only on an 8-bit basis. The newly developed Toolbox now is Unicode-based and should work well with 16-bit based Keyman layouts.

2.   The encoding of text elements:
Surface appearance vs. content markup

2.1. Text structure visualized

Let us now turn to the second topic of this chapter, viz. the encoding of the structural elements of texts. To clarify what this means, it is helpful to look again at the Svan text we have dealt with above (cf. Table 9). Even without any knowledge of the language, we will immediately have the impression that this text consists of verses. This is clearly indicated by two signals we are used to in reading poetical texts, viz. the relative shortness of lines, and the numbers (from 1 to 11) given to each line. There are many further elements of textual structure involved, however. First, we will easily guess that the text consists of five sentences, partially extending across verses and partially consisting of subordinate clauses: This is indicated by the punctuation marks used. Then, we will be able to state that the text consists of 38 words, in their turn indicated by either empty spaces or punctuation marks adjoining their first and last characters.

2.1.1. The basic elements

This may all sound trivial, but as a matter of fact, it can be crucial indeed for the documentation of textual materials to consider and mark up their internal elements when preparing them for future usage, and this should be done as consistently as the encoding of the characters appearing in words. So what elements are we talking about? Among the basic elements of every kind of text, we have already mentioned words (consisting of characters when written down), phrases, clauses, sentences; on a higher level, we will meet sections, paragraphs, chapters, text parts, and the like. For many of these elements, we intuitively adapt signals we have been used to since we were at school, such as spaces indicating word boundaries, full stops indicating sentence breaks, or "hard" line breaks indicating the end of a section or paragraph. For a consistent encoding of a digital text, this may not be sufficient, though. Another example may suffice to illustrate why.

2.1.2. An illustrative example

In Table 14, we see a specimen from an 18th century grammatical treatise in Georgian, digitized using MS Word 6. Without even a faint knowledge of the Georgian script, a reader may guess that the first line of the text is a heading, given that it obviously consists of but one word, is centered on the line, and seems to be represented in a boldface font. As to the other lines of texts, the reader will as easily suspect that this is an interplay of questions and answers, the former being clearly indicated by question marks. One more suggestion might impose itself: As the first word of every question and answer is separated by a colon and marked by an extra spacing of characters, and as these words are repeated throughout questions and answers, they might indicate the names of people speaking (as in a theater play). All these assumptions are correct: We do have an interplay of questions and answers, uttered by two different persons here (one Ioane, one Nikolaoz), and the first line is the heading (it simply means "On grammar"). The reason why it was so easy to find all this out is that here again, marking methods were used that we are used to in reading – centering of lines, usage of boldface, spacing of characters, etc. For computational purposes, however, these markings, which we may call **surface-oriented**, are arbitrary and insufficient in a twofold sense.

Table 14. Georgian text specimen

ღრამმატიკისათვს

ი ო ა ნ ე მ:	ოთხნი იგი გვარნი მოძღვრებითნი, რომელნიცა შეუდგებიან, დაემდევრებიან ღრამმატიკასა.
ნ ი კ ო ლ ა ო ზ მ ა ნ:	რაჲ არს სახელები მათი?
ი ო ა ნ ე მ:	განსაზღვრება, განწვალება, აღმოჩენა და აღლევა.
ნ ი კ ო ლ ა ო ზ მ ა ნ:	კვალად რაჲ საჴმარ არს ცნობად?

2.1.3. Program features vs. standards

First, the centering of lines may be a common feature of all existing word processors today, but it is by no means standardized: The encoding of this feature simply depends on the program structure. To illustrate what this means, Table 15 shows a part of the internal code of the given MS Word document. Here we detect the word contained in the heading (Georgian ღრამმატიკისათვის "On grammar", stored in 8-bit form) at the end of what appears to be a sixth line, followed by a "clear text" form of the questions and answers. There is no indication adjoining the "head" word that it must be centered or boldfaced, and none that it represents a heading. All this must be inferred, by the interpreting program, from the unreadable code preceding it (or from a similar looking block of coding elements added at the end of each MS Word document). Imagine somebody were to decode this document in 200 years time, without having any access to the internal program code structure of MS Word 6 – he or she would certainly not be able to extract anything from it but the "plain text", and all the additional information contained in the centering of lines and boldfacing of words would be lost (as a matter of fact, many of us have witnessed this effect when trying to open MS Word documents of the 1980s in later versions). The same would be true for the "spaced" characters indicating the speakers in the text: the spacing is here, too, covered by a program-internal function and would be lost together with the knowledge of the code. It would not be a good idea, by the way, to avoid this latter effect by inserting the character spaces manually instead of using the word processor function for it: If, as we have seen above, we use spaces to distinguish words from each other, the spaced name I O A N E would automatically appear as five words (consisting of but one character each) to any computational analysis, and it could not be found when searching for "IOANE".

Table 15. Program-specific encoding of Georgian text specimen

Ðïà¡±ÿáÿÿÿÿÿÿÿÿÿÿÿÿÿÿÿÿÿÿÿÿÿÿÿÿÿÿÿÿÿÿÿÿÿÿ
ÿÿÿÿÿÿÿÿÿÿÿÿÿÿÿÿÿÿÿÿÿÿÿÿAÿþÿCÿÿÿÿÿÿÿÿÿÿÿAÿÿÿÿ´AÿÿÿÿÿØ
ÿÿÿÿÿÿ BÿÿÿÿÀÿÿÿÿÿFÿÿÿMicrosoft Word 6.0 Document ÿÿÿÿÿÿÿÿÿÿÿÿÿÿÿÿMSWord-
DocÿÿÿWord.Document.6ÿô9²qÿÿÿÿÿÿÿÿÿÿ ÿÿÿÿÿÿÿÿÿÿÿÿÿ
ÿÿÿ Aÿÿÿÿÿ´Aÿÿÿÿÿ´ØAÿÿÿ Aÿÿÿÿÿ´Aÿÿÿÿÿ´ØAÿC:\WORKDIR\TEMPLATE\
NORMAL.DOTÿÿ
ÿÿÿüAÿÿÿÿ BÿÿÿÿÿDBÿÿ ÿÿÿhBÿÿÿÿÿŒBÿÿÿÿÿÿÿÿÿÙRAMMA°I±ISATWS
IOANEM: OTXNI IGI GVARNI MO¾ÙVREBITNI, ROMELNICA ˛EUdGEBIAN,
dAEMdEVREBIAN ÙRAMMA°I±ASA.
NI±OLAOzMAN: RAJ ARS SAXELEBI MATI?
IOANEM: GANSAzÙVREBA, GANÂVALEBA, AÙMOÆENA dA AÙLEVA.
NI±OLAOzMAN: ±VALAd RAJ SAQMAR ARS CNOBAd?

2.1.4. What you see is NOT what you get

What, then, can be done to avoid a loss of the information concerning the structuring of texts and their elements? First, we should get rid of an ideal in text processing which has become very widespread these days, viz. "WYSIWYG": "What you see is what you get". It may be true that the text you type in on your computer today will look quite the same on the screen and in a printout, but all this is restricted to a very ephemeral use: The next generation of users of your text may have no access to the sophisticated codings of your word processor and will thus "get" anything else but what you "saw". Second, we should give up the idea that the use of mere printing devices (such as boldfacing, spacing of characters, and the like) might be enough to indicate the function of text elements. Instead, we should adapt ourselves to what may be called "content markup" whenever our texts are meant to be stored for documentation purposes.

2.2.   A halfway solution: HTML

In recent years, the marking up of text elements has indeed become more and more widespread, especially by the expansion of the World Wide Web and the prescription to use a certain unified text encoding structure, the so-called Hypertext Markup Language (HTML), for documents to be provided in it. Tables 16a and 16b show the Georgian text specimen converted into a plain HTML text (as source code and visualized with a standard web browser); here, you will easily find the markup devices corresponding to the centering and boldfacing of the heading, viz. the markers <p align=center> … </p> and <b> … </b>. What you will miss is the special markup of the speakers' names; this cannot be present as the spacing of characters is not markable as such in HTML. But even if it were (actually, so-called "cascading style sheets", CSS, can be used for this purpose), it would be no good idea to use this kind of markup alone – future users might hardly grasp the idea what it stands for as the spacing of characters has no standardized meaning. In the same way, it remains unclear what the centering and the bolding of the first line is to indicate – that this is a heading remains a mere guess. As a matter of fact, the markup provided by HTML contains but very few "content" elements. One is the group of markers from <H1> to <H6> which should be used to denote several levels of headings. In our case, it would be much better to mark our heading with one of these elements (replacing <p align=center> ... </p> by <h1 align=center> ... </h1>) – the outer appearance would then be secondary and adaptable to future uses.

Table 16a. Plain HTML encoding of Georgian text specimen

```
<HTML>
    <HEAD>
        <META HTTP-EQUIV="Content-Type" CONTENT="text/html;
        charset=iso-8859-1">
        <TITLE>Grammatika</TITLE>
        <META NAME="KeyWords" CONTENT="Georgian Grammar">
            <BODY>
                <DIV>
                    <P ALIGN="CENTER"><B>ÙRAMMAºI±ISATWS</B></P>
                </DIV>
                <DIV>
                    <P><SPAN>IOANEM: </SPAN><SPAN>OTXNI IGI GVARNI
                    MO¾ÙVREBITNI, ROMELNICA ¸EUdGEBIAN, dAEMdEVREBIAN
                    ÙRAMMAºI±ASA.</SPAN></P>
                    <P><SPAN>NI±OLAOzMAN: </SPAN><SPAN>RAJ ARS SAXELEBI
                    MATI?</SPAN></P>
                    <P><SPAN>IOANEM: </SPAN><SPAN>GANSAzÙVREBA,
                    GANÂVALEBA, AÙMOÆENA dA AÙLEVA.</SPAN></P>
                    <P><SPAN>NI±OLAOzMAN: </SPAN><SPAN>±VALAd RAJ SAQMAR ARS
                    CNOBAd?</SPAN></P>
                    ...
                </DIV>
            </BODY>
</HTML>
```

Table 16b. Browser output of Georgian HTML text specimen

ღრამმატიკისათვს

იოანემ: ოთხნი იგი გვარნი მოძღვრებითნი, რომელნიცა შეუდგებიან, დაემდევრებიან ღრამმატიკასა.
ნიკოლაოზმან: რაჲ   არს   სახელები   მათი?
იოანემ: განსაზღვრება,   განწვალება,   აღმოჩენა   და   აღლევა.
ნიკოლაოზმან: კვალად   რაჲ   საჴმარ   არს   ცნობად?

2.3. Real content markup: XML

The more information of this type is to be encoded, the less will HTML markup suffice. For a consistent markup of the contents of a text, you will have to go one step further and adapt the eXtensible Markup Language, XML (a derivate of the Standard Generalized Markup Language, SGML). This alone will allow you to provide for future users all the knowledge you might have on the text materials you are working on. In an XML markup, you will easily be able to declare not only the heading of the text as its heading but also the speakers as speakers, their utterances as questions and answers relating to each other, and any other text element that might be useful to define. Table 17 shows the Georgian grammar example provided with a minimal XML markup; you will easily note the difference as against the HTML markup which consists in the meaningfulness of the tags.

Table 17. XML encoding of Georgian text specimen

```
<?xml version="1.0" encoding="utf-8"?>
  <part>
    <pnum>1</pnum>
    <chapter>
      <cnum>1</cnum>
      <heading>ღრამმატიკისათვს</heading>
      ...
      <utterance>
        <unum>1</unum>
        <utype>question</utype>
        <speaker>ნიკოლაოზმან</speaker>
        <sentence>
          <snum>1</snum>
          <item>
            <inum>1</inum>
            <itype>word</itype>რაﻪ</item>
          <item>
            <inum>2</inum>
            <itype>word</itype>არს</item>
          <item>
            <inum>3</inum>
            <itype>word</itype>სახელები</item>
          <item>
            <inum>4</inum>
            <itype>word</itype>მათი</item>
          <item>
            <inum>5</inum>
            <itype>question mark</itype>?</item>
        </sentence>
```

```
          </utterance>
          <utterance>
            <unum>2</unum>
            <utype>answer</utype>
            <speaker>ოთაßეძ</speaker>
            <sentence>
              <snum>1</snum>
              <item>
                <inum>1</inum>
                <itype>word</itype>განსაზღვრება</item>
              <item>
                <inum>2</inum>
                <itype>comma</itype>,</item>
              <item>
                <inum>3</inum>
                <itype>word</itype>განწვალება</item>
              <item>
                <inum>4</inum>
                <itype>comma</itype>,</item>
              <item>
                <inum>5</inum>
                <itype>word</itype>აღმოჩენა</item>
              <item>
                <inum>6</inum>
                <itype>word</itype>და</item>
              <item>
                <inum>7</inum>
                <itype>word</itype>აღქოქა</item>
              <item>
                <inum>8</inum>
                <itype>full stop</itype>.</item>
            </sentence>
          </utterance>
          ...
        </chapter>
      </part>
    </text>
```

2.4. XML in language documentation: Going beyond plain text encoding

Of course, all kinds of analyses of linguistic units such as words and phrases can also be included in an XML markup, and this is the real advantage it has for the documentation of languages. You can be sure that future users will hardly be interested in sharing the surface beauty of a text document; what they will be interested in is as much information about the language as you can provide. For many years, linguists have used the Shoebox program for the purpose of noting down and annotating texts they collected during their fieldwork, and for many of us, the facilities offered by this program, especially the half-automatic process of interlinearization, is indispensable; cf. Figure 2 which exhibits a sample sentence in the Tsova-Tush or Batsbi language of the Caucasus[2]. The basic idea of interlinearization as provided by Shoebox consists in the vertical arrangement of interdependent annotation layers (tiers); these can include, as in the present example, different transcriptions and transliterations (here: Georgian script, Latin script, IPA), morphological analyses, the reference to lemmatic forms, translations of the lemmatic forms, etc. The Shoebox format is not sufficient in the sense of a thorough markup, though, as it has two disadvantages: The encoding used is still 8-bit based, so that the correct display depends on the interpretative functions of the program; cf. Table 18 which shows the same Shoebox text when opened in a normal text editor. While the latter disadvantage has recently been overcome by the introduction of the Toolbox program, the Unicode-compatible successor of Shoebox 5.0, the second disadvantage remains: The interdependencies of the vertically aligned elements is not marked as such in a Shoebox/Toolbox text but depends on the interpretation of spaces between words. This is where XML markup would help: Only after the conversion of the Shoebox file into a Unicode based XML schema as the one displayed in Figure 3, we can be confident that all the information stored in the document will be accessible to later users for a long time (cf. Chapter 4 for other examples of XML application).

\ref	0485									
\per	AS									
\trs	ჩუხუჲ	შუი^{n}	ნანიგორე^{n}	ჩაყ	დეწ	ხილ'ა^{n},	მე	ვაშბა^{n}	დაჰდიცდოლ^{o}.	
\tl1	čuxuy	šui^{n}	nanigore^{n}	čaq	deç	xil'a^{n}	me	vašba^{n}	daḥdicdol^{o}	
\ph	t͡ʃuxuj	ʃui^{n}	nanigore^{n}	t͡ʃaq	det͡s'	xiɫa^{n}	me	vaʃba^{n}	daħdit͡sdol^{w}	
\ts	ჩუხუჲ	შუი^{n}	ნანიგორე^{n}	ჩაყ	დეწ	ხილ'ა^{n}	მე	ვაშბა^{n}	დაჰდიცდოლ^{o}	
\ts1	čuxuy	šui^{n}	nanigore^{n}	čaq	deç	xil'a^{n}	me	vašba^{n}	daḥdicdol^{o}	
\m	čux-uy	šui^{n}	nan-i-gore^{n}	čaq	d-eç	xil'a^{n}	me	vašba^{n}	daḥ-dic-d-ol-^{o}	
\m1	čux-uy	šui^{n}	nan-i-gore^{n}	čaq	d-eç	xil'a^{n}	me	vašba^{n}	daḥ-dic-d-ol-^{o}	
\lm	ჩუიხ	შუი^{n}	ნან	ჩაყ	დეწა^{n}	ხილ'ა^{n}	მე	ვაშბა^{n}	დაჰდიცოდა^{n}	
\lm1	čuyx	šui^{n}	nan	čaq	deça^{n}	xil'a^{n}	me	vašba^{n}	daḥdicoda^{n}	
\g	ბატკანი	თავისი	დედა	შორს	საჭირო_ა	ყოფნა,ყოლა,ქონა	რომ	ერთმანეთი	დავიწყება	
\g1	batkani	tavisi	deda	šors	sačiro_a	qopna,qola,kona	rom	ertmaneti	davicqeba	
\gl	lamb	own	mother	distant	to-be-necessary	to-be,to-have	that	each_other	to-forget	
\p	**N.4Gr.**	**ReflPron.**	**N.2Gr.**	**Adv.**	**V.**	**V.**	**Conj.**	**Recipr.Pron.**	**V.**	
\gr	**Nom.Pl.**	**indecl.**	**Loc.Pl.+Postp.**	**indecl.**	**Pres.4Gr.**	**Inf.**	**indecl.**	**indecl.**	**Cond.4Cl.3Ps.**	
\fg	ბატკნები თავისი დედებისგან შორს უნდა იყვნენ, რათა ერთმანეთი დაავიწყდეთ.									
\fg1	batknebi tavisi dedebisgan šors unda iqvnen, rata ertmaneti daavicqdet.									
\fe	*The lambs must be apart from their mothers to forget them.*									
\c	33 09:29:50									
\dt	24/Apr/2005									

Figure 2. Shoebox text file with interlinearized annotations

Table 18. Same example as in Figure 2, viewed in a normal text editor

\ref 0485
\per AS
\trs Äuxuy êui¤ nanigore¤ Äaq deÂ xiÚa¤, me vaêba¤ daÐdicdol†.
\tl1 Äuxuy êui¤ nanigore¤ Äaq deÂ xiÚa¤ me vaêba¤ daÐdicdol†
\ph tʃSuxuj Sui< nAnigore< tʃSAq detʃs' xiÂA< me vASbA< dAðditʃsdolW
\ts Äuxuy êui¤ nanigore¤ Äaq deÂ xiÚa¤ me vaêba¤ daÐdicdol†
\ts1 Äuxuy êui¤ nanigore¤ Äaq deÂ xiÚa¤ me vaêba¤ daÐdicdol†
\m Äux-uy êui¤ nan-i-gore¤ Äaq d-eÂ xiÚa¤ me vaêba¤ daÐ-dic-d-ol-†
\m1 Äux-uy êui¤ nan-i-gore¤ Äaq d-eÂ xiÚa¤ me vaêba¤ daÐ-dic-d-ol-†
\lm Äujx êui¤ nan Äaq deÂa¤ xiÚa¤ me vaêba¤ daÐdicoda¤
\lm1 Äujx êui¤ nan Äaq deÂa¤ xiÚa¤ me vaêba¤ daÐdicoda¤
\g baïÖani tavisi deda êors saÂiro_a çopna,çola,kona rom ertmaneti daviÂçeba
\g1 baïÖani tavisi deda êors saÂiro_a çopna,çola,kona rom ertmaneti daviÂçeba
\gl lamb own mother distant to-be-necessary to-be,to-have that each_other to-forget
\p N.4Gr. ReflPron. N.2Gr. Adv. V. V. Conj. Recipr.Pron. V.
\gr Nom.Pl. indecl. Loc.Pl.+Postp. indecl. Pres.4Gr. Inf. indecl. indecl. Cond.4Cl.3Ps.
\fg baïÖnebi tavisi dedebisgan êors unda içvnen, rata ertmaneti daaviÂçdet.
\fg1 baïÖnebi tavisi dedebisgan êors unda içvnen, rata ertmaneti daaviÂçdet.
\fe The lambs must be apart from their mothers to forget them.
\c 33 09:29:50

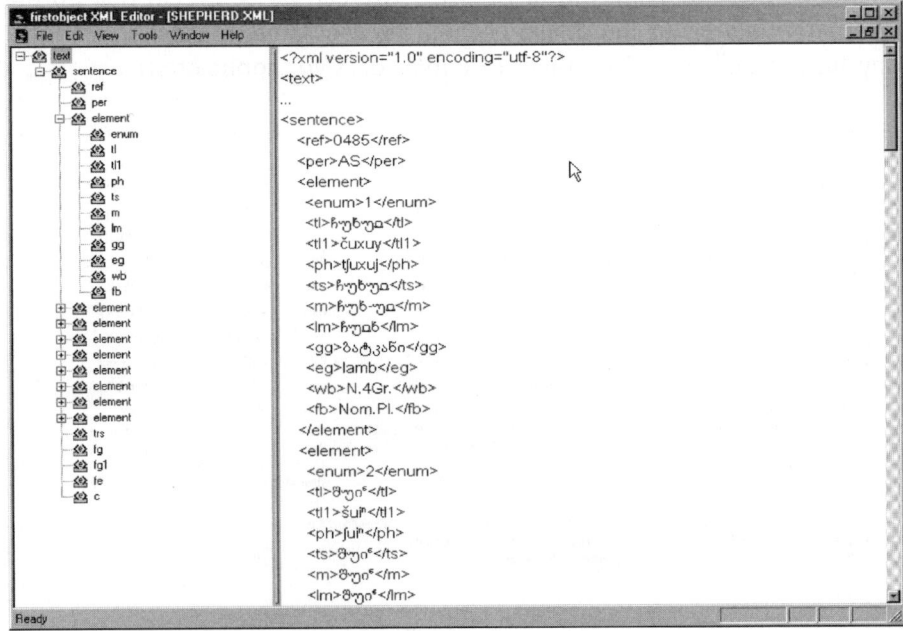

Figure 3. Same example as in Figure 2, converted into XML format

2.5. Outlook

It is true that the application of XML is not yet widely used by (fieldworking) linguists. It is also true, however, that it becomes more widespread every day, and lots of software programs that are dedicated to the production of consistent XML documents are now readily available (cf. the list attached to this book). No matter whether you intend to apply XML methods yourself in the near future or not, it may be worthwhile taking your time and visiting the website of the "Text Encoding Initiative" (TEI), just to learn more about what the structuring of textual elements means. Your linguistic work cannot but profit from this.

Notes

1. "ECLinG"; cf. the project homepage in http://titus.fkidg1.uni-frankfurt.de/ecling/ecling.htm.
2. The example is taken from the material recorded in the DoBeS "ECLinG" project; cf. fn. 1.

2.5.5 Outlook

It is true that the application of XML is not (or very widely used by enterprises today) because it is still rather advanced and it becomes more widespread once the number of software products that are dedicated for its creation and among XML interfaces are now readily available (of the B2B market to differ by also major vendors you need to apply). XML standards are apt to enhance business and it can be worthwhile taking your time and checking the web sites of the Plexs Electronic Business (TP), Rosetta.Net and so on. If the situation has not still stimulate theme, your in patience is always sufficient for much to offer.

Chapter 15

Thick interfaces:
Mobilizing language documentation with multimedia

David Nathan

Introduction

This chapter assumes that you hope that some of your fieldwork results will one day be applied to the maintenance, strengthening, or revitalization of the visited community's language. The documentation approach (Himmelmann 1998; Woodbury 2003) outlines fieldwork methodologies that increase the possibility that results can be used for these purposes. In addition, funding agencies such as HRELP insist that project results are "accessible to and usable by members of the language community as well as the wider linguistic community" (HRELP 2005).

It is also wise to plan what kind of language support might be possible and to have an idea in advance of what works best. There are many ways that fieldwork results can be applied to improving local language situations – for example, by providing teaching notes, grammatical explanations, and dictionaries, and running workshops (cf. von Gleich 2005; and Chapter 3) – but this chapter focuses on creating *multimedia products*, because

- they allow sound/video[1] to be presented and controlled;
- they integrate sound with other information;
- in many cases, they can be directly derived from rich fieldwork datasets;
- language teachers typically need accessible, interesting, and flexible language resources rather than analytical or even pedagogical resources, because teaching and learning situations vary.

Further reasons why multimedia is particularly effective in endangered languages situations will be mentioned below.

1. Mobilization

To introduce the potential uses of multimedia, this chapter discusses the *mobilization* of language documentation. Mobilization means taking linguistic documentation and working with speaker communities and other specialists to deliver products that can be used to counter language endangerment.

1.1. Purpose and scope

The term *mobilization* was recently introduced to point out that standardization of data and metadata formats should not exhaust the contribution that information technology can make to endangered languages data (Nathan 2003).[2] IT's use in documentation is normally constrained to entering, managing and browsing data, building catalogues, and digital archiving. These functions are important for working with data, and preserving and providing access to it, but they offer limited benefit for many audiences, in particular, for language communities. Recording and computer technologies allow us to create high-quality "born digital" documentation materials; but without suitable methods to effectively deliver these materials, they are also *born archival*, leaping directly from the last speakers to the preservation vault.

This chapter presents mobilization in terms of two complementary types of interfaces – the channels of communication and interaction between researchers and community, and the computer screen displays through which people interact with language resources.

A key aspect of mobilization is that it is best done, like fieldwork, in full collaboration with language communities. This is because to deliver resources that support speakers and learners, you need to know about their aims, priorities, resources, and local technological infrastructure. In addition, many of the ingredients of multimedia, such as art and design, will provide the cultural flavor of the product, and therefore should also be created or selected in collaboration and consultation with community members.

Mobilization is part of a framework for "fieldwork *delivered to* a language community," one of a set of fieldwork frameworks that resulted from successive changes in political and ethical outlook over the 20th century:

– fieldwork *on* a language;
– fieldwork *for* the language community;
– fieldwork *with/by* speakers of the language community;
– fieldwork *delivered to* a language community.

The first three frameworks are formulated in Grinevald (2003: 58).[3] Field-work *on* a language is the classic academic investigation involving a linguist and his/her "informant". In fieldwork *for* a language, communities began to exert some control over research, and linguists became "useful" to communities, typically in the sense of advocacy (rather than, say, tailoring their outputs to community needs). Then, from the 1980s, communities increasingly became collaborators in research, and, with more contexts for community control, and better local training, fieldwork is carried out *with* and *by* community members.

By contrast, the "deliver *to*" framework is concerned with timely provision of effective language resources in order to encourage and support language strengthening. It emphasizes product delivery and language outcomes over the nature of the fieldwork process or distinguishing between the roles played by community members or linguists. Typically, a fieldwork-based project will involve a mix of all of these framework activities; however, one that delivers usable resources based on documentations can be said to provide mobilization.

We turn now to the other type of interface; the computer screen displays through which people interact with language resources, first considering where information technology and, more specifically, multimedia, fit into the documentation agenda, then looking at some specific examples.

1.2. Where does information technology fit in?

Information technology plays a central role in language documentation. For example, it heads Woodbury's (2003: 36) lists of elements that "set the stage for [the] reconceptualization" of documentation:

> we should be able to link transcriptions with audio- and videotapes, and entries and dictionaries or statements in grammars with large databases of illustrative examples. (Woodbury 2003: 36)[4]

In addition, computer users, including increasing numbers of speakers of endangered languages, now have skills and experience in using many computer-based genres such as games, interactive encyclopedias, media editing applications, word processors, web browsers, and search engines (Nathan 2000a: 46; Grinevald 2005). Taking all of these together with the ongoing convergence of electronic archives, libraries, and publishing, these users have ever greater expectations of linguistic resources.

From the other direction, information technologists are paying more and more attention to language and communication. Today, a range of technology types are applied to languages, each providing increasing levels of linguistic interaction:

I	II	III
resource discovery:	*mobilization*:	*telecommunications*:
supporting access	creating usable resources	providing open channels

Development of resource discovery [I] is well under way (e.g. OLAC nd). Mobilization [II], like resource discovery, relies on the creation of linguistic materials, but, in common with telecommunications, involves relationships between producers and receivers. Although telecommunications (telephony, video links, and real time voice recognition, transcription and translation) offers considerable potential for language documentation, it is rarely used.

2. Multimedia

In this section, we look at the properties of multimedia and look further at why it is suited to supporting endangered languages. Normal human participation in linguistic events generally involves listening, seeing, and other modalities. However, languages have long been represented (and documented) using only text, or, more recently, sound. We have been restricted to *monomedia* because we have been limited by the available technologies – writing, printing, and magnetic tape. Thus, although the name *multimedia* implies complexity, it actually expresses the overcoming of previous constraints.[5] Today's multimedia technologies allow more authentic modes of expression. They can be defined as combinations of audio, video, images, and text, integrated and coordinated by a computer to allow user control and interaction.

There are several specific reasons to consider delivering multimedia as one of the outcomes of language documentation. Firstly, it sets up productive linkages between the *process* and the *outcomes* of fieldwork. Creating multimedia requires consideration of its effectiveness and its audience, and thus the language community takes the role of clients whose wider linguistic needs must be understood and from whom feedback must regularly be sought. Multimedia products must be planned early in the fieldwork process, so that suitable recordings can be made and other material collected; later, prototypes must be tested with the target audiences (although multimedia can be based on pre-existing recordings, recordings created in the context of a project with community participation will typically produce better results; Nathan 2004: 157). Therefore, multimedia products cannot be created by working in isolation, far from the community and separated from fieldwork and data collection. A clear, negotiated plan for creating a locally usable multimedia product is likely to provide the motivation and contexts for community interest and participation in all aspects of the fieldwork. It will also be the first step in creating a community "biography" of the product, which in turn will increase their enthusiasm for *using* it when it is delivered.

Secondly, using multimedia changes the way that community members and their language are represented. Multimedia products directly present a community member's relationships to the language and linguistic events, because their audio or video performances are not shifted to written forms or mediated by analysis. As a result, participants are actors rather than consultants, and they address the product's users directly, rather than through the information interpreted by a researcher.

Bird (1999a) noted that linking an analysis to the original recordings on which it is based can provide a more scientific linguistic account, because any user can examine the analysis in the light of the actual "data". For language community members, the advantages of providing ready access to rich and contextualized representations of actually occurring language events are even greater. Users can recognize individuals and experience language content in the context of real situations and relationships. In fact, multimedia can provide many connections – social, emotional, intellectual, and learning – between the user of the product and the represented actors and linguistic events.

Developing multimedia involves activities consistent with the desiderata for language documentation. It directs attention to the nature of linguistic events and performances in their social and physical contexts. When preparing the content for a multimedia product (Nathan 2004) one needs to take into account factors such as the variety, coverage, and quality of recordings of events; factors that echo the priorities of documentary linguistics (Himmelmann 1998). Multimedia typically requires a multi-skilled team and therefore reminds us of the multidisciplinary nature of documentation; it potentially exposes linguists to the expertise of designers, teachers, and programmers, and results in multimodal products that can be used in different disciplines. Even existing "legacy" materials can be given new life by using them as assets in a multimedia product.

For more discussion about practical benefits that accrue from multimedia project work, see Csató and Nathan (2003a).

3. Thin interfaces

Multimedia products might be distinguished by the presence of sound or video, but the presence of sound or video is not enough to qualify a product as multimedia. The criteria that we use to judge the quality or effectiveness of a multimedia product are yet more demanding.

First, consider a product that consists simply of primary recordings, together with their metadata.[6] According to the definition offered in the previous section, such a product would not qualify as multimedia: the recordings and the metadata are not combined in a way to allow user interaction. In fact, a standard music CD is just such a product, with the metadata printed on the cover and the audio playable from the disk.

Second, consider a product that allows you to view your primary data, as well as to add various layers of labelling, analysis, etc. to it. This would be more likely to qualify as multimedia, since it exploits the unique abilities of computers to allow us to control and manipulate data. Such products are typically software applications dedicated to inputting and managing data; an example well known to many linguists is SIL's "Shoebox" software for creating lexica and entering and glossing sentences (see Figure 1 below). Shoebox does not support sound or video, so to add annotations to sound and video, many linguists turn to software such as ELAN and Transcriber (see the reference list at the end of this volume).

However, none of these examples of software can really be regarded as ends in themselves. They are *tools* to assist in creating usable products that deliver content, just as a word processor or layout software is used to create a book. They are characterized by instrumental, limited-purpose interfaces that are transparent projections of their underlying data (Cooper 1995: 31), and that are used to construct and browse that data. Our second category, then – tools for working with data – can be thought of as "thin interfaces" because:

– they do not obscure or reorganize the details of the data – they are used to transparently view and manage such details;

- they do not add capabilities beyond those that are required to view and manage the data;
- they emphasize the acquisition of content, not its presentation or exploration;
- they are used effectively only by domain specialists.

\lx	**abátow**
\phak	[abatʊw]
\phas	[abatʊɔ]
\phfa	[abatʊw]
\ps	n
\dn	*ɔkwan a wɔfa so yi obi ma ɔdi dwuma bi.*
\ge	election/voting
\xv	**Abatow ho hia wɔ amambu mu.**
\tr	Election is essential in a democracy.
\dom	election
\sel	1000w sample
\dt	11/Apr/98

Figure 1. Sample Shoebox data (Akan Encyclopaedic Dictionary Project)[7]

4. Documentation and thick interfaces

Thin interfaces emphasize the management of data; however, we have defined mobilization as concerned with rich, flexible resources with the capability to support language strengthening and learning. For mobilization, we have to employ "thick interfaces" – creatively-designed and readily-usable software.

Thick interfaces draw not only on linguistic documentations but on the fields of graphic design, computer-usability, and, perhaps, instructional design. There are currently no settled conventions or standards for such products; the pursuit of thick interfaces challenges us to create new genres for expressing language documentation. A survey of the practice of interface design is beyond the scope of this chapter,[8] but key factors to be considered include user-group needs, choice of genre, and effective usages of hypertext and multimedia. Good thick interfaces can be explored in different ways to perform a variety of tasks. They:

- clearly reflect the collaboration and contribution of the community participants;
- use idioms to allow users to accomplish complex tasks;
- provide culturally appropriate and rational designs for presenting and navigating among content;
- allow users to make their own valid interpretations.

Cooper (1995), echoing our distinction here between thin and thick interfaces, urges that interfaces should not be determined by their underlying data, but by the needs of users and in terms of users' understanding of the represented domain. Thus multimedia mobilization entails researching and designing innovative interfaces, not only because there are no existing conventions, but also because each language, community, and set of users is different.

Design strategies, according to Cooper, should move away from data models (which recapitulate the underlying data), to metaphors (which are better, but limited by the metaphor chosen), or, preferably, to idioms that use "gizmos". Gizmos are virtual objects manipulated by users in order to perform functions of arbitrary complexity. Their idiomatic behavior must be learned, but once learned, they optimally support the performance of a task (an example is the scrollbar, where you drag a block down to move a page up). Well-designed idiomatic interfaces support learning; contemporary constructivist approaches to learning argue "that learning occurs best as a result of doing, creating, and building ... [through] the manipulation of real or virtual objects" (Goldman-Segal 1992: 258).

In the following sections, several multimedia products are briefly described, in order to illustrate how aspects of their interfaces support the aims of mobilization. As the examples show, thick interfaces reflect the contexts in which they are developed; the cultures, project participants, and development processes. There is no template or cookie-cutter approach that can do them justice.

4.1. Collaborative interfaces

The first two examples are based on *Paakantyi* (Hercus and Nathan 2002), a CD-ROM developed to help support school-based language revitalization efforts in Wilcannia, Wentworth, and other towns in the Paakantyi country of southwestern New South Wales, Australia.[9] This section presents a short case study illustrating the emergence of an interface as a result of a collaborative process involving the linguist, multimedia developer, and Paakantyi community members.

At every stage of the project we prepared and delivered product drafts representing the ongoing state of the CD in order to:

– make it easier for people to give feedback about concrete products rather than react to abstractions;
– demonstrate our ongoing commitment to the project;
– help create a community "story" or "biography" for the CD.

We also workshopped some project participants in techniques for recording, digitizing, editing, and linking the sounds they contributed.

Key graphic and navigational systems of the CD resulted from this collaborative work on its design and its linguistic and graphic content. Initially, we were given permissions to use several artworks to decorate the CD (the Paakantyi community boasts several accomplished artists). Under the guidance of Badger Bates – a Paakantyi speaker, Park Ranger, and nationally-recognized artist and sculptor – the design evolved so that recordings of important speakers from previous generations of speakers became systematically accessed via artwork created by their respective living descendants. This, we believe, contributed to the aesthetic balance of the CD, which ultimately gained keen acceptance within the community. The navigational structures are summarized in Figure 2. The top row lists the "old time" speakers from previous generations whose texts and songs feature on the CD. These people have all passed away some time ago. The oval disks in the middle row correspond to main resources in the CD – two stories (Mutawintyi, Anteater), songs (including Emu), and the talking dictionary. The bottom row lists project participants who contributed art (the two left boxes) and linguistic content (the two right boxes, with Badger Bates contributing both). The arrows represent linguistic input; the other bullet-head lines represent the provision of artwork. Vertical alignment indicates ancestry (both Dumbo Dutton and the Bates family descend from 'Gunsmoke' Johnson).

The example shows how an interface design "emerged" as a result of collaboration, to result in a design that was not only more aesthetically attractive, but also actually communicated more information – information about the genealogical relationships between past and present participants – even though this information may not be apparent to non-community members.

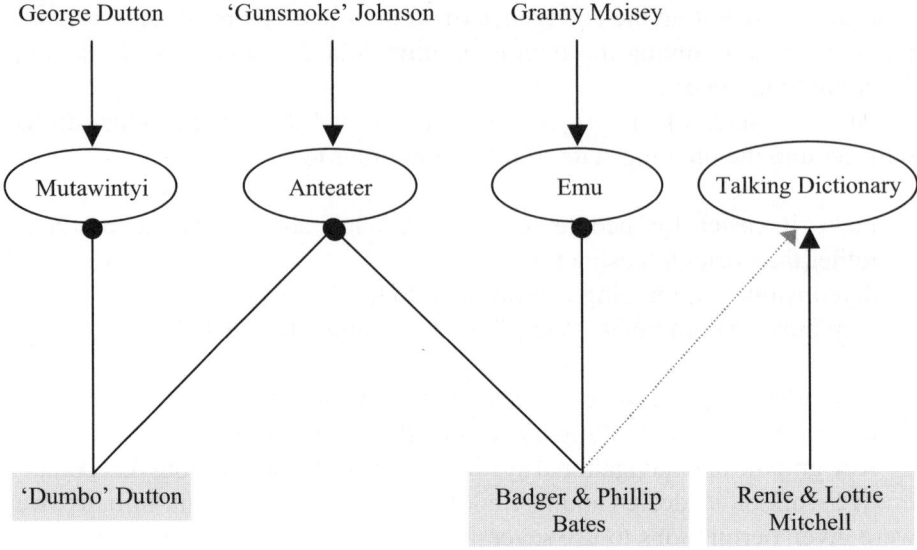

Figure 2. Participants, art and language in the Paakantyi CD (Hercus and Nathan 2002)

Figure 3. Environmental objects as controls in Bunuba Yarrangi Thanani (KLRC nd)

4.2. Appropriate interfaces

Interfaces should help users perform their tasks while respecting local cultural and aesthetic styles. But they should *not* be based on stylized impressions of a culture.[10] Some earlier productions confused the two aims by, for example, using rocks, animals and other environmental objects as buttons and menus, as shown in Figure 3. These objects do not function well as navigational metaphors because the animals displayed are unlikely to be associated with buttons or navigation. Instead, they require memorization and draw the user's attention to the interface itself rather than support the navigational task.

By contrast, the *Paakantyi* CD (see previous section, and Figure 4 below) uses a mainly text-driven interface created by a graphic designer who was given a brief to create a crisp, contemporary feel. It has been very well received and found easy to use; Paakantyi students transcend their everyday literacy levels in using it, because it allows them to focus on their chosen tasks, most especially to navigate to spoken entries in the CD's talking dictionary (cf. Goodall and Flick [1996], who urge avoidance of text elements in interfaces for Aboriginal children).[11]

Although the *Paakantyi* interface largely utilizes text, it is not a "thin" interface. Displayed text is not a simple projection of the underlying data, which is considerably more complex and incorporates thousands of links between various text and sound objects. Furthermore, much of the text functions not as content but as navigation controls that users can click on. Notice also that in Figure 4 there are variant spellings; these are the result of differences between Hercus' original research in the 1960s and the new data we recorded in 2000. The CD simply presents both variants and allows the users to draw their own conclusions.

With regard to this example, it may be worth noting that text-based interfaces can work well even in societies that do not have traditions of literacy in their own languages. Many such people do have literacies, of course, in other dominant languages (such as English in this case; it may be Arabic, Chinese, Russian, or other languages elsewhere). In addition, there is not just a single type of literacy. Other literacies, such as computer literacies, have quickly developed over the last decade across much of the world, especially as a result of familiarity with software used for internet access, and these literacies involve changes in the functional balance between text, layout, and graphics in comparison to standard "book" literacy (Nathan 2000a). At the limit, we can say that consistent text-based screen navigation objects can function like icons, and also that simply using images for navigation does not, by itself, ensure a usable interface.

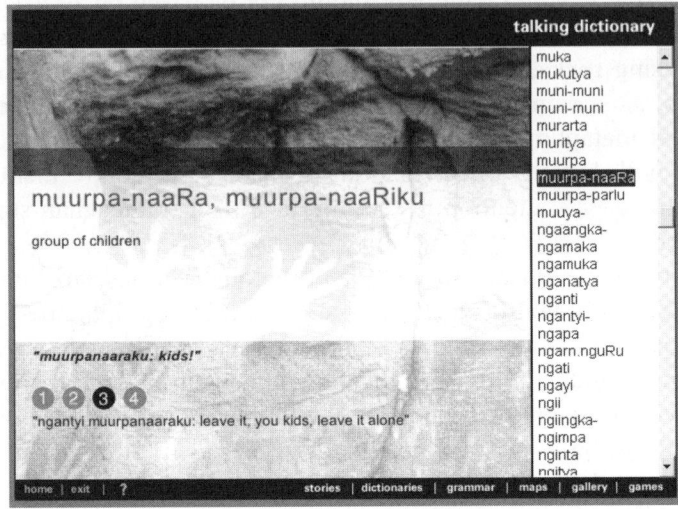

Figure 4. Navigating in the Paakantyi talking dictionary (Hercus and Nathan 2002)

4.3. Idiomatic interfaces

The *Spoken Karaim* CD-ROM (Csató and Nathan 2003b)[12] was developed as a multimedia documentation of the language, culture, and environment of the Karaim community of Trakai, Lithuania. It is centered on several narrative monologues spoken by the last full speakers of the language; these are all transcribed, morphologically annotated, and linked to a rich lexicon, grammar, and concordance; in addition, the linguistic material is accompanied by songs, videos, photographs, and eight thematic articles on Karaim history, religion, etc.

The CD also contains a system we call "Active morphology" that generates inflected nouns using an inbuilt full computational model of Karaim morphophonology (Nathan 2000b). Inflection is represented by the idiom of dragging objects onto headwords. The system is presented to the user as a set of small moveable blocks that, when dragged onto a dictionary headword, initiate the generation and display of the appropriate inflected form (see Figures 5 and 6). By keeping terminology basic, the morphophonological rules unseen, and its operation as simple as possible, the system is backgrounded for most users, and may, paradoxically, even remain undiscovered. However, given a rational context for use, it is easy to learn how to use.

The effectiveness of this system was confirmed during the recent Karaim Summer School in 2004. We developed interactive, computer-generated multimedia crossword games as language teaching aids (there were three types: normal crosswords, talking crosswords, and picture crosswords). The Karaim students were encouraged to use *Spoken Karaim* to look up words they didn't know. Their responses illustrated the three factors of *idiom*, *rational design*, and *open interpretation* mentioned in the introduction to this section. Motivated by competitive crossword games, and faced with clues whose answers required inflected forms, students found and used for the first time the idiomatic *Active morphology* controls, and they explored the CD in new ways, including its interactive concordance (which finds inflected roots within narratives). In performing these activities, the students explored the CD's language content and selected and interpreted the results in order to complete the crosswords.

4.4. "Dangerous" interfaces

A community's knowledge and modes of presentation can go even further in defining a product's interface and usage. Barbara Glowczewski's *Dream Trackers: Yapa Art and Knowledge of the Australian Desert* (2001a) is a comprehensive CD presenting the land, language, and culture of the Warlpiri (also known as Yapa) people of the Northern Territory, Australia. Its interface is structured by Warlpiri forms of knowledge representation, which highlight networks of associations. It opens with an interactive map of "dreaming paths" in an extraordinarily complex, criss-crossing pattern. Nodes on these paths are interlinked with various stories, text, and artwork throughout the CD. Glowczewski (2001b: 142) wanted the links "to follow rules and to have meanings that respected the connections that the Warlpiri themselves establish according to their own cognitive logic."

> The visual transposition of this Aboriginal cognitive mapping into an interactive map gives the user an immediate experience of this inter-connectivity ... Multimedia is an ideal tool for rendering this Indigenous mapping. This invitation to wander in the territory of the Dreaming story-telling, painting, singing and dancing made the old persons extremely happy when they saw

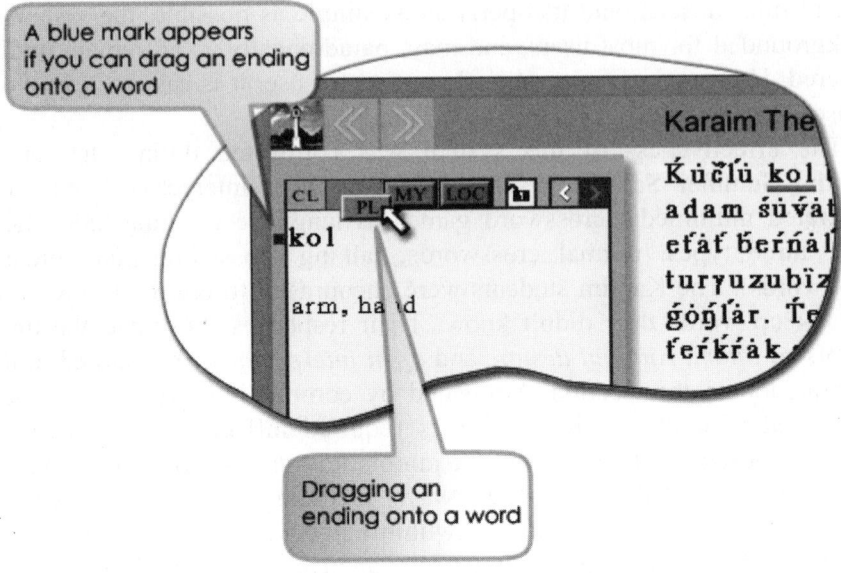

Figure 5. Operation of Spoken Karaim's "Active morphology" (extract from the CD's Help file)

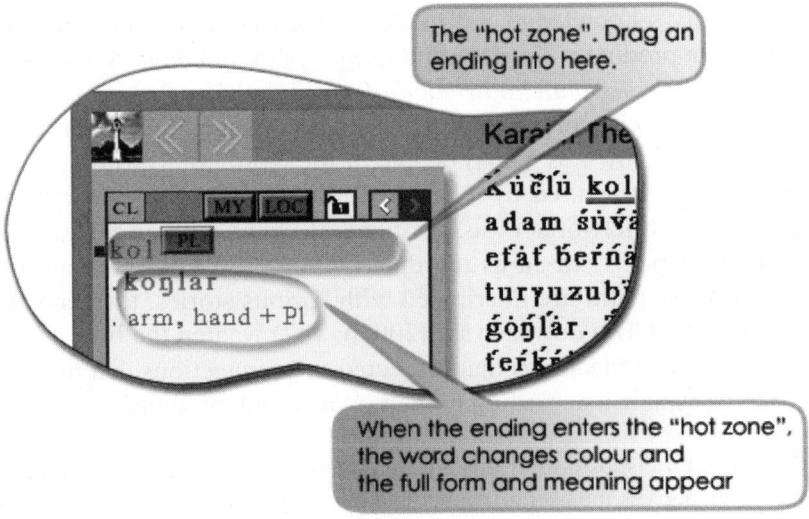

Figure 6. Result of "Active morphology" operation

tangible proof of their teaching about the inter-relatedness of the Dreaming. The elders and all the women I worked with were excited by the new medium because it did not threaten their encyclopaedic knowledge or their power in the society. On the contrary, their legitimacy was affirmed by the fact that they are recognized by name as story-tellers and painters.

(Glowczewski 2001b: 146)

However, some Warlpiri people were also deeply disturbed by the CD, because they saw that, for the first time, something fundamental about their knowledge was revealed to outsiders. Ultimately, this led to the community restricting the distribution of the CD (Glowczewski 2001b: 150). This restriction, paradoxically, was a measure of the *success* of the mobilization in Warlpiri terms. Warlpiri people took responsibility for control over it in the same way that they generally seek to be custodians over their culture and knowledge.

5. Conclusion: challenges for multimedia

This chapter has presented motivations for and examples of using multimedia and "thick interfaces" to mobilize language documentation in support of endangered languages. We could summarize factors in creating such a product as a set of heuristics all of which are essential for a "good" mobilization:

- it supports exploration;
- its functions go beyond the underlying data;
- it manifests community input and participation;
- it fully exploits the capability to present and control sound;
- users can interact with content in relevant (and innovative) ways;
- it has design integrity.

Obviously, developing custom, high-quality multimedia applications to support endangered languages can consume considerable resources and require solid dedication (see Nathan 2004 for more information about planning such a project). In fact, such projects have occasionally been described as a waste of scarce resources (e.g. Simpson 2003). However, if it is true that developing multimedia can offer a distinct contribution in endangered language situations then to call it a "waste" is to place community needs as a low priority.

Another challenge comes from an increasing preference for open source software and open data formats.[13] While most current fully-featured multimedia authoring and presentation tools are proprietary products with closed data formats,[14] the effort expended in developing content far exceeds the cost of even the most expensive of them. Without these well-developed authoring tools, the development of applications for a community would consume more, not less, resources.[15] Again, decisions have to be made on the basis of priorities for providing particular kinds of products and language support.

Multimedia is a new and complex technology and choosing to use it for mobilization will also involve making trade-offs between its positive contributions to language communities and its less-than-optimal suitability for archiving, repurposing, and even distribution. Many multimedia resources are not readily archived and have limited longevity. These limitations can be due to closed formats, but are, more broadly, an inevitable result of deciding to develop multimedia rather than other types of resources. Multimedia involves integrating a variety of media and file formats, and the use of *any* digital media in language documentation is vulnerable to the instability of a variety of formats, even open-standard ones. In addition, there are no settled conventions for designing and describing interfaces, and it is not fully known how to neutrally represent and archive abstract content such as navigation, layout, links, and interactivity. These various challenges mean that one works with multimedia not as a general strategy for satisfying diverse needs such as long-term data preservation, but in recognition of its potential for mobilizing documentation and strengthening languages, right now, when it is most needed.

Notes

1. In this chapter, I use "sound" to include both sound and video.
2. The term has since become more widely used (e.g. Wittenburg, Brugman et al. 2004; Austin 2004). It is related to, but greatly extends, the sense of "exploitation" used by Wittenburg, Brugman et al. (2004) to refer to using software to browse and analyze archive data. "Mobilization" is a more tasteful way of describing such activities in English, but does not offer that advantage in German.
3. They were adapted from Deborah Cameron, cited in Grinevald (2003).
4. In reality, there is still a wide gap between many elements of Woodbury's reconceptualization and the ways that linguists generally work with materials.
5. The term can be understood as referring to the previous constraints (rather than its actual capabilities) in the same way that *horseless carriage* and *wireless* named new technologies in terms of reversals of their predecessors (cf. McLuhan 1964).
6. Recently the meaning of "metadata" has been narrowed to refer to data that is not deemed to be "in" the linguistic event (e.g. the location or gender of the speaker) and used as file cataloguing data primarily for the purpose of resource discovery. Such metadata can be classified in terms of its various roles, e.g. in cataloguing, managing, or preserving the data (see Chapter 4).
7. Online at www.unizh.ch/spw/afrling/akandic/samples.htm; viewed September 2003.
8. Interface design is also known as Human Computer Interaction or User Experience Design.
9. Paakantyi is the language of the lower Darling River, NSW, Australia.
10. Or worse, an outsider's fantasized version of the culture.
11. The talking dictionary is described in more detail in Nathan (2006).
12. Karaim is an endangered Turkic language spoken in Trakai, Lithuania, and in Halich, Ukraine.
13. Bird and Simons (2003: 22) go as far as to advocate "an open source revolution."
14. All the examples discussed in this chapter were authored using Macromedia Director (www.macromedia.com).
15. It is possible that open-source authoring tools may become available, e.g. based on SMIL, but it is not clear when such tools may appear and how much authoring capability they might offer.

Abbreviations and resources

Up-dated versions of the following lists may be found at the book's website at http://titus.uni-frankfurt.de/ld .

Abbreviations, acronyms and technical terms in alphabetical order

N.B. For the sake of easy reference, this list comprises all abbreviations and acronyms used in this book in alphabetical order so that readers need not know in advance whether a given abbreviation stands for a technical term or concept, an organization, or some other kind of resource.

AAA	American Anthropological Association (http://www.aaanet.org)
AIATSIS	Australian Institute of Aboriginal and Torres Strait Islander Studies (http://www.aiatsis.gov.au)
AIFF	Audio Interchange File Format (Apple audio format)
AILLA	Archive of the Indigenous Languages of Latin America (http://www.ailla.utexas.org/site/welcome.html)
ANNEX	Annotation Exploration tool (http://www.mpi.nl/ANNEX)
ANSI	American National Standards Institute (http://www.ansi.org)
ASCII	American Standard Code for Information Interchange (7-bit standard)
ATRAC	Adaptive Transform Acoustic Coding (Format for MiniDisc audio recordings; http://www.sony.net/Products/ATRAC3/tech/atrac3/index.html)
AUTOTYP	AUTOmatic TYPologizing (Research program in linguistic typology; http://www.uni-leipzig.de/~autotyp)
AVI	Audio Visual Interleave (Digital video format; http://support.microsoft.com/default.aspx?scid=kb;en-us;316992#XSLTH3123121122120121120120)
Big5	(Encoding format for traditional Chinese characters, developed by five big Taiwanese companies; http://www.ldc.upenn.edu/Projects/Chinese/info_it.htm)
BWF	Broadcast → WAV File (Digital audio format incl. time stamping; www.ebu.ch/departments/technical/trev/trev_274-chalmers.pdf)

CD-R	Compact Disc – Recordable
CD-ROM	Compact Disc – Read Only Memory
CD-RW	Compact Disc – ReWritable (reusable CD-R)
CHAT	Codes for the Human Analysis of Transcripts (Transcription system, manual at http://childes.psy.cmu.edu/manuals/CHAT.pdf)
CHILDES	CHIld Language Data Exchange System (Tools for studying conversational interactions including those for coding and analyzing transcripts; http://childes.psy.cmu.edu)
CLAN	Child Language Analysis (Tools for studying conversational interactions including those for coding and analyzing transcripts; http://childes.psy.cmu.edu)
Codepage	Standardized 8-bit extension of the ASCII standard
CSS	Cascading Style Sheet (Style sheet for web documents; http://www.w3.org/Style/CSS)
DAT	Digital Audio Tape (Storage medium for digital audio recordings)
DELAMAN	Digital Endangered Languages And Musics Archive Network (http://www.delaman.org)
DoBeS	DOkumentation BEdrohter Sprachen (Documentation of endangered languages; funding programme of the Volkswagenstiftung; http://www.volkswagenstiftung.de/foerderung/foerderinitiativen/merkblaetter/merkdoku_e.html)
DOS	Disk Operating System (Standard operating system formerly used for → IBM compatible → PCs)
DTD	Document Type Definition (www.w3schools.com/dtd/default.asp)
DV	Digital Video (Digital storage format for video recordings)
DVD	Digital Versatile Disc (Storage medium mostly used for video recordings)
DVD-R	Digital Versatile Disc – Recordable
DVD-RW	Digital Versatile Disc – ReWritable (Reusable DVD-R)
EAGLES	Expert Advisory Group on Language Engineering Standards (http://www.ilc.cnr.it/EAGLES96/browse.html)
ELAN	EUDICO Linguistic Annotator (Linguistic annotation tool; http://www.mpi.nl/tools/elan.html)
E-MELD	Electronic Metastructure for Endangered Languages Data (http://emeld.org)
EMU	Edinburgh / Macquarie University (Tools for speech analysis; http://emu.sourceforge.net)

EU	European Union
EUDICO	EUropean DIstributed COrpora (Linguistic tool creation project; http://www.mpi.nl/world/tg/lapp/eudico/eudico.html)
EUROTYP	(European Science Foundation research project on linguistic typology; http://www.lotschool.nl/Research/ltrc/eurotyp)
EXMARaLDA	EXtensible MARkup Language for Discourse Annotation (http://www1.uni-hamburg.de/exmaralda)
Extended ASCII	(non-standardized 8-bit extension of the → ASCII standard often used for the → IBM / → DOS encoding chart)
FMPro	FileMaker Professional (Database manager; http://www.filemaker.com)
GOLD	General Ontology for Linguistic Description (http://www.linguistics-ontology.org)
HRELP	Hans Rausing Endangered Languages Project (Funding programme for endangered languages; http://www.hrelp.org)
HTML	Hypertext Markup Language (http://www.w3.org/MarkUp)
IASA	International Association of Sound Archives (www.iasa.org)
IBM	International Business Machines corporation (www.ibm.com)
ICON	(High-level programming language for text applications; http://www.cs.arizona.edu/icon)
ICT	Information and Communication Technology
IMDI	ISLE Metadata Initiative (Metadata system; www.mpi.nl/IMDI)
INTSINT	INternational Transcription System for INTonation (Transcription system used for coding the intonation pattern of an utterance; http://www.lpl.univ-aix.fr/~hirst/intsint.html)
IPA	International Phonetic Association / International Phonetic Alphabet
IPR	Intellectual Property Rights
IRB	Institutional Review Board
ISLE	International Standards for Language Engineering
ISO	International Standardization Organization
ISO TC37/SC4	ISO Technical Committee 37 / SubCommittee 4 (Consortium for language resources management; http://www.tc37sc4.org)
IT	Information Technology
JISC	Joint Information Systems Committee (British committee supporting the use of Information and Communications Technology; encoding standards; http://www.jisc.ac.uk)

JPEG, JPG	Joint Photographers Expert Group (Digital file format for compressed images)
LDC	Linguistic Data Consortium (http://www.ldc.upenn.edu)
LEXUS	(Lexicon tool; http://www.mpi.nl/LEXUS)
Mac	Apple Macintosh computers (http://www.apple.com)
MPEG	Moving Pictures Expert Group (Video compression standards; http://www.chiariglione.org/mpeg)
MPG3, MP3	→ MPEG (Audio) Layer III (Audio compression standard)
MPI	Max Planck Institute
MS	MicroSoft corporation (http://www.microsoft.com)
OLAC	Open Language Archive Community (http://www.language-archives.org)
OS	Operating System
PC	Personal Computer
PCM	Pulse Code Modulation (Digital storage method of analog recordings)
PDF	Portable Document Format (Encoding format for web publications; http://www.adobe.com/products/acrobat/adobepdf.html)
PERL	Practical Extraction and Reporting Language (Programming language for text applications; http://www.perl.com)
PNG	Portable Network Graphics (Digital graphics file format; http://www.libpng.org/pub/png/png.html)
PUA	Private Use Area (User definable area in the → UNICODE standard)
QuickTime	Quick Time Video (Digital video format; http://developer.apple.com/documentation/QuickTime/QTFF/qtff.pdf)
RA	Real Audio (Digital audio format; http://ekei.com/audio)
RelaxNG	REgular LAnguage for XML New Generation (Schema language for XML; http://www.relaxng.org)
RTF	Rich Text Format (7-bit based text encoding standard for cross-system exchange; http://support.microsoft.com/kb/269575/EN-US)
SAMPA	Speech Assessment Methods Phonetic Alphabet (http://www.phon.ucl.ac.uk/home/sampa/home.htm)
SAMPROSA	Speech Assessment Methods PROSodic Alphabet (http://www.phon.ucl.ac.uk/home/sampa/samprosa.htm)
SGML	Standard Generalized Markup Language (Text markup language; http://xml.coverpages.org/sgml.html)

SIL	Summer Institute of Linguistics (http://www.sil.org)
SMIL	Synchronized Multimedia Integration Language (Markup language for interactive audiovisual presentations; http://www.w3c.org/TR/2001/REC-smil2020010807)
SPEAKING	Setting/Scene, Participants, Ends, Act Sequence, Key, Instrumentalities, Norms, Genre (mnemonic abbreviation for major components of the speech situation; see Chapter 5)
TEI	Text Encoding Initiative (http://www.tei-c.org)
TIFF	Tagged Image File Format (Digital graphics file format; http://partners.adobe.com/public/developer/tiff/index.html)
ToBI	TOnes and Breaks Index (System for transcribing features of prosody, including intonation patterns; http://www.ling.ed.ac.uk/facilities/help/xwaves/tobi.shtml)
UNICODE	UNIversal CODE (World-wide 16-bit character encoding standard; http://www.unicode.org)
UTF-7, UTF-8, UTF-16, UTF-32	Unicode Transformation Format (Format used to store → UNICODE encoded data in different bit structures: 7-bit, 8-bit, 16-bit, 32-bit; http://www.unicode.org/glossary/#UTF)
VCD	Video Compact Disc
W3C	World Wide Web Consortium (organization that develops and standardizes digital formats)
WAV	WAVeform audio (Digital audio format; http://support.microsoft.com/default.aspx?scid=kb;en-us;316992#XSLTH3123121122120121120120)
WIPO	World Intellectual Property Organization (http://www.wipo.int)
WMA	Windows Media Audio (Digital audio format; http://support.microsoft.com/default.aspx?scid=kb;en-us;316992#XSLTH3123121122120121120120)
WMV	Windows Media Video (Digital video format; http://support.microsoft.com/default.aspx?scid=kb;en-us;316992#XSLTH3123121122120121120120)
WWW	World Wide Web (Internet)
WYSIWYG	What You See Is What You Get
XLS	eXceL Spreadsheet (Spreadsheet format of MS Excel; http://www.microsoft.com/Office/Excel/prodinfo/default.mspx)
XML	eXtensible Markup Language (Text markup language; http://xml.coverpages.org/xml.html)

XSL	eXtensible Stylesheet Language (Stylesheet language for → XML; http://www.w3.org/TR/xsl)
XSLT	→ XSL Transformation (Language for transforming → XML documents into other → XML documents; www.w3.org/TR/xslt)

Webresources
Resources on *ethics* and *rights* are listed at the end of Chapter 2.

Language archives and archiving initiatives

AILLA	Archive of the Indigenous Languages of Latin America (http://www.ailla.utexas.org/site/welcome.html)
DELAMAN	Digital Endangered Languages And Music Archives Network (http://www.delaman.org)
DoBeS Archive	Archive of the → DoBeS programme housed by the → MPI for Psycholinguistics, Nijmegen (http://www.mpi.nl/dobes)
ELAR	Endangered Languages Archive (archive of → HRELP; http://www.hrelp.org/archive)
PARADISEC	Pacific And Regional Archive for Digital Sources in Endangered Cultures (http://paradisec.org.au)
see also:	Language Archives Newsletter (http://www.mpi.nl/LAN)

Endangered Languages (general information)

E-MELD	Electronic Metastructure for Endangered Languages Data (http://emeld.org)
Endangered languages e-mail list	(Coombs, Australian National University; http://www.bris.ac.uk/Depts/Philosophy/CTLL/endangered-languages-l.html)
Ethnologue	→ SIL's encyclopedic reference work (http://www.ethnologue.com)
FEL	Foundation for Endangered Languages (http://www.ogmios.org/home.htm)
GBS	Gesellschaft für Bedrohte Sprachen (http://www.uni-koeln.de/gbs)
Linguist list	e-Mail list for linguistics (http://www.linguistlist.org)

Sponsors and funding programmes for work on endangered languages

DoBeS   DOkumentation BEdrohter Sprachen (Documentation of endangered languages; funding programme of the Volkswagenstiftung; http://www.volkswagenstiftung.de/foerderung/foerderinitiativen/merkblaetter/merkdoku_e.html)

ELF   Endangered Languages Fund (http://sapir.ling.yale.edu/%7Eelf)

ELDP   Endangered Languages Documentation Programme (documentation programme of → HRELP; http://www.hrelp.org/grants)

FEL   Foundation for Endangered Languages (www.ogmios.org/home.htm)

GBS   Gesellschaft für Bedrohte Sprachen (http://www.uni-koeln.de/gbs)

HRELP   Hans Rausing Endangered Languages Project (Funding programme for endangered languages; http://www.hrelp.org)

NSF/NEH   National Science Foundation / National Endowment for the Humanities / Smithsonian Institute Documenting Endangered Languages programme (www.nsf.gov/pubs/2005/nsf05590/nsf05590.htm)

NWO   The Netherlands Organisation for Scientific Research Endangered Languages programme (http://www.nwo.nl/subsidiewijzer.nsf/pages/NWOP_55AD9Y?Opendocument)

Software links

Software supporting transcription, annotation, time-linking

CHILDES   CHIld Language Data Exchange System (Tools for studying conversational interactions including those for coding and analyzing transcripts; http://childes.psy.cmu.edu)

CLAN   Child Language Analysis (Tools for studying conversational interactions including those for coding and analyzing transcripts; http://childes.psy.cmu.edu)

ELAN   EUDICO Linguistic Annotator (Tool for time-linking audio or video recordings and annotations; various search and export options; http://www.mpi.nl/tools/elan.html)

LEXUS   (Lexicon tool; http://www.mpi.nl/LEXUS)

SIL Shoebox   Tool for interlinearizing text and managing lexical data base – now replaced by → SIL Toolbox (http://www.sil.org/computing/shoebox/index.html)

SIL Toolbox	Tool for interlinearizing text and managing lexical data base; Unicode-compatible successor of Shoebox (http://www.sil.org/computing/toolbox/index.htm)
see also:	Leipzig Glossing Rules (http://www.eva.mpg.de/lingua/files/morpheme.html)
	Geoffrey Leech, 2004, Adding Linguistic Annotation (www.ahds.ac.uk/creating/guides/linguistic-corpora/chapter2.htm) (= Chapter 2 in Wynne 2004)

Metadata and corpus management

ANNEX	Annotation Exploration tool (http://www.mpi.nl/ANNEX)
EMELD	Electronic Metastructure for Endangered Languages Data (http://emeld.org)
IMDI	→ ISLE Metadata Initiative (Metadata system and corpus management tool; http://www.mpi.nl/IMDI)
OLAC	Open Language Archive Community (http://www.language-archives.org)

Fonts, encodings, keyboard assignments

Microsoft Keyboard Layout Creator (for MS Windows)
http://www.microsoft.com/globaldev/tools/msklc.mspx

SIL fonts	http://www.sil.org/computing/catalog/show_software_catalog.asp?by=cat&name=Font (Recommended Unicode font for phonetic transcriptions Doulos SIL Unicode)

Tavultesoft Keyman (Keyboard layout creator for MS Windows)
http://www.tavultesoft.com/keyman

TITUS Cyberbit Font
http://titus.fkidg1.uni-frankfurt.de/unicode/unitest2.htm#TITUUT

UNICODE	UNIversal CODE (World-wide 16-bit character encoding standard; http://www.unicode.org)
UnicTITUS	→ UNICODE keyboard layout for MS Word (http://titus.fkidg1.uni-frankfurt.de/unicode/tituutk.asp)
UniRed	Plain text editor that can handle Unicode and can be used to convert between different character encodings (http://www.esperanto.mv.ru/UniRed/ENG)

Speech analysis software (freeware)

EMU	Edinburgh/Macquarie University (Tools for speech analysis; http://emu.sourceforge.net)
Praat	Tool for speech analysis (http://www.fon.hum.uva.nl/praat)
Speech Analyzer	Tool for recording, transcribing and analyzing sound files (http://www.sil.org/computing/speechtools)
Wave Surfer	Freeware tool for sound visualization and manipulation (http://www.speech.kth.se/wavesurfer)

Software for capturing video

Adobe Premiere	Professional tool for editing digital video recordings (http://www.adobe.com/products/premiere/main.html)
VirtualDub	Freeware tool for capturing and editing digital video recordings (http://www.virtualdub.org)

XML editors

Altova XML-Spy	http://www.altova.com/download_spy_enterprise.html (fully Unicode-compatible; 30-day free trial)
Cooktop 2.5	http://www.elfdata.com (Victor Pavlov; not yet fully Unicode compatible)
ElfData	XML editor (for Apple-Macintosh) http://www.elfdata.com/xmleditor
firstobject	XML-editor (Unicode compatible) http://www.firstobject.com/dn_editor.htm
Morphon 3.1.4	XML-editor (not yet fully Unicode compatible) http://www.morphon.com/xmleditor/index.shtml
Stylus Studio	XML editor (fully Unicode-compatible; 30-day free trial) http://www.stylusstudio.com/xml_editor.html
XAmple	XML editor (Felix Golubov; not yet fully Unicode compatible; expects XSD schemas to be present before opening an XML document) http://www.felixgolubov.com
XML-Fox	http://www.xmlfox.com/download.htm (Unicode-compatible)

XMLWriter 2.5   (no Unicode support yet)
http://xmlwriter.net/download/download.shtml

XRay   XML editor (not Unicode compatible)
http://architag.com/xray/SendEmail.asp

Elicitation tools (see also section 4 of Chapter 6)

Space Games   de León 1991, Levinson 1992

Pear Story   Chafe ed. 1980, see also http://www.pearstories.org

Frog Story   Mayer 1969, Berman and Slobin 1994

Map Task   http://www.hcrc.ed.ac.uk/dialogue/maptask.html

For these and other elicitation tools see also the *Fieldmanuals* (http://www.mpi.nl/world/data/fieldmanuals) and the *Annual reports* (http://www.mpi.nl/research/publications/AnnualReports) of the Max Planck Institute for Psycholinguistics in Nijmegen (http://www.mpi.nl).

References

Allen, Charlotte
    1997   Spies like us: When sociologists deceive their subjects. *Lingua Franca* 7: 31–39.

Ameka, Felix, Alan Dench, and Nicholas Evans (eds.)
    2006   *Catching Language: The Standing Challenge of Grammar Writing.* Berlin/New York: Mouton de Gruyter.

Amith, Jonathan D.
    2002   What's in a word? The whys and what fors of a Nahuatl dictionary. In *Making Dictionaries: Preserving Indigenous Languages of the Americas*, William Frawley, Kenneth G. Hill, and Pamela Munro (eds.), 219–258. Berkeley: University of California Press.

Apothéloz, Denis and Françoise Zay
    1999   Incidents de la programmation syntagmatique: Reformulations micro- et macro-syntaxiques. *Cahiers de Linguistique Française* 21: 11–34.

Aulie, H. Wilbur and Evelyn W. Aulie
    1978   *Diccionario Ch'ol de Tumbalá, Chiapas con Variaciones Dialectales de Tila y Sabanilla.* Mexico, D.F.: Instituto Lingüístico del Verano.

Austin, John L.
    1961   *Philosophical Papers.* London: Oxford University Press.

Austin, Peter K.
    2004   Editor's preface. In *Language Description and Documentation*, vol. 2, Peter K. Austin (ed.), 3–6. London: School of Oriental and African Studies.
    2005   New documentation from old sources. Unpublished Ms., SOAS, London.

Austin, Peter K. (ed.)
    2000   *Working Papers in Sasak.* vol. 1. Melbourne: University of Melbourne, Lombok and Sumbawa Research Project.
    2003   *Language Description and Documentation.* vol. 1. (Endangered Languages Project.) London: School of Oriental and African Studies.
    2004   *Language Description and Documentation.* vol. 2. (Endangered Languages Project.) London: School of Oriental and African Studies.

Austin, Peter K., Anthony Jukes, and David Nathan
    2000   *The Sasak Conversation CD.* University of Melbourne.

Basbøll, Hans
   2000   Word boundaries. In *Morphology. An International Handbook on In-flection and Word Formation*, vol. 1, Geert Booij, Christian Lehmann, and Joachim Mugdan (eds.), 377–388. Berlin/New York: Mouton de Gruyter.

Basso, Ellen
   1987   *In Favour of Deceit. A Study of Tricksters in an Amazonian Society.* Tucson: The University of Arizona Press.
   1988   Evidentiality: The linguistic coding of epistemology. Review of Wallace Chafe and Johanna Nichols (eds.). *American Anthropologist* 90: 216–217.
   1995   *The Last Cannibal.* Austin: The University of Texas Press.

Beckman, Mary E.
   1986   *Stress and Non-stress Accent.* Dordrecht: Foris.

Berlin, Brent
   1967   Categories of eating in Tzeltal and Navajo. *International Journal of American Linguistics* 33: 1–6.
   1968   *Tzeltal Numeral Classifiers.* The Hague: Mouton.

Berman, Ruth A. and Dan I. Slobin
   1994   *Relating Events in Narrative: A Crosslinguistic Developmental Study.* Hillsdale, NJ: Lawrence Erlbaum Associates.

Bickel, Balthasar, Bernard Comrie, and Martin Haspelmath
   2004   *The Leipzig Glossing Rules. Conventions for Interlinear Morpheme by Morpheme Glosses.* Leipzig: Max Planck Institute for Evolutionary Anthropology. [http://www.eva.mpg.de/lingua/files/morpheme.html].

Bird, Steven
   1999a   Multidimensional exploration of online linguistic field data. In *Proceedings of the 29th Meeting of the North East Linguistic Society (NELS29)*, vol. 1, Pius Tamanji, Masako Hirotani, and Nancy Hall (eds.), 33–50.
   1999b   Strategies for representing tone in African writing systems. *Written Language & Literacy* 2: 1–44.

Bird, Steven and Gary Simons
   2003   Seven dimensions of portability for language documentation and description. *Language* 79: 557–582.

Bird, Steven and Mark Liberman
   2001   A formal framework for linguistic annotation. *Speech Communication* 33: 23–60. [http://arxiv.org/pdf/cs.CL/0010033].

Bishop, Judith B.
   2002   Aspects of intonation and prosody in Bininj Gun-wok: Autosegmental-metrical analysis. PhD diss., University of Melbourne.

Boas, Franz
    1911a   Introduction. In Boas (ed.), 1–83.
    1911b   Kwakiutl. In Boas (ed.), 425–557.
Boas, Franz (ed.)
    1911   *Handbook of American Indian Languages*, part I. Washington: Bureau of American Ethnology.
Bourdieu, Pierre
    1970   La maison kabyle ou le monde renversé. In *Échanges et Communications*, Jean Pouillon (ed.), 739–758. The Hague: Mouton.
Bow, Catherine, Baden Hughes, and Steven Bird
    2003   Towards a general model of interlinear text. *Proceedings of EMELD Workshop 2003: Digitizing and Annotating Texts and Field Recordings*. LSA Institute: Lansing MI, USA. July 11–13, 2003. [http://www.cs.mu.oz.au/research/lt/projects/interlinear/emeld03-BBH.pdf].
Boyer, Pascal
    1990   *Tradition as Truth and Communication: A Cognitive Description of Traditional Discourse.* Cambridge: Cambridge University Press.
Bradley, David and Maya Bradley (eds.)
    2002   *Language Maintenance for Endangered Languages: An Active Approach.* London: RoutledgeCurzon Press.
Brandt, Elizabeth A.
    1980   On secrecy and control of knowledge. In *Secrecy. A Cross-cultural Perspective*, Stanton K. Tefft (ed.), 123–146. New York: Human Sciences Press.
    1981   Native American attitudes toward literacy and recording in the Southwest. *Journal of the Linguistic Association of the Southwest* 4: 185–195.
Brewer, John D.
    2000   *Ethnography.* Buckingham: Open University Press.
Briggs, Charles
    1986   *Learning How to Ask: A Sociolinguistic Appraisal of the Role of the Interview in Social Science Research.* Cambridge: Cambridge University Press.
Bringhurst, Robert
    1999   *A Story as Sharp as a Knife.* Vancouver/Toronto: Douglas and McIntyre; Lincoln: University of Nebraska Press.
Broschart, Jürgen
    1997   Why Tongan does it differently: Categorial distinctions in a language without nouns and verbs. *Linguistic Typology* 1: 123–166.
Brown, Penelope and Stephen J. Levinson
    1987   *Politeness: Some Universals in Language Usage.* Cambridge: Cambridge University Press.
Brown, Robert and Albert Gilman
    1960   The pronouns of power and solidarity. In Sebeok (ed.), 253–276.

Bruce, Gösta
    1977   *Swedish Word Accents in Sentence Perspective.* Lund: Gleerup.
Cameron, Deborah, Elizabeth Frazer, Penelope Harvey, M. Ben H. Rampton, and
Kay Richardson
    1992   *Researching Language: Issues of Power and Method.* New York:
            Routledge.
Canger, Una (ed.)
    2002   An interactive dictionary and text corpus for sixteenth and seven-
            teenth century Nahuatl. In Frawley, Hill and Munro (eds.), 195–218.
Carneiro da Cunha, Manuela
    1999   Xamanismo e tradução. In *A Outra Margem do Ocidente*, Adauto
            Novaes (ed.), 223–235. São Paulo: Companhia das Letras.
Chafe, Wallace L.
    1994   *Discourse, Consciousness, and Time.* Chicago: The University of
            Chicago Press.
Chafe, Wallace L. (ed.)
    1980   *The Pear Stories: Cognitive, Cultural, and Linguistic Aspects of
            Narrative Production.* Norwood, NJ: Ablex.
Chafe, Wallace L. and Johanna Nichols (eds.)
    1986   *Evidentiality: The Linguistic Coding of Epistemology.* Norwood, NJ:
            Ablex.
Conklin, Harold
    1962   Lexicographic treatment of folk taxonomy. *International Journal of
            American Linguistics* 28: 119–41.
Cook, Capt. James
    1955   *The Journals of Captain James Cook, The Voyage of the Endeavour
            1768–1771.* Cambridge: University Press, Hakluyt Society.
Cooper, Alan
    1995   *About Face: The Essentials of User Interface Design.* Foster City,
            CA: IDG Books.
Coulmas, Florian
    1996   Typology of writing systems. In *Writing and its Use. An Interdisci-
            plinary Handbook of International Research*, vol. 2, Hartmut Gün-
            ther and Otto Ludwig (eds.), 1380–1387. Berlin/New York: Mouton
            de Gruyter.
    2003   *Writing Systems. An Introduction to Their Linguistic Analysis.* Cam-
            bridge: Cambridge University Press.
Couper-Kuhlen, Elizabeth
    2001   Intonation and discourse: Current views from within. In Schiffrin,
            Tannen and Hamilton (eds.), 13–34.
Couper-Kuhlen, Elizabeth and Margret Selting (eds.)
    1996   *Prosody in Conversation: Interactional Studies.* Cambridge: Cam-
            bridge University Press.

Couper-Kuhlen, Elizabeth and Cecilia E. Ford (eds.)
2004   *Sound Patterns in Interaction*. Amsterdam: Benjamins.
Cruse, D. Allan
1986   *Lexical Semantics*. Cambridge: Cambridge University Press.
Cruttenden, Alan
1997   [1986] *Intonation*. 2nd ed. Cambridge: Cambridge University Press.
Crystal, David
2000   *Language Death*. Cambridge: Cambridge University Press.
Csató, Éva and David Nathan
2003a   Multimedia and documentation of endangered languages. In Austin
          (ed.), vol. 1, 73–84.
2003b   *Spoken Karaim*. Version S. Institute for the Study of the Languages
          and Cultures of Africa and Asia, Tokyo University of Foreign Stud-
          ies, and HRELP, School of Oriental and African Studies [Interactive
          multimedia CD-ROM].
Daniels, Peter T. and William Bright (eds.)
1996   *The World's Writing Systems*. Oxford: Oxford University Press.
Dauenhauer, Nora Marks and Richard Dauenhauer
1998   Technical, emotional, and ideological issues in reversing language
          shift: Examples from Southeast Alaska. In Grenoble and Whaley
          (eds.), 57–99.
Dawson, Jean
1989   Orthography decisions. *Notes on Literacy* 57: 1–13.
Delgaty, Alfa H. and Agustín Ruíz Sánchez
1978   *Diccionario Tzotzil de San Andrés (Larrainzar) con Variaciones
          Dialectales*. México, DF: Instituto Lingüístico de Verano.
Descola, Philippe
1998   Estrutura ou sentimento: A relação com o animal na Amazônia.
          Mana: Estudos de Antropologia Social 4: 23–45.
Dimmendaal, Gerrit J.
2001   Places and people: Field sites and informants. In Newman and Ratliff
          (eds.), 55–75.
Dimroth, Christine
2002   Topics, assertions and additive words: How L2 learners get from
          information structure to target-language syntax. *Linguistics* 40: 891–
          923.
Dixon, Robert M.W.
1971   A method of semantic description. In Steinberg and Jakobovits (eds.),
          436–471.
1972   *The Dyirbal Language of North Queensland*. Cambridge: Cambridge
          University Press.
1991   *A New Approach to English Grammar, on Semantic Principles*. Ox-
          ford: Oxford University Press.

Dixon, Robert M.W. and Alexandra Y. Aikhenvald
    2002   Word: A typological framework. In Dixon and Aikhenvald (eds.), 1–
            41.
Dixon, Robert M.W. and Alexandra Y. Aikhenvald (eds.)
    2002   *Word. A Cross-linguistic Typology.* Cambridge: Cambridge Univer-
            sity Press.
Dorian, Nancy C.
    1993   A response to Ladefoged's other view of endangered languages.
            Language 69: 575–579.
Douglas, Mary
    1966   *Purity and Danger – an Analysis of Concepts of Pollution and Taboo.*
            London: Routledge & Kegan Paul.
Drubig, Hans Bernhard
    2003   Toward a typology of focus and focus constructions. *Linguistics* 41:
            1–50.
Du Bois, John W., Stephan Schuetze-Coburn, Danae Paolino, and Susanna Cumming
    1993   Outline of discourse transcription. In Edwards and Lampert (eds.),
            45–89.
Duranti, Alessandro
    1992   Language in context and language as context: The Samoan respect
            vocabulary. In *Rethinking Context*, Alessandro Duranti and Charles
            Goodwin (eds.), 77–99. Cambridge: Cambridge University Press.
    1994   *From Grammar to Politics. Linguistic Anthropology in a Western
            Samoan Village.* Berkeley/Los Angeles/London: University of Cali-
            fornia Press.
    1997   *Linguistic Anthropology.* Cambridge: Cambridge University Press.
Dyken, Julia R. and Constance Kutsch Lojenga
    1993   Les frontiers du mot: Facteurs-clés dans le développement d'une
            orthographie. In *Alphabets de Langues Africaines*, Rhonda L. Hartell
            (ed.), 3–22. Dakar: UNESCO – Bureau regional de Dakar. [English
            original: Word boundaries: Key factors in orthography development.
            In *Alphabets of Africa*, Rhonda L. Hartell (ed.), 3–20. Dakar:
            UNESCO and SIL].
Ebing, Ewald
    1997   *Form and Function of Pitch Movements in Indonesian.* Leiden:
            CNWS.
Eckert, Penelope and Sally McConnell-Ginet
    1992   Think practically and look locally: Language and gender as commu-
            nity-based practice. *Annual Review of Anthropology* 21: 461–490.
Edwards, Jane A.
    2001   The transcription of discourse. In Schiffrin, Tannen and Hamilton
            (eds.), 321–348.

Edwards, Jane A. and Martin D. Lampert (eds.)
1993   *Talking Data*: *Transcription and Coding in Discourse Research*. Hillsdale: Lawrence Erlbaum.

Ehlich, Konrad
1993   HIAT: A transcription system for discourse data. In Edwards and Lampert (eds.), 123–148.

Ehlich, Konrad and Jochen Rehbein
1979   Erweiterte halbinterpretative Arbeitstranskription (HIAT 2): Intonation. *Linguistische Berichte* 59: 51–75.

Ehrenreich, Barbara
2002   *Nickled and Dimed: On (not) Getting by in America*. New York: Owl.

Ellis, Nick C., Miwa Natsume, Katerina Stavropoulou, Lorenc Hoxhallari, Victor H. P. van Daal, Nicoletta Polyzoe, Maria-Louisa Tsipa, and Michalis Petalas
2004   The effects of orthographic depth on learning to read alphabetic, syllabic, and logographic scripts. *Reading Research Quarterly* 39: 438–468.

Eraso, Natalia
2003   Informe taller de unificación del alfabeto para las lenguas Tucano Oriental del Piraparaná. Unpublished report. Bogotá: Fundación GAIA.

Erikson, Philippe
1987   De l'apprivoisement à l'approvisionnement: Chasse, alliance et familiarization en Amazonie indigène. *Techniques et Culture* 9: 105–140.

Errington, J. Joseph
1985   *Language and Social Change in Java*. Athens and Ohio: Ohio University Press, Center for International Studies. (Monographs in international studies, Southeast Asia series, no. 65.)

Evans, Nicholas R.
1992   Multiple semiotic systems, hyperpolysemy, and the reconstruction of semantic change in Australian languages. In *Diachrony within Synchrony*, Günter Kellerman and Michael Morrissey (eds.), 475–508. Bern: Peter Lang Verlag.
2002   Country and the word. Linguistic evidence in the croker sea claim. In Henderson and Nash (eds.), 51–98.

Evans, Nicholas R. and David Wilkins
2000   In the mind's ear: The semantic extensions of perception verbs in Australian languages. *Language* 76: 546–592.
2001   The complete person: Networking the physical and the social. In *Forty Years on: Ken Hale and Australian Languages*, Jane Simpson, David Nash, Mary Laughren, and Barry Alpher (eds.), 495–521. Canberra: Pacific Linguistics.

Fausto, Carlos
   1999   Of enemies and pets: Warfare and shamanism in Amazonia. *American Ethnologist* 26: 933–957.
   2001   *Inimigos Fiéis. História, Guerra e Xamanismo na Amazônia* (Loyal Enemies. History, War and Shamanism in Amazonia). São Paulo: EDUSP.
Feldman, Laurie B. and Dragana Barac-Cikoja
   1996   Serbo-Croatian: A biscriptal language. In Daniels and Bright (eds.), 769–772.
Fillmore, Charles J.
   1982   Frame semantics. In *Linguistics in the Morning Calm*, Linguistic Society of Korea (ed.), 111–137. Seoul: Hansin Publishing Co.
Fillmore, Charles J. and Beryl T. Atkins
   1992   Toward a frame-based lexicon: The semantics of RISK and its neighbors. In *Frames, Fields, and Contrasts: New Essays in Semantic and Lexical Organization*, Adrienne Lehrer and Eva Feder Kittay (eds.), 75–102. Hillsdale, NJ: Lawrence Erlbaum.
Finnegan, Ruth
   1992   *Oral Poetry*. Bloomington: Indiana University Press.
Fishman, Joshua A.
   1991   *Reversing Language Shift. Theoretical and Empirical Foundations of Assistance to Threatened Languages*. Clevedon, UK: Multilingual Matters.
Florey, Margaret
   2004   Countering purism: Confronting the emergence of new varieties in a training program for community language workers. In Austin (ed.), vol. 2, 9–27.
Foley, William A.
   2003   Gender, register and language documentation in literate and preliterate communities. In Austin (ed.), vol. 1, 84–98.
Ford, Cecilia, Barbara A. Fox, and Sandra A. Thompson
   1996   Practices in the construction of turns: The 'TCU' revisited. *Pragmatics* 6: 427–454.
Fox, Barbara A., Makoto Hayashi, and Robert Jasperson
   1996   Resources and repair: A cross–linguistic study of syntax and repair. In Ochs, Schegloff and Thompson (eds.), 185–237.
Fox, James J.
   1977   Roman Jakobson and the comparative study of parallelism. In *Roman Jakobson: Echoes of his Scholarship*, Daniel Armstrong and Cornelis H. van Schooneveld (eds.), 59–90. Lisse: Peter de Ridder.
Fox, James J. (ed.)
   1998   *To Speak in Pairs: Essays on the Ritual Language of Eastern Indonesia*. Cambridge: Cambridge University Press.

Franchetto, Bruna
1993   A celebração da história nos discursos cerimoniais Kuikuro (Alto Xingu). In *Amazônia Etnologia e História Indígena*, Eduardo Viveiros de Castro and Manuela Carneiro da Cunha (eds.), 95–116. São Paulo: NHII/USP, FAPESP.
2000   Rencontres rituelles dans le Haut Xingu: La parole du chef. In Monod-Becquelin and Erikson (eds.), 481–510.
2001   Línguas e história no Alto Xingu. In *Os Povos do Alto Xingu. História e Cultura*, Bruna Franchetto and Michael J. Heckenberger (eds.), 111–156. Rio de Janeiro: Editora da UFRJ.
2002   How to integrate ethnographical data into linguistic documentation: Some remarks from the Kuikuro Project (DOBES, Brazil). In *Proceedings of the International LREC Workshop on Resources and Tools in Field Linguistics*, Peter Austin, Helen Dry, and Peter Wittenburg (eds.). ISLE and DoBeS. [http://www.mpi.nl/lrec/papers/lrec-pap-19LREC_Workshop_Kuikuro.pdf].
2003   L'autre du même: Parallélisme et grammaire dans l'art verbal des récits Kuikuro (caribe du Haut Xingu, Brésil). *Amerindia* 28, Numéro *Langues Caribes* (Paris: AEA): 213–248.
2005   Les marques de la parole vraie en Kuikuro, langue caribe du Haut-Xingu (Brésil). In *Modalités Episthémiques*, Zlatka Guentcheva and Ion Landaburu (eds.). Paris: Editions Peeters.
Frawley, William, Kenneth G. Hill, and Pamela Munro (eds.)
2002   *Making Dictionaries: Preserving Indigenous Languages of the Americas*. Berkeley, Ca.: University of California Press.
Frege, Gottlob
1892   Über Sinn und Bedeutung. *Zeitschrift für Philosophie und Philosophische Kritik* 100: 25–50. (Translation: On sense and reference. In *The Logic of Grammar*, Donald Davidson and Gilbert Harmon (eds.), 1975, Encino, CA: Dickenson.)
Gal, Susan and Judith T. Irvine
1995   The boundaries of languages and disciplines: How ideologies construct difference. *Social Research* 62: 967–1001.
Geertz, Clifford L.
1960   *The Religion of Java*. New York: Free Press.
Gibbon, Dafydd
1995   SAMPA-D-Vmlex, Dokumentation V1.0.
         [http://coral.lili.uni-bielefeld.de/Documents/sampa-d-vmlex.html].
Gleason, Henry A.
1961   *An Introduction to Descriptive Linguistics*. New York: Holt, Rinehart & Winston.
Gleich, Utta von
2005   Documentation and development of teaching material. In *Language Archives Newsletter* 5: 2–5.

Glowczewski, Barbara
   2001a   *Dream Trackers: Yapa Art and Knowledge of the Australian Desert.*
            Unesco [Interactive multimedia CD-ROM].
   2001b   Returning Indigenous knowledge in central Australia: 'this CD-ROM
            brings everybody to the mind'. In *The Power of Knowledge, the
            Resonance of Tradition* (Electronic Publication of Papers from the
            AIATSIS Indigenous Studies Conference, September 2001), Graeme
            K. Ward and Adrian G. Muckle (eds.), 139–154. Canberra: Research
            Program, AIATSIS. [www.aiatsis.gov.au/rsrch/conf2001/PAPERS/
            FullPublication.pdf].
Goldman-Segal, Ricki
   1992   Collaborative virtual communities: Using learning constellations, a
            multimedia ethnographic research tool. In *Sociomedia: Multimedia,
            Hypermedia, and the Social Construction of Knowledge*, Edward
            Barrett (ed.), 257–296. Cambridge, MA: MIT Press.
Gomez-Imbert, Elsa
   1998   Writing the Tukanoan languages: Educational politics in the Vaupes
            area in Colombia and Brazil. Paper read at the 14th International
            Congress of Anthropological and Ethnographical Sciences, at Wil-
            liamsburg.
Gomez-Imbert, Elsa and Dominique Buchillet
   1986   Propuesta para una grafía tukano normalizada. *Chantiers Amerindia*
            11: 1–36.
Goodall, Heather and Karen Flick
   1996   Angledool stories. Paper delivered at AUC Academic Conference
            "From Virtual to Reality", The University of Queensland. [http://
            auc.uow.edu.au/conf/Conf96/Papers/Goodall.html].
Gossen, Gary H.
   1974   *Chamulas in the World of the Sun: Time and Space in a Maya Oral
            Tradition.* Cambridge, Mass.: Harvard University Press.
   1985   Tzotzil literature. In *Supplement to the Handbook of Middle American
            Indians*, vol. 3, Victoria R. Bricker and Munro Edmonson (eds.), 65–
            106. Austin: University of Texas Press.
Grabe, Esther
   1998   *Comparative Intonational Phonology: English and German.* (MPI
            Series in Psycholinguistics 7.) Proefschrift Universiteit Nijmegen.
Graves, William, III
   1988   The sociocultural construction of grammar: A metalinguistic case
            study. PhD diss., Department of Anthropology, Indiana University.
Greenbaum, Sidney
   1984   Corpus analysis and elicitation tests. In *Corpus Linguistics: Recent
            Developments in the Use of Computer Corpora in English Language
            Research*, Jan Aarts and Willem Meijs (eds.), 193–201. Amsterdam:
            Rodopi.

Grenoble, Lenore A. and Lindsay J. Whaley (eds.)
1998   *Endangered Languages: Current Issues and Future Prospects*. Cambridge: Cambridge University Press.
Grinevald, Collette
2003   Speakers and documentation of endangered languages. In Austin (ed.), vol. 1, 52–72.
2005   Globalization and language endangerment: Poison and antidote. HRELP Annual Public Lecture, February 11, 2005.
Gussenhoven, Carlos
2004   *The Phonology of Tone*. Cambridge: Cambridge University Press.
Hagège, Claude
2000   *Halte à la Mort des Langues*. Paris: Odile Jacob.
Hale, Kenneth
1971   A note on a Walbiri tradition of antonymy. In Steinberg and Jakobovits (eds.), 474–484.
1982   The logic of Damin kinship terminology. In *Languages of Kinship in Aboriginal Australia*, Jeffrey Heath, Francesca Merlan, and Alan Rumsey (eds.), 31–37. Sydney: Oceania Linguistics Monographs 24.
Halwachs, Dieter
1994   Zur Funktion und Notation nonverbaler Zeichen. In *Satz – Text – Diskurs*. Akten des 27. linguistischen Kolloquiums, Münster 1992, Band 2, Peter-Paul König and Helmut Wieger (eds.), 45–53. Tübingen: Niemeyer.
Hanks, William F.
1990   *Referential Practice*. Chicago: University of Chicago Press.
Harvey, Penelope
1992   Bilingualism in the Peruvian Andes. In Cameron, Frazer, Harvey, Rampton and Richardson (eds.), 65–89.
Haspelmath, Martin
2002   *Understanding Morphology*. London: Arnold.
Hausmann, Franz Josef, Herbert Ernst Weigand, and Ladislav Zgusta (eds.)
1990–91 *Dictionaries*. vols 1–3. Berlin/New York: Mouton de Gruyter.
Haviland, John B.
1974   A last look at Cook's Guugu Yimidhirr wordlist. *Oceania* 44: 216–232.
1979   Guugu Yimidhirr brother-in-law language. *Language in Society* 8: 365–393.
1987   Tzotzil ritual language without ritual. Austin Discourse Conference, Ms.
1994   Verbs and shapes in (Zinacantec) Tzotzil: The case of 'insert'. *Función* 15–16: 83–117.

Haviland, John B.
    1996   "We want to borrow your mouth": Tzotzil marital squabbles. In *Disorderly Discourse; Narrative, Conflict, and Inequality*, Charles L. Briggs (ed.), 158–203. New York and Oxford: Oxford University Press.
    1998   *Old Man Fog and the Last Aborigines of Barrow Point*. Washington, D.C.: Smithsonian Institution Press.
    2000   Warding off witches: Voicing and dialogue in Zinacantec prayer. In Monod-Becquelin and Erikson (eds.), 367–400.
Heath, Jeffrey
    1980   *Nunggubuyu Myths and Ethnographic Texts*. Canberra: AIAS.
    1984   *Functional Grammar of Nunggubuyu*. Canberra: AIAS.
Heckenberger, Michael J.
    1998   Manioc agriculture and sedentism in Amazonia: The Upper Xingu example. *Antiquity* 72: 633–648.
    2005   *The Ecology of Power: Culture, Place and Personhood in the Southern Amazon, A.D. 1000–2000*. New York and London: Routledge.
Henderson, John and David Nash (eds.)
    2002   *Language in Native Title*. Canberra: Aboriginal Studies Press.
Hercus, Luise and David Nathan
    2002   *Paakantyi*. Multimedia CD-ROM. Canberra: ATSIC.
Hill, Jane H.
    1980   Culture shock, positive face, and negative face: Being polite in Tlaxcala. *Central Issues in Anthropology* 2: 1–14.
    2005   *A Grammar of Cupeño*. Berkeley and Los Angeles: University of California Press.
Hill, Jane H. and Judith T. Irvine
    1992   *Responsibility and Evidence in Oral Discourse*. Cambridge: Cambridge University Press.
Hill, Kenneth C.
    2002   On publishing the Hopi Dictionary. In Frawley, Hill and Munro (eds.), 299–311.
Hill, Marcia, Kristin Glaser, and Judy Harden
    1995   A feminist model for ethical decision making. In *Ethical Decision Making in Therapy: Feminist Perspectives*, Elizabeth J. Rave and Carolyn C. Larsen (eds.), 18–37. New York: Guildford Press.
Himmelmann, Nikolaus P.
    1996   Zum Aufbau von Sprachbeschreibungen. *Linguistische Berichte* 164: 315–333.
    1998   Documentary and descriptive linguistics. *Linguistics* 36: 161–195.
Himmelmann, Nikolaus P. and John Wolff
    1999   *Toratán (Ratahan)*. (Languages of the World Materials 130.) München: Lincom.

Himmelmann, Nikolaus P. and Robert D. Ladd
   forthc.   Prosodic fieldwork. In *A Guide to Linguistic Field Research*, Dan
           Everett. Cambridge: Cambridge University Press.
Hinton, Leanne
   2003   Orthography wars. Ms., University of California-Berkeley Depart-
           ment of Linguistics.
Hinton, Leanne and William Weigel
   2002   A dictionary for whom? Tensions between academic and nonaca-
           demic functions of bilingual dictionaries. In Frawley, Hill and
           Munro (eds.), 155–170.
Hinton, Leanne with Matt Vera, Nancy Steele, and the Advocates for Indigenous
California Language Survival
   2002   *How to Keep Your Language Alive: A Commonsense Approach to
           One-on-One Language Learning.* Berkeley: Heydey Books.
Hirst, Daniel and Albert Di Cristo
   1998   A survey of intonation systems. In *Intonation Systems. A Survey of
           Twenty Languages*, Daniel Hirst and Albert Di Cristo (eds.), 1–44.
           Cambridge, Cambridge University Press.
Hirst, Daniel, Albert di Cristo, and Robert Espesser
   2000   Levels of representation and levels of analysis for intonation. In
           Prosody: Theory and Experiment, Merle Horne (ed.), 51–87. Kluwer,
           Dordrecht. [Pdf version: http://aune.lpl.univ-aix.fr:16080/~hirst/ arti-
           cles/2000%20Hirst&al.pdf].
Hockett, Charles F.
   1958   *A Course in Modern Linguistics*. New York: MacMillan.
Holton, Gary
   2003   Approaches to digitization and annotation: A survey of language
           documentation materials in the Alaska Native Language Centre Ar-
           chive. Paper prepared for the Language Digitization Project Confer-
           ence (E-MELD), Lansing, July 11–13, 2003. [http://emeld.org/
           workshop/2003/paper-holton.pdf, accessed 15 Nov. 2003].
Hopi Dictionary Project
   1998   *Hopi Dictionary/Lavàytutuveni: A Hopi-English Dictionary of the
           Third Mesa Dialect.* Tucson: University of Arizona Press.
Hughes, Baden, Steven Bird, and Catherine Bow
   2003   Encoding and presenting interlinear text using XML Technologies.
           *Proceedings of the Australasian Language Technology Workshop
           2003.* Melbourne, Australia. December 10, 2003.
Hugh-Jones, Steven
   1995   Inside-out and back-to-front: The androgynous house in Northwest
           Amazonia. In *About the House: Lévi-Strauss and Beyond*, Stephen
           Hugh-Jones (ed.), 226–252. Cambridge: Cambridge University
           Press.

Hyman, Larry M.
2001   Tone systems. In *Language Typology and Language Universals*, Martin Haspelmath, Ekkehard König, Wulf Oesterreicher, and Wolfgang Raible (eds.), 1367–1380. Berlin/New York: Mouton de Gruyter.

Hymes, Dell H.
1971   *Foundations of Sociolinguistics: The Ethnography of Speaking*. Philadelphia: University of Pennsylvania Press.
1977   Discovering oral performance and measured verse in American Indian narrative. *New Literary History* 8: 431–457.
1992   *"In vain I tried to tell you": Essays in Native American Ethnopoetics*. Philadelphia: University of Pennsylvania Press.

Inoue, Miyako
2004   What does language remember? Indexical inversion and the naturalized history of Japanese women. *Journal of Linguistic Anthropology* 14: 39–56.

International Phonetic Association
1999   *Handbook of the International Phonetic Association: A Guide to the Use of the International Phonetic Alphabet*. Cambridge: Cambridge University Press.

Jacobs, Joachim
2001   The dimensions of topic comment. *Linguistics* 39: 641–681.
2005   *Spatien – Zum System der Getrennt-/Zusammenschreibung im Deutschen*. Berlin/New York: Mouton de Gruyter.

Jakobson, Roman
1960   Linguistics and poetics. In Sebeok (ed.), 350–377.
1966   Grammatical parallelism and its Russian facet. *Language* 42: 398–429.
1968   Poetry of grammar and grammar of poetry. *Lingua* 21: 597–609.
1973   *Questions de Poétique*. Paris: Editions du Seuil.

Johnson, Heidi
2004   Language documentation and archiving, or how to build a better corpus. In Austin (ed.), vol. 2, 140–153.

Jun, Sun-Ah (ed.)
2005   *Prosodic Typology. The Phonology of Intonation and Phrasing*. Oxford: Oxford University Press.

Katz, Leonard and Ram Frost
1992   The reading process is different for different orthographies: The orthographic depth hypothesis. In *Orthography, Phonology, Morphology, and Meaning*, Ram Frost and Leonard Katz (eds.), 67–84. Amsterdam: Elsevier North Holland Press.

Keller, Frank
2000   Gradience in grammar. Experimental and computational aspects of degrees of grammaticality. PhD diss., University of Edinburgh.

Kendon, Adam
    2004   *Gesture: Visible Action as Utterance.* Cambridge: Cambridge University Press.
Kibrik, Alexandre E.
    1977   *The Methodology of Field Linguistics.* The Hague, Paris: Mouton.
King, Heather B.
    1994   The declarative intonation of Dyirbal: An acoustic analysis. Master of Arts thesis, Australian National University.
KLRC
    nd   *Bunuba Yarrangi Thanani.* Kimberley Language Resource Centre [Interactive multimedia CD-ROM].
Kockelman, Paul
    2003   The meanings of interjections in Q'eqchi' Maya. *Current Anthropology* 44: 467–490.
König, Ekkehard, Dik Bakker, Östen Dahl, Martin Haspelmath, Maria Koptjevskaja-Tamm, Christian Lehmann, and Anna Siewierska
    1994   *EUROTYP Guidelines.* Strasbourg: European Science Foundation, Programme in Language Typology. [http://www-uilots.let.uu.nl/ltrc/eurotyp/h4.htm].
Kroeger, Paul R.
    2005   *Analyzing Grammar.* Cambridge and New York: Cambridge University Press.
Kroskrity, Paul V.
    1998   Arizona Tewa Kiva speech as a manifestation of a dominant language ideology. In *Language Ideologies: Practice and Theory,* Bambi B. Schieffelin, Kathryn Woolard, and Paul V. Kroskrity (eds.), 103–122. New York: Oxford University Press.
Labov, William
    1971   The study of language in its social context. In *Advances in the Sociology of Language,* Joshua A. Fishman (ed.), 152–216. The Hague: Mouton.
    1975   *What is a Linguistic Fact.* Lisse: Peter de Ridder.
    1996   When intuitions fail. In *CLS 32: Papers from the Parasession on Theory and Data in Linguistics,* Lisa McNair (ed.), 77–105. Chicago: University of Chicago.
Ladd, D. Robert
    1996   *Intonational Phonology.* Cambridge: Cambridge University Press.
Ladefoged, Peter
    2003   *Phonetic Data Analysis: An Introduction to Fieldwork and Instrumental Phonetics.* Oxford: Blackwell.
Ladefoged, Peter and Ian Maddieson
    1996   *The Sounds of the World's Languages.* Malden, MA: Blackwell.

Lakoff, Robin
1973   The logic of politeness; or minding your p's and q's. In *Papers from the Ninth Regional Meeting of the Chicago Linguistic Society*, 292–305. Chicago: Chicago Linguistic Society.

Lambrecht, Knud
1994   *Information Structure and Sentence Form: Topic, Focus, and the Mental Representations of Discourse Referents.* Cambridge: Cambridge University Press.

Landau, Sidney I.
1984   *Dictionaries: The Art and Craft of Lexicography.* New York: Scribner.

Lara Ramos, Luis Fernando (ed.)
1986   *Diccionario Básico del Español de México.* México, D.F.: El Colegio de México.

Larmouth, Donald W., Thomas E. Murray and Carin Ross Murray
1992   *Legal and Ethical Issues in Surreptitious Recording.* (Publication of the American Dialect Society, 76.) Tuscaloosa: University of Alabama Press.

Laughlin, Robert M.
1975   *The Great Tzotzil Dictionary of San Lorenzo Zinacantan.* Washington, D.C.: Smithsonian Institution.

1988   *The Great Tzotzil Dictionary of Santo Domingo Zinacantan with Grammatical Analysis and Historical Commentary.* Washington, D.C.: Smithsonian Institution.

Laver, John
1994   *Principles of Phonetics.* Cambridge: Cambridge University Press.

Leech, Geoffrey and Andrew Wilson
1996   Recommendations for the morphosyntactic annotation of corpora. EAGLES Document EAG-TCWG-MAC/R, March 1996. [http://www.ilc.cnr.it/EAGLES96/annotate/annotate.html].

Lehmann, Christian
1983   Directions for interlinear morphemic translation. *Folia Linguistica* 16: 193–224.

1989   Language description and general comparative grammar. In *Reference Grammars and Modern Linguistic Theory*, Gottfried Graustein and Gerhard Leitner (eds.), 133–162. (*Linguistische Arbeiten* 226.) Tübingen: Niemeyer.

2001   Language documentation: A program. In *Aspects of Typology and Universals*, Walter Bisang (ed.), 83–97. (Studia Typologica 1.) Berlin: Akademie Verlag.

2004a   Data in linguistics. *The Linguistic Review* 21: 175–210.

2004b   Documentation of grammar. In *Lectures on Endangered Languages 4. From Kyoto Conference 2001,* Osamu Sakiyama, Fubito Endo,

Honore Watanabe, and Fumiko Sasama, 61–74. (Endangered Languages of the Pacific Rim Publication Series, C-004.) Osaka: Osaka Gakuin University.

2005   Interlinear morphemic glossing. In *Morphology. An International Handbook on Inflection and Word Formation*, vol. 2, Geert Booij, Christian Lehmann, Joachim Mugdan, and Stavros Skopeteas (eds.), 1834–1857. Berlin/New York: Mouton de Gruyter.

de León, Lourdes

1991   *Space Games in Tzotzil: Creating a Context for Spatial Reference.* (CARG-Working Paper No. 4.) Nijmegen: MPI.

Levin, Beth

1985   Lexical semantics in review: An introduction. In *Lexical Semantics in Review*, Beth Levin (ed.), 1–62. (Lexicon Project Working Papers, 1.) Cambridge, Ma.: MIT Center for Cognitive Science.

1991   Building a lexicon: The contribution of linguistics. *International Journal of Lexicography* 4: 205–224.

1993   *English Verb Classes and Alternations.* Chicago: University of Chicago Press.

Levinson, Stephen C.

1992   Primer for the field investigation of spatial description and conception. *Pragmatics* 2: 5–47.

2003   *Space in Language and Cognition. Explorations in Cognitive Diversity.* Cambridge: Cambridge University Press.

Levinson, Stephen C., Sérgio Meira, and The Language and Cognition Group

2003   'Natural concepts' in the satial-topological domain. Adpositions in crosslinguistic perspecive: An exercise in semantic typology. *Language* 79: 483–516.

Liberman, Isabelle, Alvin M. Liberman, Ignatius Mattingly, and Donald Shankweile

1980   Orthography and the beginning reader. In *Orthography, Reading and Dyslexia*, James F. Kavanagh and Richard L. Venezky (eds.), 137–153. Baltimore: University Park Press.

Liberman, Mark

2000   Legal, ethical, and policy issues concerning the recording and publication of primary language materials. Workshop on Web-based Language Documentation and Description. [http://www.ldc.upenn.edu/exploration/expl2000/papers/liberman/liberman.html].

Lieb, Hans-Heinrich and Sebastian Drude

2000   Advanced glossing. A language documentation format. Unpublished DoBeS Working Paper. [http://www.mpi.nl/DOBES/INFOpages/applicants/Advanced-Glossing1.pdf].

Llisteri, Joaquim

1996   EAGLES preliminary recommendations on spoken texts. [http://www.ilc.cnr.it/EAGLES96/spokentx/node1.html].

Lord, Albert
    1985   *The Singer of Tales*. New York: Atheneum.
Luraghi, Silvia
    1990   *Old Hittite Sentence Structure*. London: Routledge.
MacWhinney, Brian
    1991   The CHILDES Project: Tools for Analyzing Talk. Hillsdale, NJ: Lawrence Erlbaum Associates.
McCarty, Teresa, Lucille Watahomigie and Akira Yamamoto (eds.)
    1999   *Reversing language shift in Indigenous America: Collaborations and views from the field*. Special issue of the journal *Practicing Anthropology*, vol. 21(2).
McIntosh, Angus
    1961   Patterns and ranges. *Language* 37: 325–337.
McLaughlin, Fiona and Thierno Seydou Sall
    2001   The give and take of fieldwork: Noun classes and other concerns. In Newman and Ratliff, 189–210.
McLuhan, Marshall
    1964   *Understanding Media: The Extensions of Man*. New York: McGraw-Hill.
Maddieson, Ian
    2001   Phonetic Fieldwork. In *Linguistic Fieldwork*, Paul Newman and Martha Ratliff (eds.), 211–230. Cambridge: Cambridge University Press.
Malinowski, Bronislaw
    1935   *Coral Gardens and their Magic*. vol. 2. 2nd ed. London: Allen & Unwin.
Marandin, Jean-Marie and Michel de Fornel
    1996   L'analyse grammaticale de l'auto-réparation. *Le Gré des Langues* 10: 8–68.
Matthews, Peter H.
    1991   [1974] *Morphology*. 2nd ed. Cambridge: Cambridge University Press.
Mayer, Mercer
    1969   *Frog, where are you?* New York: Dial Press.
Meyerhoff, Miriam
    2002   Communities of practice. In *The Handbook of Language Variation and Change*, John K. Chambers, Peter Trudgill, and Natalie Schilling-Estes (eds.), 526–548. Malden, MA & Oxford: Blackwell Publishing.
Mithun, Marianne
    2001   Who shapes the record: The speaker and the linguist. In Newman and Ratliff (eds.), 34–54.

Monod-Becquelin, Aurore
   1987   Le tour du monde en quelques couplets: Le parallélisme dans la tradition orale maya. In *Kalevala et Traditions Orales du Monde*, M.M. Jocelyne Fernandez-Vest (ed.), 467–488. Paris: Éditions du CNRS (Colloques internationaux du CNRS).

Monod-Becquelin, Aurore and Philippe Erikson (eds.)
   2000   *Les Rituels du Dialogue, Promenades Ethnolinguistiques en Terres Amérindiennes*. Nanterre: Société d'ethnologie.

Mosel, Ulrike
   1984   *Tolai Syntax and its Historical Development*. Canberra: Pacific Linguistics.
   1987   *Inhalt und Aufbau deskriptiver Grammatiken. How to Write a Grammar*. Köln: Institut für Sprachwissenschaft, AP 4 (NF).
   1994   *Saliba*. Munich: Lincom Europa.
   2004a   Dictionary making in endangered speech communities. In Austin (ed.), vol. 2, 39–54.
   2004b   Inventing communicative events: Conflicts arising from the aims of language documentation. *Language Archive Newsletter* 3: 3–4. [http://www.mpi.nl/LAN/].
   2006   Grammaticography: The art and craft of writing grammars. In Ameka et al. (eds.).

Mosel, Ulrike and Even Hovdhaugen
   1992   *Samoan Reference Grammar*. Oslo: Skandinavian University Press.

Mosel, La'i Ulrike and Ainslie So'o (eds.)
   2000   *Utugagana*. Apia (Western Samoa): Department of Education.

Mugdan, Joachim
   1989   Grundzüge der Konzeption einer Wörterbuchgrammatik. In *Wörterbücher*, vol. 1, Franz J. Hausmann, Oskar Reichmann, Herbert E. Wiegand, and Ladislav Zgusta (eds.), 732–749. Berlin/New York: Mouton de Gruyter.

Mühlhäusler, Peter
   1996   *Linguistic Ecology. Language Change and Imperialism in the Pacific Region*. London and New York: Routledge.

Nathan, David
   2000a   Plugging in Indigenous knowledge – connections and innovations. *Australian Aboriginal Studies* 2000: 39–47.
   2000b   The spoken Karaim CD: Sound, text, lexicon and 'active morphology' for language learning multimedia. In *Studies on Turkish and Turkic Languages*, Asli Göksel and Celia Kerslake (eds.), 405–413. Wiesbaden: Harrassowitz.
   2003   Endangered languages documentation: From standardization to mobilization. Paper presented at Digital resources for the Humanities 2003. University of Gloucestershire, September 2003.

Nathan, David
    2004   Planning multimedia documentation. In Austin (ed.), vol. 2, 154–168.
    2006   A talking dictionary of Paakantyi NSW. In *Information Technology and Indigenous People*, Laurel Dyson, Max Hendriks, and Stephen Grant (eds.). Hershey PA: Idea Group.

Nathan, David and Eva Csató
    forthc.   Multimedia: A community-oriented information and communication technology. In *Lesser-known Languages of South Asia. Status and Policies, Case Studies and Applications of Information Technology*, Anju Saxena and Lars Borin (eds.). Berlin/New York: Mouton de Gruyter.

Newman, Paul and Martha Ratliff
    2001   *Linguistic Fieldwork.* Cambridge: Cambridge University Press.

Nichols, Johanna and Ronald L. Sprouse
    2003   Documenting lexicons: Chechen and Ingush. In Austin (ed.), vol. 1, 99–121.

Nimmer, Melville B.
    1998   *Cases and Materials on Copyright and Other Aspects of Entertainment Litigation, Including Unfair Competition, Defamation, Privacy, Illustrated.* New York: Matthew Bender & Company.

Ochs, Elinor
    1979   Transcription as theory. In *Developmental Pragmatics*, Elinor Ochs and Bambi B. Schieffelin (eds.), 43–72. New York: Academic Press.

Ochs, Elinor, Emanuel A. Schegloff, and Sandra A. Thompson (eds.)
    1996   *Interaction and Grammar.* Cambridge: Cambridge University Press.

Odé, Cecilia
    1997   On the perception of prominence in Indonesian. In *Proceedings of the 7th International Conference on Austronesian Linguistics*, Cecilia Odé and Wim Stokhof (eds.), 151–166. Amsterdam: Rodopi.
    2002   *Mpur Prosody: An Experimental-phonetic Analysis with Examples from two Versions of the Fentora Myth.* (Endangered Languages of the Pacific Rim Publication Series, A1-003.) Osaka: Osaka Gakuin University.

Ong, Walter J.
    1982   *Orality and Literacy: The Technologizing of the Word.* London: Methuen.

Pawley, Andrew
    1985   On speech formulas and linguistic competence. *Lenguas Modernas* 12: 84–104.
    1986   Lexicalization. In *Languages and Linguistics: The Interdependence of Theory, Data, and Application*, Deborah Tannen and James E. Alatis (eds.), 98–120. (GURT 85.) Washington: Georgetown University Press.

1993   A language which defies description by ordinary means. In *The Role of Theory in Language Description*, William A. Foley (ed.), 87–129. Berlin/New York: Mouton de Gruyter (=TiL SaM 69).

Pawley, Andrew and Frances H. Syder

2000   The one-clause-at-a-time hypothesis. In *Perspectives on Fluency*, Heidi Riggenbach (ed.), 163–198. Ann Arbor: The University of Michigan Press.

Peirce, Charles Sanders (ed.)

1932   *Collected Papers of C. S. Peirce.* Cambridge, Mass.: Harvard University Press.

Pierrehumbert, Janet

1980   The phonology and phonetics of English intonation. Unpublished PhD diss., Cambridge, Mass.: MIT.

Pullum, Geoffrey K. and William A. Ladusaw

1996   *Phonetic Symbol Guide.* 2nd ed. Chicago: University of Chicago Press.

Quine, Willard V. O.

1960   *Word and Object.* Cambridge, Mass.: MIT Press.

Quirk, Randolph, Sidney Greenbaum, Geoffrey Leech, and Jan Svartvik

1985   *A Comprehensive Grammar of the English Language.* Harlow/Essex: Longman.

Raible, Wolfgang

1994   Literacy and language change. In *Writing vs. Speaking. Language, Text, Discourse, Communication*, Svetla Čmejrková, František Daneš, and Eva Havlová (eds.), 111–125. Tübingen: Narr.

Reicher, Gerald M.

1969   Perceptual recognition as a function of meaningfulness of stimulus material. *Journal of Experimental Psychology* 81: 274–280.

Rischel, Jørgen

1987   Phonetic transcription in fieldwork. In *Probleme der Phonetischen Transkription*, Antonio Almeida and Angelika Braun (eds.), 57–77. (Zeitschrift für Dialektologie und Linguistik, Heft 54.) Stuttgart: Franz Steiner Verlag.

Rogers, Henry

2005   *Writing Systems. A Linguistic Approach.* Oxford: Blackwell.

Ross, Malcom

1988   Proto-Oceanic and the Austronesian Languages of Western Melanesia. Canberra: Pacific Linguistics.

Rubel, Paula G. and Abraham Rosman (eds.)

2003   *Translating Cultures: Perspectives on Translation and Anthropology.* Oxford: Berg Publisher.

Rubino, Carl R. G.
   2005   Iloko. In *The Austronesian Languages of Asia and Madagascar*, Alexander Adelaar and Nikolaus P. Himmelmann (eds.), 326–349. London: Routledge.

Samarin, William J.
   1966   *Field Linguistics: A Guide to Linguistic Field Work.* New York: Holt, Rinehart, and Winston.

Sammons, Kay and Joel Sherzer
   2000   Translating Native Latin American Verbal Art. Washington: Smithsonian University Press.

Sapir, Edward
   1921   *Language.* New York: Harcourt etc.

Sasse, Hans-Jürgen
   1993   Syntactic categories and subcategories. In *Syntax*, Joachim Jacobs, Armin von Stechow, Wolfgang Sternefeld, and Theo Vennemann (eds.), 646–686. Berlin/New York: Mouton de Gruyter.

Saville-Troike, Muriel
   2003   *The Ethnography of Communication: An Introduction.* Malden, MA/ Oxford: Blackwell Publishing.

Schachter, Paul
   1985   Parts-of-speech systems. In Shopen (ed.), 1–63.

Schiffrin, Deborah, Deborah Tannen, and Heidi E. Hamilton (eds.)
   2001   *The Handbook of Discourse Analysis.* Oxford: Blackwell.

Schmidt, Thomas
   2004   Transcribing and annotating spoken language with EXMARaLDa. *Proceedings of the LREC-Workshop on XML based richly annotated corpora*, 69–74. LREC 2004, International Conference on Language Resources and Evaluation. Lisbon, Portugal. Paris: European Language Resources Association. May 29, 2004.

Schuetze-Coburn, Stephan
   1994   *Prosody, syntax, and discourse pragmatics: Assessing information flow in German conversation.* PhD diss., University of California, Los Angeles.

Schüller, Dietrich
   2004   Safeguarding the documentary heritage of cultural and linguistic diversity. *Language Archive Newsletter* 3: 9–10. [http://www.mpi.nl/ LAN/].

Schütze, Carson T.
   1996   *The Empirical Base of Linguistics: Grammaticality Judgments and Linguistic Methodology.* Chicago: The University of Chicago Press.

Sebeok, Thomas A (ed.)
   1960   *Style in Language.* Cambridge: MIT Press.

Seifart, Frank

2002   *El Sistema de Clasificación Nominal del Miraña*. Bogotá: CCELA/ Universidad de los Andes.

2005   The structure and use of shape-based noun classes in Miraña (North West Amazon). Proefschrift, Radboud Universiteit Nijmegen.

Selting, Margret, Peter Auer, Birgit Barden, Jörg Bergmann, Elizabeth Couper-Kuhlen, Susanne Günthner, Christoph Meier, Uta Quasthoff, Peter Schlobinski, and Susanne Uhmann

1998   Gesprächsanalytisches Transkriptionssystem (GAT). *Linguistische Berichte* 173: 91–122.

Serzisko, Fritz

1992   *Sprechhandlungen und Pausen*. Tübingen: Niemeyer.

Sherzer, Joel

1990   *Verbal Art in San Blas: Kuna Culture Through Its Discourse*. Albuquerque: University of New México Press.

1992   Modes of representation and translation of Native American discourse. In Swann (ed.), 426–440.

Shopen, Timothy (ed.)

1985   *Language Typology and Syntactic Description*. Cambridge: Cambridge University Press.

2006   *Language Typology and Syntactic Description III vols.* 2nd ed. Cambridge: Cambridge University Press.

Silverman, Kim, Mary Beckman, John Pitrelli, Mari Ostendorf, Colin Wightman, Patti Price, Janet Pierrehumbert, and Julia Hirschberg

1992   TOBI: A standard for labeling English prosody. In *Proceedings of the International Conference on Spoken Language Processing 1992*, John J. Ohala, Terrance M. Nearey, Bruce L. Derwing, Megan M. Hodge, and Grace E. Wiebe (eds.), 867–870.

Silverstein, Michael

1976   Shifters, linguistic categories, and cultural description. In *Meaning in Anthropology*, Keith H. Basso and Henry A. Selby (eds.), 11–56. Albuquerque: University of New Mexico Press.

1979   Language structure and linguistic ideology. In *The Elements: A Parasession on Linguistic Units and Levels*, Paul R. Clyne, William Hanks, and Carol Hofbauer (eds.), 193–247. Chicago: Chicago Linguistic Society.

1993   Metapragmatic discourse and metapragmatic function. In *Reflexive Language, Reported Speech and Metapragmatics*, John A. Lucy (ed.), 33–58. Cambridge: Cambridge University Press.

1996   Indexical order and the dialectics of social life. In *SALSA III: Proceedings of the Third Annual Symposium about Language and Society*, Risako Ide, Rebecca Parker, and Yukako Sunaoshi (eds.), 266–295. Austin: Department of Linguistics, University of Texas at Austin.

Silverstein, Michael
    2003   Indexical order and the dialectics of sociolinguistic life. *Language and Communication* 23: 193–230.
Simons, Gary F.
    1994   Principles of multidialectal orthography design. *Notes on Literacy* 20: 13–34.
Simpson, Jane
    2003   Representing information about words digitally. Digital Audio Archiving Workshop Sydney, 1st October 2003. [www.paradisec.org.au/Simpson_paper_rev1.html#conc].
Sperberg-McQueen, C. Michael and Lou Burnard (eds.)
    2002   *TEI P4: Guidelines for Electronic Text Encoding and Interchange.* Text Encoding Initiative Consortium. XML Version: Oxford.
Steinberg, Danny J. and Leon A. Jakobovits (eds.)
    1971   *Semantics.* Cambridge: Cambridge University Press.
Steinen, Karl von den
    1940   *Entre os Aborígenes do Brasil Central.* Separada Renumerada da Revista do Arguivo No XXXIV a LVIII. São Paulo: Departamento de Cultura. (Original edition, *Unter den Naturvölkern Zentral-Brasiliens.* Berlin: Dietrich Reimer Verlag, 1894.)
    1942   *O Brasil Central: Expedição de 1884 para a exploração do rio Xingu.* Companhia Editora Nacional. (Original edition, *Durch Central-Brasilien. Expedition zur Erforschung des Schingú im Jahre 1884.* Leipzig: Brockhaus, 1886.)
Stoel, Ruben B.
    2005   *Focus in Manado Malay.* Leiden: CNWS Publications.
Svensén, Bo
    1993   *Practical Lexicography.* Oxford/New York: Oxford University Press.
Swann, Brian (ed.)
    1992   *On the Translation of Native American Literatures.* Washington: Smithsonian Institution Press.
Talmy, Leonard
    1985   Lexicalization patterns: Semantic structure in lexical forms. In Shopen (ed.), 57–149.
Tedlock, Dennis
    1983   *The Spoken Word and the Work of Interpretation.* Philadelphia: University of Pennsylvania Press.
TEI Text Encoding Initiative Consortium
    2005   *TEI P5. Guidelines for Electronic Text Encoding and Interchange,* C. Michael Sperberg-McQueen and Lou Burnard (eds.) (revised and re-edited by Syd Bauman and Lou Burnard). [www.tei-c.org/P5/].
Thieberger, Nick
    2004   Documentation in practice: Developing a linked media corpus of South Efate. In Austin (ed.), vol. 2, 169–178.

Thiesen, Wesley
1996 *Gramática del Idioma Bora.* Yarinacochoa, Pucallpa (Perú): Instituto
Lingüístico de Verano.
Thiesen, Wesley and Eva Thiesen (compilers)
1998 *Diccionario Bora – Castellano, Castellano – Bora.* Yarinacochoa,
Pucallpa (Perú): Instituto Lingüístico de Verano.
Thomas, Jim and James Marquart
1987 Dirty information and clean conscience: Communicating problems in
studying "bad guys". In *Communication and Social Structure*, Carl
Couch and David R. Maines (eds.), 81–96. Springfield: Charles
Thomas Publisher. [www.soci.niu.edu/~jthomas/papers/jt.dirty].
Trager, George L.
1958 Paralanguage: A first approximation. *Studies in Linguistics* 13: 1–12.
Underhill, Ruth
1946 *Papago Indian Religion.* New York: Columbia University Press.
Urban, Greg
1991 *A Discourse-Centered Approach to Culture: Native South American
Myths and Rituals.* Austin: University of Texas Press.
Vaux, Bert and Justin Cooper
1999 *Introduction into Linguistic Field Methods.* München, Newcastle:
Lincom Europa.
Venezky, Richard L.
1970 Principles for the design of practical writing systems. *Anthropological Linguistics* 126: 256–270.
Wallraff, Günter
1977 *Der Aufmacher. Der Mann, der bei "Bild" Hans Esser war.* Köln:
Kiepenheuer & Witsch.
Weinreich, Uriel
1963 Semantic universals? In *Universals of Language*, Joseph H. Green-
berg (ed.), 114–173. Cambridge: CUP.
Wells, John C.
1997 SAMPA computer readable phonetic alphabet. In *Handbook of Standards and Resources for Spoken Language Systems*, Dafydd Gibbon,
Roger Moore, and Richard Winski (eds.) (Part 4, section B). Ber-
lin/New York: Mouton de Gruyter.
2004 SAMPA computer readable phonetic alphabet. [www.phon.ucl.ac.uk/
home/sampa].
Wells, John C., William J. Barry, Martine Grice, Adrian Fourcin and Dafydd Gibbon
1992 Standard Computer-Compatible Transcription. ESPRIT Project 2589
(SAM). Multilingual Speech Input/Output Assessment, Methodology
and Standardisation. Final Report. Year Three: 1.III.91–28.II.1992.
London: University College London.

Wenger, Etienne
  1998   *Communities of Practice: Learning, Meaning, and Identity*. Cam-
           bridge: Cambridge University Press.
Wennerstrom, Ann
  2001   *The Music of Everyday Speech*. Oxford: Oxford University Press.
Wilkins, David P.
  1992   Linguistic research under aboriginal control: A personal account of
           fieldwork in Central Australia. *Australian Journal of Linguistics* 12:
           171–200.
  2000   Even with the best of intentions: Some pitfalls in the fight for lin-
           guistic and cultural survival. In *As Línguas Amazônicas Hoje*, Fran-
           cisco Queixalos and Odile Renault-Lescure (eds.), 61–84. São Paulo:
           Instituo Ambiental & Paris: IRD.
Wittenburg, Peter, Hennie Brugman, Daan Broeder, and Albert Russel
  2004   XML-based language archiving. LREC 2004 Workshop on XML-
           based richly annotated corpora, LREC2004 Conference, Lisbon,
           May 2004.
Wittenburg, Peter, Romuald Skiba, and Paul Trilsbeek
  2004   Technology and tools for language documentation. *Language Ar-
           chive Newsletter* 4: 3–4. [http://www.mpi.nl/LAN/].
Wittgenstein, Ludwig
  1958   *Philosophical Investigations*. Oxford: Blackwell.
Wolcott, Harry
  2004   [1995] *The Art of Fieldwork*. 2nd ed. Walnut Creek: Alta Mira.
Woodbury, Anthony C.
  2002   The word in Cup'ik. In Dixon and Aikhenvald (eds.), 79–99.
  2003   Defining documentary linguistics. In Austin (ed.), vol. 1, 35–51.
Wynne, Martin (ed.)
  2004   *Developing Linguistic Corpora: a Guide to Good Practice*. Oxford:
           Arts and Humanities Data Service [www.ahds.ac.uk/creating/guides/
           linguistic-corpora/index.htm]
Yip, Moira
  2002   *Tone*. Cambridge: Cambridge University Press.
Zanten, Ellen van, Robert W. N. Goedemans, and Jos J. Pacilly
  2003   The status of word stress in Indonesian. In *The Phonological Spec-
           trum II: Suprasegmental Structure*, Jeroen M. van de Weijer, Vincent
           J. J. P. van Heuven, and Harry G. van der Hulst (eds.), 151–175. Am-
           sterdam: Benjamins.
Zgusta, Ladislav
  1971   *Manual of Lexicography*. The Hague: Mouton.
Zumthor, Paul
  1983   *Introduction à la Poésie Orale*. Paris: Seuil.

Language index

Subject index

A Mouton de Gruyter Textbook

Toni Rietveld and Roeland van Hout

■ Statistics in Language Research

Analysis of Variance

2005. ix, 265 pages.
Cloth. ISBN 3-11-018580-6
Paperback. ISBN 3-11-018581-4)

Statistics in Language Research gives a non-technical but more or less complete treatment of Analysis of Variance (ANOVA) for language researchers.

This book offers a thorough introduction to the basic principles of analysis of variance, based on examples taken from language research, and goes beyond the conventional topics treated in introductory textbooks, as it covers topics like 'violations of assumptions', 'missing data', 'problems in repeated measures designs', 'alternatives to analysis of variance' (such as randomization tests and multilevel analysis). Each chapter consists of four sections: treatment of the subject under discussion, a summary of relevant terms and concepts, a section devoted to reporting statistics, and finally an exercise section. After the first introductory chapter, in which fundamental concepts like 'variables', 'cases' and SPSS data formats are presented, the book continues with two 'refreshment' chapters, in which the principles of statistical testing are revised, focusing on the well-known t test. These chapters also deal with the essential, but often neglected concepts of 'statistical power' and 'sample size'. In every chapter examples of SPSS input and output are given.

ANOVA is the most frequently used technique when handling the outcomes of research designs with more than two treatments or groups. This technique is used in all parts of linguistics which deal with observations obtained in survey studies and in (quasi-)experimental research, like applied linguistics, psycholinguistics, sociolinguistics, language and speech pathology, and phonetics. Most statistical textbooks in the social sciences take examples typical of their own field and, in addition, omit subjects which are particularly relevant for language researchers, like power analysis, quasi F, F1, F2, and minF'.

Mouton
de Gruyter
Berlin · New York

WWW.MOUTON-PUBLISHERS.COM